THE FILMS

Birth of a Nation . . . The Gold Rush . . . Scarface . . . It Happened One Night . . . Gone with the Wind . . . Casablanca . . . Citizen Kane . . . Ben Hur . . . The Best Years of Our Lives . . . The Exorcist . . . Blazing Saddles . . . Star Wars . . . Julia . . .

THE DIRECTORS

Griffith . . . Lubitsch . . . von Stroheim . . . DeMille . . . Berkley . . . Huston . . . Capra . . . Kazan . . . Penn . . . Coppola . . . Wilder . . . Bogdanovitch . . . Scorsese . . . Altman . . .

THE STARS

Pickford . . . Chaplin . . . Garbo . . . Gable . . . Bogart . . . Astaire . . . Davis . . . the Fondas . . . Newman . . . Monroe . . . Redford . . .

The studios . . . the styles . . . the challenges . . . the changes . . . all are but part of this lively book that presents the fascinating phenomenon of the American movie in all its complexity of creative effort and all its multifaceted history of trial and triumph, passing fashions and lasting glories.

STEVEN C. EARLEY
and Film at Montclair
has been a film addict s
his interest to the prese

D1262744

⊘ **SIGNET**

STARS OF THE SILVER SCREEN:
THE LADY BEHIND THE LEGEND

(0451)

☐ **THE HORNES:** *An American Family* by Gail Lumet Buckley. Written by her daughter, this is the history not only of Lena Horne's dramatic life and career, but also the story of the Horne family. It is at once a stunning portrait of America's black elite and a riveting multigenerational family saga. "A fascinating, glamorous story . . . A grand family chronicle, a remarkable achievement."—*The Philadelphia Inquirer*

(156714—$4.95)

☐ **MARILYN: Norma Jean** by gloria Steinem. The nationwide bestseller. Includes 16 pages of rare and intimate color photographs. "Gloria Steinem explores the real woman behind the bombshell persona."—*Newsweek*

(155963—$4.95)

☐ **KATE: The life of Katharine Hepburn** by Charles Higham. For the first time Hepburn has authorized a writer to interview her friends and colleagues about her career, her life, and her romantic involvements. This is a portrait of the most tempestuous superstar of them all.

(148495—$3.95)

☐ **AS TIME GOES BY: THE LIFE OF INGRID BERGMAN** by Laurence Leamer. This riveting biography, complete with 32 pages of unforgettable photos, reveals Ingrid Bergman as she really was. "The frankest and most candid book about the dazzling star . . . completely fascinating."—Liz Smith

(400224—$4.95)*

Buy them at your local bookstore or use this convenient coupon for ordering.

NEW AMERICAN LIBRARY
P.O. Box 999, Bergenfield, New Jersey 07621

Please send me the books I have checked above. I am enclosing $_____
(please add $1.00 to this order to cover postage and handling). Send check or money order—no cash or C.O.D.'s. Prices and numbers are subject to change without notice.

Name_____

Address_____

City _____ State _____ Zip Code _____

Allow 4-6 weeks for delivery.

This offer, prices and numbers are subject to change without notice.

AN INTRODUCTION TO AMERICAN MOVIES

★★★★★★★★★★★★★★★★★★★★★★

Steven C. Earley

A MENTOR BOOK

NEW AMERICAN LIBRARY

NEW YORK
PUBLISHED IN CANADA BY
PENGUIN BOOKS CANADA LIMITED, MARKHAM, ONTARIO

COPYRIGHT © 1978, 1979 BY STEVEN C. EARLEY

Library of Congress Catalog Card Number: 77-95025

MENTOR TRADEMARK REG. U.S. PAT. OFF. AND FOREIGN COUNTRIES
REGISTERED TRADEMARK–MARCA REGISTRADA
HECHO EN WINNIPEG, CANADA

SIGNET, SIGNET CLASSIC, MENTOR, ONYX, PLUME, MERIDIAN AND NAL BOOKS
are published *in the United States* by NAL Penguin Inc.,
1633 Broadway, New York, New York 10019,
in Canada by Penguin Books Canada Limited, 2801 John
Street, Markham, Ontario L3R 1B4

First Printing, May, 1978

5 6 7 8 9 10 11 12 13

PRINTED IN CANADA

This book is for Evelyn Collins,
Joe Labriola, and Edward Moran

Acknowledgments

A NUMBER of people contributed to the development of this book. My special thanks to Norma Johnston and Rita Cohen for their editorial help, to Ernest Jaeger for his assistance on the chapter "Novels into Film," and to William Faulhaber for his editorial services and contribution to the sections on science fiction and war films.

Several people aided me with secretarial services and deserve my gratitude: Jennie Mahoney, Rose Errante, Rose Ferri, Evelyn Collins, Joe Labriola, William Bernardino, and Edward Moran. I am indebted to David Gaudio and Ross Woodbury. Both scholars corrected errors and suggested changes in the manuscript.

I am grateful to Emma Fantone of Montclair State College for her generous assistance in booking and screening many of the films mentioned in the manuscript, and to John Dorr of the Academy of Motion Picture Arts and Sciences, who helped select the photographs. My thanks also to the Museum of Modern Art for the use of photographs from their film archives.

My thanks to Herbert Gilbert, who encouraged me to find a publisher. I am also indebted to my editor, Barry Lippman, who guided this book through to final publication.

Contents

Preface

HISTORIES of American movies have been published before, and their usefulness has been proved. However, for readers unacquainted with the language of film, or with the historical development of the industry, or even the names of various directors, stars and films, most of these detailed publications have been too technical, their discussions too abstract and their styles too scholarly.

For those unfamiliar with American movies, this book should be easier, for it follows the history of the movies step-by-step, both as an industry and as an art, from the penny peepshows to the present. Included are suggestions for the appreciation of the older classics, as well as today's complex films. These suggestions, however, are not to be taken as "authorized" interpretations but rather as some of the ways in which critical method can enhance the film experience.

The book is divided into two parts. Part I is a history of the main currents and attitudes in American filmdom, from its beginnings in the 1890's as the illegitimate child of the theater to today's most popular art form. Representative films of various decades are examined for creativity, psychological impact, plot innovation, direction, and importance to history.

Part II traces the development of a variety of film genres—the Western, the Gangster, the Horror, the Epic, etcetera. Here, too, representative movies are analyzed for plot, acting, directing, and cinematic techniques. *All* genres are not included, since this would require a much more detailed study. The main purpose here is to give readers an overview, in the hope that interest in more comprehensive study will be whetted. Omission of certain directors, producers, actors, technicians, or film titles does not mean they are unimportant. Selections had to be made, and those who, in the opinion of the writer, made exceptional contributions are included.

Understanding plot is not necessarily understanding film.

An appreciation of any art form is enhanced by some knowledge of the historical background, of what the artist is trying to do and the methods used to accomplish results. It is the same with film. Viewers leave the theater more satisfied if they have noticed the lighting, observed the sets and decorations, recognized the symbols, appreciated the subtleties of the acting, and understood how the director developed theme, story, and characterizations. By explaining to readers how they can become aware of these aspects of film, this book hopes to improve their visual literacy, broaden their understanding of cinema, and intensify their enjoyment of the movies.

PART I

★

THE HISTORY OF AMERICAN MOVIES

1/The Beginnings: 1890-1915

IT WAS scientific curiosity, not any artistic endeavor, that brought about the development of the first photographic apparatus capable of recording motion.

Leland Stanford, a railroad tycoon, was convinced that at a certain point in a horse's stride all four feet are off the ground. In 1887, he hired Eadweard Muybridge, an English photographer, to take pictures of a trotter in motion. Muybridge's twelve cameras (later increased to twenty-four) attached to a trip wire proved Stanford's theory to be correct.

The next year Thomas Alva Edison met Muybridge, and the Englishman's photographs, shown on a disc apparatus called a "Zoopraxiscope," evidently gave the American inventor the idea for a machine which would record and reproduce images just as his phonograph already reproduced sound. Two years later Edison and an assistant, William K. Dickson, invented the "Kinetograph," an apparatus that could photograph physical action. The American film industry was launched.

The idea of motion pictures was not new. That the human eye retains an image for a fraction of a second longer than the image actually appears, a "persistence of vision," had been known for centuries. Leonardo da Vinci tried to capture motion with his *camera obscura* (a darkened chamber in which the image of an object is received through a lens opening and focused on a surface). As early as 1671, Athanasius Kircher worked with magic lanterns in Rome in an attempt to make projected pictures move. By 1824, Peter Mark Roget, famed as the compiler of Roget's *Thesaurus*, was claiming that a series of still photographs, with each picture showing a slightly more developed state of action, might, if projected in rapid succession, give the illusion of continuous motion. J.A.E. Plateau in 1833 offered the "Phenakistiscope" to the public, in which hand-made drawings turned on a disc caused successive pictures to appear as continuous motion. In

3

1877, Emile Reynaud, a Frenchman, experimented further with Plateau's invention and developed a "Praxinoscope," which projected successive images on a screen.

After seeing the Muybridge photos, Edison and Dickson came up with their first "toy" machine in 1890, and began to experiment with strips of flexible photographic film invented by George Eastman. Losing interest shortly thereafter, Edison dumped responsibility for the motion picture project into Dickson's lap and took off for Paris. Upon his return a few months later, he was greeted by the "Kinetograph" camera and the "Kinetoscope," an individual peepshow viewer that Dickson had built.

Much of the data concerning the developments by Edison, Dickson, Eastman, and others have been lost in a maze of lawsuits, misstatements, and distorted recollections. But it is an accepted fact that by 1893 Thomas Edison had asked Fred Ott, a laboratory assistant, to do something funny for the newly invented camera. Ott, indulging in a bit of horseplay, did a nose-twitching sneeze. That short strip of film made Ott the first film actor, credited Edison with the first movie closeup, and ushered the absurd world of slapstick into movies.

On the afternoon of April 14, 1894, when the motion picture made its unannounced debut, a Kinetoscope Parlor opened at 1155 Broadway, New York City. That same year the Edison-Dickson "Kinetoscope" was being sold to anyone desiring to purchase one.

Edison wasn't the only one interested in an apparatus for showing pictures. In France, the Lumière brothers, Georges Méliès, Charles Pathé, and Leon Gaumont, contributed mechanical improvements to the magic box. In Germany, Emil and Max Skladanowski produced the "Bioskop," and in England, Robert W. Paul offered improvements. By 1895, Herman Casler's "Mutoscope" was in strong competition with the "Kinetoscope." Still, Edison's machine, with its perfected system of preperforated film, remains the standard to this day.

The late 1890's were the heyday of the peepshow parlor and the penny arcade, which were lined with rented Kinetoscopes. The peepshows ran for about one minute each and the public found them highly amusing. To see a "movie," a penny was inserted in a slot. The viewer cranked the handle at the side of the iron machine, and by peering into the eyepiece was rewarded with flashing, jerky pictures of street scenes, sea waves, parades, a boy playing a trick on a by-stander, a "hootchie-kootchie" dancer, prizefights, vaudeville acts, and gags.

Most established actors had contempt for these film strips and refused to participate in them. But there were many sub-jects for Edison's camera: suffragettes marched; President McKinley talked; Ruth St. Denis danced; Wild West stars Buffalo Bill and Annie Oakley rode horses and shot guns; Jim Corbett boxed. In 1896, the acting team of May Irwin and John C. Rice played a scene from their stage success, *Widow Jones*. The film, titled *The May Irwin–John C. Rice Kiss,* eventually dubbed simply *The Kiss,* brought forth strong de-mands for censorship.

The "flickers," an early slang word for the flickering effect produced by primitive projection, had an immediate popular-ity, but once the novelty wore off, interest in the penny ar-cade lagged. The reason was obvious. The Kinetoscope, offering thirty seconds of action in return for a nickel dropped in the slot, had limited commercial possibilities; only one per-son at a time could peep into the Kinetoscope's magic box. At first any motion alone thrilled audiences, but the public wanted something more for its money.

As early as 1896, a few smart businessmen persuaded Edison to incorporate his motion picture equipment with that of the "magic lantern," a device popular on lecture platforms in the late nineteenth century, which projected short film se-quences onto a screen. Edison received permission to com-bine certain mechanical devices invented by Thomas Armat and Francis Jenkins with his own Kinetoscope, and the "Vi-tascope" was born. Later that same year New York audiences saw the first projected films in America.

The Vitascope's debut was an overwhelming success. *The New York Times* gave a glowing account of the event. Movies soon were one of the main attractions at leading vaudeville palaces. But, as with the Kinetoscope, audiences soon grew bored with the same old ideas repeated over and over—fake adventures, prizefights, Annie Oakley hitting her targets, Annabelle doing her butterfly routine, and Carmen-cita, a music hall favorite, performing a lively dance. By 1900, movies were becoming less and less attractive to the operators of vaudeville theaters. If the infant industry was to survive, new ideas were needed—and fast. George Méliès and Edwin S. Porter saved the day.

In 1895, a magician named Georges Méliès watched as the Lumière brothers, August and Louis, pioneer French cinematographers, publicly demonstrated a motion picture camera they had developed. Méliès immediately realized the new invention's potential and tried to buy a camera from the Lumières. When his offer was refused, he bought a camera in England and began a series of experiments in his Paris studio. Challenged by the instrument's possibilities, and possessing the imagination of a master showman—not to mention a conjurer's eye—Méliès was just the person needed to give the infant industry a shove in a different and exciting direction.

Like the peepshows, Méliès's first films were only a few minutes long. His films were set apart from the others, however, by their originality and the accidental discovery of trick photography. While filming a scene in the Place de l'Opéra in Paris, Méliès was forced to stop his camera to fix a jammed crank. Within minutes the repair was made, and he resumed his recording of moving traffic. When the negative was developed, he found to his delight that a transformation had taken place: a tram had suddenly become a carriage, men had changed into women, and prancing horses had replaced humans. Stop motion, one of the main components of trick photography, had been discovered. For Méliès the magician, this opened a whole new world of photographic possibilities. In his many films that followed, he developed the overlap dissolve, the fadeout, double exposure, fast and slow motion, and animation. Méliès was the first to explore the potential of the medium, concentrating on the camera rather than the actor. Méliès also decided not to reproduce life but to intensify action. Let's give the camera a story to tell. That moment the novel no longer held a monopoly on the art of narration. The fiction film was created. Méliès delighted audiences with his stories and the use of multiple settings. His pictures were marked by visual magic, fantasy interlaced with humor, and an emphasis on the satirical, the absurd, and—above all—the theatrical.

Between 1896 and 1914, Méliès turned out more than a thousand films, ranging from brief shorts to twenty-minute films. In 1902 he released a cinema masterpiece, his version of Jules Verne's *A Trip to the Moon*, in which he employed proessional actors, animation, many varied costumes and sets, and most important, a detailed scenario, all carefully supervised by him.

Méliès's position as the first artist of the cinema is indisputable. The public, in France and elsewhere, adored his lighter films. Others working in the industry quickly copied his techniques, thereby instituting a movie tradition of imitating whatever attracted audiences.

Edwin S. Porter, an American working at the Edison Company studios, was greatly impressed with Méliès's films. Porter agreed with the French director that movies should tell stories. He searched the Edison Company archives and spliced together excerpts from several films showing firemen with their firefighting equipment. He then added some newly shot footage and called the composite film *The Life of an American Fireman* (1902).

By composing each scene out of separate shots, and by cutting and shifting these scenes in order to elicit strong emotional reactions from the audience, Porter achieved cinematic narration and made the first American dramatic film. He used several episodes to tell the story: a man dreaming of his wife and child, a hand pulling a fire alarm, the arrival of the firemen at the fire, a shot of a terror-stricken mother and child huddling together, and the descent down the ladder to safety. By arranging time and space to suit his dramatic purpose, Porter demonstrated the fundamentals of film editing, but even though his method was revolutionary, not many people really noticed what he had done.

One day Porter overheard someone discussing a new play in New York called *The Great Train Robbery*; he thought the basic idea would make an exciting movie. Rounding up some unemployed actors in Union Square, Porter took them to his studio in West Orange, New Jersey. He found a train in nearby Paterson, rented horses and guns, and made the historic Western *The Great Train Robbery* (1903). Improving on his earlier editing technique, Porter introduced parallel (concurrent) action, showing simultaneous action at two or more locales, alternating them on the screen. His inventive camera and editing techniques turned out the first outstanding American motion picture, and he became the foremost director of the new medium. This film with fourteen scenes was so revolutionary for its day that many critics consider it more important to film history than any other American film, except *The Birth of a Nation* (1915) or *Citizen Kane* (1941). The public agreed, too; they put down their dime novels and hurried to the nickelodeons, a name derived from the slang word for five cents and the Greek word for theater. Why read about bandits, trains, robberies, and last-minute rescues when you could see them at the local Bijou?

Before Porter, no one had cut and assembled film into selected sequences to heighten the film's dramatic aspects. Directors had simply cranked away until the event they were shooting was over or until they ran out of film. All action was continuous. It was Porter who, after photographing hundreds of feet of film for his picture, retired to his studio and snipped, cut, and pasted; by rearranging events and scenes, he created film editing and parallel action. Alternating in such a manner, using no dissolves, he cut abruptly from one scene to another. By showing what was happening on the train and what was happening in the station, Porter made two levels of simultaneous action possible. With this technique, he also heightened suspense and emotional responses in his audience, giving the film industry a blueprint for many films that followed.

Up to this time, filmmakers used techniques borrowed from the theater. Even Georges Méliès, the inventive French director, had failed to realize that filmmaking was a unique art form. Like other directors, Méliès set up a stationary camera a certain distance from the painted sets and actors, and then cranked away. The end result was photographed theater.

Porter freed his camera from the stationary position, taking it from place to place, first shooting a scene in his studio, then carting his equipment outdoors. He photographed scenes from a moving train, and even included a panning shot of bandits escaping on horseback. His dramatic use of blazing guns, galloping horses, and moving trains thrilled audiences. As a final punch, Porter had an irrelevant but terrifying medium shot of a bandit pointing his revolver directly into the camera and firing.

Besides introducing several cinematic techniques, *The Great Train Robbery* developed the screen's most popular theme, good versus evil, as well as the characters and props that became basic to most Western films. Bad characters who perform dastardly deeds are pursued and eventually vanquished by virtuous men of law and order. Porter's film provided audiences with good guys, bad guys, gun battles, and the chase. Eventually the stalwart hero, the gallant heroine, and the scheming villain emerged in later films.

All across the land, in cities and small towns, storefronts were painted and embellished with colorful posters, and a screen, plus several rows of straight chairs and a piano, were moved in. The nickelodeon was in business. Ten-minute, one-reel features with musical accompaniment were the usual offering, followed by an "illustrated song" sung by a soloist, all for a nickel.

For the first decade of cinema history, it was France that took the lead in film production, with Italy pressing close behind, and America following in third place. Although Porter's cinematic inventiveness brought melodrama to the American screen, the comedies emanating from the French studios were popular and much in demand. Méliès's development of fast motion, slow motion, superimpositions, dream effects, and reverse action were irresistible to American audiences, who were far more interested in the camera's tricks than in character or story development. Slapstick comedy with trick photography was what the public wanted.

These early French films, particularly those directed by Ferdinand Zecca, followed a set pattern. After a fast introduction of characters and problem, the film turned into a speedy farce, usually in the "chase" pattern. Hero and heroine were on the run, pursued by man, beast, or machine. Characters raced frantically over the landscape, jumped from bridges, leaped into conveniently waiting rowboats, clattered over rooftops, wheeled in and out of traffic, and indulged in madcap antics that finally culminated in a breathlessly happy ending. Audiences adored the manipulations, the defiance of gravity, the crazy inventions, and above all, the satire on accepted behavioral patterns. A decade later, the perceptive American director Mack Sennett would adopt this same zany style for his films.

Although dozens of would-be directors were grinding out one-reel films, imitating Porter's early style, the industry in America was not advancing. Directors had not mastered the technique of editing a story within the one-reel framework. While in Europe directors were experimenting with longer films, the American producers, who controlled the studio money, did not believe the public would accept longer films. The films also had not attracted many creative writers; established authors thought that film writing would undermine their reputations. Directors filmed without scenarios, instead using simple story lines and improvising as they went along. Plots were hackneyed, filled with ridiculous situations and stereotyped characters. Melodramatic themes prevailed: labor versus capital, graft, fair treatment for the worker, the perils of drink, the dangers facing the poor working girl, and the adventures of a country boy in the big city. By 1911 D. W. Griffith, the American director, tired of turning out literally hundreds of one-reel films, wanted to make two-reel pictures in order to develop a better narrative thrust and character development. Against the objections of his employers, he told his second version of *Enoch Arden* in two reels. Griffith had changed the movie industry. By 1914 his *Judith of Bethulia* was four reels long.

Like the French, American filmmakers also tried to bring culture to the viewer. Film companies lured New York theater people to their studios in Fort Lee, New Jersey, and to the Flatbush section of Brooklyn with promises of first-rate stories based on successful plays or literary classics. The Vitagraph studio filmed *Romeo and Juliet* in 1908, Hobart Bosworth starred in *The Count of Monte Cristo* (1909), and short versions of *Vanity Fair* (1911) and *David Copperfield* (1911) were made by ambitious directors. By 1914, highbrow American filmmakers were turning out three-reel classics, but these attempts at grand art were not too popular at the box office.

While a few directors attempted these prestigious films, the majority were hunting for more popular story forms. Suddenly the industry hit a bonanza. After seeing the French serial *Fantomas* (1914), the Selig Company, recognizing a sure-fire moneymaker, imitated the French "cliff-hanger," and in 1913 produced *The Adventures of Kathlyn*, the first American serial (fifteen episodes), with Kathlyn Williams, "the girl without fear." The serial's financial success spawned a whole succession of similar "continued next week" suspense thrillers. All America seemed to spend Saturday afternoon at the movies, experiencing the hair-raising adventures of Helen Gibson, Marguerite Snow, Anita Stewart, Lillian Lorraine, and Juanita Hansen. In 1914, Pearl White starred in the most famous serial of all, *The Perils of Pauline*. Week after week, Pearl evaded attempts on her life. She fought pirates, Indians, gypsies, rats, sharks, and her dastardly guardian. By the 1920's, at least one hundred serials were on the market. The serials craze lasted until the late 1940's, made millions for the studios, and turned unknown performers into stars.

Another significant aspect of the nickelodeon era was the birth of the movie studios, many of which were to become the huge companies that dominated the industry for the next several decades. Vitagraph was organized in 1907. Biograph

Company, which would later become famous through its association with D. W. Griffith, was founded by former Edison associates in 1896. The Kalem (KLM) Company organized in 1907, as did Essanay (S&A). In 1909, Carl Laemmle, who had left the clothing business to become a theater owner, founded the Imp Company, which later developed into Universal. Adolph Zukor started the Famous Players Company in 1913, and in 1916 he merged with Jesse Lasky; later the two would establish Paramount pictures. By the 1920's, William Fox, Louis B. Mayer, and Marcus Loew headed powerful companies.

As movies became increasingly profitable, Edison grew resentful of his rivals, who were capitalizing on what he considered to be his invention. He suggested the big companies such as Kalem, Lubin, Vitagraph, Biograph, Selig, Essanay, and Klein, as well as the French Companies Méliès and Pathé, join him to form the Motion Picture Patents Company. Its main purpose was to monopolize filmmaking in the United States. Formed in 1909, this consortium declared that henceforth no one else was to photograph or print movies in the United States or European countries. All exhibitors would have to pay a two-dollar weekly licensing fee for the privilege of screening films made by Patents Company members. Because of legal loopholes, the Patents Company was beyond the reach of the antitrust laws. Hence it was able to demand high royalties, not only on films but also on cameras and projection equipment. Pressure was exerted to make exhibitors and producers use Patents Company members' products exclusively.

The Motion Picture Patents Company exerted major influence on the industry. Its officers, concerned with patents, distribution, and films as "products," were businessmen and not creative artists. They were convinced the public wanted entertainment, not art, and they limited production to one-reel movies. For some time this practice crippled the development of the feature-length film in America.

Seeking to beat the high royalties of the Patents Company, enterprising operators would rent a film for a single showing, then surreptitiously transport it from theater to theater (often by bicycle) before returning it to the film exchange. To protect their investments, the Patents Company prosecuted these offenders. Likewise, independent producers traded and borrowed film equipment from each other.

The monopolistic practices of the Patents Company encouraged the smaller, less powerful independent companies to leave for the West Coast. To avoid court proceedings, these companies headed for southern California with their about-to-be confiscated equipment. Here they were relatively safe from the law, for even if the Patents Company detectives managed to find them, refuge in Mexico was only a short distance away. Producers had another reason to be happy in California. Los Angeles was an open-shop, nonunion city. Help was cheap.

Month after month, independent movie producers, eager to cash in on the popularity of films, arrived in California with their stolen gear. They soon discovered that California had other advantages besides its proximity to a foreign country. The climate was excellent for outdoor shooting almost year-round, and the warmer temperatures eliminated the need for expensive indoor electricity. Furthermore, a wide variety of landscapes was available within easy traveling distance. The Los Angeles suburb of Hollywood was on its way to becoming the film capital of the world.

By 1913, there were about sixty studios operating on the West Coast, and only forty-seven in the East. By 1915, producers such as Sam Goldwyn, Jesse Lasky, Adolph Zukor, Thomas Ince, and William Fox were beginning to direct the industry to what the public wanted from their West Coast offices. Big studios were constructed as the trains daily deposited new arrivals in California. More than half of all American movies were being filmed in Hollywood.

2 / The Myth Makers:
Three Creative Artists

ALTHOUGH many films had been manufactured by 1920, few were outstanding. Big studios and, to a certain extent, major performers as well discouraged experimentation. For the most part, the motion picture industry had learned how to organize but still failed to produce superior films. This situation was changed substantially by three creative giants—David Wark Griffith, Mack Sennett, and Charlie Chaplin.

These three artists fought the studio system to keep their individuality. For years they worked independently of the studios. Griffith remained aloof until 1924; by the 1930's, Sennett finally gave in, following public taste and studio dictates; but Chaplin, using his personal wealth, retained his artistic independence throughout his career. D. W. Griffith, Mack Sennett, and Charlie Chaplin turned the cinema into an art form and made American movies known throughout the world.

David Wark Griffith, proud Kentuckian, would-be writer, and energetic young actor, was one of the people who broke the theater tradition in movies. Like Méliès and Porter, Griffith advanced the basic techniques of filmmaking. Within a few years, he became, in the opinion of many critics, the greatest director in the history of motion pictures.

Touring America with a theater troupe at the turn of the century, Griffith soon realized he was not destined to become a great matinee idol; he decided to quit the stage and try his hand at writing poetry and plays. In 1907, flat broke and compelled to look for work outside the theater, Griffith appeared at the Edison Studio in New York, trying to sell his scenario of *Tosca*. Instead he found work as an actor in *Rescued from an Eagle's Nest*, directed by Edwin S. Porter. From the Edison Studio, Griffith switched in 1908 to Biograph Films, where he was given his first directorial assignment. During the next five years he turned out five hundred short films.

In 1908, Griffith met "Billy" Bitzer, a gifted cameraman, and the two eventually joined forces to become one of the great teams in show business. For sixteen years they collaborated, turning out films filled with screen techniques that revolutionized moving pictures.

Griffith not only improved cinematic techniques, but also improved the quality of screen acting. Because of the harshness of close shots (the focus or slightly out of focus shots were still unknown), he decided not to use older actors. Instead, he collected a group of energetic young people whom he turned into a film repertory company. In the group were Mae Marsh, Robert Harron, Owen Moore, Mack Sennett, Lionel Barrymore, H. D. Walthall, Blanche Sweet, Mabel Normand (who later joined Mack Sennett's company), Jack Pickford and his sister Mary, and two sisters who came to the studio to visit Mary, Dorothy and Lillian Gish. The Gish girls (especially Lillian) subsequently became Griffith's favorite performers.

Griffith's enthusiasm, energy, and creative invention were directed toward bringing about changes in the techniques of filmmaking. With Bitzer's help, he experimented with various camera devices, such as the iris and the fade, plus producing emphasis through composition and framing of shots, as well as sharp editing for speed and rhythm. He developed the "last-minute chase," using cross-cutting between parallel actions in order to build up suspense and drama. In *The Lonedale Operator* (1911) he first began to master both the cross-cutting of simultaneous story lines and the disjunctive editing used by Porter in *The Great Train Robbery.* By heightening suspense through editing, Griffith excelled in involving the viewer emotionally as a vicarious participant in the onscreen action.

In *The New York Hat* (1912) with Lionel Barrymore and Mary Pickford, Griffith edited his own film, using the cutback and the closeup. In 1913, he made *Judith of Bethulia,* the first American "feature-length" film, a grandiose spectacle, which reached the unprecedented length of four reels, approximately forty minutes' running time.

After *Judith* Griffith left Biograph Films to work for Mutual Films Corporation. He convinced Bitzer and many of the younger players to come with him. Although he began *The Escape* (1914) in New York, he decided to finish it in California. Thus the director, his cameraman, and troupe of players headed for the West Coast, where they made two films,

Home Sweet Home (1914) and *The Avenging Conscience* (1914). Griffith was now ready to work on *The Birth of a Nation*, one of the most revolutionary pictures ever to hit the screen.

For years Griffith had dreamed of telling the "true" story of the Confederacy. Some time earlier he had obtained the rights to *The Clansman*, a story by Thomas E. Dixon, a fellow Southerner and a college classmate of Woodrow Wilson. While Dixon's book had been an ordinary novel and a mediocre play, it did provide the means by which Griffith could tell his own version of the Civil War. Gathering privately with a few trusted members of his company (a necessary precaution in those days, when a rival version of the same plot could be filmed and released by a competitor in a few days), Griffith acquainted them with his new project and began filming without a script, his usual practice. Almost immediately after shooting began in July, 1914, it was evident that a film of this magnitude would be both long and expensive. When the initial financing ran out, Griffith became his own money-raiser and publicist as well as producer-director. Members of the cast chipped in by accepting salary suspensions, some of them even contributing their own savings. When finally completed, on a budget of approximately $110,000, the three-hour epic, shot by Billy Bitzer with just one camera, turned out to be one of the greatest films in cinema history.

The Birth of a Nation is a monumental melodrama of the American Civil War and its aftermath. The film is divided into several parts. The Prologue portrays the beginning of slavery in America in the seventeenth century and the rise of the Abolitionists. Part One tells how the friendship between two families, the Stonemans from Pennsylvania and the Camerons from South Carolina, is virtually destroyed by the Civil War. Part One ends with Lee's surrender and Lincoln's assassination. The story is told quickly and powerfully. Part Two, which aroused intense controversy because of its anti-Negro bias, describes the effects of the war on the Camerons. The story traces their degradation and humiliation in attempting to adjust to life after the defeat of the South. Reduced to poverty, the family suffers a series of tragedies, resulting in almost total annihilation.

The picture depicts the menacing war clouds, the exploitation of the newly freed Negroes, the ambitious, domineering Northern politicians, the rise of the Ku Klux Klan, the bitterness and hatred of racial beliefs, and the eventual salvation of the Old South. In addition, the film demonstrates Griffith's personal hatred of war.

When Griffith's masterpiece premiered in March, 1915, the public responded with wild enthusiasm. The audience's tremendous emotional response was due in part to the director's skillful use of parallel action. He edited his work carefully to evoke contrasting emotional qualities and heightened suspense, using long shots, medium shots, and closeups. The dovetailing of events, the photography, the vast panorama shots, and the action are unforgettable. The ending—with the Ku Klux Klan racing to save the Cameron family—leaves the viewer stunned by visual images.

It was while making *Judith of Bethulia* (1913) that Griffith had realized audiences could be made to care about the fate of nations through the experiences of humble men and women, little people caught in conflicts larger than themselves. Thus he hit upon the idea of developing a large historical epic through intimate emotions, familiar to his audiences, and he used the same techniques in *The Birth of a Nation*. Audiences remember the poor Southern woman with her two children huddling in the bushes as the camera pans to the valley below where their home is aflame and Sherman's army continues its march to the sea. In the battle of Petersburg, Griffith codified for future films the way to film battle scenes. A charge is shown in ferocious detail, with a battalion sweeping in from the left, the men in the trenches, the shelling, the hand-to-hand encounters, and the Southern colonel running desperately across the battlefield to thrust the Confederate flag into the mouth of a Union cannon.

Despite its brilliant cinematic techniques, *The Birth of a Nation* aroused controversy for its depiction of leering, bestial blacks. A few people, both black and white, tried to suppress the picture, and several politicians denounced the film soundly. Griffith, astounded by the uproar, seemed unaware that he was either prejudiced or patronizing. (Later, he issued a pamphlet demanding freedom for the screen as well as for the press.) Ironically, the publicity from such attacks helped make the film a commercial success. The public flocked to see what the fuss was about. On a hard-found $110,000, *The Birth of a Nation* grossed $18 million within a few years, proving to be one of the most financially successful pictures ever made. The picture not only won acceptance for film as an art form, it also established D. W. Griffith as the master of the silent screen.

Griffith's next effort, *Intolerance,* should have been anticli-
mactic. Instead, it was even more monumental. In his bitterness and shock at the backlash over his treatment of race
relations in *The Birth of a Nation,* Griffith found the theme
for his next great epic. It would be a panoramic study of the
evil people do to one another in the name of good, an examination of prejudice, of human intolerance for fellow humans.
Into this project Griffith poured all his profits from *The Birth
of a Nation,* nearly two years of time, and his personal views
of history. Using powerful visual images, he created a drama
about human imperfection, preaching the absolute necessity
of tolerance if the world was to survive.

With four separate stories set in four widely different periods of history, all running concurrently, *Intolerance* is one of
the most complex films ever made. The Babylonian story tells
of the empire's conquest by the Persians; the Nazarene story
portrays the Passion of Christ; the French story depicts
Catherine de Medici's persecution of the Huguenots, culmi-
nating in the St. Bartholomew's Day massacre; the modern
story deals with the struggle of workers against capitalism in
a Midwestern city and the last-minute rescue of an innocent
man wrongly sentenced to death. An epilogue illustrates Griffith's disposition to moralize and preach.

Griffith's creativity was displayed by his handling of time
as a spiral, with all four stories told simultaneously in parallel
action. Here the director employed his discovery that suspense could be built by cross-cutting between locales, with
each episode becoming progressively shorter, until ultimately
everything is happening at once. Griffith also used parallel
camera techniques to portray parallel action: closeup of one
story, closeup of another; long shot of one, long shot of another. At the climax of each story—a mountain girl racing to
warn Belshazzer of the approach of the Persians, Christ climbing Calvary, the French soldiers galloping to massacre the
Huguenots, the condemned youth's wife in a breakneck drive
to obtain a pardon for her husband—the four streams of action come together into a mainstream that engulfs the audience.

Nevertheless, the film was a commercial failure when it
was released. Meeting a cool and puzzled public, this failure
was, perhaps, due to its own excellence, for in terms of technique, *Intolerance* was years ahead of its time. Its interwoven
stories were too complex, its pace too fatiguing, and its

changing images too rapid for audiences not yet cinematically sophisticated.

The fans may have been puzzled and confused, but film directors sat up and took notice. *Intolerance* showed them how the epic should be done. Griffith's film utilized large sets, lavish costumes, complex war machinery, racing chariots, and surging crowd scenes. He used panning techniques and traveling shots that captured the vastness of his story. After his inventive camera had done its work, there were few cinematic techniques left to offer to the genre. Griffith had used all of them.

Griffith's most popular film was *Way Down East* (1920), a well-known melodrama, best remembered today for its ice-flow sequence. The public cheered Richard Barthelmess as he rescued Lillian Gish from being swept over a waterfall. In 1921, Griffith's *Orphans of the Storm,* with a plot based on the French Revolution, demonstrated the master's ability to handle crowds, create individual characters, and sustain suspense. Audiences liked the picture, but critics started to attack the director for his prudish morals and inability to adapt to current trends. By this time, Griffith, plagued by financial problems and faulty scripts, under the constant strain of trying to live up to his reputation, was beginning to lose his creative touch. In 1925, this great independent artist went to work for Paramount, then later for Joseph Schenck. Griffith made two talking pictures, *Abraham Lincoln* (1930) and *The Struggle* (1931). *Lincoln* was praised by the critics, but *The Struggle* was not. Its plot was considered old-fashioned, and the sound suffered from poor engineering. The once-great artist, in competition with younger men with New York theater backgrounds, realized there was no place in the newly sophisticated movie industry for his by now dated films.

Today Griffith is credited with having invented practically all cinematography, even though many of his innovations had been used before by various directors. However, Griffith took such techniques as the fadein, the fadeout, the long shot, the full shot, the moving camera, the closeup, the flashback, and cross-cutting, and refined them all, creating a total screen technique. And as well as developing cinematic technique, he brought to the screen a wide range of subjects, going from the works of Tennyson, Browning, and Poe to social problem films, the philosophical essays such as *Man's Genius* (1912).

Griffith died in 1948, remembered at that time only by a

few who had loved his pictures and recognized the artistry he had brought to the screen.

Mutual in 1912 selected Mack Sennett as head of a company for comedy and named their subdivision Keystone Film Company. The comedies were to be released by Mutual. The first Keystone production *Cohen Collects a Debt* (1912) was a hit and every week until January 1913 two comedies were produced.

Mack Sennett's films owe their popularity to sight gags. His comedies depend on gross exaggeration, destructive mayhem, speed, and surprise. He keeps his performers racing from one hilarious situation to another, indulging in mad capers, harmless violence, and undisciplined destruction. Each film ends with a frenzied chase, filled with improbable dangers that have the audience hanging onto their seats.

In Sennett's mad world, nothing has logic or normal consequences. People whack enemies and friends alike over the head with gigantic clubs, automobiles crash head-on, and people run into immovable objects. But the blows merely stagger the victim, making him roll his eyes, adjust his bowler hat, and hurry off. Crockery, clubs, bullets, and custard pies never seem to be harmful. People fall from high buildings or dive off cliffs, only to struggle to their feet and run once more.

Sennett's characters are largely based on circus clowns, with their chalk-white faces, heavy, black shaggy eyebrows, grotesque clothes, floppy shoes, and ridiculous hats. His performers dress in costumes that conceal water pistols, trick flowers, and even live dogs; they are prancing mimes, tumblers, and acrobats who strut about doing outrageous things with their rubbery faces.

Sennett had been influenced by the early French comedies, with their eccentric characters and trick photography. Borrowing from many of these early French films, he combined their techniques with his own situations and collection of clowns. Sennett's pictures usually begin by planting gags based on props. Within a few minutes, something goes wrong, and the misunderstood hero or heroine is pursued by scores of police, dubbed the Keystone Kops, who tumble out of a station house and leap into a tin lizzie. The chase is on: people, machines, children, dogs, ditches, and ponds are obstacles to leap over, run around, or fall into. By means of trick photography in the chase sequences, characters run backwards as well as forward, leap walls, or cycle up the sides of buildings. In his mad flight, the hero might confiscate a car, motorcycle, bicycle, or roller skates, escaping by a hair's breadth oncoming trolleys, crosstown traffic, puffing trains, lawn sprinklers, or pedestrians threatening him with umbrellas.

From his past experience in burlesque, Sennett learned that deflating authority always produced a laugh. A pie in the eye makes the recipient look ridiculous. With his collection of clowns facing a maelstrom of mad machines and flying custard, Sennett is, in a sly way, giving his personal opinion of the world. Pompous people who take life and themselves too seriously are left in shambles. Women who dare to affect lorgnettes are objects to be destroyed. Pious people are often hypocrites. Stupid sheriffs are constantly outwitted by country bumpkins.

Sennett's genius is both in his use of the camera and in his editing. Using concurrent action, he quickly cuts from the person being chased back to the pursuers. Speed makes his films work. As the film increases in tempo, so does Sennett's cutting. Extensive slow shots give way to short, quick scenes that match the speed of the action. As his characters take flight, his quick-cut editing increases. Sennett sometimes changes his camera speed from the usual twenty-four frames per second to twelve or eight frames. By using this device in chase sequences, he brings his films to a smashing climax.

As director and, later, supervisor of his own studio, Sennett churned out literally hundreds of comedies between 1912 and 1935. The public soon grew to know the cast and to applaud when the titles appeared on the screen. A large gallery of talented knockabout comedians had their early training in Sennett's "fun factory": Mabel Normand, Slim Summerville, Louise Fazenda, Polly Moran, Buster Keaton, Chester Conklin, Mack Swain, "Fatty" Arbuckle, Charlie Murray, and a young English comedian named Charlie Chaplin.

Sennett's wonder world of comedy lost much of its popularity, however, by the end of the 1920's. Sound eliminated much of the fun of the Keystone Kops. Gags planted, developed, and finished off within a hundred feet of film no longer amused the public. Actors left Sennett for other studios offering better scripts and more money, and a few formed companies of their own; others were eager to turn to drama. Like Pearl White and her serials, and D. W. Griffith and his melodramas, Sennett and his comedies became dated. For him, comedy meant one thing: slapstick. The public, however, demanded more variety. Booking offices dropped the Keystone comedies. In 1938, the Sennett studios were bought by Republic Pictures, and Sennett's tin lizzie, filled with Kops, drove off into cinema history.

Sennett's comedies contain an indefinable something, more profound in meaning than ordinary nonsense or slapstick. Modern critics see in his mad scenes the Theater of the Absurd, the domain of such playwrights as Samuel Beckett, Jean Genêt, Albert Camus, Jean-Paul Sartre, and Eugene Ionesco. Basically, their plays offer a philosophy of the pointlessness of life, the senselessness of what happens to people. Characters live in a world that is ridiculous, incongruous, and unreasonable. In their works, too, houses have collapsing walls, pavements hide holes into which unsuspecting pedestrians fall waist-deep, cars fall apart and just as often reassemble, corpses refuse to stop growing, chairs proliferate like rabbits, and children keep their parents in garbage cans.

Sennett shows men living in a mechanized world whose ambition often drives them to destruction, characters in a world in which traditional sanctions and meanings seem to have been overthrown. Like Absurdist plays, Sennett's films have few elements of plot and little narrative. Individualized psychology is largely abandoned. Characters engage in fierce but motiveless contests or combat. The image of man is distorted, and the bizarre is normal. There are moments when his clowns shuffle down the street, then turn and look at us, as if to say that man is alone. Snub Pollard seems to be waiting for Godot; Charlie Chaplin, Marie Dressler, Mack Swain, Mabel Normand, and Chester Conklin, when they get together in *Tillie's Punctured Romance*, seem strongly related to the people in Eugene Ionesco's *The Bald Soprano*.

Charlie Chaplin, the English comedian, came to America in 1910 with a traveling music hall troupe. Within a decade, he was known as the greatest single performer in the history of films. No motion picture actor before or since has rivaled his universal popularity.

Making a Living (1914) was Chaplin's first film for Mack

Sennett, but the officials at Keystone Studios were not impressed. The Englishman was not in tune with the tempo of the Keystone Kops' roughhouse routines. Chaplin's comedy style, learned in the English music halls, was mainly based on pantomime. Emphasized body movement, subtlety of emotion, hand movement, a soulful turn of the head, a glance, a slight twitch of the body, a lowering of the eyes, and a coy and sometimes slightly feminine delicacy were his trademarks. His whimsical, poignant charm was overwhelmed in the melee created by the Sennett gang.

At first, Chaplin was given small character roles that were a notch above walk-on parts: a drunken count, an English fop, a waiter, a villain. By his third picture, Chaplin had worked out what he thought was a "fun" costume. One day, while preparing for a routine appearance in a hotel lobby scene, he borrowed some clothes from Roscoe Arbuckle, found a cane, put on an old derby hat, and pasted on a little black mustache. He hurried to the set of Mabel Normand's current picture, *Mabel's Strange Predicament* (1914), and came rushing on in the routine that he had learned in vaudeville. Bystanders watching the director shoot the picture howled; co-workers bent over with laughter. The now-famous skating, skidding, gliding walk, with mustache twitching and cane twirling, hat repeatedly raised to one and all and teeth showing in a wide smile, was used for the first time. Thus the best-known character in all cinema history was born. The "Tramp" or "The Little Fellow" with the faint smile, floppy walk, and soulful eyes appeared in dozens of films, becoming better known throughout the world than presidents, kings, and statesmen.

After making twelve one-reel pictures for Sennett, Chaplin was permitted to direct his own films, a job that he never relinquished.

Consisting mostly of sight gags and funny situations, these early Sennett comedies with Chaplin were made before the comedian could develop depth in his characterization. Realizing that he was on the road to success, Chaplin left the Sennett Studios for Essanay, where he wrote his own scripts, cast the minor roles, and, like D. W. Griffith, collected a coterie of actors, cameramen, and technicians who continued with him from picture to picture. Bit by bit, the little tramp developed into the sad little clown. In each new picture, the shabby but neat little man with exquisite manners, invariably alone or with only a stray dog for company, faced life's bleakness with a touch of elegance and irony, and a spirit that could not be destroyed.

Almost all of his films end with Charlie, thwarted from attaining whatever he wanted most, hitching up his oversize pants, twitching his mustache, and snapping his fingers at the entire universe. He would turn, look at the audience, smile sadly, then wave goodbye as he ambled down a dusty road.

People flocked to see Chaplin's screen adventures. His outstanding films were: *The Tramp* (1915); *Easy Street* (1917); *Shoulder Arms* (1918); *The Kid* (1921); *A Woman of Paris* (1923), which he directed only; *The Gold Rush* (1925), considered by some his best work; *The Circus* (1928); *City Lights* (1931); *Modern Times* (1936); *The Great Dictator* (1940); and *Monsieur Verdoux* (1947).

In *Monsieur Verdoux*, one of the screen's first black comedies (see Film Vocabulary in the Appendix), he made his most unconventional picture. Plagued by distasteful publicity—he was accused of being a Communist, criticized because of his failure to become an American citizen, and faced with paternity suit and tax problems—Chaplin turned out this classic satire in which he appears as a debonair bluebeard, a murderer with a philosophical outlook, who marries and then kills several women. Chaplin was, of course, denouncing concentration camps, dictators, war-mongers, and munitions makers; he was pointing out the close similarity between a murderer and a patriot. In his role as Verdoux, the businessman whose business happened to be killing, Chaplin succeeded in arousing further the anger of patriotic organizations throughout America.

Eventually, a disillusioned Chaplin left the United States to live in Switzerland. He made a few more pictures: *Limelight* (1952), praised by the critics, and *A King in New York* (1957), considered by most to be a flawed masterpiece. In *A Countess from Hong Kong* (1966), he shared the scene with two superstars, Marlon Brando and Sophia Loren, but the critics were not impressed. The Little Fellow however, had long ago taken his place among the immortals of the screen. Chaplin, along with Griffith, was one of the first persons to use cinema as a personal instrument for expressing his own attitudes and feelings. Of all the early stars, none is more esteemed or honored than Charlie Chaplin. In his old age, he has received recognition from any number of film festivals and world organizations. In 1971 the Motion Picture Academy gave him a special Academy Award, and in 1975, for his brilliant work in film, the Queen of England honored him with a knighthood.

3 / The Rise
of the Star System

SEVERAL organizational developments significant to the history of American films occurred within the five-year period from 1915 to 1920. First, Hollywood grew into an artificial, one-industry town with its own values, a stratified society with a unique concept of reality. Second, accompanying this growth of the industry was the growing popularity of performers who demanded higher and higher salaries, not necessarily because of the quality of their work but because of the huge audience they could attract. Third, was the block booking system, in which important producers required exhibitors to buy films in blocks of five or more, frequently sight unseen. In this way, exhibitors were forced to buy poor commercial prospects in order to obtain the movies with the moneymakers. In 1919, the powerful and important United Artists Corporation was formed by D. W. Griffith, Charlie Chaplin, Douglas Fairbanks, and Mary Pickford, in order to circumvent the system of block booking and to distribute their own and other people's films. Unhappy with their lack of independence while working for others, the four artists set up their own company to make quality films and to distribute them outside the system whereby films were available only to cinemas linked to the production company.

For the first decade of filmmaking, stars as we know them today were not part of the industry. In early films, performers were not given credit; film companies rightly feared that performers who became known by name would develop followings and be in a position to demand higher salaries.

By 1910, however, certain actors had emerged as favorites and were known either by nicknames or descriptive titles. Fan letters arrived at the studios addressed to "The Waif," "The Man with the Sad Eyes," "Broncho Billy," "Little Mary," "The Fat Boy," or "The Railway Girl." This identification factor was enhanced by Griffith's experimentation with the closeup, a technique disliked initially by the studio bosses, who were sure that the public paid its nickels to see an entire actor, not merely his head. Florence Lawrence, a member of the American Biograph Company, known to filmgoers as "The Biograph Girl," became the first film star when producer Carl Laemmle gave her a thousand dollars a week and proper billing under her own name. The star system, with all its glory and glamour, had arrived.

Soon after 1910, five typical roles were developed, which set a pattern for future years. The sweet, innocent girl who was more whimsical tomboy than woman, and who fought for her virtue against all odds, was a public favorite. Mary Pickford, the first great star of the American cinema, shaped her acting talents to the role. The solemn-faced, strong and silent William S. Hart became the screen's outstanding cowboy. Possessing nobility and an aura of romanticism, he appeared out of nowhere to right all wrongs and banish evil. Douglas Fairbanks was the exuberant boy-man athlete, who performed hair-raising feats and last-minute rescues without losing his smile or the twinkle in his eye. The fourth great star was the comic Charlie Chaplin. The lonely, whimsical, funny little tramp always lost the girl at the end of the picture, but after drying a tear, he hurried off to another adventure. The fifth, and the least important, was the "vamp," or *femme fatale*, played frequently by Theda Bara. She lured men to their death, or at least to a life of grief.

Mary Pickford—"Little Mary," "America's Sweetheart," or "The World's Sweetheart"—was the reigning queen of the screen for at least twenty years. Small, pretty, and fragile, she was not only a gifted actress with a flair for comedy, she also possessed great intelligence and was an astute businesswoman. Along with her work as a performer, she had the time, brains, and money to become co-founder of one of the great studios, United Artists. The little girl with the golden curls played the role of a dimpled, lovable tomboy who somehow remained feminine. This child-waif character, more than any other film personality, epitomized the concept of a screen goddess at that time.

Because of her small stature and the public's constant demand to see her in child roles, she was restricted to playing certain characters. As the perennial Pollyanna, she was often surrounded by downtrodden children. Beloved by the public, she became the single biggest draw at the box office, the first performer to attract crowds who waited on line to see her pictures.

Like Peter Pan, Mary Pickford never grew up in her films but continued to play the part of the innocent, wide-eyed girlish heroine for at least two decades. At age 29, she filmed *Little Lord Fauntleroy*; in 1926, at age 33, she appeared as the boisterous tomboy in *Sparrows*.

Mary Pickford held America enthralled. She worked relentlessly, guiding scriptwriters to preserve the stereotyped image of the sexless young girl on the verge of womanhood. She was in tune with the optimism of the 1920's, and almost from the beginning of her first film, *Her First Biscuit* (1909), until the last, *Secrets* (1933), Miss Pickford portrayed the essence of America. She had that special magnetism that makes a star. For almost a quarter of a century, she entertained the public and worked diligently to advance the film industry as an established art form. Her best films are *Daddy Long Legs* (1919), *Pollyanna* (1919), *Little Lord Fauntleroy* (1921), *Little Annie Rooney* (1925), and *Sparrows* (1926).

Toward the end of the 1920's, however, her little-girl image lost its appeal to moviegoers, and she retired in 1933. As audiences demanded a more sophisticated approach to life, the charm of Mary Pickford faded, for the country no longer believed in myths of innocence or virtue. The advent of sound, the realities of the Great Depression, and changing times forced old values and images off the screen. Like her friends D. W. Griffith, Pearl White, Mack Sennett, and others, Miss Pickford's "Little Mary" became unfashionable. In 1976, the Academy Awards honored her as one of the great members of the film industry.

Douglas Fairbanks portrayed the swashbuckling, acrobatic, zestful, ever-smiling hero of many comedies. His screen characters, tailored to fit his talent for acrobatics and clowning, were happy-go-lucky, optimistic one-hundred-percent Americans. In almost all his pictures, Fairbanks managed a last-minute rescue of a damsel in distress, coming to the aid of his leading ladies with acrobatic prowess. *The Mark of Zorro* (1920) added a costume-picture dimension to his career, and in *Robin Hood* (1923) and *The Thief of Bagdad* (1924), he reached his zenith. He gave the public amusing films, and he provided the film industry with high box office returns.

Fairbanks also had a head for business. He pointed out to Pickford, Chaplin, and Griffith that since they were tremendous box office attractions, they should organize their own company and reap some of the receipts. In 1919, the foursome incorporated United Artists.

Fairbanks's age and his indifference helped end his career prematurely. Costume pictures, acrobatics, and rescuing damsels in distress became somewhat dated. Eventually his role was filled by a younger actor, Errol Flynn. Fairbanks's best films are *His Majesty the American* (1919), *The Mark of Zorro* (1920), *The Three Musketeers* (1921), *Robin Hood* (1921), and *The Thief of Bagdad* (1923).

No discussion of the rise of the early American film star is complete without mention of Theda Bara. She deserves a place among the early outstanding performers of the screen simply because of her unusual rise to fame. Theda Bara was the first star to be manufactured by a manager, a press agent, and a studio.

The daughter of a tailor, Theodosia Goodman was born in Cincinnati, Ohio, went to California as a girl, and found work as an extra in pictures. In 1914, Frank J. Powell decided to film the stage play *A Fool There Was*, and to cast an unknown actress in the role of the exotic seductress. Miss Goodman was selected for the role.

William Fox's publicity department changed her name to Theda Bara, (an anagram of "Arab death") and launched her on the road to stardom. Powell gave her a different personality, taught her distinctive mannerisms, and even selected her clothes. A fictitious Oriental background was created for her. The word "vamp" (from vampire) was coined to describe her, due to her role as an unscrupulous female who uses her charms to seduce or beguile hapless men and then destroy them.

After *A Fool There Was*, Bara made thirty-nine pictures in three years for Fox Studios, repeating her role in increasingly outlandish costumes. As early as 1919, however, the public began to tire of the repetitiveness of her role, eventually switching their loyalty to less exotic stars. Without Theda Bara, however, the Fox Film Corporation could never have gained the eminence in the motion picture industry that it did.

Other studios, seeing the success of the Fox Studio publicity department, followed suit, launching stars with fanfare and contrived publicity. Promotional campaigns became a part of studio procedure. Many similar studio tricks were used to help the careers of Marion Davies, Rudolph Valentino, Mae Murray, and (years later) Kim Novak, Marilyn Monroe, and Brigitte Bardot. If Theda Bara is no longer remembered for her acting, at least she commands a place in American cinema history for having inaugurated the synthetic star.

Although "Broncho Billy" Anderson is credited with portraying the first screen cowboy, it was William S. Hart who added depth to the role and became the public's favorite Western hero. In Hart's films there is an almost documentary approach to lighting, sets, and landscapes. His harsh photography caught the feeling of both land and people. Hart's two-reel films were the most realistic pictures of Western life for years, until directors John Ford, Howard Hawks, William Wyler, and George Stevens added new dimensions to the genre.

Hart portrayed the silent, strong, dependable "good badman," eventually emerging as one of the most popular stars the screen ever produced. He reigned as king of the cowboy stars into the 1920's, when he was replaced by a flashier Tom Mix.

A Hart film usually featured a complex hero who rode into town as an outlaw, but, because of his basically good character, would join the townspeople in their fight against evil. By the end of the film, Hart's cowboy experienced a personal turnabout that brought about his own moral reform. Once the problem was settled, however, true to the code of the West, he could neither accept marriage nor settle for the quiet ways of town life; with a firm chin, he would ride off alone into the sunset.

Hart made his best pictures between 1916 and 1925. *Hell's Hinges* (1916), *The Gun Fighter* (1916), and *Tumbleweeds* (1925) aptly demonstrate that "horse opry" could be more than mere melodrama or epic; it could present the psychological aspects of the cowboy torn by deep inner conflicts.

Pickford, Fairbanks, Hart, Chaplin, and Bara worked hard, had special talents, and gave their audiences hours of pleasure. Pickford epitomized the age of innocence. Fairbanks implied that life could be adorned with grace, wit, and style. Chaplin portrayed the loneliest man in the world; rejected and shut out, he was Everyman who lost everything, except his indomitable spirit to survive and begin again.

Bara's vamp may have been short-lived, but for some years she thrilled audiences with her screen love affairs. Hart's Western films offered a lost Eden and developed an American mythological character who is still depicted on the screen today. These prototypical stars of the early 1920's established the great tradition of screen stardom.

By 1926, the worship of film stars had grown to such proportions that if Charlie Chaplin even ventured into the street, he was mobbed; Douglas Fairbanks was also treated as a conquering hero. Fans waited in train stations to get a glimpse of Gloria Swanson on her transcontinental journeys, and Norma Talmadge, Blanche Sweet, and Lillian Gish were goddesses to the multitude. When Rudolph Valentino died suddenly in August, 1926, his fans touched off an unparalleled frenzy of hysterical behavior at his funeral. The American movie stars were worshipped as quasi-deities.

4 / The Expanding Industry: 1915-1927

By 1915, films had become big business, growing bigger each year. Several new firms emerged during the five years between 1915-1920; among these were Metro, Universal Pictures, and Goldwyn Pictures Corporation. Bigger companies meant bigger salaries, and in 1917, First National Exhibitors Circuit offered Charlie Chaplin $1,075,000 to make eight two-reel films. However, despite this period of tremendous growth, not all companies were successful. Biograph, Kalem, and Lubin, three pioneer outfits, failed. Vitagraph and Essanay were active but hardly thriving, and Pathé was saved from bankruptcy only by a string of exciting serials.

By the mid-1920's, thirty years after Edison unveiled his Kinetoscope, filmmaking had developed into America's fifth largest industry. The infant, initially underestimated as a novelty by its procreators, was burgeoning into a financial giant. In the eyes of more perceptive critics, however, the Hollywood film industry had become an inhuman monster that annually devoured the creative talents of the thousands who flocked West in search of fame, fortune, and adventure. Hopeful actors, designers, writers, and technicians sacrificed their artistic freedom for money and notoriety. They were grist for the Hollywood mill during the 1915-1927 boom period, and many of the products turned out were only mediocre. More indicative of this growth period were the numerous dehumanizing but evolutionary aspects of the new industry: the development of Hollywood itself, the flowering of the star system, the influx of foreign talent, the switch to new themes and characters, and the rise of censorship.

The years 1915 to 1927 were filled with great activity and physical growth. The big studios—United Artists, Fox, Metro-Goldwyn-Mayer, Paramount, Warner Brothers, Universal, Columbia—became miniature empires, with separate departments for stories, wardrobe, lighting, sets, and publicity.

Cameramen, always a crucial part of the industry, now began receiving proper credit for their work. Griffith's photographer Billy Bitzer was still one of the best; Karl Brown, who photographed the epic *The Covered Wagon* (1923), was in demand; Charles Rosher helped make *Sunrise* (1927) one of the most beautiful films of the decade. Others who turned motion picture photography into an art form were William Daniels, Bert Glennon, Lee Garmes, and Lucien Ballard.

Writers also were needed, as expanding theater chains opened more and more outlets, setting up a demand for an unending succession of new pictures. Studios built up stables of dependable hacks who competed against and often surpassed the efforts of established authors. Writing for the studios was particularly attractive to beginning writers of genuine talent who had limited finances. Paramount, eager for prestige, boasted of filming stories written by Joseph Conrad, Arnold Bennett, Robert Hitchens, E. Phillips Oppenheim, and W. Somerset Maugham.

Among the most successful screenwriters were women. June Mathis scripted *Blood and Sand* (1922), and *Ben Hur* (1926). Elinor Glyn, who reconciled new eroticism with old romanticism, made a fortune with her stylized flapper tales, beginning with *The Great Moment* (1921), *Beyond the Rocks* (1922), and *Three Weeks* (1924). Frances Marion wrote the scenario for *The Scarlet Letter* (1926). Anita Loos and her husband, John Emerson, specialized in tailoring scripts to the talents of specific stars such as Douglas Fairbanks and Mary Pickford, and, later, Joan Crawford and Greer Garson.

Women were winning recognition in other areas as well. Julia Crawford Ivers, May Tully, Mildred Webb, and Lois Weber were directors. June Mathis, a staff writer at MGM, was made head of the scenario department of Goldwyn Studios. Dorothy Arzner, who edited the Valentino picture *Blood and Sand* (1922) and *The Covered Wagon* (1923) became a leading director in the 1930's.

In the big studios the hierarchy of producer, director, actor, and writer was supported by a number of other departments. Cedric Gibbons, who helped on costumes and sets for Edison from 1915 to 1917, joined MGM in 1924 to help create the handsome Metro look in that studio's productions. Albert D'Agostino later brought flair and good taste to RKO's art department. Hans Dreier and Van Nest Polglase made the Paramount sets the best of the decade. William

Cameron Menzies became known in the 1920's with his elaborate sets for *Thief of Bagdad* (1924). During the 1930's he developed into the most influential designer in the American cinema. Assistant directors, makeup and property people, and special effects departments contributed to the success of many films. Publicity writers joined the studios to inform magazines, newspapers, and later, radio about the dream world of Hollywood and its stars.

As the companies grew bigger, it became more and more difficult for individual creative artists such as Griffith to function independently. Studio heads such as Paramount's Adolph Zukor, a Hungarian immigrant, were buying up hundreds of theaters across the country in order to have ready outlets for their pictures. Other entrepreneurs such as Marcus Loew, who began as an exhibitor and helped form MGM in 1924, went into production to ensure a supply of films for his own cinemas. By the middle of the 1920's, the big studios dominated the industry to such an extent that independent companies were forced either to merge or to fold.

The movies themselves achieved new heights in terms of numbers and magnitude. New directors, new writers, new stars, and new technicians created hundreds of films for a voracious public more interested in glamorous stars than in masterful editing, artistic photography, or quality scripts. The bigger the business, apparently, the more mediocre the product.

There were some definite reasons for this lack of quality. The studios had become too big to risk taking chances on the unknown, and scripts had to be approved by industry heads, who operated like cost accountants. Money, not art, was important, and the scenario departments quickly learned that sex guaranteed box office success. Tawdry themes, titillating titles, and big-name stars sold pictures. By 1920, about thirty-five million Americans were going to the movies every week, primarily to see a particular movie star.

The 1920's represented the zenith of the star mystique. Newly created publicity departments and the fan magazines—*Photoplay, Screenland, Motion Pictures, Cinema,* and *Picture Play*—spewed forth a constant stream of stories about these legendary beings. Hollywood stars were royalty. Separated from the rest of the world by living in a company town, subjected to constant adulation yet treated as properties, many stars began to believe their own publicity.

Across the screen came the perennial favorites, Chaplin,

Pickford, Fairbanks, and Hart. Of lesser magnitude were such matinee idols as John Barrymore, who scowled his way through the dual role of Dr. Jekyll and Mr. Hyde, and Rudolph Valentino, the patent-leather-haired lover who glided around studio dance floors. A notch lower on the popularity ladder were Ramon Novarro, Buddy Rogers, and Ronald Colman. Lon Chaney, although hardly a matinee idol, broke box office records with his portrayals of physically deformed and mentally twisted characters. Lillian Gish continued to play and be loved for her role of the innocent adrift in a hostile world. Exotic stars such as Mae Murray, Norma Talmadge, Alla Nazimova, Pola Negri, and Gloria Swanson gave life to sultry characters and in turn received slavish adoration from their fans. Flappers such as Colleen Moore, Clara Bow, and Joan Crawford were a success with the younger crowd.

Acting teams also became popular, especially after MGM presented "the screen's greatest lovers," Greta Garbo and John Gilbert, in *Flesh and the Devil* (1927). Janet Gaynor and Charles Farrell, another combination, starred in a popular love story, *Seventh Heaven* (1927). Ronald Colman (1925), a romantic British star with polished manners, and Vilma Banky cavorted in *The Dark Angel* (1925), *The Magic Flame* (1927), and *The Night of Love* (1927), all tales of mythical kingdoms.

Fantastic fortunes were made and lost by stars, studios, and magnates during Hollywood's gilded decade. In the 1920's, Hollywood—its mystique, its artificial world, and its inhabitants—was its own most important product. Thousands flocked to Los Angeles every year, drawn by dreams of high living, easy money, and instant success.

According to the fan magazines, stars lived glamorous lives on fantastic salaries. Gloria Swanson typified the rags-to-riches myth. From an unknown Sennett extra in 1916 to a world sex symbol by 1925, Swanson was soon rich enough to produce her own films, marry a marquis, and collect a salary of $20,000 a week. Paramount's publicity department kept the world informed of her romantic escapades. The high living of Swanson and other stars made Hollywood synonymous with extravagance. Stars lived in such style that East Coast sophisticates and worldly Europeans soon judged the whole atmosphere to be vulgar and cheap.

America was hypnotized by the tinsel and mistook it for the real thing. Along with the ambitious and the eager came the drug pushers, gangsters, and other exploiters who preyed on both the extra and the powerful star. The town was a hodgepodge of greedy agents, talented actors, suave playboys, cowboys, country bumpkins, wide-eyed girls from small towns, and foreigners.

By 1925, Hollywood had acquired a reputation as a center for sin, crime, drugs, and riotous living. In 1920, Olive Thomas, unable to find a supply of cocaine, committed suicide in Paris. Wallace Reid, a promising star, died of a drug overdose. In 1921, after a drunken party, Virginia Rappe was carried from a San Francisco hotel suite dying from internal wounds. The popular Keystone clown Fatty Arbuckle was arrested and charged with manslaughter, and although Arbuckle was acquitted, his film career was ruined. William Desmond Taylor, a director at Lasky Studios and President of the Screen Directors' Association, was murdered. Because of their friendship with Taylor and some love letters that were discovered, Mary Miles Minter (Pickford's rival) and Mabel Normand were both mentioned at the inquest; Miss Minter's career was ended. Although cleared of any connection with the Taylor murder, Mabel Normand was soon involved in a second scandal that ended her film career. Alone and almost forgotten, this gay, bright comedienne died of tuberculosis at 36. In 1924, Charlie Chaplin's sensational divorce from Lita Grey and his amorous offscreen escapades almost forced his retirement from the screen.

The types of movies being filmed also underwent drastic changes early in the 1920's. Henry King's homespun melodrama, *Tol'able David* (1921), was a fitting goodbye to America's age of innocence. Judged by today's standards, King's rural romance would probably be dismissed quickly because of the story's contrived melodrama and sentimentality. Young David, after a merciless beating, defeats three bandits who had entered the village, killed his father, and crippled his brother. David's victory earns more than "jest tol'able" approval from his proud mother. Richard Barthelmess's shyness and boyish face captured the beauty and charm of the rustic title character, and the very simplicity of the film was a key to its success.

From 1910 to 1925, almost half of the films produced in America had been concerned with rustic dramas like this. Saving the homestead and contrasting the virtues of the farmboy with the evils of city slickers were favorite themes. *Tol'able David* was the swan song of the horse-and-buggy days, for urban ways and values were on the rise. By 1925, city-oriented movie fans rejected these old-fashioned stories; the rustic drama had lived out its day.

A prosperous, growing middle class of Americans was demanding new themes and characters. The Victorian moralizing of D. W. Griffith appeared ludicrous to a generation that discarded corsets, read F. Scott Fitzgerald, rode in automobiles, and drank bathtub gin. These moviegoers wanted to see the new leisure class in their beautiful homes, clothes, and motor cars; they were interested in girls who petted, drank, smoked, rolled their stockings, bobbed their hair, and had "It." A new generation of men returning from the battlefronts of World War I, and emancipated women, influenced by the radio, automobile, and advertising, demanded different social and moral standards.

Youth no longer believed in the old maxims handed down from earlier generations. The pursuit of pleasure became one of life's principal occupations, with chastity and self-restraint belonging to the elderly and/or the religious. The separation between generations became greater than ever before, for there was a new-found freedom for younger people. The Jazz Age had arrived.

Film titles alone illustrate the change: *Lessons in Love* (1921), *Foolish Wives* (1922), *One Week of Love* (1923), *Flaming Youth* (1923), *His Hour* (1924), *The Golden Bed* (1925), and *The Plastic Age* (1925). In *Prodigal Daughter* (1923), Gloria Swanson embarked on a search for sexual freedom. In *Dancing Mothers* (1926), Alice Joyce left husband and family for a new life. Harry Beaumont's *Our Dancing Daughters* (1928) presented a wide-eyed Joan Crawford as a reckless flapper.

Not all was dancing and partying, however. Erich von Stroheim's *Greed* (1923) is a realistic study of money as the root of all evil; *The Big Parade* (1925) and later *What Price Glory?* (1926), faithfully presented the brutality of war by using simulated scenes. *Underworld* (1927) opened a new genre by depicting the vicious gangster underworld and its shadowy characters. *The Crowd* (1928) explored the drabness of mechanical living in the metropolis. *The Wind* (1928), perhaps Lillian Gish's finest film, was a study of a sensitive girl's struggle against a hostile environment. Paul Fejos caught the impressions of urban loneliness in *Lonesome* (1928).

New characters replaced earlier stereotypes. Ruthless gunmen, collegians, gold diggers, playboys, and jazz-mad boys and girls were popular characters by the late 1920's. Mary Pickford's sweet, innocent tomboy type was favored by small-town filmgoers, but Clara Bow, the "It" girl, was preferred by sophisticated city dwellers. The Gish sisters and the Talmadge girls were losing their public. Cinderella was replaced by the aggressive, attractive, smart, seductive woman, and the polite, shy, proper American boy gave way to a dynamic, commanding, handsome male who flaunted his sex appeal by appearing half-nude in the boudoir. Many fans not only accepted but also approved of the modern "fallen girl/woman" who did *not* repent with tear-dimmed eyes and renounce her sin in the last reel.

Cecil B. DeMille, with his ability to recognize public changes in manners and mores, became the most popular director of the 1920's. Sensitive to the growing postwar shift in American morals, DeMille focused his efforts on titillating comedies. Bedrooms became standard sets in his pictures and in dozens of imitations. He "discovered" the bathtub and used it as an excuse to disrobe his heroine, usually Gloria Swanson. The climax of his *Saturday Night* (1922) featured a masked ball, with extras undressing and throwing themselves into a swimming pool.

If Hollywood and the younger generation had discarded Victorian standards, it was soon apparent that a great many other Americans had not. Clubwomen, church members, and civic organizations were shocked by newspaper accounts of Hollywood scandals. Civic groups called upon the authorities to ban certain films. The press and Church and political leaders agreed that crime and sin needed to be checked, not only in films but also in the stars' private lives. The public demanded that some sort of restraints be placed on the film capital and its actors before the entire industry became an international disgrace. As early as 1915, Congress reacted to public criticism by holding hearings on the industry's financial activities as well as on the morality of films. In order to avoid having the federal government meddle in their productions and regulate films through censorship, the movie magnates established their own National Board of Review, and in 1919, the studios formed The National Association of the Motion Picture Industry. Those desiring censorship were still not mollified, though.

To protect their films, the studio heads agreed to curb the outrageous behavior of some of the leading stars and to present more enlightening films. In October, 1922, fifteen producers met and elected Will H. Hays the first president of the Motion Picture Producers and Distributors of America. Hays, Postmaster-General in President Warren Harding's cabinet, was appointed czar and given the authority to police the morals of the movie industry. His job was to reform those who were misbehaving and to improve public relations.

Although in theory the Hays Office attempted to correct corruption both on and off the screen, in practice it merely succeeded in keeping most of the sensational stories out of the newspapers and in having certain stars promise not to misbehave in public. As for films, there was little one could do to prevent the studios from offering more risque themes and stories, especially since these films made money. One step the Hays Office took was to establish a code, issued to all studios, declaring that bad or sinful characters in the movies always had to be punished. No matter what happened during the picture, if the immoral characters were punished at the conclusion, the picture received a seal of approval. Directors proceeded to bypass restrictions by adding the requisite endings involving punishment for the evildoers. Characters who had lived riotous lives and broken the moral code were conveniently killed in the last few minutes of the film. By staving off the strong objections of moral critics throughout the 1920's, Hays was able to avoid any drastic action by most of the religious or civic groups.

When the committee for morality did establish standards, one of the most important directors affected by the code was the perceptive Cecil B. DeMille. In order to get around the rules, DeMille, always one step ahead of his fellow directors, simply turned to preaching without omitting sex. Bible in hand, DeMille presented his first sandal epic, *The Ten Commandments* (1923), in which he employed the perfect formula for box office success: violence, sex, and religion. He followed with *King of Kings* (1927). DeMille led, and other directors followed. They gave the public what it wanted—sin, nudity, and corruption—and to appease the Hays office, punished the offenders in the last ten minutes.

It has been suggested that the American hunger for a cultural tradition is evident in the yearning for things that are European. Having no royal family or nobility on which to lavish their attention, Americans tend to adulate other heroes, one of whom is the movie star. American audiences were eager in the 1920's for a more sophisticated version of romance than that proffered by Mary Pickford and the Gish Sisters.

Even the pseudo-sophistication of the flappers Clara Bow and Joan Crawford did not fill the bill.

The American audience was searching for new types—the adult romantic lover who combined sexual experience with courtesy and flair, who could seduce and still remain a hero, and the wordly woman to whom sex was neither a danger nor a joke, who combined mystery with real flesh and blood. By the very nature of things, the actors who played these parts simply had to be Europeans, real or manufactured. Gloria Swanson tried to recreate her image by taking several European jaunts, but the audience really wanted new faces and new types. French, German, and English theater talent disembarked in New York and caught the train for Hollywood.

The arrival of directors, stars, and technical personnel from Europe, especially from Germany, in the period immediately following World War I, had helped to make the early American films the best in the world. The combination of European artistry and American money had secured Hollywood's preeminence in filmdom. The Europeans brought into postwar America a new concept of reality and a new star image that contrasted with America's ingenues and farmboy heroes. Among the first directors who came were Maurice Tourneur, Ernst Lubitsch, E. A. DuPont, F. W. Murnau, Paul Leni, William Dieterle, Karl Freund, and Ludwig Berger. From Hungary came Michael Curtiz and Paul Fejos, and the actress Vilma Banky. From Mexico came the actors Ramon Novarro, Gilbert Roland, and Dolores del Rio. Jacques Feyder journeyed from France. Sweden contributed not only the incomparable Garbo but also the directors Mauritz Stiller and Victor Seastrom, one of the first directors to introduce deeper psychological characterizations to the screen. To these newcomers, Hollywood offered fame and a great deal of fortune, if they were successful.

Disillusioned when they found themselves required by contract to make films mechanically, penalized when they failed to produce slick American products, restricted not only by the studios but also by the Hays Office, and tired of empty stories, many foreigners refused to join the Hollywood establishment and returned to studios in Berlin, Vienna, London, and Paris. Mauritz Stiller, misused by MGM and given no chance to show his true ability, went home to Sweden. Emil Jannings disliked the hackneyed scripts that were handed to him and left for Germany. Pola Negri returned to Berlin and was eventually driven into obscurity by the advent of sound. Nevertheless, many Europeans stayed on to become internationally famous, leaving their marks not only on the silent films but also on film in the decades that followed.

American fans loved the comedies of Ernst Lubitsch, and the German director was an immediate success. His deft direction and editing elevated many performers into top stars, including Maurice Chevalier, Jeanette MacDonald, Miriam Hopkins, and Claudette Colbert.

Lubitsch's formula for success was the witty, superficial sex comedy. Like von Stroheim, he dealt with the lives and mores of upper-class Europeans, but unlike von Stroheim, he portrayed them as nice but naughty, just as Americans imagined them to be. His films had touches of irony, satire, and amusing observations of human foibles.

For a decade, "The Lubitsch Touch" was synonymous in the industry with brittle comedies that treated sex with a certain slyness. Lubitsch specialized in sophisticated triangle plots, and his movies in the 1920's and 1930's liberated films from such provincial ideas as the one that sex and money often mean unhappiness. For years, Lubitsch's concept of comedy was the pattern at Paramount Studios. Young American directors often copied his witty, urbane, and commercially successful style. His best American films were *The Love Parade* (1929), *Monte Carlo* (1930), *The Smiling Lieutenant* (1931), *Ninotchka* (1939), and *To Be or Not To Be* (1942).

F. W. Murnau, an outstanding German director, arrived in the United States on the eve of the sound era (1927) and was employed by Fox Studios. With the brilliant scenarist Carl Mayer, also from Germany, he fashioned the expressionistic *Sunrise* (1927) for Janet Gaynor. Unfortunately, Murnau was able to make only four films in Hollywood before his tragic death.

Sunrise brought prestige to Fox Studios and eventually took its place as a visually beautiful screen masterpiece. The film is a study of opposites, in which the rhythm and harshness of the city are contrasted with the ease and tranquility of country life: dark is contrasted with light, evil with good, illusion with reality, salvation with sin. Murnau's sensitive direction, Charles Rosher's photography, Roger Gliese's sets, and the compelling acting of the three principals helped make the picture one of the most lyrical and poetic epics of the 1920's. It was the last great silent picture turned out by West Coast studios. Thirteen days after its release, Al Jolson's

The Jazz Singer, the first film with sound, had its premiere in New York. Murnau's masterpiece was a fitting swan song for silent films.

By stretching categories, Josef von Sternberg can be classified as a member of the talent emigration from Europe. Born in Vienna, he worked in American films for fifteen years (1914-1929) and had, by the late 1920's, established a reputation in Hollywood, where he directed *The Salvation Hunters* (1924) and then *Underworld* (1927). He achieved outstanding success directing *The Last Command* (1927-28) with Emil Jannings, and on the strength of this film was invited to Germany to make Jannings's first sound film, *The Blue Angel* (1930). There he further demonstrated his directorial style, camerawork, and extraordinary taste in decor before he returned to Hollywood. After the advent of sound he turned out seven glossy adventure films with his star, Marlene Dietrich. Von Sternberg believed in lavish sets, eroticism, skillful lighting, and long silences. His collaboration with Dietrich eventually ended, but not before he had made her one of the outstanding sex goddesses of the 1930's.

The theories of filmmaking that the Europeans brought to Hollywood in the last years of the silent era were to dominate American films in the 1930's, and continue well into the 1940's. Their treatment of stories, their views on sex, their handling of dialogue, and certainly their knowledge of lighting helped raise the American screen to new heights of artistry.

Any history of the American movies must include the European director-actor Erich von Stroheim. On the screen, von Stroheim, with his stern features and bull neck, was the perfect brutal Prussian officer. The publicity department dubbed him "The Man you Love to Hate." World-weary, elegantly dressed, often toying with gloves, monocle, and riding whip, von Stroheim underlined his portrayal with a touch of cruelty. No matter how often he played the same role, he managed to bring originality to each performance. He shaded his intelligent portrayals with cynicism and irony; his eyes reflected his disillusionment and sometimes his depravity. Merely by kissing the hand of a beautiful woman he could suggest a secret meeting without saying a word. He could be debonair, gallant, and nonchalant, all the while suggesting the sadist lurking underneath the charm. With true stoicism and resignation he would meet his comeuppance at the film's end. For two generations of fans, von Stroheim embodied the Teutonic military type.

In 1918, von Stroheim persuaded Carl Laemmle of Universal Studios to let him direct a script (written by himself) called *Blind Husbands*. Impressed with the young man's audacity, Laemmle gave the thirty-three-year-old Austrian a contract that permitted him to design sets, direct, and if he chose, appear as the star of his own film. Thus began the career of one of the most original, brilliant, stubborn, enigmatic, and undisciplined directors in all screen history.

Blind Husbands (1918), with its eternal triangle theme, was an artistic and financial success, establishing the young director as a perceptive interpreter of European society. The picture suggests that neglected wives have the right to seek solace and love where they can. The mood throughout is wry, occasionally sentimental, and sometimes vicious. Von Stroheim's third film, *Foolish Wives* (1921), tells a tale of decadent high life on the Continent; it, too, has touches of sardonic wit and fills the screen with sensuality, symbolism, and seduction. *Merry-Go-Round* (1922) recreates the moral decay of the Hapsburgs' Vienna, but because Irving Thalberg, a studio executive, lost patience with von Stroheim's whims, temperament, and extravagance, Rupert Julian completed the film.

In *The Wedding March* (1926-28) von Stroheim again returns to his native Europe and dissects the moral corruption in Vienna of 1914. Maude George, George Fawcett, and George Nicholas give brilliant performances as older, jaded characters, ravaged by both age and spent passion. A highlight in the film is a visit to an elegant bordello, where the director makes cynical observations on human vice. In *The Wedding March,* von Stroheim jarred and amused his public by having dowagers smoke cigars and dressing both men and women in corsets, older women in chin reducers, and men in moustache pressers.

Von Stroheim's greatest accomplishment is *Greed* (1923), his film version of Frank Norris's novel *McTeague*. Much of the Austrian's reputation today rests on the merits of this film, and the picture indeed deserves to be recognized as one of the screen's most magnificent films. Directorial effects, realistic sets, masterful acting, brilliant photography, and a daring theme make this film superior screen fare.

McTeague, published in 1899, was written in imitation of the naturalistic style of Emile Zola. The novel had been Frank Norris's rebellion against the popular fiction of the

1890's, which he called "the literature of chambermaids." Filled with dull, ordinary people, murder, an unhappy ending, and a depressing theme (greed for money), the book was not thought to be screen material. Von Stroheim, however, loved the novel and was determined to turn what some considered a distasteful book into an interesting film.

The director, with a cast headed by Zasu Pitts, Jean Hersholt, and Gibson Gowland, and cinematographers Ben Reynolds. William Daniels, and Ernest Schoedsack, departed for San Francisco, to the very streets where the novel was set; von Stroheim insisted on capturing the realism of the book.

The story tells of McTeague (Gibson Gowland), who leaves his job as a gold miner in California to become an unlicensed dentist on Polk Street in San Francisco. McTeague is a man of slow wit and abnormal strength, a victim of circumstance and environment. He marries, but his wife, (Zasu Pitts) becomes a miser, loving gold more than her husband. The boorish dentist eventually murders his greedy, penurious wife, and dies after a brutal fight in Death Valley. The ugliness and greed of mankind is exposed.

Because he wanted authenticity, the director insisted upon photographing the murder sequence in a building where a similar murder had actually occurred. For the Death Valley scenes, both crew and cast spent weeks working in the hot sun of the desert. The director's relentless driving of his cast paid off, for the actors were either inspired by or determined to reward von Stroheim with magnificent portrayals.

Greed was filmed in less than ten months at a cost of $750,000. The Herculean task of editing however, took longer. Initially, von Stroheim cut the endless celluloid to forty-two reels and finally pared the film to twenty-four reels. Next, Rex Ingram cut the remaining reels to eighteen. MGM then turned the footage over to June Mathis, a screenwriter. It was finally released as a ten-reel film. Only the main thread of the story remains, and all the subplots have been dropped. Unfortunately the discarded thirty-two reels of film were scraped for their silver coating.*

---

* Before 1948, motion pictures were made on nitrate film coated with a thin layer of silver. Depending on where it was stored, nitrate film lasted only about twenty-five years. However, if not kept at the proper temperature, it soon disintegrated. Many films were placed in the studio vaults and forgotten. As a result, they crumbled into powder. Sometimes the studios decided that certain films' silver could be scraped and

Greed was a financial and critical failure. Many of the reviewers, as well as the audiences, hated it. One writer referred to it as "an epic of the sewer." It was the carefree 1920's, and moviegoers preferred entertaining, romantic stories. Today the film ranks as a screen masterpiece.

Years later, von Stroheim was paid homage by such directors as Max Ophuls, Orson Welles, and Jean Renoir. Although only a portion of his work remains, its high quality places him among the four or five most important directors of American films.

No survey of the 1920's is complete without an examination of its most famous male and female sex symbols, Rudolph Valentino and Greta Garbo.

June Mathis, a scenario writer at Metro, impressed with the Blasco Ibañez novel *The Four Horsemen of the Apocalypse,* persuaded Metro Studios to cast a minor player in the main role. The novice was Rodolpho Alfonzo Rafaelo Pierre Filibert Guglielmi di Valentina D'Antonguolla. Metro agreed, and the young Italian shortened his name to Rudolph Valentino. Within a week after the film's release, he was a raging success. From 1921 until his death in 1926, it is doubtful whether Chaplin, Fairbanks, or Pickford at the heights of their popularity attained the tremendous popularity bestowed on the Italian newcomer.

Although some critics debated the merits of *The Four Horsemen of the Apocalypse* (1921), the appearance of Valentino electrified the audience. This young matinee idol changed the image of the screen hero. Valentino was exotic, sensual, aloof, and elegant. He fulfilled the fantasies of female fans, offering them dreams of love and escape. With his style and magnetism, he was the greatest romantic idol the screen had yet seen.

Valentino initiated a new era in the cinema. Until 1921,

collected for new films. Thus many pictures were lost because of careless storage or scraping. After 1948, nitrate film was replaced by acetate, which can last as long as 500 years. Recently developed reproduction machines permit nitrate films to be transferred to acetate, and thus many older motion pictures have been saved. Eastman House in Rochester, New York, the Museum of Modern Art in New York City, and the American Film Institute in Washington, D.C., are all making efforts to preserve these early pictures by means of this method.

Latins were always presented as villains, with slicked down hair and bad intentions. But Valentino appeared as a romantic, courteous lover whose looks suggested hidden fire, passion, and the promise of something even more exciting. Because he made love and danced with such natural grace, women literally swooned over him, and although men tended to ridicule his dapper clothes and pomaded hair, the "Continental Lover" was here to stay. The public demanded that the rural personifications of Charles Ray and Richard Barthelmess, the cowboy William S. Hart, and the dashing Douglas Fairbanks move over and make room for the smoldering Valentino. The good, clean-living, fun-loving, shy American hero had a rival.

Greta Garbo, like Valentino, has passed into the realm of screen myth. Other actresses have been more dedicated and more talented, but none possessed more glamour. Garbo's reputation rests on a mere twenty-six films, twenty-four made in America. Most of these were far-fetched melodramas, unworthy of her talent. Critics and fans considered her the most beautiful and magnetic star the screen has ever presented.

In 1927 Garbo was cast in roles completely opposite to the emotionally childish flappers portrayed by Clara Bow and Joan Crawford. Publicized as a "Continental Beauty" with a restrained style of acting, MGM groomed her to portray a siren to whom men surrendered willingly. Unlike vamps in the tradition of Theda Bara or Alla Nazimova, Garbo had class, elegance, warmth, and electricity. She brought beauty, mystery, and reserve to her characterizations.

Garbo's early films were clumsy melodramas, but she graced their clichéd plots with her very presence. In most of her twenty-four films at MGM, the scenario department worked her into a set formula. She personifies the doomed, destructive heroine who sacrifices all for love. Her characters are complex, slightly neurotic romantics, who almost always bring about their own downfall. The plots usually concern a restless woman who falls desperately in love (either she or the hero is already married), the two steal a few illicit meetings, spend a few short, happy hours or days together, discard social standards, and let adulterous love bring ruin upon themselves and others.

Garbo objected in vain to this incessant role stereotyping. She was, however, confined to her screen image, and MGM would not heed her demands to play the role of a "plain woman." Consequently, she reappeared in the same role with only slight variations. Nevertheless, she held the audiences with her magnetism. In *Anna Karenina* (1935) Garbo captured the torment of the Leo Tolstoy heroine, and in *Camille* (1936) she managed to raise soap opera to the level of art. Her only comedy is *Ninotchka* (1939), a landmark of sophisticated fun.

In the 1920's, the studio publicity department was a powerful branch of the industry, and by 1924 it had evolved the "personality cult." Garbo and Valentino were among their first great successes. This manufactured stardom paved the way for publicity campaigns for such stars as Jean Harlow and Marlene Dietrich in the 1930's, Rita Hayworth and Betty Grable in the 1940's, and Kim Novak and Marilyn Monroe during the 1950's.

The studios learned to package their product, to create a personality, to select stories that further enhanced that image, and then, with high-powered publicity, to sell the product to the public. With proper publicity, the studio could persuade the public that almost anyone was a star. Unfortunately, real actors and actresses were sometimes overlooked in favor of the more salable products.

The 1920's had been profitable for the expanding American film industry. The war had virtually wiped out production abroad, and Hollywood, with its combination of seemingly unlimited capital and professional expertise, had learned how to make, sell, and exhibit its products. On the West Coast there was an abundance of talent, reputable directors, superior performers, qualified artists and craftsmen, and the best of equipment. But the studio tycoons hindered growth. They were primarily concerned with making money. Unlike the theater in the East, which supported and encouraged experimentation, Hollywood was afraid to break away from its mediocre scripts and streamlined methods of production. Studios gained in efficiency but sacrificed in originality and quality. Producers dominated production, and listened too closely to the demands of the public.

A few superior films were made—*Greed* (1923), *Sunrise* (1927), *The General* (1927), *The Wind* (1928), and *The Crowd* (1928). There were others, but in general the industry offered mostly Griffith's outdated melodramas, DeMille's spectaculars, and the exotic tales of Rex Ingram, all structured for the box office public. Toward the end of the decade, filmmaking was becoming ordinary and mundane, and losing its audience. If it was to hold its audience, the industry had to make a change. In October, 1927, the movies learned to talk, and just in time.

5 / Movies Talk:
1927-1940

THE TIME was October, 1927, the place New York, and the occasion the opening of an otherwise dreary film about a nice Jewish boy who preferred show business to becoming a cantor. About halfway through the picture he peered into the camera and quite audibly said, "Wait, you ain't heard nothin' yet," and proceeded to sing several songs. The audience gasped with the realization that the movies had learned to talk!

Al Jolson's lullaby to Mammy in *The Jazz Singer* was a swan song to a way of production, to a style of acting, and to the careers of those who proved unable or unwilling to adapt to change. Sound brought with it a reorganization of the hierarchy and policies of the big studios, more subtle acting techniques, a change in camera handling (and hence in direction), new actors and writers trained in handling dialogue, and, interestingly, a change in the star mystique. It also introduced new types of pictures, among them the gangster film, the horror movie, and the musical. Within thirteen years, motion pictures progressed from rather stilted and dull productions, such as *His Glorious Night* (1929), to the smooth screen masterpieces of *Camille* (1936), *Stagecoach* (1939), and *Gone with the Wind* (1939).

A year after *The Jazz Singer* appeared, Warners released *The Lights of New York,* the first all-talking feature film. By 1929, the new invention was so popular that 5,000 theaters in the United States were equipped with sound. By 1930, sound doubled the attendance at the box office, and by 1931, eighty-three percent of the nation's theaters were wired for the new invention. Public interest was so great that for several years the 1929 stock market crash had little effect on box office receipts. Three years after the Jolson film, studios were no longer making silent pictures.

The microphone became king, and all bowed before it— technicians, engineers, directors, and most of all, the stars.

They had to learn new acting techniques quickly. Many who lacked training in the theater found that their nasal twangs or foreign accents were unacceptable to moviegoers. Screen favorites were quickly dethroned.

John Gilbert, Constance and Norma Talmadge, Colleen Moore, and Corinne Griffith decided to quit films. Harold Lloyd, still in his prime, made fewer and fewer pictures. The scintillating Clara Bow went into a rapid decline. Emil Jannings returned to Germany, and Vilma Banky and Billie Dove walked away from the sound stages. William Haines turned to interior decorating. A few stars hired speech coaches, but for many it was too late for a fresh start.

Established Broadway performers, and even those who merely looked promising, were imported to the West Coast studios in much the same fashion as the industry had seduced the talents of the German film industry in the 1920's. Irving Thalberg, eager to gain prestige for MGM, coaxed the theater's top acting couple, Lynn Fontanne and Alfred Lunt, to turn their stage success *The Guardsman* (1932) into a picture. Helen Hayes, a leading stage performer, walked off with an Academy Award for her first film, *The Sin of Madelon Claudet* (1932). Ina Claire, Bette Davis, Mae West, Katharine Hepburn, Ruth Chatterton, Bert Lahr, Ray Bolger, the Marx Brothers, and Fredric March all contracted to make films. Ethel Barrymore and Tallulah Bankhead, who had left the movies years before, returned to Hollywood.

A new wave of European stars were recruited also. Having no language barrier, English actors found to their delight that their accents gave them prestige. British film stars included George Arliss, David Niven, Ivor Novello, Frank Lawton, Diana Wynyard, Charles Laughton, Basil Rathbone, Colin Clive, and later, the young Laurence Olivier. From France came the popular Maurice Chevalier and from Germany Marlene Dietrich, who emerged as one of the sex goddesses of the 1930's. Many Europeans found making pictures and California living agreeable, and so they stayed.

Stardom, however, was not reserved for the new arrivals alone. Marie Dressler, Lionel Barrymore, Polly Moran, and the durable Lillian Gish were a few of the silent stars able to meet the challenge of the microphone. Myrna Loy and Constance Bennett found not only new careers but also new personalities in talkies; so did Joan Crawford, who, in the first of her many metamorphoses, went from a flaming flapper to a hoofer in musicals.

Within a few years, inventive technicians overcame the restrictions of the stationary microphone, and it did not take long for directors to discover that sound could be cut, injected, or superimposed onto a soundtrack that could be attached to the film itself. Rouben Mamoulian and Ernst Lubitsch led the way; in *Applause* (1929), Mamoulian refused to limit his camera movements, and he put his camera booth on wheels in order to move it about. He also used two cameras to increase the number of possible angles, and introduced the superimposition of soundtracks.

Lubitsch and other directors, some experienced veterans of silent films and some imported from theaters in New York and Europe, solved other problems by placing more microphones around the set and making free use of the boom, a long mechanical arm with a microphone attached that could be swung from one place to another on the set. In *The Love Parade* (1929), after shooting the action, Lubitsch retired to the sound studio and added various noises and music—even dialogue. He soon discovered how, by clever dubbing, he could synchronize sound onto already developed film. Lubitsch lifted talkies out of their infantile prattling stage by showing that talking pictures did not have to be just talk. He injected whispers, sly jokes, songs, sound effects, and, cleverest of all, silences, advancing the technology of the talkies substantially.

The switch to talking pictures created numerous problems for top management as well as for the stars. Most important was the fact that it put the manufacturing of pictures firmly in the hands of Wall Street financiers, thus reshaping the organization of the industry.

During the silent era, Wall Street had invested money in movies cautiously, accomplishing little in terms of managing the business. By 1930, times were different; America was in the grip of the Great Depression. Counter to the economic trend, while many industries were failing, the innovation of sound suddenly made motion pictures a solid investment. Every week millions of people were lined up at the box office.

The talkies irrevocably wedded the West Coast's filmmaking to the East Coast's money. Wall Street, however, dictated the terms. It demanded the right to accept or veto film projects. Knowing that good business depends on efficient organization, the financiers also demanded a production-line system and a standardized product.

These restrictions produced a high degree of stylization, for putting everything on schedules and tight budgets often hindered the creative artist. Most films up to this time, could be identified by a studio's style rather than by the "touch" of a drector. Studios tended to specialize in specific genres and to issue pictures that carried their particular trademarks, the exclusive result of a particular studio team.

This is not to say that good pictures were not made under these restrictions, for during the late 1930's, many excellent films were produced. Directors, however, were often compelled to work within the rigid boundaries imposed by the studios. A producer could no longer indulge his personal whims or follow hunches. He and his director were given a story, a star, a crew, a budget, and a time limit.

At first, it had been enough that talkies talked. Early efforts were often awkward or clumsy, and did not seem promising enough to pry pennies from Depression pockets once the novelty had worn off. Fortunately, just when the financial situation looked the most bleak, the industry developed a few new twists to attract movie audiences: the escapist "women's pictures" (then embodied in teacup dramas and confession tales), the gangster and horror cycles, the cult of the child star, the bawdy freshness of Mae West, the genius of Walt Disney and his animated cartoons, and that uniquely American art form, the musical.

Writing changed, too. The studios continued to make the usual quota of romances with their diplomatic intrigue and melodramatic plots, but studio producers saw the need for more involved stories and more contemporary topics. The Latin lover and the flapper were replaced by real people with serious problems. By 1935, studios were encouraging authors and journalists to write for the screen. Some of these writers had been trained on Chicago and New York newspapers and wrote with knowledge about the harsh realities of life. They pounded out contemporary stories, offering realistic situations and conflicts that were terse, fast-moving, and tough. Reputable writers were placed under contract. Clifford Odets, Dorothy Parker, and Lillian Hellman turned out scenarios. By 1937, there was a colony of writers, including Donald Ogden Stewart, F. Scott Fitzgerald, Sidney Howard, Robert E. Sherwood, Thornton Wilder, Edna Ferber, Elmer Rice, George S. Kaufman, and Moss Hart. William Faulkner*

---

* Faulkner, who never liked Hollywood, wrote for the screen solely for money. According to legend, he grew tired of reporting to his little of-

wrote about thirty scripts, and Ernest Hemingway even tried
his hand at screenwriting.

With new approaches to character and plot, new actors
were needed. These scenarios required performers with the
harshness, toughness, and reality of Ida Lupino, Humphrey
Bogart, Rosalind Russell, and Barbara Stanwyck. Disciplined
young artists trained in the theater, such as Sylvia Sidney,
Henry Fonda, Jimmy Stewart, and Margaret Sullavan, were
cast in realistic stories with which the young movie audience
could identify. The Latin lover, who had only good looks and
the tango to offer, gave way to men like Spencer Tracy,
Clark Gable, and Gary Cooper. Writers designed stories for
the staccato Jimmy Cagney, the sinister Edward G. Robinson,
the vibrant Katharine Hepburn.

The new heroines, like the American women of the Depression, were dependable, wise, and self-sufficient. Aware of
their sex appeal, women openly pursued men; they knew
what they wanted. The image of the regal film queen
crumbled in the face of the wisecracking, hardboiled, earthy
characters of Joan Blondell, Barbara Stanwyck, Myrna Loy,
Rosalind Russell, Jean Arthur, and Bette Davis. The sex symbol remained, however, but in modified form. Jean Harlow
embodied glamour, but she was a real person, never without
her nasal twang and wisecracks. Near her in the glamour department, but also with essentially realistic outlooks, were
Kay Francis, Claudette Colbert, Carole Lombard, and Ginger
Rogers. The only stars to retain the exotic, aloof image were
Greta Garbo and Marlene Dietrich.

The great silent comedians, whose humor had been visual
rather than oral, found their films slowed down by the microphone; dialogue did not enhance the madhouse antics of the
Sennett gang. Chaplin ignored the innovation, Keaton's contract ended, Harold Lloyd retired, and Larry Semon and
Harry Langdon slipped into obscurity. Comedy needed new
direction, and it was at this moment that Walt Disney appeared with his animated cartoons.

Mickey Mouse made his debut in 1928 and was at once a
public favorite. By 1931, Disney had turned out ninety short
films, and with each one the public approved of his ever-
growing inventiveness, ingenuity, and wonderful sense of fan-

---

fice on the studio lot, and one day he asked his boss if he could write
his script "at home." Thinking that he meant his apartment, the boss
agreed, only to discover a week later that Faulkner had gone home to
Oxford, Mississippi.

tasy. In 1933, *The Three Little Pigs* singing "Who's Afraid of the Big Bad Wolf?" not only symbolically challenged the Depression but had audiences humming along with them. It won a special Academy Award.

In the 1930's the Disney films took full advantage of movement, color, sound, musical synchronization, and vocal effects. It should be noted, however, that Disney's major contribution to the art of animation was his business acumen in organizing teams of artists. Trained as a commercial artist, he stopped drawing after 1928 and delegated his graphics to others. Under Disney's guidance, hundreds of artists poured out cartoons that delighted millions. In 1937, Disney attempted his first full-length feature, *Snow White and the Seven Dwarfs*, revealing that motion pictures had found a brilliant artist-technician whose efforts opened new vistas in filmmaking. Three years later, *Fantasia* (1940), a film that was years ahead of its time, was Disney's first attempt at abstract art.

No consideration of the films of the 1930's is complete without an examination of that product of the Depression that lingered in diluted form until after World War II, the cult of the child star. Immortalized in Chaplin's *The Kid* (1921), the first important child star was Jackie Coogan. His screen buddies were Wesley Ruggles and a tot called Baby Peggy. By the late 1920's, audiences were charmed by "Our Gang." In the 1930's, Jackie Cooper's impish "Peck's Bad Boy" face appealed to audiences, who eagerly opened their pursestrings at the box office. The model for the sweet child actor was the dimpled darling, Shirley Temple. If Mary Pickford had been America's sweetheart, Shirley was its little Princess. All curls and cuteness, she served as the catalyst for bringing innumerable pairs of movie lovers together, lovers who decidedly played second fiddle to the pint-size scenestealer. By 1934 she displaced Janet Gaynor and Greta Garbo, two of the top stars of the decade, in popularity. Her cuteness helped amass the fortunes of Twentieth Century-Fox. Her natural charm made the cloying sweetness of her film plots palatable.

The Shirley Temple cult established a vogue for child and teen-age stars, such as Jane Withers, Deanna Durbin, Roddy McDowall, Virginia Weidler, Edith Fellows, Gloria Jean, Judy Garland, Mickey Rooney, Margaret O'Brien, and Elizabeth Taylor. Despite their obvious acting ability, with the exception of Judy Garland and Elizabeth Taylor, few were as popular in their adult acting careers.

Sex is one commodity that even in time of financial panic remains as popular as ever. As romance and melodrama gave way to increasing sophistication and realism, films grew bolder. The early talkies that spoofed sex offended many by taking sex lightly, yet more somber treatments of sexuality shocked family audiences with their bluntness.

In 1933, Paramount released a film version of William Faulkner's novel *Sanctuary,* a story of perversion and corruption. The picture was titled *The Story of Temple Drake* (1933), and although Paramount pretended to avoid all the sexual abnormalities, civic groups were offended because the director had slanted his film to condone a murder. Meanwhile, Mae West, who had had her own troubles with censorship on the stage in New York, filmed her satirical and bawdy comedies with innuendos that caused censors to raise their eyebrows and use their scissors.

The Hays Office, which was supposed to control film censorship, had discovered after its initial reforms that policing public morals could be difficult. It had become more of a public relations office than an effective censorship agency, content to police the public image of the stars rather than trying to cope with the films in which those stars appeared. By 1929, however, it was shocked out of its lethargy by unyielding demands from both church and civic groups that something be done.

Unable to withstand this pressure, the Hays Office joined with the Roman Catholic Church's newly formed Legion of Decency to devise the famous Motion Picture Production Code, the first draft of which was written by Martin Quigley, publisher of the powerful trade journal, *Exhibitor's Herald World,* the Reverend Daniel Lord, and the Reverend F. J. Dineen. The Code was a statement of censorship principles enforced by American Roman Catholic Bishops (Legion of Decency), who suggested boycotting all films unless there was an improvement in moral standards. (The Code was revised in 1956 and 1966.) By 1934, Catholics, Protestants, and Jews were insisting that unless the Code was actually enforced, they would demand Federal censorship. In Chicago, a half-million women threatened to boycott films unless the movie producers cleaned up their products. Eventually, the Hays Office put Joseph Breen in charge of administering the

Code. He was empowered to withhold a seal of approval from pictures that violated the Code's standards.

The Code's eight pages listed all the offenses that could not be committed against the morals of a society. For example, the audience was never to be enticed into sympathizing with the proponents of crime, wrongdoing, evil, or sin. Films were not permitted to ridicule any aspect of law—divine, natural, or human. The Code, in general, was to curb crime, brutality, sex, vulgarity, obscenity, and profanity, and to strive for "clean and artistic" entertainment.

Frightened by the demanding church groups, the studios initially adhered strictly to the Hays document. As late as 1939, David O. Selznick had to fight desperately with the Hays Office to permit Rhett Butler (Clark Gable) to say the famous line at the end of *Gone With the Wind,* "Frankly, my dear, I don't give a damn."

Following the big-business formula of becoming known for a specific product, each studio began to specialize in certain types of films. Knowledgeable fans could soon differentiate between the products of MGM, Paramount, Monogram, Warner Brothers, United Artists, Columbia, RKO, etcetera. Various studios were distinguished not only by the contract stars who appeared in their films but also by directorial techniques, types of stories, and even, in some cases, by lighting methods, styles of settings, and costume design. Most films bore the mark of special studio teams.

Paramount employed European directors and technicians, particularly from the German UFA-EFA studios. Their films, under the guiding hand of Hans Dreier, chief art director, utilized photography that revealed German theories of lighting and camerawork. Paramount had four outstanding directors: Cecil B. DeMille, Ernst Lubitsch, Rouben Mamoulian, and Josef von Sternberg. Superepics were of course directed by DeMille, and sophisticated comedies by Ernst Lubitsch; Mamoulian's films took place in a grubby world, usually on city streets, or they could be humorous fantasy, such as *Love Me Tonight* (1932); and von Sternberg, with his glossy lighting and intricate camera angles, created exotic adventure films. Other directors—for example, Mitchell Leisen and Alexander Hall—were under contract, and there were other types of pictures, but these four basic patterns were by and large Paramount's preserves. Paramount stars were Maurice Chevalier, Miriam Hopkins, Claudette Colbert, Marlene Dietrich, Gary Cooper, Fredric March, and the Marx Brothers.

While Paramount made sophisticated comedies, Warner Brothers produced entertainment for simpler tastes. They offered musicals, social problems, and biography, and specialized in "headline drama." Their pictures were at times closer to yellow journalism than to social criticism. Even their musicals, with dance numbers directed by Busby Berkeley, were stories about hardworking chorus girls, ambitious singers, and the little man. Their films were concerned with the problems of cabdrivers, dance-hall girls, bellhops, and gangsters. Their star roster consisted of the hard-boiled nasal set—Bette Davis, Joan Blondell, Barbara Stanwyck, Ginger Rogers, Aline MacMahon, Ruby Keeler, Dick Powell, James Cagney, Humphrey Bogart, and Peter Lorre. Their best directors were Mervyn LeRoy, Roy Del Ruth, Lloyd Bacon, Archie Mayo, Michael Curtiz, Howard Hawks, and William Dieterle. Dieterle handled the prestige biography pictures, usually with Paul Muni as the lead; LeRoy turned out musicals and dramas on social themes; Michael Curtiz, a prolific worker (forty-three films between 1930 and 1939), directed mystery, melodrama, and adventure films; Hawks was the incomparable provider of comedies and action pictures.

Universal Studios offered many horror films; Monogram preferred cheap Westerns, the Bowery Boys, the East Side Kids, and Charlie Chan. David O. Selznick, an independent producer, specialized in beautifully photographed literary classics. RKO put its trust in screwball comedies and an occasional prestige picture, such as *The Informer* (1935). Samuel Goldwyn Studios, like the Selznick group, offered quality pictures with social comment. United Artists, Fox, and Columbia specialized in musicals and adventure stories.

The studio that best represented the American cinema of the 1930's, however, was Metro-Goldwyn-Mayer. Nicholas Schenck developed the company with Marcus Loew in the 1920's, and without a doubt, MGM was the most productive, biggest, and richest studio. At its height, it boasted of twenty-two sound stages, an endless wardrobe department, and a one-hundred-acre back lot, where standing sets were used and stored. It produced forty-two feature films a year, almost enough features to change the bill weekly in the string of MGM theaters. Its output was the biggest of any studio in the history of films. Louis B. Mayer supervised this gigantic machine, aided by Irving Thalberg and Robert Rubin. These three controlled both the product and its distribution. Mayer, who fought to control costs, would have cheapened the

MGM films, but Thalberg worked constantly to keep each picture up to a high artistic standard, and it was mainly through his efforts (until his sudden death in 1936) that MGM remained at the top with productions of distinction.

When a company makes forty-two pictures a year, there must be supervision and a "factory production line" approach, yet the product must not be ordinary or the public will not buy it. MGM pictures were polished to a degree of technical perfection. Each film displayed skilled lighting effects by one of the five experts in the business—Oliver T. Marsh, William Daniels, Karl Freund (cinematographer), Harold Rossen, or George Folsey. This team set standards that no studio could surpass.

Metro's sets for almost every major picture were designed, or at least supervised, by Cedric Gibbons; Douglas Shearer handled sound; Gilbert Adrian designed costumes; Herbert Stothard was head of music. The sets and clothes typify this decade in motion pictures more than do many of the films themselves. The players under contract were the glamorous superstars: Greta Garbo, Norma Shearer, Joan Crawford, Jean Harlow, Luise Rainer, Myrna Loy, and Jeanette MacDonald; the men were Clark Gable, Spencer Tracy, Robert Taylor, William Powell, Wallace Beery, and Leslie Howard. The directors, too, were some of the best: Clarence Brown, George Cukor, and W. S. Van Dyke (thirty-two features from 1930 to 1939). There were also Sam Wood, Sidney Franklin, Jack Conway, King Vidor, and Victor Fleming.

MGM films were the result of teamwork; all departments worked together. With lighting experts, set designers, a stable of stars, first-rate directors, and outstanding cameramen, the studio turned out films that one could easily recognize. In spite of the tight supervision by producers and the board of directors, many of them were pictures of distinction. MGM contributed more than its share of outstanding films in the 1930's.

Because emphasis was always on entertainment, escape films, romance, and exciting melodramas, big studios during the 1920's avoided films of social reform. A few individual directors, realizing the value of such pictures, persuaded studio bosses to let them venture into the genre, but in general, the industry felt the public was not ready for films that examined social problems.

By the 1930's the American movies grew a bit bolder and began to wash their dirty linen on the screen. By the mid-

1930's there were many abuses worth exposing. Eventually, a few directors and writers offered pictures that dealt with the country's pressing problems; bonus marchers, bank failures, embittered veterans, Hoovervilles, injustice, bigotry, man's inhumanity to man, the ever-present unemployment problem, evils of secret societies, the machinations of big business, and the perennial favorite, political corruption.

One of the first experiments in social realism stands as one of the best. King Vidor's *The Crowd* (1928) investigates the drab life of a city clerk, emphasizing the regimentation of metropolitan living and presenting the hero as a mere digit in a world of nondescript office workers. Mervyn LeRoy's *I Am a Fugitive from a Chain Gang* (1932) deals realistically with social abuse. *Heroes for Sale* (1933) depicts the country's unsuccessful attempt to handle the Depression. William Wellman's *Wild Boys of the Road* (1933) offers a disturbing picture of homeless young kids, the dispossessed searching the country for work.

Fritz Lang's first American film *Fury* (1936) tells how gossip in a small town grows into a lynching. His film on mob hysteria denounces the lynchings common in America at this time. Lang's picture was followed by others that attacked lynch law, namely, *They Won't Forget* (1937), *The Ox-Bow Incident* (1942), and *The Sound of Fury* (1937). Archie Mayo's *Black Legion* (1936) exposes small-town bigotry; it awakened the public to the evils of the Ku Klux Klan. In 1937, Fritz Lang again turned his camera on American society in *You Only Live Once*, a touching story of a young kid who becomes a criminal because of economic necessity. Mervyn LeRoy's *They Won't Forget* (1937) is a searing condemnation of lynch law in the deep south. *Dead End* (1937) provides a stinging commentary on delinquency and American slum life, as do *Angels With Dirty Faces* (1938) and *They Made Me a Criminal* (1936). Prison reform is advocated in *Each Dawn I Die* (1939) and *Castle on the Hudson* (1945).

Hollywood not only exposed the social problems existing in America, but also turned its cameras on other nations, and, with compassion, emphasized human suffering as the common bond of the brotherhood of man. *The Good Earth* (1937) concerns the poor of China; *How Green Was My Valley* (1941) tells of miners in Wales.

John Ford directed two films of social significance, one a near-disaster, the other a masterpiece. *Tobacco Road* (1941) is an adaptation of Erskine Caldwell's savage picture of "poor white trash." Despite the fact that Ford and his cast played the picture for laughs, the film contains some satiric observations on Southern society. Ford's social comment on the Depression, *The Grapes of Wrath* (1940), stands today as one of our finest films, dealing with impoverished migrant farmers traveling from the Midwestern dustbowl to the promised land of California.

Twelve years after the invention of sound, American movies had progressed to an incontestable position as the greatest of popular arts. Hollywood in the 1930's had no equal. Across the screen came a steady flow of superior films. In this era of excellent craftsmanship, the one film that can best represent Hollywood's collective expertise is *Gone With the Wind*.

This film epitomizes prewar producing talents. Hollywood craftsmen had obviously worked together well before in order to present such a work of art. Directors Cukor, Fleming, and Wood, applying the filmmaking techniques set down by D. W. Griffith, emerged with a screen masterpiece. Mammoth in design, done with taste and distinction, it stands as a superior picture that few spectacles have duplicated since. Wardrobe, sets, Technicolor, script, musical score, casting, publicity, and photography all reflected an industry that had reached technical perfection.

By the end of the 1930's, Hollywood had developed, tested, reshaped, and refined the financially successful picturemaking formula upon which successful films have been based. The decade offered teacup dramas, gangster stories, costume dramas, Westerns, "handkerchief" pictures, horror stories, suspense tales, musicals, cartoons, knockabout farces, screwball comedies, biographies, and adaptations of the classics. These were the offerings from the American cinema, and by and large they remain the same today. The decade was one of progress, a decade of which the industry could be proud.

6 / The War Years
and After: 1940-1949

THE ONSET of World War II brought production limitations, a direct and indirect concentration on the war effort, and, by and large, a decline in quality of films. There was a handful of excellent films, but in general, the sentimental stories of the silent era returned in full force. Nice people involved in heartbreak, flag-waving, and jingoism were recurring themes. Melodrama, the horror film and the woman's picture, featuring women superstars, were public favorites.

Despite its limitations, however, the period saw the rise of such new directors as John Huston, Elia Kazan, Orson Welles, Billy Wilder, Louis de Rochemont, Jules Dassin, Joseph Losey, Robert Rossen, and Edward Dmytryk. John Huston and Billy Wilder, aware that part of the American world was corrupt and blatantly brutal, developed black cinema or *film noir*, as the French called it. Depicting a world of crime, violence, revenge, and despair, this offshoot of the gangster film captured the attention of the fans.

In contrast with the general mediocrity, a few films were produced that must be considered masterpieces by any standards, notably John Ford's *The Grapes of Wrath* (1940), and *How Green Was My Valley* (1941), Orson Welles's *Citizen Kane* (1941), and John Huston's *The Maltese Falcon* (1941).

Hollywood plunged into the war effort wholeheartedly. The Hollywood Canteen was formed as a club for servicemen on leave, stars participated in war bond drives, and even the superstars appeared on USO tours to entertain the troops, both in the United States and abroad. Clark Gable, James Stewart, Douglas Fairbanks, Jr., Robert Montgomery, and Robert Taylor were among many film stars who went off to the battlefield. Gable's wife, Carole Lombard, died in an air crash while on a war bond drive.

Those left behind found production curtailed by restrictions and limitations. Box office receipts from continental

Europe dwindled, and currency restrictions cut deep into company earnings, particularly from the United Kingdom. Far East returns fell drastically. Vital items were proscribed by government needs or placed on a restricted list. Camera manufacturers were making equipment for the war effort. A total of $5,000 was set as the maximum for materials to be used on a single set. A $25,000 ceiling was proposed on performers' salaries; this was later raised to $67,000. Studios made fewer films, conformed to building restrictions on set construction, cut salaries, and contracted only with directors who could turn out either quick comedies or patriotic war films on time and within a limited budget. The epic, the lavish musical, and the super-production were curtailed for the duration of the war.

There was an upsurge, however, in box office receipts by 1942-43. The American economy was excellent, prices were frozen, and salaries in war-related industries spiralled. There was little to spend one's money on. Unemployment dropped to near-zero, and most luxuries were scarce. One of the few markets for surplus money was the movie theater. As in the Depression days, people flocked to the movies for a night's outing and to escape from the wearing experience of the war.

At the time, moviegoers were essentially uncritical in their film selections; few people paid attention to reviews. Even though time, personnel, and material restrictions resulted in the production of many inferior films, they were still gobbled up by the public. On the whole, studios were concerned with five basic types of pictures: knockabout comedies, black cinema or *film noir*, anti-Axis productions showing the evils of the enemy (the Germans, Italians, and Japanese), films to please the women left behind, and musicals.

Studios continued to make formula stories according to models established in the 1930's. These were the usual melodramas: *This Gun for Hire* (1942), *The Reckless Moment* (1944), and a succession of Hitchcock films—*Rebecca* (1940), *Suspicion* (1941), and *Spellbound* (1945). Horror films, although not of first-rate quality, were popular. Jacques Tourneur made the best of this genre during these years: *Cat People* (1942), *I walked With a Zombie* (1943), and *The Leopard Man* (1944). MGM also released two quality films of this type: a remake of *Dr. Jekyll and Mr. Hyde* (1941), and Albert Lewin's *The Picture of Dorian Gray* (1945). Unfortunately, the 1940's horror film degenerated into mechanical plots, crudity, and bad taste, and toward the end of the decade dwindled into burlesque.

The beginning of the war saw the making of many propaganda films containing a strong anti-Nazi bias: *The Mortal Storm* (1940), *Escape* (1940), *Man Hunt* (1941), and the best film of this genre, Michael Curtiz's *Casablanca* (1943).

American films had been generally rather detached from the events across the Atlantic until Pearl Harbor. Then the movie industry turned all its back lots into village streets, mountain hideouts, and battlefields. After Pearl Harbor, the Japanese were the major villains. Hollywood showed the war in the Pacific in *Guadalcanal Diary* (1943), *Dragon Seed* (1944), *Thirty Seconds Over Tokyo* (1944), and *They Were Expendable* (1945).

In addition, there were the usual prestige biographies and literary classics. Several were outstanding: *Pride and Prejudice* (1940), *Abe Lincoln in Illinois* (1940), and *Jane Eyre* (1944).

The industry put its best foot forward with the musicals. These productions were big, brassy, and popular. The 1940's saw the continuation of the usual themes of backstage life, as well as costumed nostalgia for the "good old days." Alice Faye, Betty Grable, Rita Hayworth, June Haver, Carmen Miranda, Fred Astaire, Gene Kelly, Mickey Rooney, and Judy Garland all contributed their talents. *Ziegfeld Girl* (1941) had a lavish, star-studded cast featuring Judy Garland, Hedy Lamarr, Lana Turner, and James Stewart. One of MGM's best musicals was *Meet Me in St. Louis* (1944), directed by Vincente Minnelli, the decade's outstanding director of musical films. Bing Crosby, Bob Hope, and Dorothy Lamour started their famous *Road* series, beginning with *Road to Singapore* (1940), which eventually stretched to six films. These were light musical comedies, all written to the same formula.

Two, beautiful pinup, sweater girls became the sex symbols for the forties. Rita Hayworth and Betty Grable had worked in pictures, Grable since 1932 and Hayworth since 1935, but it was the American G.I. who pushed them to the top as box office queens. Columbia Studios made Rita Hayworth a sex goddess *par excellence*. Photographed semi-nude in bed and wrapped in silks, satins, and furs, Hayworth typified the manufactured star. With red hair streaming and high heels tapping, she danced with Fred Astaire in *You'll Never Get Rich* (1941) and *You Were Never Lovelier* (1942), and enacted the cliché of unknown-into-star in *Cover Girl* (1945). She married the era's boy wonder, Orson Welles, and later went on to become the princess bride of the international Moslem playboy, Aly Khan. With her exotic appeal and down-to-earth warmth, she was one of the greatest movie personalities to emerge during the war years. Her beauty, dancing ability, and charm made her a favorite with audiences everywhere.

Rita's closest rival, and the serviceman's favorite pinup, was Betty Grable. A cute, curly-haired blonde who sang and danced with limited talent, Grable represented the pretty American girl-next-door the G.I.'s had left behind. Like Hayworth, she appeared in shallow stories that were only a framework for dances and production numbers. The backview pinup of bathing-suited, high-heeled Betty in her upsweep hairdo, smiling over her shoulder, was one of the most famous pictures to come out of World War II.

Betty Grable and Rita Hayworth may have danced their way to love and happiness, but other female performers were having a harder time solving their emotional problems on the screen. With actors at war, studios concocted stories centered around the female stars. These sentimental films usually presented one of three themes: noble girls concerned with self-sacrifice, the torments of love, or a woman making her way alone through a male-dominated world. Almost all the women fall in love with the wrong man, who then plays with their affections but does not offer marriage; frequently, he is in love with the woman but is already married to another.

The woman's picture was a box office success for a time, especially with women audiences looking for escape because their men were away at war. Many of these productions offered fluid direction, beautiful lighting, handsome photography, stunning costumes, and occasionally, strong performances. The scripts, however, with their melodramatic aspects, could not be taken as serious cinema. A few were superior fare, but in general the genre was photographed soap opera.

Among the three stars who suffered most were Bette Davis, Joan Crawford, and Barbara Stanwyck. All three struggled to find the soap opera road to happiness—Bette Davis in *The Great Lie* (1941), Joan Crawford in *A Woman's Face* (1941), and Barbara Stanwyck in *The Gay Sisters* (1942). Others who played roles of the same type were Gene Tierney, Anne Baxter, Jennifer Jones, and Irene Dunne. Sometimes wicked, sometimes good, they lived in a world untouched by war. The radiant Ingrid Bergman had the intelligence to select superior scripts, and she captivated audiences with her saint or sinner roles. Olivia de Havilland, who almost dethroned Davis and Crawford as love's sacrificial victim, won two Academy Awards for her portrayals of suffering females in *To Each His Own* (1946) and *The Heiress* (1949). By the end of the decade, the public had tired of the woman's picture. These women and their soap opera problems had no place in the world of postwar realism.

After World War II, American films flooded the European markets. The French, especially, were intrigued by the mood of cynicism, the darkness, and the dominant theme of pessimism in many of the crime thrillers. French critics quickly dubbed them *film noir*, or Black Cinema. An extension of the gangster cycle, the *film noir* takes a harsh, uncomplimentary look at the American way of life. Psychotic characters, hardboiled detectives, killers on-the-run, men and women inhabiting a night world of wet streets, glistening bars, and sleazy apartments provided the characterizations and settings for these films.

The directors who excelled at portraying the war and postwar disillusionment were Billy Wilder, John Huston, Henry Hathaway, Robert Siodmak, Nicholas Ray, and Robert Aldrich. Some of the best examples of this genre are: *Double Indemnity* (1943), *They Live by Night* (1949), *The Asphalt Jungle* (1950), *Pickup on South Street* (1953), and *The Big Heat* (1953).

The years 1940-1945 were not completely inundated by war stories, musicals, women's pictures, and *film noir*. At the very beginning of the decade, two superior films appeared— *The Grapes of Wrath* and *Citizen Kane*.

The grand master of the traditional school of film is John Ford, whose career parallels the history of Hollywood itself. Like his fellow director Howard Hawks, Ford mastered most of the genres* the screen has to offer. His films, particularly the Western marked by grandeur and romanticism, rendered a panorama of a region and its traditions. He is best known for his authentic treatment of the old-fashioned values that have evolved throughout American history. Ford is able to

---

* In 1974, the Los Angeles *Filmex* asked forty American critics to name their favorite American films of all time. *The Grapes of Wrath* was among the first ten. Ahead of every other director in terms of number of films listed was John Ford. Seven of his pictures were on the list.

convert sentiment into genuine tenderness and nostalgia into art. With an eye disciplined to capture sharp detail, he is able to depict sympathetically the basic human issues of birth, death, love, loyalty, family, law and order, morality, and personal sacrifice. Working within these traditional themes, and imbued with his own personal, emotional response to his material, he has been able to turn film into epic poetry.

John Steinbeck's *The Grapes of Wrath*, a moving story of social injustice that presents a powerful depiction of America's migrant workers during the Depression, caused a furor when it was first published. It was attacked as Communist doctrine, a dishonest sociological novel, and a slur on America. Still, others proclaimed it a masterpiece. Producers avoided it, rationalizing that a public just emerging from the Depression would not accept a film that commented on the dust bowl, Okies, Hoovervilles, strike-breaking, and the deep internal problems of a troubled nation. In short, the novel was politically too hot to handle. Darryl F. Zanuck, however, saw the possibilities inherent in the story, bought the film rights, and asked John Ford to direct.

Ford set to work with writer Nunnally Johnson to transfer the compassion, beauty, and magnificence of Steinbeck's Okies to the screen. When completed, Ford gave the American cinema a moving and occasionally sentimental study of a typical migrant family, the Joads, who make their way from the dust bowl to the "promised land" of California. *The Grapes of Wrath* is a masterpiece of realism, superior acting, graphic settings, and outstanding photography.

Ford's compelling film portrait of the Joad family stands as the finest study ever made of the Depression years in America. It captures the feeling of those dark days better than any other medium, including the novel on which the picture was based. Jane Darwell gives a compelling performance as the matriarch of the clan, and Henry Fonda excells as the son driven to radicalism by intolerable conditions.

Ford's vivid, harsh, and yet tender picture gave the screen another example of the stark realism that von Stroheim had inaugurated with *Greed*. The industry was surprised when Ford's film proved to be one of Hollywood's finest achievements.

In June, 1940, RKO announced that the young Orson Welles, in collaboration with Herman J. Mankiewicz, had finished an original screenplay called *Citizen Kane*. It turned out to be one of the most controversial films in the history of the movies.

The story, supposedly based on the life of William Randolph Hearst, the world-famous millionaire newspaper publisher, tells of one Charles Foster Kane, dying at seventy-six in his castle, Xanadu, whispering his last word—"Rosebud." Rawlston, editor of a newsreel (similar to the *March of Time*), prepares a film biography of the dead millionaire and decides to unravel the meaning of Kane's last word. He thinks "Rosebud" is the key to the mystery of the inscrutable Kane. Thompson, a reporter, is sent out to learn the word's meaning. The reporter interviews various people, who each knew Kane well; some liked him, some loved him, some despised him. Each person tells a biased, detailed story, but not one can explain the word "Rosebud." In the final shot, the audience finds out the meaning of the word and its relationship to the newspaper tycoon.

Citizen Kane, now generally considered to be the best American film ever produced, is a dazzling display of moviemaking. Although its cinematic techniques are not necessarily new, young Welles put them to startling effect. Deep-focus photography, lighting, dramatic cuts, acting, and dialogue contribute to this brilliant picture.

Welles followed *Citizen Kane* with an adaptation of Booth Tarkington's novel *The Magnificent Ambersons* (1942). Although the second film does not contain the consistently great directorial touches of *Kane*, and despite the fact that Welles claims at least forty-five minutes were cut from the finished picture, *The Magnificent Ambersons* ranks high among American films. The picture scrutinizes middle-class values while telling a sometimes bitter, sometimes touching story of a disintegrating nineteenth-century aristocratic American family, and the rise of an industrialist.

By the time of his second film, Welles had made many enemies in the industry. RKO turned against Welles, tagging him as a smart aleck, and gave the final editing of *The Magnificent Ambersons* over to Robert Wise, who had helped to edit *Kane*. Rumors of Welles's eccentricities, extravagances, temperament, and prejudices were rampant. After *Kane* and *Ambersons*, he directed *The Stranger* (1946), *The Lady from Shanghai* (1947), *Macbeth* (1948), *Touch of Evil* (1958), and other films. Like Chaplin and von Stroheim, he eventually went to live in Europe, returning on occasion to the United States to appear in a particular role that interested him, to make appearances on TV talk shows, or to narrate documentaries.

Orson Welles is one of the most original directors ever to work in the movie industry; he outstrips many veterans who have been turning out pictures for decades. During the war years, while Hollywood was busy grinding out endless stereotyped comedies, mediocre melodramas, and propaganda films, Welles refused to lower his standards. Although he did not develop any new technical devices, he employed old techniques in a more inventive manner. Welles deliberately makes the audience conscious it is watching a film, a technique picked up by the young directors of the 1960's, particularly those of the French "New Wave."

In 1962 and 1972, a poll of foremost film critics resulted in *Citizen Kane* being named the best film ever made (*Sight and Sound*). Again, in 1974, forty American critics named Welles's *Citizen Kane* the greatest American film of all time. With this masterpiece and several other superior films to his credit, Orson Welles assumes a place next to D. W. Griffith, Erich von Stroheim, and Charlie Chaplin as one of the most creative and innovative directors of the American cinema.

The most entertaining wartime film, *Casablanca* (1942), has also achieved a special place in screen history. Directed by Michael Curtiz, the picture has all the ingredients, good and bad, of filmmaking in the 1940's.

Basically, *Casablanca* is a romantic spy melodrama, a tale of war refugees trying to escape to freedom. But rather than exploit the harrowing potentialities of such a situation, the script offers witty, cynical, and ironic twists. (War can be enjoyable as well as hazardous.) Two lost and lonely lovers who met, loved, and parted in Paris after a misunderstanding are adrift in a world at war. Humphrey Bogart, the sad, bitter, tough guy, still carries a torch for Ingrid Bergman. By chance, their paths cross again in Casablanca, where their romantic torment is played out against a background of international intrigue. Employing a basic love story, Curtiz inserts a game of spies into the plot. At the end, Bogart makes the grand sacrifice: after outwitting the Gestapo, he turns sentimental, sends his love off to safety in an airplane, and walks off into the fog.

Measured by current standards, the film displays many faults—it is farfetched, a synthetic romance, oversimplified, stereotyped, dated, and has obvious studio shots. Regardless of all these artificialities, however, it remains a minor classic.

Based on a script by Philip and Julius Epstein, it is technically striking and displays disciplined direction. It reveals the
slick cinematic expertise that American studios have developed in forty-three years—exotic studio sets, lighting that
suggests psychological tension, an outstanding musical score,
clever dialogue, and excellent acting by stars and supporting
players. Hollywood, however, was soon to bid farewell to this
kind of studio-made picture.

With the end of the war, the motion picture industry experienced substantial alterations. The situation at first was eu-
phoric. In 1946, the most profitable year in the history of
filmmaking up to that time, the box office gross was $1.5 bil-
lion. Within a year, the situation changed. While films improved in terms of both quality and maturity, the
industry—its finances, its organization, and in certain cases,
its big names—was battered by unforeseen problems. The decline of the major studios had begun.

Postwar screenwriting changed. Frightened by the Con-
gressionally instigated Communist "witch hunt" conducted by
the House Un-American Activities Committee between 1947
and 1956, screenwriters were hampered in presenting new
ideas for the screen, having to turn out ordinary stories. Even
the modest liberalism of *Best Years of Our Lives* (1946) became suspect. "Liberal" was a dirty word. A series of mundane films flooded the market. In order to establish its
political good intentions, Hollywood manufactured a number
of overtly anti-Communist features such as *The Iron Curtain*
(1948), *The Red Menace* (1949), and *The Red Danube*
(1949). These pictures added up to crude and foolish panto-
mimes. Eventually fresh writing talent from the television
studios in the East arrived, and writers turned from weak political issues to contemporary stories dealing with psychological characters and social problems.

According to Hollywood mythology during the 1930's, if a
director tried to convince a studio to let him do a picture
with a social message, the front office would send back the
reply, "If you want to send a message, call Western Union."
By 1950, all that had changed. Between 1945 and 1955, thematic floodgates were opened, and pictures that offered
messages were suddenly fashionable. The effects of the war
were evident in the style and content of films. Scenarios faced
racial prejudice, Negroes and Jews, insanity, alcoholism,
juvenile deliquency, and problems of ex-servicemen. Audiences, too, were ready for the change. Edward Dmytryk,

John Huston, Stanley Kramer, Elia Kazan, and others, in order to bring reality to their films, avoided the artificial sets, studio lighting and fake scenery for the real thing. They introduced a semi-documentary approach to the postwar cinema. In order to get a feeling of authenticity to their films, directors with their new story material wedded fact to fiction. Taking cast and crew out of Hollywood, they made films on location in small towns or in the busy streets of the big cities. Henry Hathaway's *The House on 92nd Street* (1945) and *Kiss of Death* (1947) were among the first to make the transition from studio to location. Clarence Brown's *Intruder in the Dust* (1949), based on the novel by William Faulkner, was shot in the author's home town of Oxford, Mississippi, with townspeople recruited as extras for the mob scenes.

Elia Kazan, the director who excelled at the semi-documentary approach, told the story of a small-town priest who was murdered in *Boomerang* (1947). The picture set new standards in semi-documentary films. Kazan shot the picture in the actual town and streets where the man lived and the crime had taken place; the film brought stinging reality to the screen. Kazan had so mastered the blending of fiction with documentary that his *On the Waterfront* (1953), a brutal study of corruption on the New York docks, is one of the best in this genre.

Methods of acting also changed after the war. Against authentic backgrounds, and dealing with an incident that had really happened—a murder, robbery, a strike or natural disaster—performers were encouraged to forget theatrical techniques and to act like participants in the actual events. On occasion, nonactors played minor roles. Treating the scene as if it were a contemporary news event, the cameraman incorporated newsreel techniques which had been learned from war propaganda films. The desired result was entertainment plus authenticity. Thus the documentary, which had begun as a genre of its own, was eventually incorporated into popular films.

Inspired in part by the documentary techniques used in crime stories, and influenced by the postwar demand for maturity in subject matter, Hollywood began timidly at first to explore taboos that were previously avoided by the film industry. Billy Wilder's *The Lost Weekend* (1946), a raw study of an alcoholic, is among the most daring. Race prejudice is the theme of Stanley Kramer's *Home of the Brave* (1949), and Elia Kazan's *Gentleman's Agreement* (1947) depicts a

Gentile who passes as a Jew in order to investigate the unwritten laws barring Jews from jobs, social clubs, restaurants, and hotels. In *Pinky* (1949) Kazan explores the dilemma of a light-skinned black girl who passes as a white. Edward Dmytryk's *Crossfire* (1947) is peopled with alcoholics and a pathological liar; it deals with prejudices found in the seamy underside of a big city at night. Clarence Brown's *Intruder in the Dust* (1949) turns William Faulkner's intricate novel into a moving study of a dignified elderly black man wrongly accused of murdering a white. Anatole Litvak's *The Snake Pit* (1948) offers a chilling study of madness and the workings of a mental institution.

The realistic postwar stories of crime, social problems, and psychological misfits also initiated the decline of the glamorous movie star. The studios began to terminate contracts with the stars, along with their special hairdressers, makeup artists, lighting experts, and costume designers. A few held on for more than a decade, but the male superstars were fewer in the future. Clark Gable, James Stewart and Tyrone Power returned from the World War II battlefields. With Gary Cooper, Henry Fonda, Robert Taylor, Humphrey Bogart, and Spencer Tracy, they continued to be in demand for some time, but new faces were also appearing: Alan Ladd, Kirk Douglas, Burt Lancaster, Gregory Peck, Marlon Brando, Montgomery Clift, Rod Steiger, Paul Newman, Rock Hudson, and Tony Curtis.

Some of the talented older female stars retained their box office appeal well into the 1950's by demanding studio permission to change their images to fit the changing times. Joan Crawford, Bette Davis, Barbara Stanwyck, Susan Hayward, and Lana Turner continued for a while to enjoy their prewar fame, forsaking glamorous roles for nymphomaniacs, alcoholics, hypochondriacs, rich bitches, murder victims, or neurotic artists. (Bette Davis, the screen's ultimate interpreter of neurotic females, made nineteen films in the 1940's.) Joan Crawford eventually switched to dramatic roles, notably in *Mildred Pierce* (1945). Marlene Dietrich abandoned her exotic portrayals for a tough, earthy role in *The Spoilers* (1942). But on the horizon were such newcomers as Kim Novak, Grace Kelly, Marilyn Monroe, Audrey Hepburn, Kim Hunter, Lee Remick, Shelley Winters, and eventually, Mia Farrow, Faye Dunaway, Julie Christie, Glenda Jackson, and Shirley MacLaine.

A change had taken place in both star image and star importance. Younger performers who emerged after the war did not choose to be accepted as an "image." Indeed, they did not want to fit into any of the established patterns. They were actors rather than heroes or villains; actresses rather than vamps, virgins, or "love goddesses." Scenarios demanded real people rather than stereotypes. This trend was enhanced by the fact that younger, contemporary directors were interested in character interpretation rather than personality performances. Before the decade ended, studio contract lists were drastically cut, and many outstanding names, both in acting and production, passed into oblivion.

In 1946, box office receipts reached an all-time high of $1.5 billion; three years later they had dropped by nearly 70 percent. Gasoline was no longer rationed, postwar cars rolled off the Detroit assembly lines, and people found other things to do: they took vacations or stayed home to watch television instead of going to the movies.

Added to its financial woes, the film industry also faced legal difficulties. A 1948 Supreme Court order insisted that film companies either sell their theater holdings within five years or face prosecution. Eight major companies were charged with monopolistic practices concerning production, ownership, and distribution of films. Studio ownership of theaters was a violation of the Sherman Antitrust Act.

In addition to breaking up the manufacturing-exhibition combine, the government also ended, once and for all, the lucrative practice of block booking. For years, the giant studios had owned and operated their own chains of theaters, providing them with a ready-made market for all their own films. MGM alone produced almost enough films each year to keep its theaters supplied with a new picture every week. This union of production and exhibition had provided the industry with financial stability for nearly a quarter of a century. It had also made it extremely difficult for independent producers to get their films before the public. Independent theater owners had been forced to book films not individually, following the dictates of customer preference, but in blocks prepackaged by studio distribution departments. In order to get films with such name stars as Ginger Rogers, Clark Gable, Bette Davis, or John Wayne, theater owners were required also to book mediocre pictures with second-rate talent. Under this system, studios enjoyed guaranteed profits, and independent producers had a limited number of outlets for their films.

After the Supreme Court's decision, the situation was reversed. Specifically, the Court's ruling ordered the selling of theater chains owned by studios, the limitation of packaged units to no more than five films each, and the right of theater managers to preview films before buying.

The end of theater ownership and the block booking system, coupled with dwindling box office receipts, forced Hollywood film companies into an economy drive that had far-reaching effects. Studios sheared their budgets, and thousands of extras and technicians were put out of work. Epics demanding large, expensive crowd scenes were out, and stories requiring small casts were in. By the end of 1948, the studios had laid off approximately one-fourth of their staffs; huge sums were no longer being offered for novels, plays, or original scenarios; stars were released from high-salaried contracts; and only twenty-two feature films were in production.

In the late 1940's, the movie-watching public also discovered the postwar foreign film, causing an even greater erosion of the receipts being earned by American filmmakers. The European filmmakers, whose work was either curtailed or of poor quality during the war years of 1939-1945, were beginning to assert themselves. Although film exportation to America was still small compared to the influx forthcoming in the 1950's and 1960's, it was nevertheless significant.

From England came a succession of neat, highly logical comedies, including *Kind Hearts and Coronets* (1949), *The Lavender Hill Mob* (1951), and *The Man in the White Suit* (1951), which introduced Americans to the unique gifts of Alec Guinness. Alastir Sim, the lugubrious Scottish comedian, and Margaret Rutherford, who specialized in doughty spinster roles, had critics and public cheering them in *The Happiest Days of Your Life* (1950). Carol Reed's polished suspense dramas in the British tradition, such as *The Third Man* (1949) and *The Fallen Idol* (1949), and David Lean's famous *Brief Encounter* (1946), based on a manuscript by Noel Coward, a low-keyed film about two ordinary middle-class, middle-aged people caught in a doomed, adulterous affair, also were imported for receptive American audiences.

Italian filmmakers, freed of their Fascist burden, were reaching new levels of realism as demonstrated by Roberto Rossellini's stark *Open City* (1945), and Vittorio de Sica's sensitive *Shoeshine* (1946) and *Bicycle Thief* (1948).

Another threat to the status quo in Hollywood came from the political realm rather than the economic sphere. This threat came in the form of a question that was posed to all America after World War II: "How loyal are you to America?"

In the years immediately following the end of World War II, Americans became increasingly frightened of Soviet political doctrines and intentions. Led by Senator Joseph McCarthy of Wisconsin, Americans thought they saw the specter of Communism everywhere. Some Americans, anxious to rid the country of this ideological threat, embarked on the notorious "witch hunts" that were to stain the country's image and damage its cultural life during the late 1940's and all the 1950's. The "Red scare" had Congressional committees investigating teachers, civil servants, labor unions, and, particularly, the movie industry. They singled out writers, actors, and other studio employees who were suspected of having ties with the Communist Party, or who had appeared in and worked on certain films supposedly tainted with Communist doctrine. Rumors were rife about writers and directors who sympathized with Communism, or who at least had been connected with the liberal, possibly "Communist-front" organizations that had flourished in the theater during the 1930's. Deciding that Hollywood was a center of subversive activity, Congressional committees ordered an investigation.

The House Un-American Activities Committee (HUAC), under Congressman J. Parnell Thomas, launched its initial attack on October 18, 1947. By the time the hearings ended two weeks later, thirty-nine witnesses had appeared. Ten men (eight writers, a producer-writer, and a director), refusing to testify whether they were or were not Communists and thus avoiding implicating friends, were jailed for contempt of Congress when they took the Fifth Amendment. All served short prison sentences. When released some found themselves on a blacklist, unable to work in Hollywood except under pseudonyms.

At the start of these investigations, some of those working in motion pictures were openly indignant over this invasion of privacy by Congress, and a loud clamor arose from both directors and established stars. Gene Kelly, Lauren Bacall, Humphrey Bogart, Danny Kaye, and others came forward to make a plea for an end to careless accusations. But the investigation continued. Within a short time people began to fear for their jobs.

Acting under the guidance of Nicholas Schenck, Eric Johnston, President of the Motion Picture Association of

America, issued what came to be known as "The Waldorf Statement" (so called because the producers held their meeting at the Waldorf-Astoria Hotel), in which fifty studio administrators pledged not to hire anyone considered politically dangerous or suspected of any form of Communist or socialist affiliation. Basing its actions mostly on hearsay, gossip, and prejudice, the industry drew up a blacklist of two hundred twelve people, half of them writers, who were suspected of possible Communist associations. Many artists were no longer able to find work in the American film industry.

One of the ugliest aspects of the blacklist was that many people were unaware their names were on it and only knew that their services were no longer desired. For years, many talented and creative artists, writers, performers, and directors, both those who appeared on the list and others who were revolted by what was going on, either left Hollywood for Europe or abandoned the industry entirely.

By the end of the 1940's, it appeared that Hollywood—its great stars, giant studios, and all-powerful executives—was doomed. A combination of economic deterioration, changes in technology and audience desires, and low industry morale resulting mostly from the witch hunts, had inflicted severe blows to the industry. Hollywood limped feebly into the 1950's.

7 / The Decline of the Hollywood System: 1951-1959

FOR FIFTY years Hollywood took its position as the world capital of the film industry for granted. With the beginning of the 1950's, however, Hollywood awoke from its complacency to discover its supremacy threatened from without and its system questioned from within. The American motion picture industry, caught in a vise of competition from TV, resistance to change, soaring costs and taxes, dwindling profits, and strong competition from abroad, heaved itself reluctantly into a new era.

As in the 1930's, significant changes took place in the industry after Wall Street financiers began to invest heavily in films. Studio executives who had been with established companies for decades were dropped in rank, dismissed, or left of their own accord. Louis B. Mayer, long-term overlord of MGM, was eased out of his position by young Dore Schary, whose rise in films had been rapid. Even Nicholas Schenck, the great mogul of MGM's Eastern office, was asked by board members to leave. Howard Hughes, owner of RKO studios, lost interest in moviemaking and sold the entire business to commedienne Lucille Ball. She utilized the sound stages for filming television programs. Darryl Zanuck left Twentieth Century-Fox to produce films independently in Europe. In 1946, Universal merged with International, and in 1949, Republic and David O. Selznick Studios closed completely. In September, 1973, the familiar growling lion that announced each MGM film went back to the zoo.

For decades, the movie industry had engendered and perpetuated escapism, with glamour served up as art. Entertainment and dreams were commodities that the public bought and, judging from box office receipts, apparently enjoyed. Movies were undisputably the greatest medium of mass entertainment. By the 1950's, however, the movies feared for their future. Television had become more than an oddity in local bars and restaurants. The little box with the blue-gray light was appearing in everyone's living room now, and people on Main Street, Park Avenue, and isolated farms sat mesmerized by the usually bad programs that passed for entertainment. Romance, dreams, and adventure were no farther away than a button in the living room.

Nobody seemed to care except movie executives, performers, and shareholders, who watched grimly as box office returns tumbled. Attendance decreased alarmingly. While 90 million people went to the movies in 1948, only 60 million were recorded in 1950. It appeared as though a third of the audience had gone home, perhaps to stay.

During the 1950's, original screenplays were rare. Because of the blacklist, films dealing with social controversy were virtually nonexistent; the studios played safe by adapting stage plays or popular novels. As production money became scarcer, this practice became more prevalent. Finally, the industry faced up to the split between the old Hollywood glamour productions and the search for "realism" in subject matter and in presentation. Encouraged by the phenomenal growth of television, movie executives decided to lure television directors and writers to the West Coast.

The young dramatists arrived from television with new ideas. Themes became bolder, confronting head-on problems of family life and of society, as well as the ethics of big business and political illnesses. Many of these films portrayed the nihilism and growing feelings of disillusionment of the postwar world. In the same way that late-nineteenth-century literary naturalism came about in reaction to the flowery romanticism of the time, the new films concerned ordinary people who were fated, driven, and manipulated by outside forces. Critics called them "films about the little people."

Paddy Chayefsky's *Marty* (1954), the story of an unprepossessing butcher (Ernest Borgnine), directed by Delbert Mann, was one of the first successes. This low-budget black-and-white feature caught the public's fancy. Fielder Cook's *Patterns* (1955), exposing the primitivism of big business, and *The Bachelor Party* (1957) were two typical films of the period. Shot in TV style, with all emphasis on closeups and foreground effects, these pictures delighted audiences. Sidney Lumet's *Twelve Angry Men* (1957) vindicated the jury system. John Frankenheimer, who also worked in TV, directed his first feature *The Young Stranger* (1957), which made a plea for decent treatment for delinquents. In a quiet, realistic style, *Middle of the Night* (1959) explored the private agony of a businessman in his fifties, a widower who, finding his life empty, falls in love with a girl less than half his age. Fredric March gave an exceptional performance as the businessman, and Kim Novak was outstanding as the young woman. These films were definitely not superproductions, and the public soon realized that ordinary lives could also be exciting and dramatic—that middle-class living could be as engrossing as grand-scale epics.

Just as they welcomed the innovation of sound in the 1930's, movie executives enthusiastically welcomed any new mechanical change that might save the industry again, feeling that TV might still be held at bay. More than once in the past technology had breathed new life into a failing industry.

The first technical innovation to capture the public's imagination was Cinerama. Using three projectors to throw a tripartite image on a specially curved 146-degree screen, the device gave a realistic illusion of depth. Just as audiences in 1896 ducked at the onrushing Empire State Express, in 1952 they enjoyed enormous wall-sweeping travelogues that transported the viewer from tropical beach to mountaintop. Cinerama's main problem was a lack of proper stories, and audiences soon tired of roller coasters, bounding surf, and helicopters hovering over canyons.

In November, 1952, fans were issued red-and-green-lensed glasses to watch the 3-D (three-dimensional) action of *Bwana Devil*. This was an apparatus to provide viewers not so much with a sense of depth but to create the illusion of people reaching forth or objects flying out into the audience, a kind of binocular vision. But 3-D was short-lived. The audiences did not like the Polaroid glasses. Other large-screen inventions that failed to capture a permanent place in American movie palaces were VistaVision, Todd-AO and Technirama.

Twentieth Century-Fox offered *The Robe* (1953) in Cinemascope, a seamless Cinerama. Cinemascope produced an image twice as wide as it was high by using certain projection equipment and adding an anamorphic lens to "unsqueeze" the image which had been optically compressed on the film to fit the usual 35mm frame. Cinemascope was eventually replaced by Panavision.

Panavision, a wide-screen system superior to Cinemascope because of its superior anamorphic lens, appears to be one of

the best technical improvements. The company also developed, in 1973, the Panaflex, a camera so light it can be
hand-held; it permits dialogue recording without interference,
and it adjusts from 35mm to 16mm. Because of its light
weight, it is especially useful for on-the-spot filming and
crowd sequences, where heavier, more awkward equipment
might be difficult to use.

There were a few movie executives, however, who realized
that equipment and technology were not enough to save the
industry. What was needed, in their opinion, were expert
directors, trained technicians, and new stars and stories that
reflected America's changing world view. Different financing
arrangements that would drastically cut the expenses of producing films also had to be developed, in order to make artistry profitable.

Many of Hollywood's familiar story plots, and even the
newer documentary-realism films, were so well suited to
black-and-white photography that they did not transfer well
to the big screen or to the new color processes. This meant
that other kinds of stories had to be developed to meet the
demands of the large screen, and directors had to discover
new cutting and editing techniques. Hollywood directors and
writers reached for their ancient history books and the Bible,
resurrected the old D. W. Griffith, Cecil B. DeMille specta-
cle-epic, and renamed it the blockbuster. Thus the big picture
with an enormous budget, crowds of extras, spectacular
scenes, and all the latest sound, lighting, color, and cinematic
advances came back into vogue.

It was also soon discovered that blockbuster films were often cheaper if made abroad. Technical equipment had become more sophisticated, more portable, and more readily
available around the world. Because the cost of labor, along
with land and taxes in Hollywood and environs, had risen
tremendously, studios found ownership of mammoth California tracts financially prohibitive. Moreover, many companies
had earned revenues abroad that were tied up by currency restrictions. It became cheaper to use some of this blocked income and take cast and crew to the authentic foreign setting,
whether it was a South Seas island or a London street. In addition, local artisans and labor were easily available at advan-
tageous prices, and authentic extras could be hired.

Filming abroad also appealed to high-income performers,
who quickly discovered the tax benefits available to those
who do most of their work outside the territorial limits of the

United States. With international air travel becoming common early in the 1950's, on-location shooting evolved into an accepted practice. This trend received further impetus from the new independent production companies, who were free to travel and shoot wherever they pleased. And it soon gave rise to the establishment of a number of companies which served as financial backers and also as distributors of the independents' completed films.

Hollywood was soon dispatching crews to Italy, Spain, Egypt, France, and Israel. The big screen had one major advantage at this time: by its very size and scope it could offer something to audiences that was unavailable on television. The blockbuster made full use of the new visual processes, stereophonic sound, and color. Scenario writers avoided nostalgia and went the Judeo-Christian route, turning out Biblical epics wrapped in escapism, such as *Quo Vadis* (1951), *The Robe* (1953), *The Ten Commandments* (1956), and *Ben Hur* (1959). Others took the "knight" route, with *Ivanhoe* (1952), *Knights of the Round Table* (1953), *Quentin Durward* (1955), and *Prince Valiant* (1954).

In another development after World War II, a new acting approach labeled "the Method" became a major catalyst in changing acting, directing, characterization, and story styles. This technique stressed the creation of realistic character from within rather than from without. The Russian actor-director-manager Constantin Stanislavski had evolved this novel acting style in reaction to the highly stylized and artificial techniques prevalent at the end of the nineteenth century. He further refined his system at the Moscow Art Theater over a period of several years.

Emphasizing ensemble playing, honest motivation, and thoroughly developed characterizations, even for walk-on parts, the Stanislavski system burst upon the Western world like a thunderclap when the Moscow Art Theater Company made its first American tour in 1923. Several members of the troupe, already disenchanted with Communism, managed to stay in the United States to act, direct, and teach. Many young actors, attracted by the realism of the system, began to study it, and a few Americans, most notably Joshua Logan, Harold Clurman, and Stella Adler, eventually traveled to the Soviet Union to meet Stanislavski himself.

In the 1930's, some of these enthusiastic, idealistic, and untraditional young people formed New York's Group Theater

Company. Luther and Stella Adler, Morris Carnovsky, Lee Strasberg, Franchot Tone, Lee J. Cobb, John Garfield, writer Clifford Odets, director Elia Kazan, producer Cheryl Crawford, and other mid-twentieth-century theatrical figures owed their start in theater to this organization. By the early 1940's, the Group Theater dissolved as its members became involved in their individual careers.

A decade later, Strasberg, Kazan, and Crawford founded the Actors Studio, where professional actors could perfect their craft between engagements. Here Strasberg became famous as teacher and high priest of the Stanislavski Method, or at least for his interpretation and Americanization of it. Many of his young students made their reputations in the infant television industry or helped to change the face of Broadway stage acting. They also brought their Method approach to Hollywood. Among those highly gifted individuals were the talented, introspective Marlon Brando, who leaped to fame with his portrayal of Stanley Kowalski in the film version of Tennessee Williams's *A Streetcar Named Desire* (1952), the fragile blonde Eva Marie Saint, who appeared opposite Brando in *On the Waterfront* (1954), and the multi-talented Paul Newman and his wife, Joanne Woodward. Other Method actors included Ben Gazzara, Geraldine Page, Rod Steiger, Eli Wallach, Kim Stanley, Arthur Kennedy, James Dean, and Julie Harris. Even established stars, such as Shelley Winters and Marilyn Monroe, traveled East to study at the Actors Studio.

The chief directorial exponent of the Method in its early Hollywood days was Elia Kazan, who had won an Academy Award for *Gentleman's Agreement* (1948). He was later responsible for such Method films as *A Streetcar Named Desire* (1952), *Viva Zapata* (1952), *On the Waterfront* (1954), and *East of Eden* (1955).

These films, directors, and actors spawned a host of imitations both during the decade and afterward. At its best, the Method approach turned out remarkable ensemble playing, believable stories, a high degree of reality, and complex and subtle characterizations that emphasized the conflicting motivations and objectives of human behavior. At its worst, it produced sloppy performances that lacked the most elementary techniques of movement and diction, self-indulgence, and preoccupation with the details of reality at the expense of the larger truths that turn drama into art.

Elia Kazan's production *On the Waterfromt* (1954) is an

outstanding representation of the "Method Movie," and a milestone in American film. The film deserves special attention because of its sets, scenario, photography, and above all, its acting. *On the Waterfront* concerns an ex-prizefighter who works as a stevedore and accepts most of the vicious practices of waterfront racketeers. Terry Malloy (Marlon Brando), aided by his girlfriend Edie Doyle (Eva Marie Saint) and a militant priest (Karl Malden), slowly comes to his senses, realizing the extent of the corruption that exists; he decides to oppose the syndicate. Terry's brother (Rod Steiger) is brutally murdered when he fails to persuade Terry to keep quiet. After agonizing torment, Terry breaks the code of silence and talks to the police. Shunned by his fellow dockworkers as a squealer, he has a brutal battle with the union boss, wins and keeps a job without the favor and consent of the racketeers, regaining the respect of his co-workers.

The film's engrossing story of an inarticulate dockworker and his awakening to existing evil made such an overpowering impression that it stands as one of the most important American films in screen history. Brando's portrayal of the slow-thinking hero is one of the most heroic performances ever captured on film, and represents Method acting at its finest. Brando's characterization, filled with tension and torment, and Kazan's semi-documentary style, produced an army of imitators, revolutionizing the concept of acting in American films.

Method movies inspired numerous stories of restless, dissatisfied, maladjusted teen-agers. Although earlier films had portrayed young dissatisfied people, the 1950's screen was overrun with movies depicting young, sensitive, misunderstood youth, alienated from parents, friends, society, and even themselves. Often victims of a lack of love, these characters were overwhelmed by emotional problems.

The picture that pushed the angry anti-hero and his motorcycle into center stage was *The Wild One* (1954), produced by Stanley Kramer. This film was followed by *The Wild Angels* (1966), *Devil's Angels* (1967), *Born Losers* (1967), and dozens of others, reaching its zenith with *Easy Rider* (1969), starring Peter Fonda. The genre featured gangs of long-haired youths in leather jackets, who came roaring onto the screen with terrifying speed, flaunting their death wish, anxiety and sex at a young audience who cheered them on and made them box office hits.

The Wild One (1954), starring Marlon Brando and directed by Laslo Benedek, portrayed a motorcycle gang that terrorizes a small Western town. (The film's treatment of the theme was so strong that it was initially banned in England, not receiving a certificate of approval until 1967.) Brando's performance, plus the violence, speed, and sheer revolt of youth, had young people standing in line for hours to see the brooding punk and his gang of hooligans fight, humiliate, and morally destroy the town's inhabitants. With his sullen look, mumbling speech, leather jacket and jeans, along with what appeared to be his hatred of everything and everybody, Brando became the idol of American youth overnight. He soon had to share this position, however, with the equally morose but gentle James Dean.

Young people seeing *East of Eden* (1955) were so carried away by the shy, tender, rebellious James Dean, the boy who somehow managed to do everything wrong, that he was immediately proclaimed a star. More than any other actor, Dean was the symbol of misunderstood youth, and within weeks, young people had transformed him and his screen character into a national cult. In his second film, *Rebel Without a Cause* (1955), directed by Nicholas Ray, Dean gave an outstanding performance as a restless teen-ager. (The film was among the first to present rich kids as town hoodlums.)

The young actor parlayed his image into screen immortality, for like the self-destructive characters he portrayed, Dean fulfilled his romantic-rebel image in real life by dying young. His untimely death produced an emotional outcry unequaled since the death of Rudolph Valentino.

Dean was the best of the screen's young rebels, and his shy-yet-tender character has never been replaced. He was the sensitive lost youth who was alienated, a victim of the harsh world around him. His outward coolness masked inner torment, and his silences mirrored unutterable pain.

Anthony Perkins and Montgomery Clift also acted alienated, sensitive youths unable to cope with their problems, the world, and people. Perkins portrayed the neurotic, tormented by hidden desires, who committed murder. His best role was the tortured, twisted killer in *Psycho* (1960). Clift, on the other hand, excelled as the introspective youth, bordering on the existential antihero, who cannot believe in absolutes. He must struggle painfully to arrive at truths that adults thought he should have taken for granted. Clift's performances in *Red River* (1948), *A Place in the Sun* (1951), *From Here to Eternity* (1953), and *The Young Lions*

(1958) made him one of the leading actors of the 1950's. Like Dean before him, he died an untimely death in 1966.

Any discussion of the 1950's must include mention of the archetypal sex image, the delectable but vulnerable Marilyn Monroe. She was one of the last of the great Hollywood-conceived star images. America's favorite legend, the Cinderella story, had come true once more. Norma Jean Baker, illegitimate child of a mother who suffered a nervous breakdown, was boarded out to at least a dozen families, sent to an orphanage where she scrubbed floors, and then turned into a beautiful movie princess.

After minor roles, Monroe was selected by John Huston for a part in *The Asphalt Jungle* (1950), and from then on audiences were aware of this beautiful and capricious girl. In Howard Hawks's *Gentlemen Prefer Blondes* (1953) she flashed star quality and began to make box office cash registers ring. In Billy Wilder's *The Seven Year Itch* (1955), her considerable talent for pairing sexy humor with a certain pathos had audiences chuckling, loving her.

Monroe's studio, thinking they had found the perfect replacement for Betty Grable, was shocked when they discovered she was going East to study the Stanislavski Method. Fifteen months later she returned from Lee Strasberg's Actors Studio to make Joshua Logan's *Bus Stop* (1956), the picture that turned a glamour girl into an actress. As Cherie, a floozy with high ideals, she was funny, sad, and touching. No longer just the girl who manipulated her hips and eyes simultaneously and opened her moist lips and spoke in a high-pitched baby voice, Monroe, as a Western *chanteuse*, was touching, forlorn, and sadly comical, giving a performance that ranked among the best of the decade.

Although she was exploited throughout her career for her sexiness, Monroe was one of the screen's most gifted comediennes. She brought her own special charm and freshness to each picture. Her dreamy vulnerability gave a new slant to sex. Her lure was the antithesis of the harder images created by Jane Russell, Jayne Mansfield, Lana Turner, and Ava Gardner.

In *Some Like it Hot* (1959), a brilliant farce, Monroe brought her hilarious innocence to Billy Wilder's satire on American life. *The Misfits* (1962), the story of cowboys on a savage hunt for wild horses, was Monroe's last film (before her untimely death) in 1962. It was also the last film appearance of Clark Gable, who died shortly after the picture was completed.

Marilyn Monroe, the very essence of Hollywood glamour, and Clark Gable, king of the industry, passed into twentieth-century mythology, and with them went the old image of Hollywood. By the end of the decade the industry was a shadow of its former self.

Besides the financial restrictions and dwindling box office returns, the industry saw the shift from the huge, monolithic studios to the independent filmmaker-producer-director-performer, whose office was often beneath his or her own hat. These one-person studios roamed the world making one film at a time (often of exceptional quality), which was then distributed by one of the major studios.

Independent filmmakers, representative of a new type in Hollywood, were unhampered by industry traditions or methods, free to work where and how they pleased. Their financial backing came from banks, private investors, foundations, friends, or out of their own pockets. Studios such as United Artists became distribution agencies rather than producers, often furnishing money and facilities in exchange for the privilege of releasing the independent's work. These entrepreneurs were at liberty, of course, to select their own stories and stars, and to give their films personalized treatment.

Such creative artists as Samuel Bronston, Sam Spiegel, Anthony Mann, and Jules Dassin set up their own production units, and their films easily found distributors. This approach also appealed to such established craftsmen as Joshua Logan, Elia Kazan, John Huston, Billy Wilder, and Orson Welles. From the stage and television, as well as the film studios, came additional personnel. Television actor-director John Cassavetes filmed the semi-improvisational *Shadows* (1960). Former editor and documentarist John Sturges brought out *Bad Day at Black Rock* (1955) and *The Old Man and the Sea* (1958). Joseph Losey, who had left Hollywood during the witch hunts, worked abroad independently to film *Town Without Pity* (1957), a study of American occupation troops in Germany. Stanley Kramer filmed literate Broadway dramas, *Death of a Salesman* (1952), and *The Member of the Wedding* (1953). Blake Edwards and Stanley Kubrick wrote, directed, and produced their own films.

Performers, too, climbed on the independent production bandwagon, because the studios, subjected to the financial pressures of the time, were loath to subsidize high-priced contract stars. With the end of the superstar era, a handful of performers, aware of the box office value of their names and faced with the ever-tightening squeeze of taxes, frequently wanted more control over the quality of their films. Many formed their own companies when their studio contracts expired. A few, relinquishing their usual high salaries, hired themselves out to the independents for a share of the profits and the right to impose their own ideas on the shaping of the film. Among the first stars to do this were Marlon Brando, Burt Lancaster, Kirk Douglas, and Richard Widmark. Later William Holden, by accepting only a percentage of the gate receipts instead of a salary for *The Bridge on the River Kwai* (1957), became a millionaire.

These enthusiastic and daring independent directors and stars were willing to experiment, encourage new talent, and try new themes. Their films revealed a strong movement toward greater realism, both in stories and in acting styles, and featured complex, misunderstood characters who were often out of step with society. Stories moved quickly and characters were charged with tension and violence. Like Orson Welles, the independent directors restudied all the old cinematic techniques and put some of them to daring new uses. Above all, they feared neither studio pressures nor audience reaction.

Although complete freedom in vocabulary, nudity, and sex was not to come until a decade later, the films of the 1950's strained and finally broke the standard limitations of the time. Otto Preminger's *Anatomy of a Murder* (1959) dealt with rape, while *The Man With the Golden Arm* (1956) dramatized the horrors of drug addiction, as did *A Hatful of Rain* (1957). The former-child-star-turned-sex symbol, Elizabeth Taylor, appeared in Tennessee Williams' *Suddenly, Last Summer* (1959), a chilling Gothic tale of incest, homosexuality, and cannibalism. In Williams's *Cat on a Hot Tin Roof* (1958), Kazan drew a brilliant performance from Paul Newman in a script that contained a pervasive sexual theme. Karl Malden directed *Time Limit!* (1957), a story of brainwashing and psychological torture, raising the question of whether America expected too much of men at war.

Determined to present their individual ideas and personal thoughts, these artists also discovered a new audience, younger in attitude if not always in age, which responded to realistic acting and identified with more complicated characters who asked new questions and sought new answers about life.

Mature films were emerging from an industry that for decades had been afraid to experiment for fear of alienating its audience. American films revealed a startling degree of good health and admirable maturity in the 1950's: the traditional Hollywood system was gone forever.

8 / The European Film: 1945-1977

IN ORDER to better understand American films after 1960, attention must be given to the powerful influence of European films, for they set the pace for many American directors to follow.

Until 1945, the term "movie industry" to most Americans was synonymous with Hollywood. By 1960, however, European directors and their pictures began to dominate the world cinema, and American films had to yield their long-held supremacy. Foreign films became customary fare in America. With their daring stories, complex characters, modern themes, and innovative cinematic and directorial techniques, imported films had tremendous influence on the younger American filmmakers.

By the 1950's, various changes in moviemaking had occurred that helped to popularize the foreign film. The language barrier had been overcome by means of skillful dubbing and improved methods of subtitle display. And young people, particularly students, became seriously interested in film as an art form, and demanded to see the international products. But what really popularized foreign pictures in America was their frank treatment of sex. Unrestricted by a puritanical industry code, the Europeans often depicted sex in a highly graphic manner. Nudity and frank lovemaking were box office attractions.

The English were the first to break the invisible blockade surrounding American movie houses. A common language and a shared artistic and literary heritage gave English filmmakers easy access to American audiences. English acting and English humor were familiar and readily comprehensible to Americans.

In the late 1950's, a group of British writers and directors presented new themes that struck strong chords of identification with young people around the world. The group became known as Britain's "angry young men," a name derived from

John Osborne's play (later a film) *Look Back in Anger* (1958). These films are typically British by virtue of their tight construction and their use of virile, comical dialogue. Essentially, they attack the failure of politico-economic liberalism to solve the serious problems of the postwar world.

Among these films are the aforementioned *Look Back in Anger* (1958), the feature film debut of the young director Tony Richardson; his later, allegorical tale of the old vaudevillian *The Entertainer* (1960); and his sensitive *A Taste of Honey* (1961), adapted from Shelagh Delaney's stage play, which introduced the alienated waif Rita Tushingham to America. Jack Clayton's directorial debut with *Room at the Top* (1959) and its frank treatment of sex set a pattern for a number of films that followed. Other striking films of the same type included Karl Reisz's *Saturday Night and Sunday Morning* (1960), Tony Richardson's *The Loneliness of the Long-Distance Runner* (1962), Lindsay Anderson's *This Sporting Life* (1962), Clive Donner's *The Caretaker* (1963), and John Schlesinger's *Darling* (1965), which gave American audiences their first look at the radiant Julie Christie.

No discussion of British films in this period would be complete without mentioning Tony Richardson's virtuoso filming of the adventures of that hilarious eighteenth-century angry young man, *Tom Jones* (1963). Filmed partially in slapstick Sennett manner, Richardson exploits the repertoire of silent-film tricks and employs sharp wit and sly sophistication to produce a masterpiece.

In 1943 and 1944, a few Italian directors made several films that were passionate outbursts against society, the Germans, fascism, the "system," and, above all, man's inhumanity to man. Because of their authentic treatment of social problems and their inclination toward a visually accurate style, these films are classified as neorealism.

Cesare Zavattini, author of many scripts for Vittorio De Sica, is given credit for the ideal of neorealism as a cinema that would present total truth, with Zavattini insisting that dramas containing plots were false. Since life had no plot, films also should be plotless; they should also abolish the deceit of the actor's performance and transfer real life directly to the screen. The subject must be contemporary and must give characters a sense of their own dignity and importance as human beings. Movies should capture the truth, agony, humiliation, and success of everyday living by venturing into the streets, photographing the most ordinary human conditions and ignoring conventional narrative patterns.

Italian directors began to follow Zavattini's advice: they avoided contrived stories and concentrated on the problems of ordinary humans. Because there was no money for either stars or expensive sets, they worked on a tight budget. With inexpensive equipment, exciting semi-improvised stories, and dedicated casts, wholly or largely nonactors, they presented films that came as close as possible to actuality.

By 1950, five creative directors had inaugurated an Italian film renaissance. Luchino Visconti, Roberto Rossellini, and Vittorio De Sica were the initial successes; Federico Fellini and Michelangelo Antonioni followed. Luchino Visconti's second film, *La Terra Trema* (1948), a monumental picture filled with lyrical romanticism and flashes of harsh reality, established this talented man as among the most renowned of Italian author-directors. His story of a Sicilian fisherman's struggle against poverty and exploitative businessmen is epic neorealism. Visconti's *Senso: The Wanton Countess* (1954), a story of degradation, is one of the most beautiful color films in the history of the cinema. *Rocco and His Brothers* (1960), a realistic study of how a lower-class farm family is ruined by the corruptions of city life, gave Visconti an international reputation; it is his grandiose study of love, violence, and death. *The Damned* (1969), a powerful film about corruption in Nazi Germany, develops one of Visconti's favorite themes, the solidarity and destructive power of family relationships.

It was not, however, Visconti's films that kicked off the postwar recognition of Italian films but rather Roberto Rossellini's semi-documentary *Rome, Open City* (1945), depicting with harsh realism the omnipresent evil and corruption during the German occupation. This film established Rossellini as the leader of the Italian neorealist movement. It is noteworthy not only for its harsh, documentary-like photography but also for a magnificent performance by Anna Magnani. A year later the American public was captivated by *Paisan* (1946), a story of the liberation of northern Italy by the American and Italian forces. In six episodes, this film told the crude, tender, and often tragicomic aspects of the clash between the two cultures.

Vittorio De Sica, another director who shunned studios and artificial sets, journeyed with nonprofessional actors to the slums and the countryside for location shots. His films illustrate how simple people with their problems can become engrossing tragic heroes, far more interesting than the synthetic characters of Hollywood. Critics and public alike praised De Sica's *Shoeshine* (1946) and *The Bicycle Thief* (1948) for their superb characterizations. *The Bicycle Thief*, a tender examination of a father-son relationship during the search for a lost bicycle in the pouring rain, is unsurpassed for capturing frustration and love. *Miracle in Milan* (1951) and *Umberto D* (1952) are masterpieces of pathos and human understanding. *Two Women* (1960) won an Academy Award for Sophia Loren; the film tells of De Sica's favorite characters, pathetic people who live on the fringes of respectable society. De Sica has the gift for creating stark and terrible tragedy out of everyday incident. *Two Women* also presented the most realistic rape scenes ever filmed up to that time.

Although Italian films appeared to be on the wane in the late 1950's, directors, stars, and writers had taken the Italian cinema farther in a ten-year period than it had gone in the previous fifty years. Just when it appeared to be running out of talent, a new group of brilliant directors came to the fore. If Vittorio De Sica, Roberto Rossellini, and Luchino Visconti were the leading directorial voices for the Italian cinema during the 1940's and 1950's, then Federico Fellini and Michelangelo Antonioni were the spokesmen for the 1960's.

Federico Fellini, who is often concerned with the problems of the Italian middle class, told in his semi-autobiographical film *I Vitelloni* (1953), a story of idle Italian boys living without purpose and trapped without a future in a small town. In 1954 he completed *La Strada*, the story of a simple-minded waif Gelsomina (Giulietta Masina), who joins a brutish strong man (Anthony Quinn) to entertain people along "the road." The pair travel constantly but arrive nowhere. Fellini takes his characters from the sea back to the sea, transforming Gelsomina from a child of innocence into a knowledgeable woman. It is one of the most unforgettable films in the history of the screen.

Fellini's *La Dolce Vita* (1959), in which Fellini captures the demise of Roman society also deserves special attention. It is a funny, profound, and tragic film, revealing the lies, corruption, and evil that exist in the world today. The story tells of a young reporter (Marcello Mastroianni) who encounters the rich, idle, immoral artists, writers, and intellectuals of Rome. He, too, eventually imitates the characters he meets, losing sight of proper values, honest standards, and beliefs, becoming one of the "lost souls." He abandons his early training, morals, religion, and his desire to write. Slowly, he sinks into the sweet—*dolce*—soft life. Finally corrupted, he not only rejects love but also loses the ability to recognize love.

In *8½* (1963) Fellini focuses his camera on his own psyche and records an artist's fears, joys, and fantasies. The film uses James Joyce's stream-of-consciousness technique and Luigi Pirandello's theme of reality versus truth.

Antonioni's pictures almost contradict what movies are meant to do; they do not move. Along with his slow style, he offers esoteric stories severed completely from the old patterns of the literary cinema. He is the cinematic poet of the absurd, whose characters have lost their sense of meaning, all *raison d'être*.

His basic theme is the failure of modern man and modern society. The human mind, not physical action, interests Antonioni; he is concerned with people and their emotional problems as revealed by their psychological complexes. His characters appear to be always living a life of boredom, suffering from emotional sickness; by their actions, glances, and dialogue, they show the purposelessness, emptiness, and futility of their lives. They are often freaks adrift in a Franz Kafka world, a T. S. Eliot wasteland, or a Samuel Beckett desert, unable to give or find compassion. Antonioni's films capture the characters' inner logic and attitudes, their reasons for various actions.

In 1960 Antonioni presented *L'Avventura*, a film that many critics consider his masterpiece. It is part of a trilogy that included two later films, *La Notte* (1961) and *L'Eclisse* (1962). All three films are filled with symbols, fantasies, puzzles, haunting guilt, and irony; each film is paced to approximate the rhythm of life depicted in each story. Through the three scenarios, the main ideas that dominate Antonioni's pictures emerge. Besides the purposelessness and futility of life, Antonioni plays on other recurring minor themes: how easy it is to betray either a loved one, one's self, or an idea; how fleeting is love; how difficult it is to communicate with one's friends or even with oneself. Interwoven throughout the films are the director's observations about some elements of human nature; the lack of genuine emotions, intellectual shallowness, and weakness in confronting a crisis. He presents characters who are destroyed from within because of their impotence in decision-making.

The Antonioni trilogy reflects the malaise of our times; its characters are systematically pulverized by machines, by other people, and by themselves.

The French, too, began to export more films to America after World War II. Although French studios had produced excellent pictures for decades, because of the language barrier their films were given restricted circulation in American theaters during the period between the World Wars.

The revolution in French cinema began in 1947 when André Bazin (1918-1958), critic and theorist, founded a magazine, *La Revue du Cinéma*. In 1950 the publication changed its name to *Cahiers du Cinéma*, and Bazin, as editor, encouraged those interested in movies to submit critical articles. At once, a group composed largely of young critics and headed by François Truffaut attacked old guard directors Henri Clouzot, Rene Clement, Claude Autant-Lara, André Cayette, Marc Allegret, and others, accusing all of them of repeating old themes of the need for social reform. (The same critics did, however, respect and admire the more personal and individual directors, such as Abel Gance, Jean Vigo, Robert Bresson, Jacques Tati, Max Ophuls, and Jean Renoir.) Perceptive criticism submitted by François Truffaut, Jean-Luc Godard, Claude Chabrol, Eric Rohmer, Jacques Rivette, and others demanded that new talent be given a chance in the French cinema. Before long these young critics were making their own films. Armed with new ideas and enthusiasm, they changed the industry. In 1958, with the appearance of Claude Chabrol's film *Le Beau Serge*, youth began to dominate the French movie industry. The long rule of older, established directors ended.

At the 1959 Cannes Film Festival, audiences were aware that a whole new generation of French directors had surfaced when three French motion pictures received a stormy, enthusiastic reception from international audiences. *Orfeu Negro (Black Orpheus)* by Marcel Camus took first prize; François Truffaut's *Les Quatres Cents Coups (The 400 Blows)* received the award for direction; and Alain Resnais's *Hiroshima, Mon Amour (Hiroshima, My Love)* won the International Critics' Prize. French critic Françoise Giroud dubbed the new cinema style *la nouvelle vague*, the New Wave, and the tag line stuck.

François Truffaut's influential essay explaining his *politique des auteurs* theory appeared in *Cahiers* (January, 1954) and launched a new school of cinema criticism. The phrase is translated simply as the *auteur* theory. (The key word in French, *auteur,* is retained in order to avoid the literary connotation of "author" in English.) Briefly, the *auteur* theory states that the director is the sole creative artist responsible for the complete film. Each of his films reveals his personal touches, his artistry. The *auteur* director places form above content, pattern and structure above performance. The French school of critics selected as examples of *auteur* directors not Orson Welles and Charlie Chaplin with their humanistic themes, but older Hollywood veterans and some minor directors of B films. They avidly pointed out the relation of the *auteur* theory to the early films of D. W. Griffith, von Stroheim, and chief of them all, Howard Hawks.

The French government, realizing these "New Wave" directors could revitalize a stagnant film industry, gave them assistance with State funds. By the 1960's, France was the foremost maker of creative films. Headed by Jacques Beratier, Roger Vadim, Marcel Camus, Agnes Varda, François Truffaut, Raymond Vogel, Louis Felix, Claude Chabrol, Alain Resnais, Jacques Rivette, and Jean-Luc Godard, the New Wave directors turned out some of the most exciting films of the decade.

Certain cinematic techniques are characteristic of the New Wave. The scenario does not necessarily follow a structured story. The film may plunge into a situation with no introduction; motives for conduct may go unexplained. Sometimes neither climaxes nor neat endings are evident. Points of view can be deliberately confused. The viewer might leave the theater with unanswered questions, unsure of what to think. Sometimes there are no apt conclusions because the director intentionally creates an ambiguous film, taking no other stand other than objectivity. The camera, removed from tripod and restricting dollies, is a hand-held apparatus, small enough to follow hero or heroine wherever he or she goes. There is no effort to achieve smooth, rolling shots—the bumpier and jumpier the better. Directors want audiences to know they are watching a movie. The jump cut is a prominent characteristic. After introducing a scene, the director may abruptly jump from one locale to another with no explanation.

Certain directors of the New Wave employ the old silent

film technique of Mack Sennett—fast action, slow action, and the freeze shot. Memory or recall of a character's past is represented through split-second shots simulating remembrance in the character's mind. Characters may step out of their roles to speak or wink directly at the audience. The camera may linger over a long sequence during which characters may indulge in enigmatic talk or mumble in a bored manner. There may be closeups of characters improvising endless long monologues.

One of the first of the New Wave directors was Alain Resnais, a former editor. Resnais's *Nuit et Brouillard (Night and Fog)* (1955), a 30-minute short, had a powerful impact on French film. It is a superior documentary that re-creates the terror of Auschwitz, reminding all of us of our universal responsibility for the catastrophes perpetrated on the Jews by Nazi Germany. The film is a lucid, objective, profound essay on a revolting subject. In 1959, Resnais's *Hiroshima Mon Amour* offered the study of the effects of a war-torn past on the love affair of a Japanese businessman and a Frenchwoman. The film is original and influential, one of the best of the New Wave.

Jean-Luc Godard, semi-surrealistic director and critic, the most controversial of the New Wave, had a decided effect on the cinema world. His first full-length film, *A Bout de Souffle (Breathless)* (1959), was a formidable success, offering various New Wave techniques. His hero, a car thief, kills a policeman, then risks returning to his apartment to carry on a love affair with his amoral girlfriend; eventually, he dies in the street. Godard's film defies logic; its unstructured story exudes cruelty, rage, violence and indifference, suggesting that life and death are hardly worth the effort.

Godard's controversial films have been labeled electrifying masterpieces, as well as puzzling, boring, and downright dull by others. His heroes (or antiheroes) are criminals, gangsters, petty thieves, foreigners, or students living on the fringes of society. The stories are often episodic, consisting of cynical, depressing themes. Characters move from one physical situation to another, sometimes expounding political or social doctrines. Of all the new directors, Godard has been most opposed to the standard patterns of moviemaking. He wants to attract new audiences who will accept change.

Godard's *Weekend* (1967) is a horrific tragedy with sardonic twists; there are hints of humor and irony throughout.

In one seventeen-minute sequence, Godard presents a corpse-strewn traffic accident photographed so graphically it appears real. In this vignette, the director presents the automobile as a death machine, operating amid the dehumanizing indifference of modern humans. The picture ends as the young heroine, who has turned into a cannibal, eats a sandwich made from her husband's body.

Along with Jean-Luc Godard, François Truffaut soon became one of the foremost directors in French cinema. His films are somewhat autobiographical, and most are concerned with the role of love in relationships between individuals.

Although *Jules and Jim* (1961) is by critics' choice Truffaut's best, *The Four Hundred Blows* deserves discussion because it reveals his compassion and gentleness and is enormously entertaining. *The Four Hundred Blows* is the story of Antoine Doinel, a lonely, neglected twelve-year-old Parisian boy, living in a home with indifferent parents. He is constantly subjected to their distrust, and in school he faces a cold and often cruel teacher. Eventually the boy turns delinquent, and because of a petty crime, goes to jail.

Although other directors tried to capture the agony of youth, it is this French director's film that succeeds above all others. Truffaut's harsh social commentary is a study of a misunderstood adolescent and his inability to adjust to an adult-dominated world. Adding to the film's greatness is the director's refusal to treat his subject sentimentally or to give ready answers. The last shot of Antoine at the edge of the sea, caught in a freeze frame, provides a haunting memory.

Several Swedish filmmakers also left a distinctive mark on the cinema in the 1960's. Bo Widenberg in 1967 gave the screen a beautiful film in *Elvira Madigan*. After censorship trouble, Vilgot Sjoman managed to release his *491* (1966) to the American public. The following year his sensational *I Am Curious-Yellow* had far-reaching effects concerning the permissibility of sex on the screen.

Ingmar Bergman, however, dominates the Swedish cinema. He has been named by critics, moviegoers, and others in the industry as one of the most creative and influential directors working in the medium today.

Bergman's stories provide serious drama: they make solemn statements about life. Principally, they concern tormented characters searching for answers to personal problems. His favorite themes recur throughout his productions: dreams versus reality (do we look at truth or illusion?); the alienation of the artist in a hostile world; the happiness and sorrow of loving; the question of God's existence. Many of Bergman's films dwell on this last theme, for he believes there must be some power in the universe that influences the human mind and situation.

The photography, lighting, costuming, acting, and script are fused so carefully in Bergman films that they emerge as intellectual exercises the audiences must follow carefully in order to understand his philosophical games. Like the tortured August Strindberg or the severe Selma Lagerlof, the great geniuses of Swedish literature, Bergman relentlessly probes man's inner torments, conflicts, doubts, and beliefs within a framework of Gothic fantasy.

The Seventh Seal (1956) exemplifies many of Bergman's cinematic techniques, themes, and views on the world, religion, and God. The film tells of the struggle of an individual trying to find himself in an indifferent universe. A knight returning home after ten years of fighting in the Crusades finds his country ravaged by the Black Plague. Accompanied by a cynical squire, the Crusader begins his joruney cross-country to a castle. Enroute he is joined by various characters. Even the ominous figure of Death occasionally joins the group. The knight seeks definite answers to some puzzling questions regarding proof of God's existence; he will not accept dogmatic beliefs. Eventually Death strikes the knight down, before he has found either God or the answer to his questions. Only a "holy family" of three escapes the Plague and survives, as vindication of simple faith that can sustain man in adversity. The film represents a tale of Everyman and his journey to the grave. Like a medieval allegory, the characters are abstractions representing various levels of religious belief. The film contains striking photography, startling closeups, scenery, intricate characters, and mysterious symbols.

While William Wyler and Cecil B. DeMille were shooting Biblical epics in Hollywood in the 1950's, in Europe, directors were concentrating on modest black-and-white films, rejecting the big-budget spectaculars and offering productions that contained personal statements, films that favored characters over action and direction over production. Indulging in their unique brand of individuality, the Europeans presented a complex world—sometimes tragic, often humorous, peopled with unconventional characters. These directors helped liberate cinema by demonstrating, in both form and content, that everything is permitted to the creative artist.

9 / The Sixties

DIVERSITY and vitality marked the movies of the 1960's. Like the 1930's, it was a decade of experiment and growth. Older fans may have been shocked at the nudity, profanity, and explicit sex scenes of the movies, abandoning moviegoing in favor of television, but for the young, movies were stimulating and, above all, provocative. There were conventional films, experimental films, art films, and documentaries. Established directors as well as untried talent offered their movies to the public. Tradition stood next to rebellion. There was the rise of the director as *auteur*, a strong influence of European cinematography, the breaking of the Production Code, and above all, a proliferation of young directors who offered new viewpoints with ease and competence through varied film techniques. The American screen became absorbed in an international style.

By mid-decade the movies had burst forth into free-wheeling style. Staid conservatism gave way to the pop culture world. The new "mod" lifestyle found its complete expression in movies. Stanley Kubrick led the way into the new forms of expression; his *Lolita* (1962) and *Dr. Strangelove* (1963) ended the dull film styles of the fifties and inaugurated the uninhibited style of the 1960's.

By the 1960's, directors were fully in control of filmmaking; the *auteur* theory had swept the industry. Partially filling the power vacuum left by the once-important studio moguls, directors were of top importance. "Old Masters," still working within the traditional Hollywood formula, survived industry changes by offering action-adventure films. Their films, noted for their idealized characters, fast action, sentimentality, and structured story lines, were usually based on the West, the war, the Bible, or sagas of revenge and retribution, embodying variations of the chase sequence. For a while the old guard directors enjoyed star status in their own way. Discriminating fans and the general public knew that their names guaranteed slick entertainment. However, their popularity began to wane. Ignoring most of the creative aspects of European filmmakers and unaware of the demands of the young audience, the old guard turned out flawed, often insignificant films which failed at the box office. They appeared to be out of touch with the problems of the day.

Headed by John Ford, the establishment directors continued to offer ornate escapism, costume epics, blockbusters, and stories idealizing cornerstones of the American way of life. Ford's traveling companions were Fred Zinnemann, Howard Hawks, Lewis Milestone, Anatole Litvak, George Cukor, Henry King, William Wyler, King Vidor, Henry Hathaway, and Otto Preminger. Many of these men had been in films since the 1920's, but it was obvious their day had ended.

A second category of directors, who emerged after World War II, had by the 1960's become an establishment themselves. Most of them were products of television or the Method school of theater; a few had even been screenwriters. They offered low-keyed films concentrating on realistic stories concerned with social problems, a corrupt world with complex characters (Paul Newman or Marlon Brando) burdened with psychological problems. Focusing on a cinema of intimacy, these directors avoided the wide-screen, multiple-set, cast-of-thousands epics. Their work is marked by brisk editing and cutting, brilliantly lighted photography, and the heavy use of sound to heighten the story. Their pictures are in tune with the passing scene. Stanely Kramer headed this group, followed by Robert Rossen, Elia Kazan, Robert Aldrich, Billy Wilder, John Huston, Richard Brooks, and Robert Wise.

A third group, the experimental directors, emerged during the 1960's. They were not concerned with normal film production methods but explored untouched areas of the medium in a particularly self-expressive manner. Their independently produced films are structured for specialized audiences outside the ordinary theater circuit. The independent, surrealism, underground, or experimental directors emerged in America during the 1930's, blossomed in the 1950's and surfaced in the 1960's. They are mostly poets, painters, journalists, and nonprofessionals. The early films are concerned with sexual dreams, adolescent visions, and abstract imagery, often reflecting a world of homosexuality and transvestism, or a lyrical dream world. Members of the group include Maya Deren, Marie Menken, James Broughton, Gregory Makropoulos, Kenneth Anger, Stan Brakhage, Robert Nelson, Larry Kadish, Sidney Peterson, Curtis Harrington, Jonas and Adolfas Mekas, Ken Jacobs, Ron Rice, Bruce Baillie and Andy Warhol.

From this group emerged the New American Cinema (1955), with Jonas Mekas, John Cassavetes, Shirley Clarke, Robert Frank, and Alfred Leslie, among others.

These directors were making films not to entertain but rather to stimulate, to make people see and think, even to be repulsed by what they saw. They wanted to describe slums fully, along with juvenile delinquents, protest marches, drug problems, civil rights struggles, police brutality and bigotry. They were determined to capture the turmoil of the world at the time.

Two of the features to be shown to the public were Shirley Clarke's *The Connection* (1961) and *The Cool World* (1964). Jonas Mekas's *The Brig* (1964) and Kenneth Anger's *Scorpio Rising* (1963), with their offbeat sexual themes, found an interesting public. In the 1960's the films of Andy Warhol, the Mekas brothers, and Shirley Clarke were released in America's main cities. But the experimental film has had its most substantial impact on other professional movie-men. Directors Arthur Penn, Sidney Lumet and Elia Kazan, among others, have praised the genre as having opened new areas of creativity.

Later, another group emerged who might be called directors of the Now or Direct film, sometimes called *cinéma verité*. They are interested in recording events without a script, trusting themselves to catch the dramatic moment. This group includes Robert Drew, Donn Alan Pennebaker, Fred Wiseman, Albert Maysles, James Lipscombe, Gregory Shuker, and Hope Ryden.

An example of the Now or Direct film is *Monterey Pop* (1968), Richard Leacock, D. A. Pennebaker, and Albert Maysles's upbeat color documentary of the 1967 pop-music festival in California. It gave young fans a new genre to follow, and the rock documentary found instant success. These filmed festivals, revealing different subcultures in American life, are for the young, especially the youth who comprised most of their audiences. These documentaries aim to translate live performance into the medium of film. The prime value is to focus on the music, and then the audiences concerned with the music. The camera shows the link between the two. The films capture movement by means of cinematography, a rapid pace of cutting, and the use of flashing lights for psychedelic effect. They tell a story within the framework of stark naturalism, recording people and music as they actually are, restructuring time in order to evaluate the total event. The best examples of the genre are *Monterey Pop* (1968), *Woodstock* (1969), and *Gimme Shelter* (1970).

By the 1960's, the art/experimental/underground/now movement was propelled into the mainstream of filmmaking, releasing its films through standard production channels.

Nonetheless, the industry continued to manufacture products whose artificialities attempted to be idealized truths of America, such as the blockbuster, musicals, crime, comedies, the spy film, the Western and science fiction. Box office returns went sky-high with such structured films as Alfred Hitchcock's *Psycho* (1960) and *The Birds* (1963), and John Ford's *The Man Who Shot Liberty Valance* (1962). But younger fans wanted something new.

The fourth category of directors, and by far the most important, made pictures for the young audience brought up on television. These fans had new tastes, namely an insatiable appetite for sensation. Hence these new directors offered films with daring themes, interesting characters, and growing attention to sex, nudity, violence, and action.

Photography, editing and visual techniques can be as stimulating and innovative as the subject matter itself. With an abundance of creative energy, onto the sound stages came Arthur Penn, Mike Nichols, Roman Polanski, Richard Fleischer, Stanley Kubrick, Franklin Schaffner, Byron Haskin, Sidney Lumet, John Frankenheimer, John Schlesinger, Francis Ford Coppola, Peter Bogdanovich, and others. Their films captured the intellectual, and ever-growing student body interested in movies.

To these directors, many Hollywood pictures, with their simplistic answers to sociological questions, failed to offer proper solutions to existing conditions. The new directors examined the problems of the individual or the problems of a small group as a method of analyzing the temper of the time. They didn't concentrate on the leader of the community but chose to study the town outcast, the misfit, the loner. Often from the "lower classes," these social deviants who come from outside the cultural mainstream, questioned values with complex sensitivity. Alienated from himself and others, rejecting old truths and unsure of the new ones, the new hero or heroine appeared to be lost in the complexity of modern times, unable to communicate or even to hope for something better.

While the independent filmmakers of the post-World War II period, such as Elia Kazan, Stanley Kramer, Billy Wilder, John Huston, and others, brought American films to maturity in terms of serious intent and philosophic themes, it was the directors of the 1960's who pushed for more freedom of expression and made films that tackled complex themes, stories, and characters. These narratives challenged the existing Production Code, and to understand how that moral fortress collapsed, one must take a view of conditions in the 1950's.

Despite the rebellion of independent producers and directors, and the influence of foreign films, most major studios at the beginning of the 1950's still tried to meet the requirements of the Hays Office. Its seal of approval continued to be important to religious and civic groups, and many theater managers still refused to exhibit pictures not approved by the Production Code.

The downfall of the Production Code began in 1950, with Roberto Rossellini's *The Miracle*, a story of a simple, unmarried shepherdess (Anna Magnani) who is made pregnant by a passing hobo but believes, in simple faith, that St. Joseph had caused her to conceive. The New York Commissioner of Licenses banned the film as sacrilegious. The importers of the Italian film took the case to the United States Supreme Court. Anticensorship lawyer Ephraim London argued that pre-release policing of motion pictures constituted illegal prior restraint, which could not be imposed on newspapers, books, or magazines, and, ergo, the same freedom belonged to film. The high court agreed.

Consequently, in 1952, the Supreme Court unanimously overruled the New York Film Licensing Board, declaring that movies were a source of information as well as entertainment, and that they enjoyed the constitutional guarantees of free speech. This decision, reversing a ruling that had stood since 1915, drastically altered the making of motion pictures. The importance of the decision lay in its placing films under the same constitutional protection as other communications media. Eventually subsequent rulings reduced and proscribed the power and procedures of the film licensing boards. These were the first steps toward a liberated screen.

Otto Preminger, one of the first to defy the Production Code of 1930, released *The Moon Is Blue* (1953) and *The Man With the Golden Arm* (1956) without seals of approval. Both films were box office successes. The former film introduced the daring word "virgin" to screen vocabulary; the latter dealt graphically with the heretofore taboo subject of heroin addiction. In 1961, the realistic Italian film *Two Women* showed Sophia Loren and her film daughter being raped by German Occupation troops. The American public may have been shocked, but another taboo disappeared. In that same year, Elia Kazan, directing *Splendor in the Grass,* induced Natalie Wood to step out of a bathtub and walk away from the camera down a corridor, thus introducing rear-view nudity. In 1964, the Hollywood Production Code was further challenged by *The Pawnbroker.* Director Sidney Lumet insisted that it was absolutely necessary to the story line—an elderly Jew's shocking remembrance of his wife's humiliation in a concentration camp—to photograph a young actress (Thelma Oliver) nude from the waist up. When the Legion of Decency protested, producer Ely A. Landau carried his case to the Motion Picture Association of America Appeals Board, and was granted a seal of approval.

By 1966, it was clear that the Production Code had collapsed. Hollywood asked Jack Valenti (President Lyndon Johnson's public relations man and later the president of the Motion Picture Association of America) to reestablish some sort of moral order for film production. Valenti's job was to update the old Code with modern concepts of morality, to appease Church groups, and to ward off federal censorship. Valenti and the famous trial lawyer Louis Nizer set about drafting a new Code. By November 1, 1968, they had established standards by which each film could be judged on its own merits; the appropriateness of what might be properly portrayed was left to the discretion of the film director. With this self-imposed rating system, the new Code Board hoped to appease church, state, and individuals, to promote creativity and artistry in the cinema, and to satisfy the sophisticated, mature moviegoer.

A rating system of G-M-R-X was set up: G=films for general audiences; M=mature audiences only, with parental supervision advised; R=restricted to persons over 16 (in some states, higher) unless accompanied by parent or adult guardian; X=persons under 21 not admitted under any circumstances.

In March, 1970, this original rating system was revised to G-PG-R-X: G=general audiences; PG=all ages admitted, but parental guidance suggested; R=prohibited for persons under 17 unless accompanied by parent or adult guardian; X=prohibited for persons under 17. In 1972, an increasing number of newspapers, including the *Boston Herald-Traveler*, the *Cleveland Plain Dealer*, the *Detroit News*, and the *Cincinnati Enquirer* made it their policy to refuse advertisements of X-rated films, as well as films without any rating. The general public surmised that the MPAA's X-rating indicates pornography, and critics, fearing new restrictions on film freedom, have asked that the rating system either be revised or abolished.

Because of nudity and profanity in films, pressure groups encouraged the public to rebel against the flood of supposedly obscene pictures, and on June 21, 1973, the Supreme Court issued another edict: there was no longer a national standard for obscenity. Each community would be allowed to decide what is considered obscene on the basis of what the average person might think of as "patently offensive." The 1973 ruling threw Hollywood into confusion. Producers, not knowing how local courts might interpret the ruling, decided to shoot various versions of risque or questionable scenes.

Certain films ran into immediate trouble. *Deep Throat* (1973), a hard-core pornographic film, was seized on obscenity charges in at least a dozen cities. The industry, thinking the June 21 decision would restrict only the "hard-core porno industry," was shocked when the ruling began to affect "responsible" films as well. *Carnal Knowledge* (1972), directed by Mike Nichols from a screenplay by Jules Feiffer, became a test case. The Georgia Supreme Court on July 2, 1973, upheld the obscenity conviction of a theater operator showing the R-rated film.

The Street Fighter, in 1974, was the first film to get an "X" rating for extreme violence, rather than nudity or explicit sex scenes. This action set off another debate in the industry. The movie studios had created the Code and Rating Administration (CARA) in 1968 to classify films according to "suitability" for young movie fans, and usually gave the "X" for sex and nudity. When *The Street Fighter*, which is short on sex but long on violence, received its "X," CARA seemed to be declaring a change in policy. The distributor recalled the film from circulation and cut out certain revolting scenes. This judgment may be establishing a new criterion for American film censorship.

By 1975, the public, police, and civic organizations appeared to have lost interest, at least temporarily, in deciding what is obscene. Officials in Philadelphia, Boston, and Denver fought hard to keep X-rated theaters from opening, but public outrage over obscenity subsided. Police in certain cities felt pursuing obscenity cases to be a waste of taxpayers' money.

When the film industry began selling its old movies to television, a practice that appeared to be self-defeating, the public, especially families and elderly couples, decided to wait for films to appear on their home sets instead of taking the time and expense to go to a movie. By 1955, box office receipts had fallen off so drastically that the movie industry was in trouble.

Noting the decline of older fans at the box office, perceptive producers turned to the potential audience of carefree teen-agers, and thus many films were structured to capture the youth market. The 1950's belonged to bobbysoxers, hot rods, crew cuts, and the high school crowd; films were lighthearted and gay, appealing to the young and their love for escapism. Movies offered pop music, broad comedy, semi-nudity, drag races, and surfboards. The kids paid to see Sandra Dee, Deborah Walley, Cindy Carol, Elvis Presley, Tab Hunter, Ricky Nelson, Sal Mineo, Tommy Kirk, and Tuesday Weld.

By the mid-1960's, however, the mood of the youthful audience changed. The political and social climate of the country was in a troubled state. The Vietnam War forced young men of draft age to face the possibility of being called to military service, and many young people began to question seriously such ideals as patriotism and heroism. Kids began to doubt that dying for one's country made one a hero. At the same time, a growing demand for equality in work, schools, living conditions, and voting rights, especially among blacks and Spanish-speaking citizens, raised the consciousness of the entire nation. Gradually these subcultures of youth and minorities gathered momentum, shaking many middle-class white American values.

Producers were quick to see the box office potential in this, and they released pictures with such timely themes as youth in revolt, the generation gap, racial tension, the drug scene, and the abolition of sexual taboos. As early as 1953, Stanley Kramer's *The Wild One*, followed by Richard Brooks's *The Blackboard Jungle* (1955), and John Frankenheimer's *The*

Young Stranger (1955), were among the first to present the problems of the decade. Some of the high school crowd dropped their greasy-haired singing idols and flocked to see the neurotic Anthony Perkins, the lonely Marlon Brando, and the introspective Montgomery Clift. Teen-agers applauded wildly the forerunner of tortured youth and the plight of the adolescent, as played by James Dean in *Rebel Without a Cause* (1955). Fans who laughed at *I Was a Teen-age Werewolf* (1957) were shouting approval of *Dr. Strangelove* (1963), a black comedy that made fun of nuclear war.

The very young continued to prefer Ann-Margret, Michael Parks, and Russ Tamblyn, but the 18-to-25-year-olds discovered Frank Perry's *David and Lisa* (1963), and Mike Nichols's *The Graduate* (1967). Young audiences liked the aimless student who rejected a world of plastics and was seduced by his girlfriend's mother. They were captivated by the hoodlums in *Bonnie and Clyde* (1967) and the lonesome travelers in *Easy Rider* (1969).

Characters who rebelled against society became the favorites of the younger audience. The talented Tuesday Weld, having graduated from inane comedies, pleased both the critics and the youth crowd with her special blend of innocence, carnality, and evil in *Pretty Poison* (1968). Young filmgoers lined up to buy tickets for the rock documentaries *Monterey Pop* (1968), *Woodstock* (1969), and *Gimme Shelter* (1970). Youth understood Antonioni's selfish photographer in *Blow-Up* (1967), who lost all values in his world of technological art. They formed a cult for Stanley Kubrick's fantasy of the future, *2001: A Space Odyssey* (1968). They understood *Medium Cool* (1969) and *Alice's Restaurant* (1969).

It did not matter that many films were badly developed or flawed by extreme prejudice or a lack of objectivity; they were accepted as long as they attacked traditional values. The more bizarre, daring, and scathing films yielded higher box office receipts. By the mid-1960's young people seemed to control the American cinema. Even the directors and producers were younger people, dictating trends and selecting daring stories with explicit language, nudity, and graphic lovemaking. Their films found a ready audience among youngsters who identified with the teen-agers having problems on the screen. Thus, in a way, youth forced the movies into new explorations, opening the floodgates to what some called screen freedom.

The themes presented by many contemporary filmmakers are complex, and the questions they raise are frequently profound. It is difficult to pinpoint one theme or one subject characteristic of the major films of this decade. Films of the 1960's reflected upon and questioned all facets of the contemporary scene. Some films reveal human callousness to violence: *Bullitt* (1969), *Bonnie and Clyde* (1967), and *The Wild Bunch* (1969). Other films explored previously forbidden areas of love: *The Killing of Sister George* (1968), *The Sergeant* (1969), *Staircase* (1970), *I Am Curious-Yellow* (1969), and *The Boys in the Band* (1970). They alluded to the generation gap, an epigraph of the decade, in *Alice's Restaurant* (1969), *The Graduate* (1968), and *Goodbye, Columbus* (1969). *The Pawnbroker* (1965) points out that one person's inhumanity to another is never-ending. *Putney Swope* (1969) and *Medium Cool* (1969) dissect the disintegration of family and society; the latter film is also a polemic on self-government.

Interpersonal relationships were explored from every perspective, often with shocking intensity. Anthony Harvey's *Dutchman* (1967), from the LeRoi Jones play, provides a violent treatment of racial prejudice from the point of view of a white trollop who teases, goads, curses, and eventually stabs a young black man. *The Loved One* (1966) features macabre black comedy on the American way of death. Sentimental animal films of the 1940's and 1950's gave way to *Futz* (1969), the tale of a farmer who makes love to Amanda, a pig. *Midnight Cowboy* (1969) traces the abortive career of a young, handsome male prostitute seeking success in New York City. *Medium Cool* (1969) is the powerful story of a cameraman and his direct involvement during the Democratic National Convention riots of 1968 in Chicago. Bernardo Bertolucci's *Last Tango in Paris* (1973) offers boldness and brutality, intimate sex scenes, profanity, and nudity in an opulent visual style.

"Unheroic" heroes (or antiheroes) became prevalent in films in the 1960's; the psychotic, the neurotic, and the loner were all grist for the film mill. The schoolboys in *If* (1969) shoot their professor and the school curate, while in Luchino Visconti's *The Damned* (1970), the main character sexually molests little girls and rapes his mother. Heroes and villains are often one and the same; morals no longer appear to be fashionable. Frequently the protagonists do not fit into society. They take their sex on the run, hate the Establishment, openly denounce the government, break the old moral code, deny tradition, and in many cases, are unable to develop satisfying, meaningful ways of life to replace those they have destroyed. Finding neither true love, freedom, nor self-knowledge, they frequently have no wish to examine themselves or to change their lifestyles.

The most radical changes in movie characters recently have been in roles for women. By the 1960's, the screen heroine was no longer a prim, sexless domestic type but often appeared as a jilted mistress, a drunk, an emotional whimperer, a sex-starved spinster, a psychotic, or a downright whore.

Shirley MacLaine in *Irma La Douce* (1963) is a charming prostitute. The heroine of *Love With the Proper Stranger* (1963) seeks an illegal abortion. In *Luv* (1967), Elaine May wishes she were a lesbian. Jane Fonda is a hooker who is searching for someone to love in *Klute* (1971). A heroine of the 1960's and 1970's can be a savage antagonist, break moral laws, steal, and at the end win her man, the sympathy of the audience, and even reap spiritual and material rewards.

The newest, and to many the most disturbing, element of characterization in these modern films in that they neither explain the maladjustments and sicknesses of their characters nor imply that there is anything in their actions to condemn or forgive. Rather, these films frequently give the impression that their characters represent normal people.

Defenders of this new-found freedom contend that if a film is to represent life as it is rather than to preach or amuse, then the viewer cannot expect ready-made moral or social judgments. While they may have personal views of what they are portraying, they try to lead viewers into forming particular opinions or coming to certain conclusions. In so doing, they have tried to create films that are all things to all people—both personal statements and eternal problems. In effect, directors now regard the film experience as a multisensory "happening" on an emotional level, which will lead to independent, individual reactions.

The two films that best represent the 1960's, reflecting the changing times, are *Bonnie and Clyde* (1967) and *Easy Rider* (1969). Arthur Penn's use of force in his study of Bonnie Parker and Clyde Barrow elevated sleazy killers to national heroes. Young audiences saw these characters as heroes for a disenchanted age. Moving in an existential world, the film mixes comedy, poetry, and extreme violence in the story of the two minor criminals. The film reflects the moral attitude of the decade. The ads for the film declared, "They're young! They're in love! And they kill people!" (see Chapter 11, "The Gangster Film"). *Easy Rider* (1969) ushered in the low-budget, unpolished, personalized film. The phenomenal success of this film made studio executives willing to back almost any director under thirty in any youth-oriented project.

Directed by Dennis Hopper and starring Hopper, Peter Fonda, and Jack Nicholson, *Easy Rider*, although cheaply made ($375,000), was highly influential. Typifying America's aimlessly rebellious youth, the film had a tremendous impact on young fans.

Two motorcyclists ride off from California to Florida, traveling over a beautiful and at times grotesque landscape, to live a life of ease in the sun. Because of their unconventional appearance, they are objects of suspicion, turned away from motels, forced to sleep outdoors, and ridiculed by society. Eventually the two travelers meet a violent end at the hands of barbaric rednecks. The beauty of the countryside is infiltrated with corruption, violence, stupidity, and death.

The picture owes much of its success to the comments it makes about the mood of America. Fonda and Hopper suggest that society is paranoid, that free and individual souls are doomed, that contemporary youth and the lifestyle it follows is denounced by an intolerant society. *Easy Rider* is upsetting because of its observations of rednecks, uptight kids, the Establishment, guns, drugs, and sex. It speaks brazenly and openly about the disturbed years.

By the end of the decade, Hollywood had almost fully dismantled its dream factory. Fewer and fewer movies were made on the West Coast. Instead they were shot in Europe, New York, Africa, and South America. The industry turned international, with American production companies hiring distinguished foreign directors, stars, and technicians. The studios, in order to make money, not only released their collections of films to TV but also made features directly for television, designed for later release in theaters at home and abroad. Movies and TV, out of economic necessity, decided to wed each other. However, the potential of the medium of film as an art form continued to excite young artists, with the cinema taking over from the theater and literature as the favorite form of personal expression. Thus the industry entered the 1970's with energy and optimism.

10 / The Seventies

By THE early 1970's, fans and critics had come to regard the movies more as an art form rather than mere entertainment. Films were made to appeal to a circumscribed audience, many of them under thirty. At the beginning of the decade, falling revenues and rising production costs created a demand for low-budget movies. Directors, working outside the studio system, independent of budgets and deadlines, were in control. Some studios continued to produce the old-style extravaganza, the dread-and-disaster epic, the Western, and the period piece, but a group of young directors appeared along with a seemingly inexhaustible supply of fresh acting talent.

Surprisingly, the films produced by these new combinations were less experimental and more conventional than those of the decade before, but they were filled with ingenuity and creative energy, which the public loved. Most of these young directors, thoroughly conditioned by American films during their youth, ignore the fragmented style, the murky characters, and heavy symbolism of foreign films. They make films with strong narrative lines, clear characterizations, tight editing, strong command of action, and superb camerawork. Visually beautiful, these films are realistic and forceful. Concerned with young people and today's problems, their films, offering ideas that entertain as well as enlighten, reveal a sense of immediacy, filled with vitality and excitement.

The early films of the 1970's can be divided roughly into five categories: (1) reworking old favorites; (2) comedy (slapstick, farcical, and serious); (3) films about blacks; (4) the blockbuster or the disaster/doomsday feature; and (5) personal tragedy, which reflects futility, corruption, and despair.

Reworking the nostalgic vein can be dismissed quickly. *King Kong* (1977) added only color and contemporary wisecracks to the brilliant original. *A Star Is Born* (1976) ended up as an unpleasant vehicle to satisfy the voracious ego of

Barbra Streisand. William Friedkin's *Sorcerer* (1977) is an outstanding remake of the brilliant Henri-Georges Clouzot film *The Wages of Fear* (1953). Scheduled for future release are remakes of *Kind Hearts and Coronets*, *The Prisoner of Zenda*, and *The Cat and the Canary*. Hollywood appears to be running out of material.

As for comedy, the most appealing new talents are Elaine May, Woody Allen, and Mel Brooks. Interestingly, all three are performers as well as directors. Miss May, one of the few women to make her mark as a director, offered *A New Leaf* (1970) and *The Heartbreak Kid* (1972), two films with a malicious view of contemporary American life. Woody Allen, the darling of the intellectuals, appearing in his own skillfully directed films, is almost always a hero who is betrayed by fate; he is also a schlemiel. His comedies are the word-oriented humor of the writer-performer.

As the screen's most cerebral joker, Allen is the meek dope in *Bananas* (1971), *Sleeper* (1973), *Love and Death* (1975), and *Annie Hall* (1977). His films reveal a hilarious imagination, and younger fans set him up at once as a cult symbol. Mel Brooks's *Blazing Saddles* (1974) is also a box office success, but Brooks's film is filled with rude sounds, words, sight gags, and *double-entendres*. *Young Frankenstein* (1975) is tailored from the same cloth, and fans proclaim Mel Brooks, along with Woody Allen, as a top director of comedy.

In other screen comedies of the 1970's, *The Happy Hooker* (1975) has Lynn Redgrave taking care of the sexual fantasies of maladjusted men; *The Return of the Pink Panther* (1975), *Shampoo* (1975), and *Silver Streak* (1977) are notable successful comedies.

Blacks took a big step forward in the films of the 1970's. *Shaft* (1971) and *Shaft's Big Score* (1972), the adventures of a black private eye, intended as escape films, set a pattern for others that followed. Gordon Parks, Jr.'s *Super Fly* (1972), the first black-oriented film financed by blacks, broke box office records but raised the wrath of critics for its glorification of a drug pusher. *The Final Comedown* (1972) is a black rebellion film that offered little solution to the problems of racial injustice. *The Legend of Nigger Charlie* (1972), a black Western, was condemned for its violence and stereotyped whites; it failed to present a true film of either the black man or the old West. In *Lady Sings the Blues* (1972), a biography of the late jazz singer Billie Holiday, critics praised Diana Ross's performance but criticized the film for liberties it takes with the facts of Miss Holiday's life. *Georgia, Georgia* (1972) marks the first time in American cinema that a black woman (Maya Angelou) has had an original screenplay produced (generally to favorable critical reaction).

Among the best films of 1972, *Sounder*, Martin Ritt's story of a family of black sharecroppers in the Deep South struggling to eke out an existence, has received high critical acclaim. It is a model of solid filmmaking that towers above most contemporary black films. Arriving on the cinema scene when movie screens were being flooded with black exploitation product, dealing only with sex, violence, and drugs, *Sounder* was welcomed by almost every critic.

When *Easy Rider* (1969), a low-budget movie with a folk-rock soundtrack, pushed box office returns so high, the studios deluged the public with low-budget films made by young inexperienced directors. The result was a score of flops, for young audiences spurned these feeble efforts. Hollywood, following foreign films, turned to sex and nudity but these films were eventually overshadowed by hard-core pornography. By 1973, the Supreme Court reopened the troublesome censorship problems, and by 1975 it was safer to avoid sex in favor of a blockbusting disaster film filled with brutality and violence.

The 1970's saw a wave of films dealing with a world turned upside down by catastrophe. The star of these films is, of course, the special effects man. In each one, the plot is a string of blatant contrivances, and the dialogue is consistently inane. The success of the film, however, lies in the extent of the catastrophe. One of the first to launch the disaster theme was *The Poseidon Adventure* (1972), in which a luxury liner is overturned by a monstrous wave. This ark movie (disaster always seems to strike just as the assorted characters are enjoying a carefree moment) is an outstanding example of the disparity between critical and popular taste. Although praised for its special effects, the critics cast thumbs-down on the film, but the public certainly did not. By mid-1974 *The Poseidon Adventure* had earned $38 million in domestic rentals alone. *Airport 1975* (1974), directed by Jack Smight, has Charlton Heston saving the passengers on a pilotless 747. The flight crew is killed in midair, and Heston is dropped in for the rescue. Among the passengers are Gloria Swanson, Myrna Loy, and Sid Caesar. *Gold* (1974) offers a dam bursting into the channels of a South African mine. *Earthquake* (1974) is a blueprint for cinematic technology. The producers restructured theaters with a device called "Sensurround" to give audiences the feeling of being in an actual earthquake. *The Hindenburg* (1975) tells of the explosion of the famous dirigible; *The Towering Inferno* (1974) is about a fire in the world's tallest office building; and *The Swarm* (1978) releases killer bees that threaten to destroy the human race. Since these dread-and-disaster films filled the studio coffers, many other studios climbed on the bandwagon.

These films, reflecting a contemporary fascination with apocalyptic horror and doom, give audiences the added pleasure of watching such horrendous sights without any physical risks. They also contain the aesthetic appeal of spectacle and destruction, sights that movies can display more effectively than any other art form.

The fourth category, personal tragedy, is occupied with a world without honor, order, or integrity, depicting a society in which individuals ride not on paths of glory but rather into the depths of hell. Most of the directors who make these films began in television, where they learned to film, cut, edit, and tell a story within a specified time frame. Many of these pictures are composed of the same basic ingredients: the main characters are either fun-loving, daredevil young people or pathological, alienated types, who are exalted as symbols of the new generation. They often live in a police state, are hounded by killer cops, and are running away from a problem, a crime, or society, but arriving at no solution or destination. Some come from homes in which the parents have realized the American dream but don't know what to do next. They follow a random lifestyle of this undirected generation. These antiheroes live in a world of constant motion, panic, and pursuit. On horseback, on foot, or in battered cars (that eventually become as individualistic as the escaping characters), these existential child-adults are pursued by cops as corrupt as the robbers themselves. They are jaunty, freewheeling kids who select fun and violence, ripping off whatever they please. Many directors set these pictures in the now nostalgically beautiful days of the 1930's, 1940's, or 1950's. The chase is usually across America, and the time is post-Hoover and pre-Vietnam. These emotionless, bored adolescents, invariably from small towns, discover sex, hide out from the law, live in a moral vacuum, and race across a landscape of desolation and despair. Secondary characters often have the double-edged bite of parody and reality. During these cinematic journeys, the directors usually manage to show a satiric portrayal of the ugly-beautiful architecture of plastic America, and to stress the steady decline of national morality.

These films of the 1970's have obvious roots in various productions of the 1950's and 1960's, mostly in those stories that rejected the formulas of the big studios and offered the antihero in simplistic sociological studies that passed as serious cinema. The contemporary directors take the same loner, the alienated kid, the outcast, or the misfit, whose problems of alienation and confusion are often caused by American society itself, and change this killer into a lovable kid with a hilarious sense of humor. The beginnings of this type of film can be traced to Arthur Penn's *Bonnie and Clyde* (1967), the movie that elevated two killers into national heroes.

These sagas of outlaw folk-heroes not only provide audiences with charming killers and immoral characters, but also criticize society's ills. Armed with a basic story spiced with sex and heavy doses of violence, the directors follow the adventures of otherwise nondescript individuals, using them as a means of denouncing various aspects of American life. Skillful acting, the throbbing beat of country music, and a probing mobile camera provide both immediacy and authenticity.

This school is headed by such experienced and talented directors as Robert Altman, Sam Peckinpah, Alan Pakula, and George Roy Hill, followed by Bud Yorkin, Francis Ford Coppola, George Axelrod, Paul Mazursky, Michael Sarne, and Mike Nichols. The younger disciples are Martin Scorsese, George Lucas, John Milius, William Friedkin, William Fraker, Peter Bogdanovich, Peter Fonda, Monty Hellman, and Terence Malick.

In George Lucas's second film, *American Graffiti* (1973), young characters hang out at the local hamburger stand in constant motion, cruising in cars, living in limbo and going nowhere. Martin Scorsese's *Mean Streets* (1973) portrays evil and decay in a vicious study of life among the young in New York's Lower East Side. *Steelyard Blues* (1974), Alan Meyerson's first picture, features dropout criminals, who imagine they are old-style outlaws. In *Electra Glide in Blue* (1973), James William Guercio's black comedy and Conrad Hall's dazzling photography reveal the death of dreams. In *Paper Moon* (1973), Peter Bogdanovich turns to nostalgia with his portrait of a fraudulent Bible salesman and a precocious nine-year-old girl bumping along in their jalopy through the Midwest during the Great Depression. Jerry Schatzberg turns his camera on two losers and their odyssey across America in *Scarecrow* (1973), while Sidney Pollack revisits the recent past in *The Way We Were* (1973), a political love story of the 1950's. Robert Altman's *Thieves Like Us* (1974) tells of young lovers in the 1930's who kill and run. His *Nashville* (1975) mixes country music with politics, showing the vulgarity, deceit, and greed of American life. *The Last Detail* (1974) directed by Hal Ashby, is a funny and heartbreaking story of three sailors who, during a five-day beer-soaked journey through cities from Virginia to New Hampshire, discover insights into their essential characters too late.

Of this crop of directors, one of the most promising is Steven Spielberg, who first directed for television. His film for TV *Duel* (1972), is a terrifying story of a commercial traveler (Dennis Weaver) and his fight to the death against machines (a diesel truck). It is a cunningly contrived scenario that offers great suspense. In *The Sugarland Express* (1974), his fugitive couple are on an endless chase, living in a world of pursuit and panic, killing and violence. *Jaws* (1975) singles Spielberg out from other young directors. His film excels at editing and tempo. Because of its emotional pacing and exciting chase, *Jaws* is a box office smash, showing promise of being one of the greatest financial successes ever turned out by the industry.

Terence Malick scores brilliantly with *Badlands* (1974). Set in the 1950's, his hero, accompanied by a fifteen-year-old girlfriend, is off on a killing spree, living in a moral vacuum. Malick follows the couple's lethal meandering in a detached dreamlike style, catching the brutality of their lives. As the fugitives make their somewhat aimless way to safety, the killer/hero coolly guns down anyone who stands in his way.

Martin Scorsese's *Boxcar Bertha* (1972) follows the adventures of minor-league characters to tell a gruesome story of the 1930's. It is yet another attempt to criticize the mores of society through violence, sex, humor, and bloodshed. Scorsese's *Alice Doesn't Live Here Anymore* (1974) is one of the first groundbreakers for the self-determined woman. The picture is a minor classic because of its steady vision of the world seen through the eyes of Alice. His *Taxi Driver* (1976), a tale of an insomniac Vietnam veteran who takes up taxi driving to pass the long night hours, is a realistic film of an alienated character and a depressing city. In *New York, New York* (1977) he presents Liza Minnelli as a 1940's singer who juggles her marriage and career.

Robert Benton's *Bad Company* (1973) offers a study of two malevolent young men who escape the Civil War draft and seek their fortunes as amateur brigands; roving independents, refugees from civilization, they travel through the West. In comic strip fashion, they live off the land and try to convince the viewer that being a criminal is the only answer. At the end, the two set off to rob a Wells Fargo office.

Films of the 1970's also reflected the darkening political and social climate in the United States. Conspiratorial forces shape history in *The Conversation* (1974), which depicts the paranoia and anxiety symptomatic of a Watergate world. Alan J. Pakula's *The Parallax View* (1974) suggests that the assassinations of Kennedy, King, and others may have been shaped by a conspiracy beyond the reach of the law. In mirroring certain facets of American society, these films present characters disenchanted with the country, scornful of traditional moral values, and negative in outlook with regard to the value of existence itself.

Violence is popular. In *Burnt Offerings* (1976) a wife pushes her husband out of a third-story window. His son, sitting in a station wagon, watches as his father comes crashing through the windshield. In *The Omen* (1976), a child pushes his mother from a balcony. In *Carrie* (1977), a mother stabs her daughter with a pair of scissors. The daughter lives long enough to crucify her mother with a collection of sharp kitchen knives. In Andy Warhol's *Bad* (1977) a short-tempered mother, unable to stand her nonstop squalling baby, throws it out the window of the high-rise apartment.

By 1975, many films were distinguished by an abundance of villainy and a lack of heroes. The protagonist is neither hero nor antihero. He is a person who discovers the diseases of today's society and tries not so much to fight them but merely to stay alive. The ordinary man is pitted against a web of evil. He is often unintentionally involved and discovers a bigger web and then another, etcetera. All the powers are tainted—up and down. Our ordinary man is obliged to struggle for nothing but his life as he uncovers the evil around himself. Various aspects of this theme exist in *Three Days of the Condor* (1975), *Killer Elite* (1975), *Marathon*

Man (1976), *The Next Man* (1977), and *Network* (1976). There are few heroes in a world of nihilism.

One exception however, is the popular and inspiring film *Rocky* (1976), a romantic tale directed by John Avildsen, starring Sylvester Stallone. Rocky, a thirty-year-old club fighter, gets a shot at the championship boxing title. A Philadelphia nobody, he gains his manhood, self-respect, and the love of a worthwhile girl. In spite of its hackneyed ideas, the film has an emotional effect on audiences and served as an inspiration to many contemporary fans.

By 1975, if one had asked where American movies were going, the answer would have been into the hands of the conglomerates, where they have remained ever since. The era of the once-omnipotent studio mogul has ended. The power held by pioneer producers such as Jesse Lasky, Carl Laemmle, Samuel Goldwyn, Adolph Zukor, Louis B. Mayer, and Stanley Kramer has long since passed. In the front office today, there sits a young, college-educated agent-chairman, trained in television, carrying out orders from big businesses in the East. Trans-American Corporation, Gulf and Western, and other powerful firms dictate studio policy.

The agent-chairman is not a showman but a package buyer, a budget watcher, and a deal maker. Much of his time is spent making deals with directors, offering an outlet for their films, hoping he's found another *American Graffiti* (1973). Today his reputation and that of the studio rides on a boom or bust program. And the boom, if not present in an independent director's efforts, is often found in the studio blockbuster. The company that can produce one or two gigantic moneymakers every year is able to survive. Because of tremendous publicity programs, the public's appetite for big pictures has never been more keen. Some companies are so determined to find the panacea to success that they are trying market-research techniques to predict what type of stories, themes, directors, cast, timing, and methods best combine to make a hit. Each executive and his staff searches for the Holy Grail—the action-packed blockbuster that will surpass in box office revenue the all-time moneymaker *Star Wars* (1977).

For decades, the heads of the studios decided what pictures the public would see. Today television, newspaper headlines, independent directors, and the once-lowly screenwriter dictate the choice. In order not to lose out to television, movies resort to larger-than-life showmanship. Movies can offer anything television can—only bigger. What's happening in the news can be tomorrow's successful film. *Dog Day Afternoon* (1975) and *All the President's Men* (1976) picked their plots off the front page. At least six pictures are planned about the murder of Don Bolles, the Phoenix investigative reporter, who was hot on the trail of Mafia bigwigs. Independent directors such as Woody Allen, Robert Altman, Terence Malick, Mel Brooks, Martin Scorsese, George Lucas, and others offer their yearly films structured to capture the intellectual and student audiences.

At present, studio chairmen have decided to limit the corporation's money to several kinds of pictures: war, the relationship of women, the world of jocks, and the murky shenanigans of freaky kids.

World War II is being refought, with Gregory Peck as the imperious five-star general in *MacArthur* (1977); in *The Eagle Has Landed* (1977), Michael Caine heads a German team which enters England to kidnap Winston Churchill; in *Cross of Iron* (1977), audiences have a chance to see the Germans' side of the war. The $25 million *A Bridge Too Far* (1977) is one of the biggest projects of its kind in cinema history. Richard Attenborough attempts to tell the story of Operation Market Garden, a single bold thrust aimed at ending World War II. Young and old fans are enjoying the holocaust, mayhem, destruction, and violence. But World War II is ancient history. Hollywood has finally found the nerve to face Vietnam. The studios offer reality with the release of a spate of movies of burning significance. The Southeast Asia conflict is being refought in *Rolling Thunder, Who'll Stop the Rain, Tracks, Coming Home, The Deer Hunter, The Boys in Company C,* and the long-delayed Francis Ford Coppola's *Apocalypse Now.*

The world of the athlete is another lodestone to mine. Films, examining the high pressures of the big-business world of amateur and professional sports, have fans lining up for tickets. Michael Ritchie's *The Bad News Bears* (1976) tells the story of a group of tough kids, smoking and mouthing profanity, out to win the baseball pennant, showing the effects of the American success syndrome on a group of youngsters. The public reacted so enthusiastically that the studio rushed out a sequel *The Bad News Bears in Breaking Training* (1977), and they are following this with *The Bad News Bears in Japan*. The possibilities are endless. *Rollerball* (1974) tells of a mindless sports hero who defies the system in a future society in which all problems have vanished. *Rocky* (1976), a rather schlocky old-fashioned picture that romanticizes real life, is an overwhelming success both with fans and critics. The boxing ring is also the setting for *The Greatest* (1977) with Muhammad Ali. Robert DeNiro will portray middleweight champion Jake LaMotta in *Raging Bull*. *Semi-Tough* (1977) and *Knockout* are sports films, while *One on One* (1977) examines amateur basketball. *Slapshot* (1977), with its raunchy dialogue, has Paul Newman as a hockey player. The film treats violence not as a manifestation of macho sensibility, but as a result of weakness, confusion, and insecurity.

Since the 1930's and 1940's, women have had few important roles in movies. Anne Bancroft gave a brilliant performance in *The Miracle Worker* (1962), and Patricia Neal helped make *Hud* (1963) a hit. Shirley Booth, Marilyn Monroe, Geraldine Page, Joanne Woodward and Jane Fonda won plaudits in various roles, but in general, the 1960's and 1970's were lean years for women performers. Now the rising importance of the equal rights program has attracted Hollywood's attention. The machismo frolics, sometimes referred to as Caper films, between Newman-Redford and Hoffman-McQueen appear to have ended. The screen will once more examine the relationship between women and men. Woman is no longer to be merely a sex object, a dramatic prop to reveal the hero's character, a silent partner loading the shotgun to stave off the Indians, but a person with feelings, facing profound problems, and involved in a web of relationships. Robert Altman's dream film *Three Women* (1977), the story about three women whose identities merge and flow together, has been one of the lead-off films. *The Other Side of Midnight* (1977) is another. Jane Fonda and Vanessa Redgrave are female activists in *Julia* (1977), Diane Keaton is a psychological misfit in *Looking for Mr. Goodbar* (1977), Marthe Keller, a dying heroine in *Bobby Deerfield* (1977). Audiences have seen Jill Clayburgh in *An Unmarried Woman*, and Susan Sarandon in *Pretty Baby*.

Older fans remember child stars such as Mary Pickford, Shirley Temple, Freddie Bartholomew, Jackie Cooper, Margaret O'Brien, and Natalie Wood as idealized representations of children who were loyal, truthful, staunch, dependable, and wise beyond their years. Movies today have turned kids into monsters. Jodie Foster, Tatum O'Neal and Linda Blair are not exactly filled with sugar and spice but rather profanity, deception, nicotine stains, and wisecracks. These children can't be tagged as Mommy's pride or Daddy's delight. In the 1970's, movie kids are killers, streetwalkers, and demons.

Audrey Rose (1977), a spinoff from *The Exorcist* (1973), concerns reincarnation. An eleven-year-old girl, Audrey Rose, who is killed in a car accident, takes over the body of another child born two minutes after the death of Audrey. In *The Omen* (1976), the supposedly natural son of Gregory Peck and Lee Remick is the offspring of the Prince of Satan and has come to take over his kingdom. *It's Alive* (1977) tells of a newborn baby who kills the doctors and nurses in the delivery room, then creeps around Los Angeles killing senior citizens, milkmen and bystanders. In *Demon Seed* (1977), Julie Christie has been seduced by a computer that wishes to rule the world. Christie's child, supposedly a superbeing, has his own plans for the world's future. Jodie Foster in *Taxi Driver* (1976) is a teen-age prostitute; in *Bugsy Malone* (1976), a speakeasy singer. In *The Little Girl Who Lives Down the Lane* (1977), Jodie, in her struggle against giving in to the rules and regulations of an ordinary life, does away with her father, mother, and various neighbors.

Hollywood's latest spate of films offers the vigilante as hero; the man who walks softly and carries not only a big stick but also a loaded gun. *Walking Tall* (1973), directed by Phil Karlson, offers the heroics of a civilian posse to urban vigilantism. The film spawned dozens of tales of the individual who takes the law into his own hands. Michael Winner's *Death Wish* (1974) had the greatest influence on such a trend. Charles Bronson, a businessman whose wife has been murdered and daughter driven insane by muggers, becomes a one-man vendetta, depopulating New York as the police look on in amazement. Audiences send up rowdy cheers of approval as Bronson, the revengeful father, kills off his prey one by one. Frontier ethics have moved into the city. The vigilante is now a screen hero.

Frontier justice and Biblical vengeance are evident in *Dirty Harry* (1971) and its sequel, *Magnum Force* (1973). In the former, Clint Eastwood, as a cynical policeman, works within a placid system, and manipulates the law to suit his own revenge. In *Magnum Force* he's back in the Establishment, defending the world against a cell of vigilante cadets.

Other vigilantes followed: the hero of Martin Scorsese's *Taxi Driver* (1976), *White Line Fever* (1977), Michael Winner's *Stone Killer* (1977). Heroes take just so much, then take their guns and seek revenge. Movie audiences cheer the shooting and slaying in *White Line Fever, Vigilante Force* (1976), *The Human Factor*. Americans are fair game for hired guns. In Lamont Johnson's *Lipstick* (1976), Margaux Hemingway goes after her sister's rapist with a gun.

The vigilante film reaches its apotheosis with *Taxi Driver* (1976). As an insomniac Vietnam veteran, Robert DeNiro, a taxi driver, is sickened and disgusted by the seamy world he sees through his windshield. He is the very spirit of urban alienation. Alone, he sets out to bring order to chaos. He is the avenging angel, his taxi a yellow chariot. Politics and human relationships both reject him. He prepares for a conflict to cleanse. He kills. And the camera glides from bloodstained walls to a clean wall. DeNiro has become a hero for his night of massacre. He has been reborn. He establishes rapport with fellow drivers and has a shy, friendly smile for a girl who spurned him. The vigilante is the hero.

Where are American films going? Nobody can predict, but it is unlikely that the weekly habit of going to the movies will remain the pastime it once was. American movies will continue to dominate world cinema. Instability, always a part of the entertainment world, continues to be a part of moviemaking. The solvency of a studio may lean increasingly on a single blockbuster film, but revenues of a runaway success can carry a string of flops. American films dominate with their technical virtuosity, and they will continue to redefine various genres. Complex social issues will be tackled.

In this age of multiple choices, it is impossible to be specific in terms of types, stories, or styles. Based on the medium's cyclical history, however, certain predictions can be made. Cinema is and will be pulled between its co-existing extremes: show business vs. art; entertainment vs. message; national vs. international. The artistic and popular success of any individual film will, as before, depend on the delicate balance it is able to strike between these inherent polarities. Success will also hinge upon the filmmakers' abilities to fuse fresh insights with the techniques and genres that have developed over the formative years, while simultaneously remaining open to the stimulating and creative trends of newer filmmakers.

Movies have made great strides in the past twenty years. Much has been new and much has been exciting. On the other hand, much has seemed revolting to many viewers. Only time will tell what is novelty, what is shock for shock's sake, and what is enduring truth. If cinema was accused for decades of creating a dream world, that accusation no longer has validity, as the industry and its independent practitioners face today's world and its ever-increasing yearnings for honesty and truth. In the United States the potentialities of film as a medium continue to excite and attract young would-be artists, and it is these we will be hearing from.

PART II

★

THE DEVELOPMENT OF SELECTED MOTION PICTURE GENRES

11 / The Gangster Film

ALTHOUGH the gangster had appeared briefly in D.W. Griffith's *Musketeers of Pig Alley* (1912), it was another fifteen years before *Underworld* (1927) triggered the gangster film cycle of the Prohibition years. Replete with thieves, prostitutes, con artists, henchmen and gun molls, *Underworld* captured the imagination of cinema fans and set the pattern for plot and characterization that was widely imitated. Josef von Sternberg's innovations—rapidly flashing closeups, dissolves, montages, and unusual lighting—coupled with Ben Hecht's authentic dialogue of Chicago mobsters, made *Underworld* the prototype for almost every subsequent gangster movie.

This type of film was greatly enhanced by sound. Directors discovered that dramatic intensity was heightened by the splatter of tommy-gun bullets, the squealing tires of speeding cars, the music from the honkytonks, and the torch songs of nightclub singers. Sound increased the suspense of "the hunt," as mobsters searched out their victims in shadowy, sinister alleys or cheap hotel rooms.

Modeled after Al Capone and his gangster cohorts, the killer lived in an anonymous city, moved in a world of nightclubs, drank moderately or not at all, and usually took his sensual pleasures from mercenary women. If the right woman came along he could be tender and kind, but once deceived he turned violent and brutal. He was usually surrounded by a cluster of stock characters: a nightclub owner, often a racketeer; a gun moll, usually a blonde golddigger; a "mouthpiece" (lawyer); a collection of strong-armed bodyguards; and a sycophant who ran errands and listened to the boss's philosophical observations. At the conclusion of the film, the sycophant or flunkie was often the only character who survived to warn the audience that crime does not pay.

The killer was usually moody and quick-tempered, sentimental at times and fatalistic at others. World-weary, ironic, sarcastic, and brutal, he seemed to know that he would die violently. Despite his viciousness, he might have a strong familial attachment for a mother, sister, younger brother, or father. Most gangland films included at least one encounter with the gangster's family to show how loving and kindly the killer could be. In *The Public Enemy* (1931), Jimmy Cagney returns home several times to visit his family; in *Scarface* (1932) Paul Muni is devoted to his sister. In *Dead End* (1937) Humphrey Bogart pays a call on his mother (who scorns her gangster son with a sharp slap across his face).

In 1931, production chief Darryl Zanuck announced that Warner Brothers would make fewer costume or romantic pictures. Instead, it would concentrate on realistic dramas. Zanuck's first move was to put some of the top newspaper reporters of the time under contract, including Ben Hecht, Robert Riskin, Charles MacArthur, William Burnett, John Bright, Nunnally Johnson, and Dudley Nichols. The scenarios they wrote reflected contemporary social changes and problems, inspired by the grim stories dominating the front pages.

Zanuck's timing was right. By the early 1930's, America was in a severe economic Depression, and the public wanted more than Hollywood's romantic fantasies. When Zanuck presented realistic films, the public clamored for more. But gangster films remained the most popular of these contemporary dramas.

Oddly enough, audiences admired the gangster for his individualism, audacity, and easy grin. The evil he represented was perversely attractive, and like the legendary Western badman, the gangster became a hero for young movie fans.

By 1931 the gangster movie was outdrawing the Western at the box office. Audiences rushed to see such films as von Sternberg's *Dragnet* (1928), which was basically a repeat of his previous gangster film *Underworld* (1927); Lewis Milestone's *The Racket* (1929); and Rowland Brown's *Quick Millions* (1931). But the acknowledged masterpieces of this genre were *Little Caesar* (1930), *The Public Enemy* (1931), and *Scarface* (1932).

Mervyn LeRoy's *Little Caesar,* the first talking gangster film, dramatized the gang wars of the twenties. W. R. Burnett's compact story and Edward G. Robinson's outstanding performance as the cocky killer made the film a classic. It ends as the dying hoodlum utters his now-famous last line, ". . . Is this the end of Rico?" Le Roy used rapid cutting and sharp photography to help make *Little Caesar* a film of mounting tension.

The Public Enemy, directed by William Wellman, was the first film to examine seriously the causes of criminal behavior and to portray the gangster as a product of his environment. Cagney's snarling, vicious hood is doomed because of his background. The film traces his transformation into a killer and ends with his bullet-riddled body sprawled on his mother's doorstep.

The best of the trio, *Scarface* (1932), was directed by Howard Hawks.* The complete title is *Scarface: Shame of a Nation.* It was Hawks' idea to show that the ruthless Al Capone and his henchmen controlled Chicago with all the cunning, treachery, and violence of the powerful Borgia family of fifteenth-century Italy.

The film was an excellent example of studio teamwork. Warners combined the talents of producer Howard Hughes, scriptwriter Ben Hecht, cameraman Lee Garmes, and director Howard Hawks. The cast was perfect. Paul Muni, in his first film, gave an electric performance as the stupid, arrogant, and egocentric killer. He also added a subtle touch of incest to his relationship with his sister, played by Ann Dvorak. Almost as impressive as Muni was George Raft as the coin-flipping "Little Boy," whose romance with Muni's sister led to his murder. Raft's death scene was a high point of the film. Boris Karloff as the mobster Gaffney, and Karen Morley as Poppy, handled their minor roles with distinction.

To reveal character and add suspense to his story, Hawks used various symbols—particularly the cross or "X" to signify death. For example, the camera focuses on a ceiling with cross-shaped rafters; a hotel door has the Roman numeral ten, X; Karloff marks his bowling scorecard with an X, and is killed after throwing the ball; the ball hits the pins—a strike; and the scar on Muni's face is X-shaped.

In his use of expressionistic sets and lighting, Hawks was no doubt influenced by German film techniques. Garmes's

---

* André Bazin (1918-1958), French critic and theorist, editor of France's foremost film magazine, *Cahiers du Cinéma,* proclaimed Hawks one of the first and best American *auteur* directors. The *auteur* theory states that the director is the sole creative artist responsible for the complete film, revealing certain personal touches that mark each picture as his very own. Although this theory of directing burst on the scene with the *nouvelle vague* (New Wave) movement of the late 1950's, French film historians see the origins of this type of directing emerging as early as 1910 with Griffith, in 1919 with von Stroheim, and the 1930's with Howard Hawks, John Ford, Alfred Hitchcock, and French directors Max Ophuls, Marcel Carné, and Jean Renoir.

camera work captured the killer's tumultuous lifestyle, as did Hecht's cynical script. *Scarface* remains today one of the best of the gangster movies.

After gangster films proved that violence attracted the public, theaters were inundated with movies presenting depraved methods of murder and torture. Killings became a part of every scenario, and a disregard for life was commonplace on screen.

Ten years had indeed brought great changes. In 1921, motion pictures were presenting the innocent, rustic charms of Charles Ray and Richard Barthelmess, with their shyness toward women. By 1931, in *The Public Enemy*, the snarling James Cagney rammed a grapefruit into the face of his girlfriend, Mae Clarke. The stalwart Wallace Reid, the heroic Douglas Fairbanks, and the dependable William S. Hart had been replaced by cold and evil killers who lived in a world of violence.

But these killers were doomed to a short screen life, for by 1933 various civic and church organizations were demanding a halt to the brutal gangster films. The savagery of *Scarface*, in particular, touched off protests by women's clubs, religious groups, and fraternal organizations. They demanded that the Hays Office restrain the production of such films, claiming that hoodlums had become the idols of American youngsters. Instead of disapproving of Dillinger, Machine Gun Kelly, Baby Face Nelson, John Hamilton, and Pretty Boy Floyd, the youth of the country looked up to them. The gangster joined the Western gunslinger to become a national hero.

The protests of the civic groups were bolstered by two events: the Lindbergh kidnapping case, which jolted people into realizing that gangsters were a serious threat to society, and the repeal of Prohibition in 1933.

After America legalized the sale of liquor, the 1920's-style gangster became obsolete. However, he did not completely disappear from the screen; he was just demoted, as the focus of the gangster films shifted away from him onto the clean-cut, straight-shooting, idealistic G-men. The new-style films contained as much brutality as their predecessors—they overflowed with murders, shootings and bloodshed—but the ruthless killer was no longer the star. The film industry had once more skirted the demands of the Hays office and appeased civic pressures as well. The public was now clamoring to see such cops-and-robbers films as *G-Men* (1935), *Bullets or Ballots* (1936), and *I Am the Law* (1938), in which the "good guys" were the stars.

One of the outstanding examples of the new treatment was Michael Curtiz's *Angels With Dirty Faces* (1939). Considered the best gangster film since *Scarface*, *Angels* had a first-rate cast—Pat O'Brien, James Cagney, Humphrey Bogart, George Bancroft, and the Dead End Kids. Written by Roland Brown, the story concerns Rocky (James Cagney), a big-shot gangster who returns to the slums of his childhood and becomes a hero to the neighborhood kids. His boyhood friend (Pat O'Brien), who is now a priest, fights the gangster's influence and eventually wins. Rocky is condemned to the electric chair, but before going to his death he is persuaded by Father Jerry to destroy the boys' illusions about him, for the sake of their future. He does so, and in the end he dies regretting his past.

By the end of the 1930's, the urban-gangster theme had faded. Raoul Walsh's *The Roaring Twenties* (1939) was one of the last efforts to hark back to the lawless decade, showing cheap hoods working their way up in the organization.

Walsh's film told of three World War I veterans who, after failing to find work, take to petty crime in their attempt to make a living. The corporation or crime syndicate hires the trio, and bootlegging, hijacking, and crimes of violence follow eventually. They push their way to the top as Prohibition bootlegging kings. James Cagney, Humphrey Bogart, Jeffrey Lynn, Priscilla Lane, and Gladys George turned this film of social realism into the last gangster classic. The confrontations between Jimmy Cagney and Humphrey Bogart are memorable, and Bogart's reckless gangster stands as a prototype of the killer. Walsh captures the sleazy streets, speakeasies, dark warehouses, and the shootout with rival gangs. The film is a noteworthy nostalgic farewell to the "bathtub gin" era.

By the 1940's, George Raft, James Cagney, Edward G. Robinson, and Paul Muni refused to continue as sadistic killers, and this image was assumed by Humphrey Bogart. As Duke Mantee in *The Petrified Forest* (1935), Bogart portrayed one of the last apostles of rugged individualism, bidding adieu to the gunman and to his restricted way of life. In Raoul Walsh's *High Sierra* (1941), he offered a character filled with emotional complexities, who has outlived his time and is at odds with society.

Bogart became a star after *High Sierra* (his role had been

turned down by Paul Muni and George Raft), but soon he, too, abandoned the gangster image and went on to more significant parts, but not until he snarled, shot, killed, and fought his way through the 1930's and 1940's with dark, compulsive villainy. His cynical laugh and melancholy air of nonchalance were so unforgettable that he joined Cagney, Robinson, Muni, and Raft as one of the great mythical figures of gangland.

By the mid-1940's, the gangster/G-man films began losing their appeal. The cycle had worked itself out. Performers had grown old or switched to other roles, and the younger actors and writers could not match the talents of the older generation for films of this genre. There were no replacements for Cagney, Muni, Raft, or Bogart. The gun molls, too, were disappearing, and there seemed to be no new talent to replace the girls who followed their men to their hideaways and died with them in ambush—women such as Ida Lupino, Joan Blondell, Marjorie Rambeau, Mae Clarke, Mayo Methot, Bette Davis, and Ruth Donnelly. There seemed to be no minor players who could bring laughter, pathos, or cruelty to their roles, as had Allen Jenkins, Jack LaRue, and Warren Hymer. Few were as sinister as Eduardo Ciannelli, Fred Kohler, Dan Duryea, or Joseph Sawyer, or as whiny as George E. Stone, Ernie Adams, or Ed Brophy.

But the gangster died slowly. Postwar Hollywood kept reviving him in documentary-style dramas such as Henry Hathaway's *Kiss of Death* (1947), William Keighley's *Street With No Name* (1948), and Robert Siodmak's *Cry of the City* (1948). These films, however, added little to the cycle. The best was Raoul Walsh's *White Heat* (1949), with Cagney a genuine toughie, following the tradition established by *Scarface*. Some other gangster movies appeared, but on the whole it seemed that the genre was fading into film history. The 1960's, however, changed all this.

In 1967, Arthur Penn and Warren Beatty produced a film that presented new and original variations on the traditional gangster theme. The picture, *Bonnie and Clyde,* caused a furor when released. The critics and public immediately took sides as to whether the film was immoral or not, and once a film raises this argument, it is bound to be a success, at least financially.

Penn took the known story of Clyde Barrow and Bonnie Parker, small-town gangsters of the 1930's on the run. But what gave his film its style was that it involved a new treatment of plot, character development, and soundtrack. What made the film tremendously popular was that thousands of young people saw themselves in Bonnie and Clyde. The furor arose because older people termed it immoral.

Other directors had presented the killer Clyde and his Bonnie as coldblooded, merciless killers, but Penn offered new characters. In a mock-heroic style sprinkled with sardonic touches, he portrayed the couple as romantics rather than desperadoes—likable kids at odds with their environment and their times. They are misfits of the Depression, early hippies, and like many young people of today they are vibrant and on the move, always seeking adventure.

In the opening minutes the film appears to be a romantic comedy, until suddenly Bonnie (Faye Dunaway) and Clyde (Warren Beatty) rob a bank and shoot a clerk.

The kids are against the system. They have nothing, go nowhere, are forever on the move. Life for them is fun and games, and their idea of fun and games is to steal. On the run, they don't even follow the road (their determination to break rules) but take off in their car, bouncing and jolting over the countryside to the bittersweet beat of the Bluegrass sound. Clyde and his buddies have neither plans nor bad intentions; out for kicks, they end up as killers.

Critics took issue with Penn for presenting amoral characters as sentimental romantics. Reviewers objected that these outlaws who robbed and killed remained attractive and sympathetic. Penn was accused of treating them as an American folk legend, rather than showing them as ruthless, amoral people against society and its rules.

Controversy, of course, guaranteed good box office receipts—the public wanted to see Warren Beatty and Faye Dunaway as irresponsible gangsters who reject society and their environment for a joyride of bullets and violence, ending in a slow-motion bloodbath. In a very skillful way, the director made mordant, cynical observations on the American scene, and his film brilliantly satirizes the mores, moods, and pastimes of present-day society.

The critical uproar provoked by *Bonnie and Clyde* was a mere squall compared to the reception given *The Godfather* (1972). Critics attacked the film as dangerous, offensive, and pornographic (while admitting that the direction, photography and acting were excellent). *The Godfather* opened simultaneously in three theaters in New York and grossed a million dollars each day of its extended run, according to press reports. It will gross one of the highest returns in cinema history.

Paramount Studios had assigned Francis Ford Coppola to direct Mario Puzo's high-class potboiler about an Italian dynasty, featuring fast action, suspense, vulgar Italian jokes, sexual exploits, and gory scenes. Instead of employing the gangster film clichés of the 1930's, however, Coppola presented a brilliantly directed picture.

The story begins in 1945 and follows the Corleone family over a ten-year period. The Corleones, who are part of the Mafia, live in a heavily guarded compound. They control crime with businesslike efficiency, simultaneously buying off police, judges, and union officials. Their crude tribal system of justice is presided over by the "godfather" (Marlon Brando), who dispenses favors, rewards people who are loyal, and destroys those who are not. Murder is an accepted part of the business. When the seemingly omnipotent godfather is almost fatally wounded, his sons take over the dynasty. The final section of the film concentrates on the gradual transformation of the youngest son, Michael (Al Pacino), from a decent sensitive young man into a ruthless Mafia chieftain—a new godfather.

In *The Godfather*, unlike *Little Caesar* (1930), *The Public Enemy* (1931), and *Scarface* (1932), whose heroes were hoodlums standing alone against society, Coppola presents his killers within the context of normal family life. Vito Corleone is depicted as a kind, philosophical leader who must occasionally kill to restore order. He is not punished like the killers in the early gangster films, but dies a natural death in the warmth of the family circle.

The Godfather contains startling visual effects. Coppola and his cameraman Gordon Willis created nostalgic scenes of the 1940's in which shadow and light symbolize guilt and happiness, death, and innocence. The director's use of cinematic chiaroscuro reaches a climax in the baptismal sequence, with the camera alternating between the solemn ceremony in the church and a series of brutal murder scenes, in which Corleone's enemies are methodically eliminated.

Violence is rampant. Characters are murdered while eating spaghetti, starting their cars, paying a highway toll, receiving a message, and going through a revolving door. So many

murders occur that death becomes mechanical and meaningless.

The director eschews the zoom lens, fast jump cut, and jar-
ring closeup. Instead, he employs long tableaus, subtle fades,
and well-worn conventions, such as montage of newspaper
headlines and photographs to compress time. Scenes are carefully cut to heighten the tension.

The Godfather found a young audience eager to follow its
adventures of blood and massacre. It broke box office records
and was so successful that Francis Ford Coppola, his production staff, and actors repeated the pattern for *The Godfather,
Part II* (1974).

With the exception of a few social reform films such as *I
Am a Fugitive from a Chain Gang* (1932), *Heroes for Sale*
(1933), and *The Wild Boys of the Road* (1933), Hollywood's gangster theme exposes the economic and moral attitudes of the Hungry Thirties. The gangster first surfaced and
rose to popularity at a time when America may have been
preoccupied with the breakdown of law and order but was
also forced to face up to unemployment and constant money
worries. Perhaps because of basic resentment of the Establishment, moviegoers admired the dapper, dim-witted character who solved the problems of a brutal world with bullets.
Failing to find work, many a job hunter squeezed out the
price of a movie ticket and spent the afternoon applauding
killers, because the Depression made crime seem almost an
accepted way of thumbing one's nose, not at the law, but
rather at the impersonal forces of the economy.

Killers in the early gangster movies were members of organized crime. Kids often worked for the syndicate in order
to make a living. Cagney, Muni, Bogart, Raft, and others
portraying first generation immigrants, mostly of Italian ex-
traction, were victims of their environment. They pushed to
get ahead but often ended up dead. Audiences were willing to
accept these killers, putting the blame on society. Their involvement in crime appeared to be a matter of chance rather
than choice. They were misfits fighting their way up.

Eventually, the mob or organized crime and unfortunate
kids were replaced by a different killer—the psychopathic,
unpredictable misfit. Pretty Boy Floyd, Bonnie Parker, Clyde
Barrow, and Baby Face Nelson, fourth- or fifth-generation
WASPS from rural towns in the Midwest and Southwest,
took to stealing and killing. Mere punks out of reform school,

they robbed filling stations and banks, and kidnapped at will. Their crime was not bootlegging or rubbing out other members of a rival mob, but making direct and forceful assaults on society, killing in a sadistic way.

By 1940, the war made the gangster old-fashioned. Screenwriters replaced the killer and the G-man with the private eye, the lone detective, and later, the antihero. For almost two decades the gangster genre was neglected, except for *Force of Evil* (1948), *Al Capone* (1958), *Murder, Inc.* (1960), the excellent *The Rise and Fall of Legs Diamond* (1960), and *The St. Valentine's Day Massacre* (1967).

The gangster film, with its tough characters and violence, used the screen to examine causes of criminal behavior, and to suggest that bad characters are often the result of economic conditions, immediate environment, and a government that doesn't care. It revealed to rural America the problems of the big city, kids reared in slums, and life in the underworld. The genre may have exploited brutality and viciousness in its stories, but at least these movies made audiences aware of the important sociological problems that existed in their contemporary world.

Outstanding Gangster Films and Their Directors

Underworld	(1927)	Josef von Sternberg
The Racket	(1928)	Josef von Sternberg
The Lights of New York	(1928)	Mervyn LeRoy
Little Caesar	(1930)	Mervyn LeRoy
The Public Enemy	(1931)	William Wellman
Scarface	(1932)	Howard Hawks
The Petrified Forest	(1935)	Archie Mayo
Dead End	(1937)	William Wyler
Angels with Dirty Faces	(1938)	Michael Curtiz
The Roaring Twenties	(1939)	Raoul Walsh
They Made Me a Criminal	(1939)	Busby Berkeley
High Sierra	(1941)	Raoul Walsh
The Killers	(1946)	Robert Siodmak
Brute Force	(1947)	Jules Dassin
Key Largo	(1948)	John Huston

White Heat	(1949)	Raoul Walsh
Bonnie and Clyde	(1967)	Arthur Penn
The Godfather	(1972)	Francis Ford Coppola
The Godfather, Part II	(1974)	Francis Ford Coppola

12 / Film Noir, or Black Cinema

IN THE 1940's, when the public began to tire of gangster movies, the studios came up with a new type of crime thriller, distinguished by its cynical tone and dark mood. Many of these films featured a slightly disreputable private eye as antihero, or the trenchcoated loner pursuing his prey—a mysterious object or person—down dark streets.

It was the French who gave this genre its name. After World War II, when their theaters were inundated with this type of American movie, they dubbed it *film noir*, or Black Cinema.

The world of Black Cinema (not to be confused with Black Comedy) is similar to the world of the gangster. The small-time, unheroic figure, like the gangster before him, prowls the streets and meets his contacts at night in dimly lit alleys or waterfront warehouses. He follows his suspects relentlessly and, in turn, tries to elude mysterious pursuers. Invariably he drifts into dimly lit cocktail lounges, their chrome bars displaying shining glasses and mirrors that reflect the ominous mood. (Mirrors in films are often used as a device to reflect the character's guilt or fear.) Scenes are shot in lonely hillside homes, shabby train stations, or hotel rooms lit with flashing neon signs—the last refuge of the hunted.

The soundtrack exposes a world of blaring jukeboxes, torch singers, tinkling pianos, and careening cars. Occasionally we hear the melancholy whistle of a faraway train, or the mournful sob of a tugboat on the bay.

The characters are wrapped in shadows that symbolize the imprisonment of their souls; sets are filled with spectral images. Streets are dark and menacing. Alan Ladd moves along blank walls showing only predatory eyes in the darkness. Veronica Lake, Mary Astor, or Martha Hyer, beautiful decoys, move through a world of dramatic shadows. Dorothy McGuire, a mute entrapped in darkness, discovers that she is to be murdered. Gale Sondergaard, coat collar held tightly, waits in the night rain to murmur her deadly instructions. The tormented characters inhabit a world of loneliness, violence, and sentimentality.

In Black Cinema, women are often presented as harpies, bitches, and schemers hardened by greed and lust; the females are sexy, slinky, and venomous to know. They are portrayed as indifferent to the suffering they cause. In the end, violence is the result of the evil woman's ambition. In Anatole Litvak's *Sorry, Wrong Number* (1948), Leona Stevenson (Barbara Stanwyck) manipulates her husband (Burt Lancaster), who in turn is overly ambitious. Their values contain seeds of distrust, greed, and violence. In *Mildred Pierce* (1945), Joan Crawford pays a high price for success, wealth, and power.

If sets and soundtracks resemble those in the gangster films, the characters do not. The stereotyped greasy-haired mobster sporting expensive rings and broad-brimmed hats has been replaced by the tormented loner, who usually, but not always, leans toward the side of the law.

An outstanding director of *film noir* is John Huston. His tight crime stories, offbeat characters, and innovative camera and lighting techniques influenced two decades of pictures.

Huston's *The Maltese Falcon* (1941) is one of the best high-style thrillers in cinema history. Based on Dashiell Hammett's brilliantly constructed crime story, the film is noted for its terse, sharp dialogue and deft characterizations. Private eye Sam Spade (Humphrey Bogart) is a complex character, a blend of toughness, honor, fear, avarice, and brutality. The rogues he mingles with, played with great finesse by Mary Astor, Sidney Greenstreet, and Peter Lorre, doublecross him and each other throughout the film. In the end, all are revealed to be fakes, even the coveted Maltese falcon.

Huston's cynical outlook comes across clearly. In this film, as in many of his others, the hero is engaged in a search. But when he finds the long-sought object or person, his victory is invariably empty. Such is the fate of those who take themselves too seriously. *The Maltese Falcon* was a resounding success, catapulting Huston into the top ranks of those engaged in *film noir*. Among his other excellent pictures in the same genre are *Key Largo* (1948) and *The Asphalt Jungle* (1950).

Another classic of the genre is *The Big Sleep* (1946), directed by Howard Hawks. Based on a Raymond Chandler tale of blackmail, intrigue, and murder, the film follows the adventures of Philip Marlowe (Humphrey Bogart), a cynical yet sensitive and incorruptible private eye.* In adapting the story for the screen, Hawks combines strict realism with tough, sardonic dialogue, complex characters, and multiple layers of meaning. The setting is a large city filled with anonymous, rootless people. Corruption and duplicity are everywhere; every sleeve conceals a knife. The fast-paced action captures the Chandler atmosphere and contributes to the film's popularity.

The private eye movie is not the only type of *film noir*, although it is the most common. Other pictures in this genre often have criminals or psychotics as the leading characters—misfits who spring from every level of society. The killer could be the kid next door, a jazz musician, a debonair man-about-town, a suburban housewife, a spoiled playgirl, or a quiet man who likes to tend his garden.

Director Billy Wilder has done outstanding work with this form of Black Cinema. His films attempt to expose the evil in men's souls, and he leads his audience into a frightening world of rogues, criminals, cheats, and murderers. He concentrates on plot and dialogue, avoiding the overuse of camera angles which are sometimes mistaken for art.

Wilder's *Double Indemnity* (1944), a tawdry story of crime and sexual corruption, is based on a James M. Cain novel about a murder plot keyed to an insurance swindle. Phyllis Dietrichson (Barbara Stanwyck) conspires with a cynical insurance salesman, Walter Neff (Fred MacMurray), to murder her husband. After they succeed, she shows no emotion over the killing. In fact, she is now planning to get rid of Walter and keep all the money herself. But a suspicious insurance investigator (Edward G. Robinson) begins to apply pressure. Eventually the scheming couple grow to loathe one another, and in a tension-filled finale, they shoot each other to death.

Raymond Chandler, master of the detective novel, helped Wilder with the script and dialogue. John Seitz, the leading cameraman of Black Cinema, captured the evil, terror, and violence of the story. Other notable films by Wilder include

---

* There have been at least six Philip Marlowes: Dick Powell in *Murder My Sweet* (1944), Humphrey Bogart in *The Big Sleep* (1946), Robert Montgomery in *The Lady in the Lake* (1946), George Montgomery in *The Brasher Doubloon* (1947), Elliot Gould in *The Long Goodbye* (1972), Robert Mitchum in *Farewell, My Lovely* (1975) and a remake of *The Big Sleep* to be released in 1978.

The Lost Weekend (1945), *Sunset Boulevard* (1950), and *Ace in the Hole* (1951).

Director Tay Garnett selected another James M. Cain novel as the basis for his first *film noir* effort. In *The Postman Always Rings Twice* (1946), a waitress (Lana Turner) dressed in immaculate white falls in love with a penniless young drifter (John Garfield). At the same time, she wants to get rid of her elderly husband (Cecil Kellaway), who has never been ambitious or successful enough to satisfy her greed. When she devises a murder scheme, her nervous young lover reluctantly agrees to help her, but afterwards they have a falling out. Eventually they are driven to their own destruction. Garnett's film is a harsh, brash exposé of the cancerous evil that exists in the characters and their world.

Other directors who tried their hand at *film noir* were Roger Corman, Robert Siodmak, Don Siegel, Otto Preminger, Michael Curtiz, and William Dieterle. Siodmak, director of some of the most chilling crime movies of the 1940's, excelled at capturing tensions. His *Phantom Lady* (1944) is a minor masterpiece. *The Suspect* (1944), *The Spiral Staircase* (1945), and *The Strange Affair of Uncle Harry* (1945), all evoked the sinister presence of death.

Siodmak's closest rival was Fritz Lang, who as a young director in Germany proved himself a master of suspense, adept at probing the seedy night life of the big city. Lang's best *film noir* pictures are *The Woman in the Window* (1944), *Ministry of Fear* (1944), and *Scarlet Street* (1945). In *The Big Heat* (1953) he shocked the audience when Lee Marvin threw scalding hot coffee into Gloria Grahame's face.

Jules Dassin's *Naked City* (1948) was an influential police thriller, whose documentary approach inspired dozens of imitators. Robert Aldrich's extremely violent *Kiss Me Deadly* (1955) was imitated by the French New Wave directors.

The master of the *film noir* is Orson Welles. His *The Lady from Shanghai* (1948), filled with murderous intrigue, tells the story of a yachting cruise that leads to a preposterous murder design. The exciting visual effects in the final funhouse sequence, a shootup in a hall of mirrors, displays Welles's grotesque brilliance. The hero is pursued into an empty amusement park, into a crazy house of terror where madness and hell are made manifest as he hurdles giddily down huge slides into the mouths of gigantic model dragons. The shootout in the mirror maze climaxes the film. Welles shattered the myth of all-American cinema when he left the heroine (Rita Hayworth) to die in the magic mirror maze instead of in the arms of the hero.

Welles's *Touch of Evil* (1958) is a masterpiece of the genre, and considered to be the final outpost of the *film noir*. In a deliberately confusing plot, threaded with violence and perversion, the story leads the viewer from one false clue to another into a nightmare of intrigue. Vargas (Charlton Heston), a narcotics inspector, tracks down the corrupt practices of Quinlan (Orson Welles), the chief of police. The conflict between morality and justice is lifted into a complex sphere surrounded by bizarre characters, a shabby border town, psychological lighting, and high-tension action. The director adroitly brings home his study of the abuse of power.

Such movies add a new dimension to the crime drama—they neither preach morality nor glamorize characters motivated by greed, revenge, and lust. But by the late 1950's, the techniques of Black Cinema had been so repeatedly copied, not only in motion pictures but also on television, that the formula was losing much of its appeal.

Eventually, the tormented loner of *film noir* emerged in the form of a violence-prone cop. Sometimes psychotic himself, the new-style cop pursues victims out of hate, misuses the law, and is almost (or equally) as bad as the immoral characters he hunts down. Plots often center on international narcotics traffickers, whose influence extends into the upper echelons of police departments. Such films employ rapid cutting, zoom shots, throbbing musical scores, and the inevitable chase scenes.

Don Siegel became one of the leading directors of neo-Black Cinema; his *Madigan* (1968) is a hard-hitting, popular example of the genre. Set against a realistic background of police work, *Madigan* features a tough detective whose personal integrity is not above question. He is surrounded by a gallery of despicable underworld characters; profanity, sex, nudity, and sadism abound. An offbeat musical score, zoom lens, long tracking shots, and laconic dialogue quicken the pace of the film.

Siegel's *Dirty Harry* (1971) concerns the San Francisco police department's efforts to capture a man who is terrorizing the city. It is a minor *film noir* masterpiece, centering on a psychotic detective who is out to kill a killer, but the villain is really an extension of the detective's own twisted personality. This theme emerges in *Madigan,* too.

Roman Polanski's *Chinatown* (1974), a story of greed, violence, and deceit, was inspired by the *film noir* of the 1940's; it is one of the best contemporary movies of the genre. Layers of corruption and terror unfold bit by bit (as in *The Big Sleep*), and audiences are constantly deceived by the director's game of cat and mouse.

Chinatown's Jake Gittes (Jack Nicholson) is a throwback to the earlier private eyes, Sam Spade and Philip Marlowe. He is hired by a mysterious widow, Mrs. Mulwray (Faye Dunaway), to solve the puzzle of her husband's death. During the hunt, Gittes discovers that the entire city government is corrupt, but he is forced to remain silent because of a compromising district attorney.

Filled with futility and despair, this cynical film depicts justice and honesty in fetters. Corruption is rampant. Government can be bent to the will of the rich; men of power and money get off scot-free. The picture is a bitter observation on today's moral climate.

Dick Richards's *Farewell, My Lovely* (1976) is a salute to nostalgia, capturing the sleazy Los Angeles haunts, the flashing neon signs, the disillusioned hero (Robert Mitchum), the old trenchcoat, and a hunt for a teen-age girl. Marlowe glides through an atmosphere of urban corruption, sleazy nightlife, Skid Row, and death. The film is a minor masterpiece, with its narrative flashback, fascinating visual details, and the inevitable chase, with emptiness at the end.

The Late Show (1977), directed by Robert Benton, has Ira Wells (Art Carney) a private eye hired by Margo (Lily Tomlin) to find her lost cat. For this Chandler-reminiscent story, the aging detective makes Wells a valid addition to the repertory so magnificently established by Humphrey Bogart. Lily Tomlin gives an outstanding performance as a kooky would-be actress-designer.

Martin Scorsese's *Taxi Driver* (1976) is one of the best of the genre of the past five years. Robert DeNiro as the moody, frustrated, tormented loner works and lives in a world of darkness. The film takes a harsh look at the society that spawned him. It is *film noir* at its blackest.

The *film noir* is peopled with characters who live in a world gone wrong. The law is something to manipulate for profit and power. The streets are dark with danger at every corner. Death is treated with detachment and clinical bleakness. The ambivalent hero is sensitive, physically powerful, often hero and victim, lover and loved, hunter and hunted. Various supporting actors suggest psychological and sexual perversity. In its way, the *film noir* served to cloak the hidden fears and tensions of postwar America and to lead its viewers into a world of violence.

The dance through the genre was led by a knowledgable clique. The leaders were the novelists James M. Cain, W. R. Burnett, and David Goodis, with their gallery of hard-boiled characters, as well as Dashiell Hammett with his literary creation Sam Spade and Raymond Chandler with his fictional Marlowe. Next in line were the directors John Huston, Howard Hawks, Billy Wilder, Tay Garnett, and recently, Dick Richards, Roman Polanski, Robert Altman, and Robert Benton. The actors who were a part of the dark world were Humphrey Bogart, Mary Astor, Ida Lupino, Sydney Greenstreet, Orson Welles, and a long parade of others, leading eager movie fans through foggy city streets, into dark alleys, lonely hotel rooms, and up the steps to many a private eye who reluctantly took the assignment and set off into a blatantly brutal world of corruption and duplicity.

Hollywood encapsulated all the fears of the unknown and the terrors about social disquiet in its *film noir*. It offered shadows on everything the screen was afraid to face. It muffled real violence in stylization and elegant romanticism, to make death a pointless parable.

The hero of the 1940's, with his square-shouldered gabardine suit and felt hat, attractive to women but adopting a hard-bitten contempt, was a powerful image that movie fans applauded.

Eventually the fears and tensions of the *film noir* emerged out of the shadows into light postwar films, or else turned to socially committed crime films with their graphic violence. Edward Dmytryk's *Crossfire* (1947) helped carry the *film noir* into social reform, with its theme of racial intolerance. In its time, it was daring for an American commercial release. Its story and bold theme of anti-Semitism in the United States, its vivid photography of the ugly side of a city at night, and the superb dialogue and acting make it an outstanding film.

Robert Rossen's *Body and Soul* (1947) exposes the seamy side of the boxing ring, Alexander Polonsky's *Force of Evil* (1949), and Fred Zinnemann's *Act of Violence* (1949), showing the explosive cruelty of New York City, cleared away the shadows of the *film noir* and prepared us for a nonsentimental look at violence and corruption, all a part of modern life. Eventually these were replaced by the tormented, sometimes amoral killer-detective. Independent directors offered new ideas within the old framework, but in general these films failed to recapture the tension and art of the early films. Several films offered outstanding photography, excellent editing, and fascinating characters, while others were filled with clever plot twists, overpowering chase sequences, violence, killings, sex, and seedy characters; but somehow, with few exceptions, these later pictures never quite achieved the success of efforts in the 1940's.

Outstanding Black Cinema Films and Their Directors

The Maltese Falcon	(1941)	John Huston
Journey Into Fear	(1942)	Orson Welles
Double Indemnity	(1944)	Billy Wilder
The Phantom Lady	(1944)	Robert Siodmak
The Woman in the Window	(1944)	Fritz Lang
Murder, My Sweet	(1944)	Edward Dmytryk
The Spiral Staircase	(1945)	Robert Siodmak
The Postman Always Rings Twice	(1946)	Tay Garnett
The Big Sleep	(1946)	Howard Hawks
Sorry, Wrong Number	(1948)	Anatole Litvak
The Lady from Shanghai	(1948)	Orson Welles
In a Lonely Place	(1950)	Nicholas Ray
The Big Heat	(1953)	Fritz Lang
Kiss Me Deadly	(1955)	Robert Aldrich
Touch of Evil	(1958)	Orson Welles
The Saint Valentine's Day Massacre	(1967)	Roger Corman
Madigan	(1968)	Don Siegel
Bullitt	(1968)	Peter Yates
Dirty Harry	(1971)	Don Siegel
The Long Goodbye	(1972)	Robert Altman
Chinatown	(1974)	Roman Polanski
Farewell My Lovely	(1976)	Dick Richards
Taxi Driver	(1976)	Martin Scorsese
The Late Show	(1977)	Robert Benton

13 / The Epic / Spectacular

THE epic/spectacular, generally speaking, is an historical event of sweeping grandeur. With all its battles, mayhem, destruction, and death, it usually presents the basic theme of man's ability to triumph over the overwhelming obstacles that defeat most of his fellow creatures, and not only lust, hedonism, gold, paganism, devils, and monsters, but also moral disillusionment. The challenge of the director making an epic/spectacular is to combine both these elements so that each enhances the other.

The first motion picture spectacle seen in America was the Italian director Enrico Guazzoni's overwhelming nine-reel two-hour production of *Quo Vadis* (1912). When the film opened in New York in 1913, viewers were awed by the elaborate sets, the Bacchanalian feasts, the masses of extras, the incredible scenes of Rome burning, and the ruthlessness of the arena scenes in which Christians were attacked and killed by lions.

Among those impressed by the genre was the American director D. W. Griffith, who was inspired to film *Judith of Bethulia* (1913). He followed this with the powerful and popular *The Birth of a Nation* (1915), the first American epic. A year later, Griffith produced his greatest spectacle *Intolerance* (1915), which stands today as the most complex, most ambitious film ever produced by Hollywood.

Both *The Birth of a Nation* and *Intolerance* raised film to the level of art, setting the pattern for future epics. (See Chapter 1.) The fact that *Intolerance* was a financial failure did not dampen other directors' enthusiasm for big-budget spectaculars. They reasoned (correctly) that Griffith was an ambitious artist who had no idea of budget control. Convinced that the genre was here to stay, they began the quest for bigger, if not better, epics, marked by exotic settings, earthquakes, tidal waves, volcanic eruptions, avalanches, and conflagrations. Film budgets were increased, larger theaters were built, and the price of tickets went up. Movies were no longer just the Saturday afternoon pastime of children and the poor; they had become everyone's favorite form of entertainment.

Writers searching for material soon discovered the Bible. J. Gordon Edwards's *Queen of Sheba* (1921) was a box office hit, as were *Sodom and Gomorrah* (1922) and *Samson and Delilah* (1923). Maurice Tourneur produced *The Christian* (1923) and Raoul Walsh told the story of the prodigal son in *The Wanderer* (1925).

Mihaly Kertesz came to Hollywood from Vienna in 1925, changed his name to Michael Curtiz, and directed *Noah's Ark* (1928), which was famous for its superb glass shots of the Tower of Babel superimposed on live action. However, the picture was not a great success because it was caught in the transition from silent to sound.

It was Cecil B. DeMille, a preacher's son, who established himself as Griffith's greatest rival, beginning with *Joan the Woman* (1917) and *The Woman God Forgot* (1917)—films that featured stunning battle scenes and pageantry. (DeMille himself noted that a bit of Griffith could be found in every American epic.) After his success with *Manslaughter* (1922), Paramount asked DeMille to direct *The Ten Commandments* (1923). It cost $1.6 million and was the first of the mammoth Bible spectacles linked to DeMille's name.

After studying the provisions of the Hays censorship code, DeMille decided he could avoid its restrictions by using the Bible as a facade. *The Ten Commandments* was filled with sex orgies, sin, and thinly clad girls—all under the guise of Biblical history. The first part of the film, dealing with Moses and the exodus from Egypt into the promised land, depicts plagues, sadism, chariot races, the opening of the Red Sea, sensual women, the worship of the Golden Calf, and God's delivery of the Ten Commandments on Mount Sinai. The stupendous sets and magnificent scenic effects captivated audiences.

The second half, which attempts to show what happens when moral laws are broken in the contemporary world, is awkward and embarrassing melodrama, vulgar in its depiction of love, lust, and intrigue. The uneducated public may have been fooled by DeMille's phony history lesson and Nita Naldi's outrageous performance as the vamp, but more sophisticated viewers ridiculed them.

In some respects, DeMille was imitating Griffith's *In-*

tolerance, which was also erotic and horrifying in parts. It contains shots of naked women, plus scenes where heads and hands are cut off. But Griffith included such effects for artistic purposes, whereas DeMille's motives apparently were commercial.

Undaunted by the critics, DeMille followed with another Biblical epic in 1927, *King of Kings,* a hit starring H. B. Warner as Jesus. (It appeared that filmmakers had only to catch hold of the flowing robes of Jesus to make money.) The picture cost $2.5 million.

DeMille's spectacles, unfortunately, began a new trend. Although he may be credited with some excellent photography, interesting special effects, and good craftsmanship, he is also largely responsible for turning the epic into a shallow, pretentious, and vulgar type of film.

Douglas Fairbanks became famous for a different kind of spectacular. For *Robin Hood* (1922), he constructed a tremendous authentic medieval castle surrounded by great walls and moats, and then leaped, frolicked, winked, grinned and dueled his way to box office success. The highly publicized picture cost $1.3 million, and earned $3 million for its backers.

After *Robin Hood,* Fairbanks wrote and starred in a truly mythical, magical Oriental fantasy, *The Thief of Bagdad* (1924), a superbly filmed tale from *The Arabian Nights,* for which he built a fanciful city and palace. *The Thief of Bagdad* is a joyful pastiche, the story of a thief who steals whatever he wants until one night, in a daring raid on the royal palace, he sees a princess who steals his heart. He then faces countless dangers to win her.

For the film's opening on the East Coast, the producer had the New York Liberty Theater refurbished in a completely Oriental motif. (By now, studios had discovered the importance of a highly touted premiere.) First night audiences were greeted with smoldering incense, throbbing drums, and ethereal songs. Ushers dressed as Arabs served coffee. During the showing, viewers were clearly delighted by scenes of Bagdad, the Crystal City, the Cavern of Fire, the Valley of the Monsters, the Citadel of the Moon, the Winged Horse, and the hero on his flying carpet—all created by trick photography, glass shots, and the use of miniature models.

A master of the spectacular during the early twenties was James Cruze, who won awards and accolades for his films about the forty-niners, *The Covered Wagon* (1923) and *The*

Pony Express (1925). Another of his historical efforts was *Old Ironsides* (1926), the story of the frigate *Constitution*, the ship that freed the seas of Barbary pirates. Cruze's films were very popular, and he reigned supreme at Paramount Studios for ten years.

The 1920's was the decade in which the epic spectacular set box office records. People lined up to see Lillian Gish rescued at the last minute from the ice floe in *Way Down East* (1920). Tears were shed as Dorothy and Lillian Gish were united and saved from the guillotine in *Orphans of the Storm* (1922). Audiences applauded when brave frontier families fought Indians and nature in *The Covered Wagon* (1923). They suffered and sympathized with the deformed Quasimodo in *The Hunchback of Notre Dame* (1923). They were thrilled with D. W. Griffith's inspiring *America* (1924), and enthralled with the romance and mystery of *Beau Geste* (1926). In *The Volga Boatmen* (1926) they suffered with the Russian downtrodden, and in *Wings* (1927) they gasped at the audacious air attacks. If many of these films neglected historical accuracy, the fans didn't care. What they liked about the epic was its noble characters, drama, excitement, historical sweep, and above all, the grand entertainment it provided.

Perhaps the most monumental film of the decade was *Ben Hur* (1926). The film was based on a book whose sales record was surpassed only by that of the Bible. The author, General Lew Wallace, spent five years writing it, and it took almost as long to turn it into a film. When it was finally completed, this epic about man's faith during the time of Christ had become the biggest and most expensive film since *Intolerance*.

Shooting began in Italy, but after months of filming, the results were disastrous. Costly sets, bad weather, and disagreements between Italian and American artists forced MGM to scrap everything and start again in the United States. Gigantic sets were constructed on the West Coast, and shooting began once again, under the direction of Fred Niblo.

When completed, *Ben Hur* was an artistic (and financial) triumph. Perhaps the most famous sequence is the chariot race, which required 3,300 extras, twelve chariots, forty-eight horses and ten stunt drivers. A total of eight hundred men, working in shifts, filmed the sequence in four months; forty-two cameras were needed. Of the 200,000 feet of film shot for the chariot race, only seven hundred were used. The sequence is a masterpiece of editing.

Much of the credit for the film's success belongs to the second unit man, Reeves Eason, who staged the rousing battle at sea and the spectacular chariot race. As often happens with epic films, the second unit man can turn a potential white elephant into a box office hit.

The first half of the 1930's did not produce any outstanding epics. The Depression forced studios to cut costs and concentrate on smaller stories. DeMille, however, persuaded producers that there was still box office in big productions. With the coming of sound, his films gained in pace, construction, and logic. He stopped inserting absurd flights of fancy, such as surrealistic shots of girls on the front of a locomotive rushing at the audience like living figureheads.

DeMille's comeback after a string of flops was another pseudo-Biblical film, *The Sign of the Cross* (1932), a melodrama of sex and violence that features Claudette Colbert as Queen Poppaea swimming in a bathtub filled with asses' milk. His *Cleopatra* (1934), a sexual extravaganza complete with royal barges, outlandish costumes, and assorted anachronisms, helped audiences forget hard times. Hans Dreier created elegant sets for this film.

DeMille turned next to medieval history, going on location with Loretta Young, Henry Wilcoxon, Ian Keith, and thousands of extras to shoot *The Crusades* (1935). This film differs from earlier DeMille movies only because it is bigger and noisier and lacks a bathroom scene. Although its artistic and historic worth are questionable, it is saved from obscurity by Ian Keith's performance as Saladin, and several exciting battle scenes.

DeMille was the archetype of Hollywood directors, habitually clad in jodhpurs and helmet, wielding a megaphone, and flanked by dozens of assistants. Even though critics panned many of his pictures, he made some outstanding contributions to American cinema. His extravaganzas astonished the public and earned a respectful salute from those in the movie industry.

Wesley Ruggles's splendid production of *Cimarron* (1931), based on the Edna Ferber novel, also deserves mention. Although sound had not yet been fully mastered, the film captured the American frontier spirit, the harshness of the landscape, and the tensions involved in the race to open new territory. The Oklahoma land rush sequence is particularly memorable. The performances of Richard Dix and Irene Dunne stand out against the film's historic sweep.

By the mid-1930's, studios were concentrating more on the best-seller market. Mervyn LeRoy's *Anthony Adverse* (1936), based on Hervey Allen's novel of Napoleonic Europe, used 130 different sets and 700,000 feet of film (before editing). Although the film failed to wed historical pageantry and personal drama, it was cited for its cinematography, editing, and musical score.

Frank Capra's beautiful and haunting *Lost Horizon* was a bright spot of 1937, featuring lavish sets for the mythical Himalayan paradise of Shangri-La. Meanwhile, on the MGM lot, thousands of extras dressed as Chinese were pillaging a city for the filming of *The Good Earth* (1937), while Cecil B. DeMille was turning to novels for new inspiration. *The Plainsman* (1936) and *The Buccaneer* (1938) were healthy, expansive, and robust films about the winning of the American West.

In 1936, even before the publication of Margaret Mitchell's novel *Gone With the Wind*, David O. Selznick read the galley proofs and saw the ingredients for a film on the grand scale in the story of a headstrong Southern belle whose secure life is wrecked by the Civil War. He bought the screen rights for the then-unprecedented sum of $50,000. When the novel appeared, the public was carried away by the enticing heroine, the sweep of the story, the tender romance of Melanie and Ashley, the passion of Rhett and Scarlett, and the history of a society that could neither accept the catastrophe of defeat nor adapt to a new era. Selznick's publicity department played cat and mouse with the public, creating an avid interest in the casting of *Gone With the Wind*. No film roles before or since have created such public enthusiasm. There were discussions, arguments, proclamations. Newspaper columnists, editors, radio commentators, and celebrities joined in to announce their choices for the various leads.

The public demanded that the swaggering, masculine Clark Gable be cast in the role of Rhett Butler. MGM agreed to allow Gable to work at the Selznick studio if the firm would in turn accede to their demands: in return for Gable and half the production costs, up to a ceiling of $2,500,000, MGM would receive the distribution rights and 50 percent of the profits. Selznick was under contract to release all his films through United Artists, but he wanted Gable so badly for the role of Butler that he postponed filming for two years until his distribution contract with United Artists expired. Leslie Howard was to be Ashley Wilkes; the role of Melanie Hamilton went to Olivia de Havilland. Various minor roles were carefully cast with such veterans as Hattie McDaniels, Thomas Mitchell, and Laura Hope Crews.

It was the role of Scarlett O'Hara that kept public excitement high. During the two years of waiting, the Selznick studio tantalized the public with rumors, reports, denials, and gossip. Even before the first day of shooting, *Gone With the Wind* was the best-publicized picture in the history of motion pictures. Dozens of actresses were tested for the role, among them Joan Crawford, Miriam Hopkins, Margaret Sullavan, Claudette Colbert, Bette Davis, Paulette Goddard, Katharine Hepburn, and Susan Hayward. The search itself cost the studio $92,000.

By December, 1938, when shooting was to begin, the role still had not been cast. Then came the night of photographing the famed "burning of Atlanta" sequence, a conflagration in which hordes of old sets on the back lots were consumed. Among the guests invited to witness the burning was Selznick's mother and his brother Myron, a successful Hollywood agent. The rest, as the saying goes, is history. Announcing, "David, I want you to meet Scarlett O'Hara," Myron presented his brother with the young English actress Vivien Leigh, unknown to Americans, who was promptly given the coveted role. Selznick made a fortunate choice, for Miss Leigh brought to the role her natural beauty and the techniques of a professional artist, giving a performance that is today part of screen history.

George Cukor was to direct, and filming began in earnest in January, 1939. After three weeks of shooting, Cukor was replaced by Victor Fleming, a friend of Clark Gable. Cukor and Selznick disagreed about the interpretation of the script and Victor Fleming was called in to direct. After weeks of shooting, Fleming collapsed and withdrew for a rest. Sam Wood took over the duties of director. Fleming later returned and he and Wood completed the most popular epic of the American screen. The script was adapted from the novel by the playwright Sidney Howard, and he, too, died in a tragic accident before filming commenced. Howard's version was in turn worked on by Ben Hecht (responsible for the beautiful prologue), F. Scott Fitzgerald, Charles MacArthur, John van Druten, Jo Swerling, David O. Selznick, and at least a half dozen more writers. Max Steiner handled the music, and Ernest Haller and Ray Rennahan were cinematographers.

William Cameron Menzies designed the production. Hundreds of people contributed in one way or another to the completion of the picture, which opened in Atlanta, Georgia, on December 14, 1939.

When released, the three hour and forty-two minute picture was the biggest, most expensive, and the longest film yet made in America. The press and the public were highly enthusiastic. On Oscar night, February 29, 1940, *Gone With the Wind* won a total of ten awards. Fans were thrilled with the scenes of Tara, Scarlett delivering Melanie's baby, the reading of casualty lists after the Battle of Gettysburg, the flaming sunsets, the burning of Atlanta, plus the romance and the splendor of the Old South.

This film epitomizes prewar production, with Hollywood craftsmen working together to present a work of art. Mammoth in design, done with taste and distinction, it stands as the master picture that no spectacle has since duplicated. Wardrobe, sets, Technicolor, script, musical score, casting, publicity and photography all spoke for an industry that had reached technical perfection. Although originally made in 1939, the film still draws crowds whenever reissued.

Costing $4.25 million, *Gone With the Wind* earned $13.5 million in distributor's grosses during its first year. Worldwide rentals totaled $116 million. In 1976, the historical romance was released to television. NBC paid $5 million, the highest price ever, for a single showing. There have been longer, costlier, and more ostentatious historical spectacles, but few have enjoyed the acclaim of *Gone With the Wind*.

World War II curtailed the making of epics. Many members of the film community couldn't find work because of budget cuts, and spectaculars had been abandoned in favor of pictures with small casts, small stories, and, unfortunately, small characters. Even after the war ended, audiences were less interested in historical movies than in realistic stories of police corruption, juvenile delinquency, urban ills, and racial intolerance. For escapism, audiences preferred animated films, fantasies, comedies, musicals, melodramas, *film noir*, and horror films.

Even so, the spectacle did not completely die out. There were a few costume films, such as *The Mark of Zorro* (prewar 1940) and *The Adventures of Don Juan* (1949), both swashbucklers. Two Westerns should also be mentioned: *Red River* (1947) and *Duel in the Sun* (1947). *Red River* depicts the first cattle drive over the Chisholm Trail from Texas to Kansas in 1865, and stars John Wayne and Montgomery Clift. The Howard Hawks film achieves a rhythm, grandeur, and scope that few Westerns can match. On the other hand, *Duel in the Sun* attempts to be grandiose, passionate, and colorful, but succeeds only in being tasteless. It is the decade's most flamboyant and inflated Western—David O. Selznick's imitation of films made in the "grand manner" in the 1930's. Critics were astonished by the violence, and the public wouldn't accept Gregory Peck and Jennifer Jones as unsavory characters who shoot each other to death. Despite some good Western action sequences, the results were empty.

Ironically, as the movie business faltered in the late 1940's, Hollywood discovered that it paid to spend more. In 1949, DeMille made the costly *Samson and Delilah*. Based on just a few paragraphs in the Old Testament, his film ran two hours and starred Hedy Lamarr and Victor Mature, neither of whom would ever be candidates for best acting honors. But Samson shook the pillars of the great temple, destroying the Philistine's idol and bringing on a cataclysm of death, and fans cheered. *Samson* was the answer to sagging gate receipts, proving again that the Bible was Hollywood's best friend.

Following this film, the studios fell back on DeMille's old formula: sex, violence, spectacle, and religion. The milliondollar epic became the panacea for an ailing industry—particularly with the advent of Cinerama, VistaVision and Panavision. The new big screen was perfect for gigantic spectacles—something viewers couldn't get from their smallscreen television sets.

In 1951, MGM sent Mervyn LeRoy, Robert Taylor, Deborah Kerr, and Peter Ustinov to Rome to shoot *Quo Vadis*, based on Henryk Sienkiewicz's popular novel. The film had a cast of thousands, cost $8.5 million, and grossed $12.5 million. It was followed by *The Robe* (1953), the first film in Cinemascope and undoubtedly one of the worst. Based on a pseudo-Biblical novel by Lloyd C. Douglas, the film tells of Christ's stained robe which was gambled away under the cross by Roman soldiers. The story follows the robe from Jerusalem to Rome; along the way it helps turn heathens into Christians, and brings love, happiness, and sometimes death to many. A heavenly choir sings as the lovers, Richard Burton and Jean Simmons, march to their deaths. *The Robe*, like so many screen epics, cashed in on Christ. It may have been phony, poorly photographed, badly acted and boring, but it was financially successful.

Salome (1953), directed by William Dieterle, needed all of Rita Hayworth's charm and beauty to keep audiences from walking out before John the Baptist lost his head. Richard Thorpe's Biblical extravaganza, *The Prodigal* (1955), starred Lana Turner as a high priestess. It was a sheer waste of time and money, surpassing the vulgarity of the poorest DeMille epic.

Using sophisticated new equipment, DeMille himself rejoined the Biblical parade in 1956 with a remake of his old hit *The Ten Commandments.* (Earlier, in 1952, he had moved into the modern world with *The Greatest Show on Earth*, a circus extravaganza.) Hokum though it is, *The Ten Commandments* was able to lure viewers away from their television sets because of its spectacular costumes, color, sets, and special effects—particularly the powerful scene in which Moses parts the waters of the Red Sea.

Countless more Biblical epics appeared during this period, as well as other types of expensive blockbusters, including musicals, adventure tales, and war movies. Among the more costly films were: *The King and I* (1956), $6.5 million; *Around the World in Eighty Days* (1956), $6 million; *War and Peace* (1955), $6 million; and *Moby Dick* (1956), $5 million. Hollywood pushed Biblical escapism because controversial topics were out of fashion as a result of the witch hunts and the blacklist of the 1950's.

In 1959, MGM decided to remake *Ben Hur*, budgeting the production at $15 million, the highest cost yet for a single movie! It also turned out to be the best of the 1950's spectaculars, even though it did not follow the DeMille formula; there are no orgies in *Ben Hur.*

The film concerns a young man, a contemporary of Jesus, whose fortunes parallel and occasionally intersect those of the Messiah. Memorable performances were given by stars Charlton Heston (Judah Ben Hur), Stephen Boyd (the scheming Messala), and Haya Harareet (Esther), and by the supporting players, Jack Hawkins, Martha Scott, Sam Jaffe, and Finlay Currie. William Wyler's direction was superb, as were the special effects, photography, and editing. The second unit men, Andrew Marton and Yakima Canutt, planned the logistics, arranged the daring battle scenes, and photographed the famous chariot race with consummate skill. (As in the 1926 version, the chariot race is undoubtedly one of the greatest sequences on film. Audiences remember this episode better than the story.) Second unit scouts were sent to

France, Spain, Italy, England, and Mexico to film location sequences, while studio shots were completed at the Cinecitta Studio in Rome. The result was a stupendous superproduction, worthy of the eleven Academy Awards it received.

During ten months of shooting, 1.5 million feet of film were used. The production required 100,000 costumes, seventy-eight horses, twelve camels, eighteen chariots, fifty ships, 25,000 extras and 60,000 blossoms for victory parades; there were 452 speaking roles. Editing was a tremendous task. Sol C. Siegel and director Wyler labored for weeks to assemble the picture. When released, *Ben Hur* was a hit.

During the 1960's Hollywood continued churning out spectaculars to raise film attendance. It would be impossible to examine all such films individually. War themes were used for spectacle and drama in *Exodus* (1960), *The Alamo* (1960), *The Longest Day* (1962), *Lawrence of Arabia* (1962), *The Victors* (1963), *Major Dundee* (1965), and *Doctor Zhivago* (1965). Still more blockbusters were based on the Bible: *The Story of Ruth* (1960), *King of Kings* (1961), and *The Greatest Story Ever Told* (1965). John Huston tackled the first few chapters of Genesis in his film *The Bible* (1966).

Of all the epics, *El Cid* (1961) excels as a courageous attempt to recast the genre in fresh dramatic form. Rodrigo Diaz de Bivar of Castile, known as El Cid, Spain's national hero of countless ballads and stories, sweeps across the plains of eleventh-century Spain on his white stallion to rout the Islamic invaders. Anthony Mann's film captures the history, the glory, the panoramic grandeur, and the tragedy of the man and his country. It also features some of the swiftest action sequences of any epic. In an unforgettable climax inside the city of Valencia, the dying Cid, aware that his forces might collapse at the news of his death, orders that he be bound upright on his horse. With his king beside him, he rides out at dawn past the columns of men, through the gates of the city into the sea, into history, and into legend. The final images are beautiful and inspiring.

Charlton Heston was never more fortuitously cast. His stern features, intense expression, and athletic frame were just right for the heroic character of El Cid. (During the 1960's, Heston may have starred in more spectaculars than any other actor.)

Director Anthony Mann reached a new peak with this film. The movies he had made in the 1940's were mediocre, but in the 1950's he turned out several superior films concerned with violent but thoughtful men, including *Winchester 73* (1950) and *Bend of the River* (1951). *El Cid* was his crowning achievement, followed by another excellent spectacular, *Fall of the Roman Empire* (1964).

In the same mold as *El Cid* is the epic masterpiece *Lawrence of Arabia* (1962). This, too, is an inspiring study of a peace-loving man who is ultimately responsible for the shedding of much blood, an aloof scholar forced to be a man of action. In many ways, *Lawrence of Arabia* is the best epic the screen has ever presented, superbly directed by David Lean and magnificently photographed by Fred Young. (Lean had already added a new dimension to the epic in *Bridge on the River Kwai* (1957).)

In real life, Thomas Edward Lawrence, alias T. E. Shaw, alias Private Ross, alias Lawrence of Arabia, was an enigma. A hero to the British and a god to the Arabs, his character was never clearly revealed. To some he was a savior and a military genius; to others he was a *poseur*, a pathological liar, a sadist, a crass exhibitionist, and a homosexual.

Lawrence of Arabia succeeds because the director presents a perplexing, exciting character caught up in an equally exciting moment of history. Furthermore, Lean recognized the potential of the epic and treated it with artistic respect. Never has a setting added so much to a film; cameraman Young makes the brooding presence of the Jordanian desert as compelling to the audience as it must have been to Lawrence.

The saga begins in 1916 when Lawrence (Peter O'Toole), an intellectual young lieutenant in the British Army, is sent as a military agent to unite the Arab tribes against the Turks, who are oppressing them. He leads a small Arab band in a successful attack on the Turkish-held city of Aqaba, and from then on, the British supply him with guns and gold so he can continue to undermine the Turkish position in the Middle East. Adopting Bedouin dress, Lawrence and his growing force of Arab guerrillas wage relentless warfare against the Turkish army. Because of his courage and stamina, and his sympathy for their cause, the Arabs become fanatically devoted to him. Eventually, he is captured, tortured, and sexually abused by the Turks, an experience from which he never fully recovers. Despite misgivings, he is persuaded by the British to wage one more campaign and liberate the city of Damascus. After much hardship, he and his guerrillas finally reach the city, only to learn that the British have al-

ready gained control of it and are dividing the Middle East
with the French. Disillusioned by this, and by the inability of
the Arab tribes to unite, Lawrence leaves the Middle East
and returns to England, where he dies in a motorcycle accident.

Without losing sight of his theme, Director Lean not only
manipulates Lawrence through the tangled web of Middle
Eastern history, but also reveals the man's complex personality, a difficult thing to do in an epic. Lawrence is shown as
both a hero and an egoist, a flawed individual who could be
petty, masochistic, and outrageously vain. Yet at times the
film depicts Lawrence as a savior, or perhaps it is depicting
Lawrence's image of himself as a savior. Sitting atop his
camel, he is photographed from ground level, giving him a
larger-than-life appearance. When he encounters the Arab
Prince Faisal (Alec Guinness), Lawrence looms godlike out
of the dust and smoke. He announces that he will cross the
Sinai Desert like Moses, refers to the sandstorm as a pillar of
fire, and at one point in the film, after displaying almost su-
perhuman endurance and strength, he enters camp like Christ
entering Jerusalem. Finally, when the Arabs and Lawrence
prepare to blow up a train of Turkish soldiers, he is shown
running across the top of the cars. Suddenly the camera
catches him silhouetted against the bright sun, robes flowing
in the wind. He turns and spreads his arms, Christlike, gazing
at the battling hordes below. But in the scene where
Lawrence is captured by the Turks, the director skillfully
evokes his fear and his loss of belief in his own invulnerabil-
ity.

In the role of Lawrence, Peter O'Toole had the longest
speaking part in movie history, and certainly one of the most
physically demanding. (O'Toole got the part after Marlon
Brando and Albert Finney refused it.)

Filmed in 70mm, for the extra-wide screen, *Lawrence of
Arabia* fully justifies its grandiose proportions, proving that
when the epic is treated with taste, judgment, and skill, it can
be a dazzling cinematic showcase. But commercialism still
took precedence over art, as far as Columbia Pictures was
concerned. When the film was first released, it ran for nearly
three hours. Then Columbia cut off thirty-five minutes of the
film because the shorter version could be shown three times a
day.

If sheer cost could have assured quality, Joseph Mankiewicz's production of *Cleopatra* (1963) would have been the

greatest film ever made. Instead, it was one of the industry's biggest disasters. *Cleopatra* cost $31 million to produce, took three years to complete, ran through a succession of producers, directors, and writers, and ultimately carried Twentieth Century-Fox to the edge of bankruptcy. To break even, the film had to earn at least $40 million from its gate receipts. After several reissues, it finally succeeded in doing this, but the fiasco signaled the impending decline of the epic.

Only a few successful spectaculars appeared during the waning years of the genre. David Lean chose the turbulent days of the Russian Revolution for his moneymaker *Dr. Zhivago* (1965). In *Lord Jim* (1965), Richard Brooks told a stirring story of a man in search of himself. Among several auto racing spectaculars, the best was John Frankenheimer's *Grand Prix* (1966). Another popular epic was *2001: A Space Odyssey* (1968).

By the end of the 1960's the public seemed to have lost interest in sweeping epics. Many younger moviegoers avoided them altogether, reacting against the banality and wastefulness of such extravaganzas, and turning instead to smaller, more intimate films that were being turned out by independent American filmmakers. Studios became reluctant to spend millions on blockbuster productions, especially since the big stars were demanding a share of the profits as well as their salaries.

But the epic wasn't abandoned entirely. By 1974, producers had worked out a highly commercial variation of the formula, dubbed the "disaster" film. As in *Grand Hotel* (1932) and *Stagecoach* (1939), various characters, each with their own personal problems, are gathered together on a train, plane, boat, airship or skyscraper, when suddenly disaster strikes. A tidal wave upsets a luxury liner; a skyscraper goes up in flames; a dirigible blows up during a New Year's Eve party; a jumbo jet loses its pilot. The best examples are *The Poseidon Adventure* (1972), *Airport 75* (1974), and *Earthquake* (1974), all of which contain outstanding special effects.

Such films, however, are only a passing fancy. Undoubtedly studios will soon find a new formula to refresh and invigorate the genre. It's not likely that spectaculars will be abandoned altogether, because they have the potential for providing enormous profits. Of the ten biggest moneymakers in seventy-five years of cinema history, five have been epic/spectaculars. And now *Star Wars*, for example, is repaying 20th Century-Fox $12 million a week.

D. W. Griffith codified for all time the structure of the epic in *The Birth of a Nation* (1915) and *Intolerance* (1916). Technical advances were blended unostentatiously into the narrative, which in the hands of this artist took third place to emotional emphasis and historical accuracy. Griffith turned movies into art and the epic into a national favorite. Along with the Western, it offers the most solidly satisfying movie genre to the public.

The 1920's was an era of "colossal" productions, headed by Cecil B. DeMille and his Biblical epics. Other directors such as Fred Niblo, Rex Ingram, King Vidor, James Cruze, and John Ford opened enormous vistas and perspectives in the epic film, telling their interesting stories with visual beauty and a mellifluous style.

By the 1950's, the epic appeared to be the one formula to save Hollywood and pull audiences away from their TV sets. William Wyler, a director with a distinguished string of hits, applied his skill and craftsmanship to another version of *Ben Hur*, bringing to the public an intelligent epic devoid of the fatuities and idiocies often associated with the genre. The multimillion dollar epic was the safest form of investment.

With William Wyler, David Lean, Stanley Kubrick, Anthony Mann, Carl Foreman, George Stevens, Nicholas Ray, Franklin Schaffner and others, the epic acquired artistic stature. No other genre except the Western in the postwar years pushed the conformist cinema to greater heights. Independent directors and personal cinema offer new approaches to film, but the epic will always, when handled by creative artists, find an appreciative audience.

Outstanding Epic/Spectaculars and Their Directors

The Birth of a Nation	(1915)	D. W. Griffith
Intolerance	(1916)	D. W. Griffith
Orphans of the Storm	(1921)	D. W. Griffith

The Four Horsemen of		
the Apocalypse	(1922)	Rex Ingram
The Covered Wagon	(1923)	James Cruze
America	(1924)	D. W. Griffith
Ben Hur	(1926)	Fred Niblo
King of Kings	(1927)	Cecil B. DeMille
Noah's Ark	(1928)	Michael Curtiz
Cimarron	(1931)	Wesley Ruggles
The Sign of the Cross	(1932)	Cecil B. DeMille
Cleopatra	(1934)	Cecil B. DeMille
Gone With the Wind	(1939)	Victor Fleming
The Rains Came	(1939)	Clarence Brown
Gunga Din	(1939)	George Stevens
Red River	(1948)	Howard Hawks
Ivanhoe	(1952)	Richard Thorpe
Land of the Pharaohs	(1955)	Howard Hawks
Ben Hur	(1959)	William Wyler
Spartacus	(1960)	Stanley Kubrick
Exodus	(1960)	Otto Preminger
El Cid	(1961)	Anthony Mann
Lawrence of Arabia	(1962)	David Lean
Barabbas	(1962)	Richard Fleischer
Cleopatra	(1962)	Joseph L. Mankiewicz
How the West Was Won	(1962)	George Marshall, John Ford and Henry Hathaway
55 Days at Peking	(1963)	Nicholas Ray
The Fall of the Roman Empire	(1964)	Anthony Mann
Doctor Zhivago	(1965)	David Lean
Airport	(1970)	George Seaton
The Poseidon Adventure	(1972)	Ronald Neame
Earthquake	(1975)	Mark Robson
The Towering Inferno	(1975)	John Guillermin
The Hindenburg	(1976)	Robert Wise

14 / The Horror Film

ALTHOUGH the Edison Company made a one-reel version of the Frankenstein story as early as 1910, the genre known as horror films really emerged from Germany. German directors were the first to experiment with pictures that deliberately frightened their audiences. These early efforts directly influenced the American horror films, particularly those of James Whale. From Berlin studios came the outstanding thrillers: Robert Wiene's *The Cabinet of Dr. Caligari* (1919); Paul Wegener's *The Golem* (1920); F. W. Murnau's *Nosferatu* (1922), a version of *Dracula*; Fritz Lang's *Dr. Mabuse* (1922); Paul Leni's *Wax Works* (1924); Stellan Rye's *The Student of Prague* (1926); and Fritz Lang's *Metropolis* (1926).

Through their cultural heritage of folk tale, myth, superstition and interest in the occult, German directors turned to the world of demons and evil. The spectator of their films entered a world of the supernatural, featuring ruined castles, necrophilia, sadism, the walking dead, mysterious happenings, vampires, monsters, succubi, mad scientists, torture chambers, and assorted characters controlled by drugs, evil spirits, or hypnotists. The pictures were financially and artistically successful, and several were imported to America.

Film, in particular, with its many mechanisms to conjure up the fantastic, is a suitable medium for the creation of horror, but the studios before 1927 were not interested. Some members of the industry had seen the early German efforts but the horror genre in the United States remained a relatively unexplored area as late as 1930-31.

Lon Chaney, a star of the 1920's, attempted a kind of horror film somewhat different from the European type. Chaney, one of the screen's great artists, was interested in makeup and roles that required physical distortions. His films offer the grotesque rather than the gruesome. He does not frighten his fans so much as surprise them. He is not interested in the supernatural world of ghosts, ghouls, or walking dead, but with characters who are often arch criminals resorting to makeup to conceal their identity. Chaney's monsters are human beings, real people who bring on disaster because of their twisted minds and their drive for revenge. His first success as the pathetic but repulsive Quasimodo in *The Hunchback of Notre Dame* (1923) was followed by the faceless kidnapper in *The Phantom of the Opera* (1925).

In 1925, Chaney joined forces with the director Tod Browning, and together they made a series of pictures of which the best was *The Unholy Trio* (1925). Both star and director were interested in the macabre, and they produced a series of superior silent films: *The Unknown* (1927), *London After Midnight* (1927), and *West of Zanzibar* (1928). However, the Chaney-Browning films were not true horror films. All mysterious actions were logically explained at the end of the film.

Until the 1930's, the most often filmed near-horror story was Robert Louis Stevenson's *Dr. Jekyll and Mr. Hyde* (the man with the split personality). Two of the best versions featured John Barrymore (1920) and Fredric March (1932). They undertook the double role and created a sensation with their characterizations of Hyde. Yet, like the Chaney pictures, these attempts are not true horror films.

The Bat (1926) is a mystery-comedy that pleased the public, and Carl Laemmle, suspecting there might be a public for this kind of film, imported Paul Leni to direct *The Cat and the Canary* (1927). Leni, who had worked on European horror films, used his knowledge of lighting and camera angles to make the picture a success. Like a few of their predecessors, these films dealt with supposedly haunted mansions where a weekend party concealed a killer among the usual collection of weird guests. The murderer polishes off his victims one by one, and no one knows where he might strike next. At the end, however, the culprit is exposed, and all the opening and closing of doors and apparitions are fully explained. Again the director gives logical explanations for the mysterious happenings. These mystery-comedies had not yet stumbled upon the formula of terrifying their viewers.

Count Dracula, an amorous, blood-drinking Transylvanian vampire, created by the novelist Bram Stoker, had delighted several generations of readers. Universal Studios in 1930 decided to turn the *Dracula* into a film, and they wanted Lon Chaney for the urbane vampire, but the star died of cancer before shooting began. He was replaced by the lesser-known Bela Lugosi, who had played the role in the 1927 Broadway production. Tod Browning was the director, and Karl Freund, who had worked on several German horror films, did the cinematography. Although Browning's previous films were rooted in the real world, this time he fully entered the realm of the supernatural. In *Dracula*, vampires, the living dead, and walking spirits actually exist. They are not just a hoax. No comforting, rational explanations are offered by the end of the film.

Revealing a somewhat macabre sense of humor, Universal billed *Dracula* as "the strangest love story of all," and released it on St. Valentine's Day, 1931. Audiences were mesmerized, and *Dracula* became a box office smash. Although Count Dracula died with a stake through his heart, the marksman must have missed, for the bloodthirsty giant reappeared in dozens of sequels.

Once *Dracula* was completed, Browning next turned his attention to the grotesque tale *Freaks* (1932). The film hardly falls within the horror category but deserves mention. A masterpiece about human abnormality, *Freaks* uses genuine freaks onscreen, and is a forerunner of today's psychological horror films.

Freaks is about the unhappy romance of two circus performers, a trapeze artist Cleopatra (Olga Baclanova) and a midget (Harry Earles). The aerialist, repelled by the midget until she discovers he is heir to a fortune, marries him, then plots to poison the little man and take his money. The plan fails, and the band of freaks discovers Cleo's plans and takes revenge on her. In the closing sequence they chase the trapeze artist through a dark forest, capture her, and wreak their vengeance. A shocking epilogue shows Cleopatra turned into a freak like the others.

The picture was refused by many theater managers and was banned for thirty years in England. Browning's script is concerned with normal versus abnormal, but the supposedly normal characters are the villains.

Browning followed this strange tale with a series of mediocre films: *The Mark of the Vampire* (1935), *The Devil Doll* (1936), and *Miracles for Sale* (1939). He retired shortly thereafter, having helped to make horror films a popular art.

James Whale, a British stage director, also earned a reputation for his outstanding horror films. Whale had gone to the West Coast in 1930 to direct the famous antiwar film *Jour-*

GANGSTER: Little Caesar (1930) is the first talking gangster film, telling of the gang wars of the 1920's. The story of the underworld and the rise and fall of a gang boss (played by Edward G. Robinson) is distinguished because of Mervyn LeRoy's economical direction, tight editing, fast-paced action, and flashes of violence.

GANGSTER: Bonnie and Clyde (1967) represents the gangster film of the 1960's. Arthur Penn blends comedy, poetry, and violence to tell his tale of small-town killers (Faye Dunaway and Warren Beatty) who are not members of the organization but rather kids out for kicks, who end up killers. The film progresses from comic affection to realistic violence.

FILM NOIR: Double Indemnity *(1944), Barbara Stanwyck, Fred MacMurray, and Edward G. Robinson turn a tawdry crime story into a minor masterpiece. Murder, tremendous suspense, unsparing realism, psychological lighting, a sharply witty script, and above all Billy Wilder's direction make this one of the best of the Film Noir.*

EPIC: Gone with the Wind *(1939) with Vivien Leigh, Clark Gable, and Olivia de Havilland is the culmination of motion-picture art of the 1930's. The issues of the American Civil War, spectacular crowd scenes, lavish sets and costumes, a dramatic musical score, and splendid acting make the film an outstanding epic.*

HORROR: Frankenstein *(1931) is an effective exercise in terror. Avoiding gruesome details, the director gains his effect with impressive reticence. Sets, lighting, mounting suspense, and the acting of Boris Karloff make the film a classic in the horror genre.*

SCIENCE FICTION: 2001: A Space Odyssey *(1968) marks a milestone in the use of photographic special effects. Stanley Kubrick's brilliantly controlled venture into science fiction expresses his wry view of mankind. Technological detail dwarfs the characters as the spectator is taken on a flight into the beyond.*

MUSICAL: Singin' in the Rain *(1952) with Gene Kelly and Debbie Reynolds is an exhilarating and fast-moving song-and-dance story. The mixture of satire, nostalgia, brilliant choreography, lighting, color, and musical numbers integrated with dramatic scenes turn this into a musical to remember.*

SCREWBALL COMEDY: It Happened One Night *(1934) Clark Gable as the wandering journalist and Claudette Colbert as the runaway heiress in the romantic caper that introduced the screwball comedy. Piquant dialogue, clever incidents, sexual undertones, technical skill, and whacky characters turned this film into an enormously successful movie.*

BLACK COMEDY: Dr. Strangelove (1964) is a satire of nuclear warfare and excels at black humor. Stanley Kubrick ridicules with biting satire the army, government officials, the President, and even the destruction of the world.

WAR: All Quiet on the Western Front (1930) is an antiwar declaration of power and realism. Lewis Milestone's use of sound, editing, single-track shots, grim trench scenes, and effectively staged life at the front brought the horror of war to movie audiences.

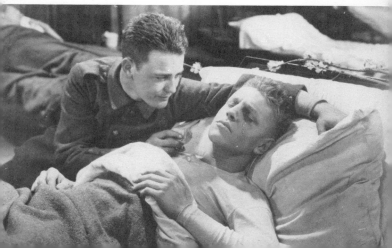

WESTERN: Shane *(1953) Using a basic plot and stereotypic characters, George Stevens offers a serious atmospheric western. Balancing a conventional western with human drama the narrative has the usual bar-room brawl, guns, horses, and exciting climax but the editing, photography, scenery, conflicts, and acting make the film outstanding.*

ROMANCE: Letter from an Unknown Woman *(1948) with Joan Fontaine and Louis Jourdan is a bittersweet story of a woman's unrequited love. Max Ophuls' haunting film with its beautiful photography, romantic images, and dramatic music set in turn-of-the-century Vienna suggests a romantic dream world. All the ingredients of the genre are captured in this distinguished film.*

POSTWAR REALISM: On the Waterfront *(1954) is one of the first films to introduce Method acting to the screen. Elia Kazan's direction shows technical mastery in realistic settings, harsh photography, grim mood, and improvisatory style acting. Marlon Brando's inarticulate characterization dominates the film.*

NOVEL: The Grapes of Wrath *(1940) is an adaptation of John Steinbeck's powerful book, and stands as one of the best examples of novel into film. John Ford's direction caught the theme, atmosphere, and brilliant characters created by Steinbeck. One of Hollywood's strongest stands against social injustice, it attempts a realistic treatment of ordinary people uprooted by the dust bowl during America's Great Depression.*

DOCUMENTARY: Nanook of the North *(1921) gives a realistic account of the life of the Eskimo. Robert Flaherty captures a vanishing way of life with fluid camera work and sharp editing. It is the first significant documentary in cinema.*

EXPERIMENTAL FILM: Scorpio Rising *(1963) Kenneth Anger's film explores the sexual deviation and Nazi-inspired demonic forces in the daily rituals of a member of a motorcycle gang. By using cuts, symbolism, a blaring sound track of rock music, violent imagery, and brilliant editing, Anger created an unnerving movie, and one of the best examples of the Underground film.*

ney's End. After completing this picture, Universal Studios gave him the script of *Frankenstein*, written by Robert Florey, based loosely on Mary Shelley's nineteenth-century novel and on Paul Wegener's play *The Golem*. Studios wanted Bela Lugosi to play the monster, but he refused, fearing no one would recognize him under the heavy makeup. The lead was then given to William Henry Pratt, better known by his stage name, Boris Karloff.

Frankenstein (1931) is the best of the American horror films. By now, its plot is familiar. The brilliant Dr. Frankenstein (Colin Clive) is obsessed with the desire to create life, and after years of secret experiments, he finally succeeds in creating a living creature, a monster that resembles a human being. But Dr. Frankenstein is unable to control his own creation, and eventually the monster kills the doctor's cruel assistant and escapes into the world. In one especially moving scene, the monster meets a little girl, the first person to show him any kindness. The two playfully toss flowers into the lake. After the monster unintentionally drowns the child,* the villagers hunt him down, chasing him into a mill which they set on fire. He supposedly dies in flames.

The brilliant performance of Karloff, then an unknown British actor, turned the story into a classic. Without dialogue, Karloff created a tragic character, a lumbering, physically repulsive being who tries desperately to cope with his bewildering environment. His awkward movements, pained eyes, and inarticulate groans elicited the audience's sympathy; it marked the first attempt at character development in an American horror film.

The heavy-lidded, booted monster was resurrected many times, stalking through six sequels at Universal Studios alone: *The Bride of Frankenstein* (1935), also directed by James Whale; *The Son of Frankenstein* (1939); *Ghost of Frankenstein* (1941); *Frankenstein Meets the Wolf Man* (1943); *The House of Frankenstein* (1945); and *Abbott and Costello Meet Frankenstein* (1945).

Karloff's role was eventually assumed by Lon Chaney, Jr., Bela Lugosi and Glenn Strange. By the 1950's, the English, Japanese, and Italians were exploiting the character in cheaply made films.

---

* In certain areas of the country, censors cut this scene in such a way that audiences were led to believe the monster had criminally assaulted the little girl. This was particularly unfortunate because it rendered the monster unsympathetic, which was not the director's intention.

Whale directed two other classic films, *The Old Dark House* (1932) and *The Invisible Man* (1933). Recognized as the master of the horror genre, he retired from film work in 1940.

Perhaps the only character to rival Frankenstin in popularity is the Wolf Man. Introduced to the screen by Henry Hull in *The Werewolf of London* (1934), the werewolf (or lycanthrope) is an ancient Central European mythological character who changes into a wolf at full moon, kills a victim, then resumes human form by morning. The best of the series is George Waggner's *The Wolf Man* (1941), in which Lon Chaney, Jr., gives a sensitive performance as the young man doomed to eternal existence as a werewolf. In a particularly memorable scene, an old gypsy woman (Maria Ouspenskaya) sits in her horse cart with the evening fog curling about her, pitying the tormented Chaney as he stalks through the forest searching for his prey.

Karl Freund, who had done the cinematography for *Dracula*, got his first directorial assignment in *The Mummy* (1932). With Karloff as the star, *The Mummy* is a minor masterpiece containing stunning visual effects. Karloff's portrayal of the resurrected Im-Ho-tep, High Priest of the Temple of the Sun, has dimension and feeling, and is believable—a difficult accomplishment in this kind of film. In the opening sequence, which held audiences spellbound, Karloff awakens from the dead and emerges from a sarcophagus. The film is notable for its creation of mood, as well as for its lighting, photography, and direction. It inspired at least ten more versions, the most recent being *Blood from the Mummy's Tomb* (1971).

Freund's second horror film, a remake of *The Hands of Orlac* entitled *Mad Love* (1934), again reveals his ability to create dramatic tension through photography. Stephen Orlac (Colin Clive), a concert pianist, loses his hands in a train accident. A sinister surgeon (Peter Lorre, in his first American appearance), grafts onto Orlac the hands of a guillotined murderer. When Orlac discovers that his new hands belonged to a killer, he goes mad from fear. In the end, the hands seek vengeance on the surgeon and murder him.

After *Mad Love*, Freund gave up directing and returned to cinematography, working on such classics as *Camille* (1936), *The Good Earth* (1937), and *Pride and Prejudice* (1940).

Michael Curtiz, Hungarian-born director of more than sixty films abroad, settled in Hollywood in 1925 and, after a series of silent films, made a successful leap into sound. In 1932 he directed *Doctor X,* a Warner Brothers attempt at the horror film. Similar in plot to *The Hands of Orlac,* it concerns a one-armed scientist (Preston Foster), who discovers a synthetic flesh substitute and fashions for himself an uncontrollable hand that strangles one victim after another.

Robert Florey's *Murders in the Rue Morgue* (1932) and Edgar Ulmer's *The Black Cat* (1934) were two other outstanding horror films of the 1930's.

Jacques Tourneur's *Cat People* (1942), may have been the first monster film in which the audience never actually sees the monster. Terror is created by suggestion, which has led some film historians to describe it as the first psychological horror picture. Produced by the Russian-born Val Lewton, a man of sophisticated literary and artistic tastes, it is an ingenious low-budget suspense thriller. After *Cat People,* Lewton and Tourneur made *I Walked with a Zombie* (1943), based loosely on the novel *Jane Eyre; The Seventh Victim* (1943), which deals with devil worship in Greenwich Village; *The Body Snatchers* (1945); and *Isle of the Dead* (1945). All these pictures suggest horror rather than actually showing it.

As horror films declined in popularity during the 1940's, filmmakers began burlesquing them, turning werewolves, ghouls, and vampires into comic characters. Even Lugosi, tired of being typecast, ridiculed the character that had made him famous by appearing in such spoofs as *Abbott and Costello Meet Frankenstein* (1948).

Efforts were made to keep the horror cycle alive, but without critical success. Occasionally, a B picture was "discovered" by fans, such as *Night of the Living Dead* (1969). Produced by two young filmmakers, this low-budget movie deals with the aftermath of radiation from a satellite, when the dead rise from their graves to devour the living. A group of people barricaded in a farmhouse attempt to fight off the hungry dead outside, but eventually they are killed. Critics were not kind to this sleeper, calling it "an unrelieved orgy of sadism." But the film caught on with the young, who enjoyed the bloody scenes of cannibalism and of zombie children murdering their parents.

Roger Corman, the most prolific moviemaker in contemporary film, did a series of films based on the short stories of Edgar Allan Poe, the first entitled *The House of Usher* (1960). This macabre film may have received cool notices from critics, but it was a success at the box office. Corman followed with *The Pit and the Pendulum* (1961), *Premature Burial* (1962), *Tales of Terror* (1962), and *The Haunted Palace* (1963), all of which used Daniel Haller's eerie sets as a backdrop for Poe's haunted, crumbling world. In *The Raven* (1963), *The Terror* (1963), and *The Tomb of Ligeia* (1964), Corman made use of the crypt and coffin theme. Although his films bear scant resemblance to the literary genius of Edgar Allan Poe, they do have excellent Gothic sets, suspense, color, and humor.

Alfred Hitchcock's films create a feeling of suspense rather than horror, but *Psycho* (1960) is an exception. It is not only Hitchcock's best film but an intelligent and disturbing horror classic. The director once more offers ordinary people caught up in extraordinary events that lead them into a vortex of frightening situations. *Psycho*, after a long and misleading introduction, beautifully unwinds a tale of mystery, horror, and grotesque comedy.

By now almost every TV watcher knows the story. In order to run off with her lover, Marion Crane (Janet Leigh) steals $30,000, checks into a motel and is slashed to death in the shower, apparently by the motel-keeper's aged mother. A detective, (Martin Balsam), trying to solve Marion's disappearance, is also killed. Marion's sister (Vera Miles) eventually solves the mystery. The motel-keeper Norman (Anthony Perkins) is a psychotic killer who keeps his dead mother's corpse in the house and, in an effort to deny his own crime of matricide, has taken her identity. Norman, as his mother, has killed Marion and the insurance agent.

Hitchcock's study of mounting terror uses elements from the modern world to develop his story of a split personality. The character of Norman is reflected in mirrors, Gothic sets, winding staircases, atmospheric music, descents into cellars, and symbols of stuffed birds, photographs, electric fans, lamps, knives and windshield wipers. The film is bathed in a dusky light, creating a menacing atmosphere that frightens yet attracts the viewer. It is a claustrophobic world—no crowds or large groups of people, and very few outdoor scenes. The viewer enters a dark, threatening private world and discovers horrible secrets.

Jack Clayton, working from an excellent scenerio by Truman Capote, satisfied intellectual audiences with *The Innocents* (1961), an adaptation of Henry James's novella *The Turn of the Screw*. The film, in its elegant simplicity, is a subtle study in evil and terror. Robert Wise's *The Haunting* (1963), graced with the acting ability of Julie Harris and Claire Bloom, is a remarkable story of darkness and the unknown. A scientist and his team of psychics investigate the ghosts of an old house. The house has doors that throb and pulse like a huge heart, a child's hand, mysterious screams, a staircase that rejects humans, and messages scrawled on walls. Wise's intricate editing brings terror to the audience.

Rosemary's Baby (1968), Roman Polanski's thriller, emerges as one of the best horror tales of the decade. It succeeds in creating a world of horror for a trapped and vulnerable heroine. In an old New York apartment, a pregnant young housewife (Mia Farrow) slowly realizes she has been selected to give birth to the anti-Christ. Her evil husband and neighbors are agents of the devil. Polanski's direction and William Fraker's photography turn the film into a nightmare for the heroine and the audience as well.

The Exorcist (1973), directed by William Friedkin, may not have been the best horror film of the 1970's, but it is one of the biggest moneymakers in movie history. The religious element exploited in *Rosemary's Baby* has been sensationally developed in Friedkin's film. The film, a shocker, tells the story of a twelve-year-old girl Regan (Linda Blair) possessed by the devil. Her mother (Ellen Burstyn) uses every means to save the child. Regan screams obscene language, brutally attacks her mother, and spews vomit at priests who come to exorcise the demon who possesses her. Friedkin's masterly direction turned this contest between good and evil into an Academy Award winner for best screenplay.

The classic horror themes of the dead scratching their way out of the tomb, the rebirth of Dracula, and the constant returning of Frankenstein amused audiences in the 1930's. The 1940's offered a world of zombies and voodoo; the 1950's discovered science, flights into space, and the world of mutation. The 1960's dwelled on the theme that human control of technology must eventually lead to world destruction. By the 1970's, audiences were no longer interested in Dracula, the return from the tomb, or the world of grotesque organisms. The world of science had lost its appeal too. What the public wanted to see was the world of the occult, satanism, and mediums.

Polanski's *Rosemary's Baby* (1968) introduced audiences to the Prince of Darkness, the anti-Christ, and William

Friedkin's *The Exorcist*, adapted from the novel by William Peter Blatty, had audiences fearing the world of demons. In *The Omen* (1976), Gregory Peck and Lee Remick have been hoodwinked into accepting and adopting a baby after their child has died. The boy is, of course, the devil, the soul of evil who has come to claim his kingdom, and even has plans to move into Washington high society. The public couldn't have cared less that the critics dismissed it; they pushed it onto the all-time high money list. *The Reincarnation of Peter Proud* (1976), *Audrey Rose* (1977), *Demon Seed* (1977), and *Carrie* (1976) continued the trend. The best of these is *Carrie*, the story of a plain high school girl who discovers she has the mental power to move objects. When her classmates belittle her, she takes revenge by destroying her school chums at a dance, then returns home and eventually kills her mother. *Exorcist II* (1977) has the exorcist girl (Linda Blair) four years older, visiting her psychiatrist (Louise Fletcher) in a hospital, where the two don brain contraptions and relive moments of the girl's past. Richard Burton, a priest, talks of good and evil and tries to save another soul. The devil, this time, is a swarm of locusts. Hollywood continues to rework old ideas in the hopes of another box office hit.

What direction the horror film will take in the future is anyone's guess. It appears that vampires, ghouls and zombies will give way to creatures in outerspace. At the moment spaceships, interplanetary travel, and flights out into the unknown are on the schedules of many studios. With *Star Wars* such a smash success, and *Close Encounters of the Third Kind* breaking records, the industry is wasting no time jumping on the spacewagon before the fad wears thin. Twentieth Century-Fox is already at work on a sequel to *Star Wars*. A new release, *The End of the World* (1977), tells of a scientist who accidentally comes upon a group of aliens disguised as a priest and six nuns. Producer Charles Bond's next production is *Laser Blast*.

Fox Studios will put some of its profits from *Star Wars* into another science fiction spectacular, *Alien*, the tale of a space creature who takes to mugging U.S. spacemen. American International Pictures is producing *The Incredible Melting Man*. A returning spaceman must drink gallons of blood to keep from liquefying. Universal plans *The Thing from Another World*, originally made in 1951 with Howard Hawks as director. Lily Tomlin will star in *The Incredible Shrinking*

Woman. Even Disney Studios has a new flick for kids entitled *The Cat from Outer Space.*

Outstanding Horror Films
and Their Directors

Dracula	(1930)	Tod Browning
Frankenstein	(1931)	James Whale
The Mummy	(1932)	Karl Freund
The Old Dark House	(1932)	James Whale
The Invisible Man	(1933)	James Whale
Werewolf of London	(1934)	Stuart Walker
Bride of Frankenstein	(1935)	James Whale
The Wolf Man	(1941)	George Waggner
The Cat People	(1942)	Jacques Tourneur
I Walked with a Zombie	(1943)	Jacques Tourneur
The Body Snatchers	(1945)	Robert Wise
The Creature from the Black Lagoon	(1954)	Jack Arnold
Psycho	(1960)	Alfred Hitchcock
The Innocents	(1961)	Jack Clayton
The Haunting	(1963)	Robert Wise
Rosemary's Baby	(1968)	Roman Polanski
The Exorcist	(1973)	William Friedkin
The Omen	(1976)	Richard Donner
Carrie	(1976)	Brian de Palma

15 / The Science Fiction Film

DURING THE 1950's, the horror film emerged as science fiction.* Werewolves, Egyptian mummies, and the walking dead became monsters arising from land and sea, usually horrible mutations, or crawling atomic beetles, scientific creations that constantly threatened the existence of man. The science fiction film at its best can be one of the cinema's greatest creations, utilizing all the myriad technical devices and aplomb of movie magic to construct a world existing only in the minds of those who originally put it on film. At its worst, however, this genre offers a combination of absurd monsters, inarticulate depravity, and phony romanticism.

There must be some plausible, rational base for science fiction films, or else they fall completely flat. The great secret of this type of film is in selecting a rational base and building on it. If this is done, the film's futuristic qualities become credible, and the film can then be seen as an extension of reality, not as something far-fetched or false. Accordingly, the characters will seem "normal" and the scientific setting will neither militate against nor parody a possible real situation.

The science fiction film has a multiplicity of themes which can be dealt with in numerous ways. One of the commonest themes is the loss of individuality. For example, mental and psychological control, and sociological domination, are frequently used in depicting future societies. Another approach is the role of science as corruptor rather than as savior. In H. G. Wells's late Victorian and comfortably middle-class world, the Invisible Man's rein of terror revealed the darker side of man's nature, once thought to be abolished by improvements in education, sanitation, and industrial development. The

---

* Science fiction is a difficult term for which to supply a precise definition. Basically, it is a kind of fantasy which depends not on legend but involves the work of man; a story in which scientific fantasies, possibilities, or speculations are visualized.

most common line in the science fiction film is the statement that there are some things that man is not meant to know, expressing the primitive fear of too much knowledge. Usually depicting science as a force for good, the good-evil duality that often emerges certainly reflects carefully hidden fears and concerns that can reveal themselves with frightening effect at certain times. Horror and terror of the unknown also fall within the sphere of this genre, together with science itself.

These intertwining motifs form the crux of a good science fiction film. The filmmaker must resist the temptation to pander to his audience's fears (hidden or not) and adhere to whatever message the author is trying to communicate. Often overlooked in the cheap sensationalism and special effects of these films is the powerful desire of the writer to make a point about the nature of things. Perhaps here, more than in other types of films, the medium *does* become the message, although this is too often ignored.

Science fiction films rely heavily upon elaborate sets and symbols, and in the hands of a great filmmaker, these works can take on new life, filled with brilliance and imagination. The films frequently differ a great deal from the stories or novels on which they are based, since the director's imagination can bring to life before one's eyes the marvels and horrors set forth in ordinary prose. A history of this genre reveals the changing ideas and themes of the filmmaker, as well as the changing concerns of the American moviegoing public.

In 1895, H. G. Wells and Robert Paul applied for a patent on a device that would duplicate the effects of time travel that Wells had described in his novel *The Time Machine*. It was the first audiovisual mixed-media art form—a chamber filled with movable floors and walls, vents for injecting currents of air, and screens depicting scenes from the different eras that the Time Traveler had visited. Through a judicious use of motion picture films and slides, the audience would experience the illusion of moving forward or backward in time, and of seeing close up the strange wonders that Wells so vividly described in his novel. This early attempt to combine science fiction and film was doomed to failure for lack of money to develop the two men's ideas. However, this concept marked the beginning of the basic science fiction style: the attempt to create in visual terms the effects of a scientifically imagined situation.

From 1895 to 1930, only a few films were made which can qualify as science fiction movies. An early film of George Méliès, the famous French fantasist, was *A Trip to the Moon* (1902), based on works by Jules Verne and H. G. Wells. Particularly noteworthy in it are the amazing Selenites, the race of advanced beings who populate the moon. This film ran for sixteen minutes in thirty tableaux, and its companion piece, *An Impossible Voyage* (an imaginary trip to the sun, also adapted from a work of Verne), represented the style of the time. These films utilized many photographic tricks in their creation of special effects.

By 1905, however, this era was over. Audiences were becoming more interested in content, seeking greater realism and drama in a world filled with violence.

The first true science fiction film in England was the work of Charles Urban, in 1909. This film, *The Airship Destroyer*, runs for about twenty minutes and includes what has become the staple of this type of movie, special effects. Through the use of miniature models, Urban depicted the bombing of London by airships. This film was succcessful and led to others in the same vein, such as *The Aerial Anarchists* (1911), which showed the destruction of London in only fifteen minutes, and *The Pirates of 1920* (1911). All these films depended on the accuracy of their special effects. Little attempt was made to heighten tension or atmosphere by cutting or intensifying the narrative, for filmmakers then considered it enough to show the wonders of modern technology to their audiences.

The French, later to dominate the field, worked on developing the theme of hypnotism in such efforts as Abel Gance's *The Madness of Dr. Tube* (1915), which used distorting lenses and trick photography to show the insanity of scientific experimentation with light waves. Another French film, *The Inhuman One* (1925), used cubism to achieve its impact, but was poor in content. Up to this time, science fiction films had made a very promising beginning. They were realistic and depicted science as the "hero" of their stories. In Berlin and Paris, however, different spirits were stirring, and soon the surrealistic and expressionistic elements in the art of the period were applied to the film. With this came a concern for the grotesque and the bizarre, and the horror film was born.

This new development produced one of the most famous films in the history of the medium, *The Cabinet of Dr. Caligari* (1919). This incredible film tells the story of a mad doctor and his somnambulist monster, Cesare, and also comments on the nature of sanity and insanity. The story is told through the eyes of a young man who is later found to be an inmate in an asylum. However, this is not revealed until the very last frames of the movie, when the youth is seated before Dr. Caligari himself, who was previously suspected to be the villain of the piece. The deliberate ambiguity of the ending is further heightened by the weird buildings and twisted shapes of the world the young man inhabits. Light and shadow are used with terrifying effect, and although some critics would not call it science fiction, its emphasis on the bizarre and the frightful certainly contain ingredients of the basic science fiction film as it was later known. Regardless of classification, however, the film is noteworthy for its use of expressionism and for its oblique commentary on the nature of sanity versus insanity, or how each man views and comprehends the world around him. It would be difficult to find a more horrible scene in film than the interview in Dr. Caligari's chambers when the viewer suddenly discovers what has been going on in terms of what he has already seen.

The horror-science fiction film genre frequently blurs. The progression of horror films actually starts with *The Golem* (1920), produced by Paul Wegener. This film is about a robotlike monster fashioned from clay that was supposed to help Jewish people in their hour of greatest need. A chilling effect is produced at the film's end with the sight of a man on horseback reading a proclamation against the Jews in medieval Prague, perhaps a forecast of the persecutions to come when the Nazis took power in another era.

Another horror film of the time was *Homunculus* (1916). This serial of six one-hour parts concerns the life of an artificial man without a soul; later it paved the way for the treatment of more complex topics. In these films, scientists and science were shown for the first time as dangerous. Homunculus was created by a scientist who wanted a creature of reason and will, but since it was made without a soul, the being turned instead to destruction. This film is now considered a primer of almost every science fiction film element. The "mad scientist" stereotype begins here, with its conclusion of divine intervention in the destruction of the godless man. The film was directed by Otto Rippert and exerted much influence on subsequent films, including *The Golem*, and continuing with *Frankenstein* and *The Creature from the Black Lagoon* in America.

Meanwhile, England continued its airship dramas with *First Men in the Moon* (1917), and was joined with Denmark's *Heaven Ship* of the same year. Both films contained pleas for international peace and understanding, but lost much of their artistic value in doing so. In addition, Russian filmmakers joined this embryonic film movement with such works as *Aelita* (1924) and *The Hyperloid of Engineer Garin* (1924), which used grotesque costumes and masks, and *The Death Ray* (1925).

American studios paid scant attention to the science fiction film at this point. D. W. Griffith wrote and produced a film called *The Flying Torpedo*, which has since been lost. In 1912, he produced *Genesis*, a story of the distant, prehistoric past which featured clumsy mechanical dinosaurs. It also starred two characters called "Weak Hands" and "Brute Force." "Weak Hands" wins the inevitable struggle between them through his superior mind. The film is probably remembered only because Charlie Chaplin parodied it in a film called *His Prehistoric Past* (1914), in which he played "Weak Chin." The last gasp of such absurdity was Frank Butler's *Flying Elephants*, starring Laurel and Hardy. Another early film from France that was noteworthy for its treatment of the nature of science was René Clair's *Paris Qui Dort* (1923), which dealt with a scientist who put the entire city of Paris to sleep. The film also contained a number of witty and charming scenes set in the environs of the Eiffel Tower.

A German filmmaker produced the first really modern science fiction film. Fritz Lang's *Metropolis* (1927), an incredible voyage into a manufactured universe, is today considered a rich source of technical innovation and has had much influence on the spectacle film, especially in Hollywood during the 1930's and 1940's. The film describes a superscientific utopia, but one where mankind is shackled by its own machines and inventions. Technology runs rampant, and in the end, the workers lead a revolt against the omnipresent domination of the machine. The film foreshadows the weak endings and plots of so many of the films in this genre. Yet despite these defects, the special effects and miniature models reached a peak of development that was hard to equal for many years.

American producers, recognizing the potential of the genre,

quickly copied the set designs and the Germans' ability to create special effects—especially miniature models, forced perspective, and the "Shiftan Process," in which models and mirrors placed close to the camera lens give the impression of whole structures built in the distance.

Another influential film of Lang's was *The Women in the Moon* (1928), of which only a few prints exist today. Because of the technical expertise that went into filming it, and the resulting German rocketry developments of the 1930's, Hitler confiscated many of the prints and destroyed them, since the realism of the film could indicate to his future enemies how advanced German missile technology had become.

Horror films that dominated the field during the 1930's and 1940's usually depicted fiendish doctors working their dreadful will on mankind, either for revenge or for their distorted ideas of progress. Only one science fiction film of this decade was genuinely new and imaginative—Alexander Korda's *Things to Come* (1936), derived from a novel by H. G. Wells. Wells personally adapted his book for the screen to avoid the excesses of some filmmakers who frequently botch or seriously alter the original story. The result was the depiction of a utopian civilization governed by a benevolent technocracy. This ideal civilization enjoyed a life based on public service and the pursuit of a mild and undemanding happiness—very revolutionary ideas for the Depression-wracked year of 1936.

By the beginning of World War II, several magazines were carrying science fiction stories to the reading public, and the success of comic strip characters such as Buck Rogers and Flash Gordon helped to make the idea of space travel plausible. For a decade, serials based on comic strip stories dominated the science fiction field. The serials presented wildly impossible plot lines and unbelievable characters which only an especially naive or uncritical viewer could accept. Although this type of film actually began with *The Black Box* (1915) and *The Master Mystery* (1918), these serials swept the field during the 1930's. Republic, Columbia, and Universal turned out dozens of this genre, controlling the form from its boom years to its unlamented demise in the 1950's.

Aside from the excursions of Flash Gordon and Buck Rogers, the serials seldom extended themselves beyond the thriller. In the 1940's, they relied more and more on the comics for material, as in *Batman* (1943), *The Spider Returns* (1941), *The Purple Monster Strikes* (1945), and *King of the Rocket Men* (1949). This childhood world of passwords, elaborate costumes, and dark secrets (although only a juvenile auxiliary of the science fiction medium) exerted a profound influence on two generations of filmgoers.

The 1930's also offered the "lost world" or "lost kingdom" stories, which fall somewhere between adventure and science fiction. These works featured dinosaurs, pterodactyls, and other strange monsters from the distant past. Most "lost kingdom" films derive their origin from H. Rider Haggard's novel *She*, filmed at least nine times, the best version appearing in 1935. Another outstanding source is Arthur Conan Doyle's *The Lost World*, which described a fantastic jungle in South America where dinosaurs and other monsters still survived into the contemporary era. Who can forget how the fragile Bessie Love and her companions captured the brontosaurus and took him to London for all the world to see?

The greatest of the "lost worlds" is the classic *King Kong* (1933), loosely based on *The Golem*. Like the medieval statue, Kong falls in love with a beautiful young heroine, only to be repulsed by her. Driven mad, both the Golem and Kong go berserk and fall to their deaths. The chilling sight of the monstrous gorilla clutching Fay Wray in his hand as he climbs the Empire State Building epitomizes the emotional power of this type of film. The amount of inventive talent spent in producing the models and trick photography for these creatures is staggering, and although these films may not be ranked among the all-time greats (except *King Kong*), they still merit viewing for their shock value and verisimilitude.

The 1950's is usually considered the zenith of the science fiction film. Several directors worked to produce a few noteworthy films, and in viewing them, it becomes obvious how much a director like Stanley Kubrick learned from his predecessors in making his 1968 film, *2001: A Space Odyssey*.

In 1950, the science fiction film became temporarily one of the biggest selling properties in Hollywood. Magazines and paperbacks were big business, as authors such as Ray Bradbury and Arthur C. Clarke began writing fiction that held its own with the Wellsian novels and tales of several decades earlier.

With his delight in the fantastic, George Pal took over most of the market, winning six Oscars for special effects. Pal's talent was his extraordinary combination of technical facility and business acumen, beginning the decade's work with *Destination Moon* (1950). This film employed mechanical effects, imaginative landscapes, and technical brilliance. The fantastic landscape and depiction of meteor showers are amazing and scientifically correct. Pal followed up his initial success with *When Worlds Collide* (1951), again employing his famous special effects to simulate the "real thing" that audiences had come to expect from *Destination Moon*. These films brought a host of imitators to the scene and revivified the genre.

George Pal's successes stemmed from his ability to combine special effects with color and massive action. His adaptation of H. G. Wells's *The War of the Worlds* (1954) is an exciting film for several reasons. First of all, Pal collaborated with Byron Haskins, head of special effects at Warner Brothers, and he also shifted the locale of the film from late-nineteenth-century England to twentieth-century Southern California, in order to better take advantage of the scenes of chaos when the Martian invaders begin their destruction of Los Angeles. (The Martians devastate London in the novel.) The atomic bomb fails to stop their onslaught, and the surprise ending of the film (the Martians are destroyed by bacteria which do not exist on their own world) is made even more unexpected by showing the wreckage of the city's downtown sections just moments before their machines fail and the creatures die. The color shots of the machines and the actual explosion of atom bombs make for a degree of horror hard to surpass. Pal certainly brings the novel to life, and the shift in scene and time makes it even more believable than its original. Some of the same team's better films are *The Conquest of Space* (1955) and *The Power* (1967).

Forbidden Planet was an attempt to explore the idea that life might exist beyond our solar system. Walter Pidgeon as Dr. Morbius, a scientist who has spent years investigating the remains of a long-vanished civilization on a planet circling the star Altair, succeeds in learning the secrets of the race who built strange, powerful machines beneath the planet's surface. He is joined by the crew of another Earth spaceship and reveals to them some of the scientific devices that he has found. However, not until near the end of the film does the audience realize why Dr. Morbius and his daughter have lived alone on Altair: the doctor's own subconscious mind refused to let him leave the planet when he first arrived with a party of his own men, and the strange machines beneath the world's crust magnified his desire to stay to such an extent that all his companions were killed when they attempted to leave. At the end, Morbius dies and the captain of the second ship's crew takes his daughter away, hours before the planet explodes. Although at times the action and plotting are thin, the film suggests that man has a dual nature, and that despite all the machinery in the world to make life pleasant and enjoyable, man is unable to conquer the evil within himself. The film is superior to ordinary science fiction films which emphasize fantasy and other-worldly technology. The science fiction film's potential for entertainment and education is fully revealed in Pal's work.

From 1953 to 1958, Jack Arnold of Universal also worked on the science fiction film. His clarity of vision and personal style created such beautiful scenes that they might have been directed for the stage. Arnold recognized the frame as a formal boundary to the image, and he skillfully employed it to hide action as a stage director might use theater flats. Some of Arnold's better films are *It Came From Outer Space* (1953), *The Creature from the Black Lagoon* (1954), and *The Incredible Shrinking Man* (1957). The Gill Man, who made his first appearance in *Lagoon*, was later used in several films.

One of the best films, *The Day the Earth Stood Still* (1951), directed by Robert Wise and starring Michael Rennie and Patricia Neal, concerns an emissary from another planet who warns earthmen about the danger of experimentation with atomic weapons. It is at once a somber and a joyous film, as utopia seems just around the corner when the mysterious spaceman and his robot depart in their flying saucer after giving their warning. The film keeps the action at a plausible level; there are no worldwide attempts at the destruction of cities and similar excesses that mar so many science fiction films. This work, together with Howard Hawks's *The Thing* (1951), were Hollywood's most serious attempts to render science fiction ideas on film.

Monsters of the nuclear age are all creatures of the Bomb. Since *The Beast from 20,000 Fathoms* (1953), the screen has been overrun with all kinds of biological mutants. *Beast* (1953), from a short story by Ray Bradbury, with special effects by Ray Harryhausen, launched the idea of atomic blasts releasing supposedly extinct creatures to emerge and frighten the universe. *Them* (1954), probably the best of this group, offered fifteen-foot-long ants; *It Came from Beneath the Sea* (1955), an enormous octopus; in *Tarantula* (1955), a spider; and a gargantuan insect in *The Deadly Mantis* (1957). Atomic radiation and mutations become the subject for a flood of Japanese imports. Nothing seems more laughable to the viewer than to see the wires and the sometimes awkwardly constructed sets that control the creatures let loose to destroy the world. *Godzilla* (1955), another beast wakened from a long sleep by an atom blast, *Godzilla vs. The Thing, Return of Godzilla,* and *King Kong vs. Godzilla* typify the preoccupations of the Japanese filmmakers. The creature phase reached its zenith under the hand of Ishiro Honda with *Rodan* (1957), *Gammera* (1959), and *Mothra* (1959).

The cycle finally began to wane as the search for unusual monsters brought forth such inferior films as *Attack of the Crab Monsters* (1957) and *Attack of the Giant Leeches* (1958). Exhausting this market, American studios then transformed people into monsters in *The Amazing Colossal Man* (1957) and *Attack of the Fifty Foot Woman* (1959). The end of the decade finally brought to a close the production of these cheap films, but they nearly finished off science fiction as a serious medium for the exploration of contemporary issues.

Until recently, forces accomplishing the end of the world were often shown in science fiction films as being of extraterrestrial origin. However, the advent of atomic weapons brought a great number of films warning about the devastating effects of the new devices. If the threat of the planet's ruin is averted, it is through the intervention of some supernatural power—like the bacteria in H. G. Wells's *The War of the Worlds,* which destroy the Martian invaders at the last moment.

The ultimate horror in science fiction is neither death nor destruction but a state in which life is suspended—dehumanization. Man is deprived of feeling, moral judgment, and free will. Don Siegel's *Invasion of the Body Snatchers* (1956) has through the years become a television favorite, and fans have pushed this film into a near-classic. In *The Village of the Damned* (1960), a mysterious force from outer space has descended on a small village causing all the natives to lose consciousness for several hours. When they awaken, time passes and all the women discover they are impregnated. They give birth to totally emotionless, superintellectual children. Finally it dawns on one father (George Sanders) that these children are capable of taking over the minds of those they mistrust, and can order them to kill themselves. These strange, blond children are to take over the Earth. Sanders decides to destroy them, and to save the world he selects a super charge of dynamite and blows the kids and himself to pieces.

Invasion of the Body Snatchers also reveals the zombies among us. Dr. Miles Bennell (Kevin McCarthy) returns to the quiet town of Santa Mira and slowly, as the night passes, he is aware that huge seedpods contain gruesomely imperfect alter egos of various people in the village. These seedpods seem to drain the likenesses and minds from sleeping humans. Miles and his fiancee discover the entire town has been taken over by these mysterious pods. Miles tries to escape the village, manages to get to Los Angeles, and tells his harrowing tale. The viewer is left to assume that the seedpod evil will be stamped out.

The serious concept of God intervening in human affairs came as early as 1933, with *Gabriel Over the White House*. However, the religious theme was really developed in William Wellman's *The Next Voice You Hear* (1950). In this film, God reaches out to counsel man with a general message resulting in the complete conversion of the world. *Red Planet Mars* (1952) introduced the concept that God would intervene in world affairs in order to destroy the international Communist conspiracy and to confirm the power of the present American administration. The film can be seen as a reflection of the McCarthyite hysteria of the day, but it also sinks to the depths of bathos and critical unbelief with its tawdry baggage of claptrap and political propaganda. Other films which presented exterior menaces at this time were *The Day the Earth Exploded* (1955), where the threat of a new element brought to the surface through atomic bomb experiments causes the crisis, and *Earth vs. The Flying Saucers* (1956).

Despite the prevalence of natural onslaughts and disasters, science fiction filmmakers have also liked to dwell on the horrors of atomic warfare as a cause for the end of the world. Part of the reason is technical: special effects were expensive to make, and a film based on a world war could economically use stock footage from previous real wars. Also, the idea of self-destruction holds a special attraction, and there would be numerous opportunities in such films to end with bursts of drama and wild scenic effects. The idea of the world ending in an atomic holocaust gained great favor and plausibility after 1945, and the films of the day reflected the new mode of destruction. Producers could also combine with this theme another hoary one: the threat of too much knowledge. The results were such works as *The Beginning or the End* (1946), *Five* (1951), *The Twenty-Seventh Day* (1957), *The World, the Flesh, and the Devil* (1959), and an outstanding film capturing the mood of atomic annihilation, *On the Beach* (1959). The last picture is a powerful one, only somewhat flawed by the too romantic treatment given Nevil Shute's novel by Gregory Peck and Ava Gardner as the lovers doomed by radioactive fallout.

The 1960's produced its quota of science fiction films, both good and bad. Technically, films like Richard Fleisher's *Fantastic Voyage* (1966) reached new heights of invention in the story of a group of humans who travel by miniature submarine and explore the human body in order to search for the best way to cure a certain disease. Doctors on "Earth" are unable to operate due to the dangerous location of the illness, and the submarine's crew is dispatched to perform the operation. The special effects—with their depiction of blood vessels and organs—are especially noteworthy, although as so often happens in this type of film, the plot line becomes quite weak.

The decade also saw renewed preoccupation with the idea of a nuclear World War III in such films as *Fail Safe* (1965) and *Dr. Strangelove, or How I Learned to Stop Worrying and Love the Bomb* (1964) (see Chapter 17, "The Comedy Film"). The latter film is especially interesting in that in addition to the science fiction elements, it also adds a high degree of black comedy to the plot, a genuine rarity in this genre.

The last part of the decade once again brought something new to the genre and showed its great power both to teach and to entertain at the same time. The film was Stanley Kubrick's *2001: A Space Odyssey* (1968), the most technically advanced and courageous cinema venture of the decade, and which deserves to be examined in detail.

In 1950, Arthur C. Clarke wrote a short story entitled "The Sentinel." Eighteen years later, much to the surprise of Clarke, Stanley Kubrick's creative direction transformed it into a $10 million dollar science fiction film. Kubrick's movie is perhaps the most ambitious of this genre to be released, for never before has the screen seen such stunning special effects. The work is an example of two themes frequently repeated in this type of film: the threat of knowledge and the idea of dehumanization.

In the beginning of the film, the viewer sees the Earth poised in space, with the moon in the foreground and the sun rising over the top of the planet bringing in a new day. The ominous brass of Richard Strauss's tone poem "Thus Spake Zarathustra" (Op. 30) rings out through the theater, and the opening scene culminates with the arrival of dawn in a pre-historic landscape. The full orchestra blares out the tri-umphant theme of Strauss's work (based on Nietzsche's book of the same name), and the knowledgeable viewer realizes right away that this film will offer something new. One of Nietzsche's themes is the doctrine of eternal recurrence, and this motif operates throughout the movie, contributing to sev-eral startling effects and mental realizations when the audience learns what is going to happen to characters.

The viewer next sees a very barren landscape and then catches sight of a group of apes around a water hole in a desert. Suddenly, an ear-piercing sound fills the air and a mysterious black slab (extraterrestial intelligence?) appears in their midst. Summoning up his courage, one of the apes proceeds to touch it and is joined by his companions. They seem to worship the mysterious object, and although it soon disappears, something has happened to these creatures. One of them sees some dried bones nearby, picks up one of the longer bones, and begins to play with it. The others soon take their cue from the leader, and when an invading party of apes attempts to take over their water hole, the leader ad-vances with his club and kills one of the invaders. The tool/weapon-wielding apes soon vanquish the interlopers, and in exultation, the leader hurls his club into the air. The whirl-ing club changes into a space station flying at tremendous speed around the Earth, and the viewer is abruptly transported from the world of the distant past into that of a not-too-distant future. The plot unfolds when a rocket bearing an American scientist reaches the space station and the viewer learns that something mysterious has been going on at the main lunar base in the crater Clavius.

The space sequences of this film, especially the use of color, soundtrack ("The Blue Danube Waltz" plays continu-ally as the ship progresses toward the moon), and camera fo-cus attention on the marvels of the universe, producing a feeling of awe in even the most sophisticated viewer. Brilliant color photography, visual images that dazzle the mind and eye, and an intriguing plot all combine to make *2001* a superb example of the science fiction genre.

The ship lands at Clavius and a conference of scientists there reveals that a strange black monolith has been found buried beneath the lunar surface. The group adjourns and several of its members fly across the moon's plains to see the wonder for themselves. As they walk down a gentle slope where the monolith is, one of them touches it, and again the viewer hears the same ear-piercing shriek that he has heard in the earlier ape sequence. The scene changes with startling rapidity, and a large spaceship is seen in the depths of space headed toward the planet Jupiter, tens of millions of miles distant.

The spaceship contains only two active men and a computer. (The rest of the crew is in a state of semi-hibernation for the long voyage to the giant planet.) The computer, named "HAL" (if the initial letters are moved ahead once, the familiar "IBM" soon emerges with renewed connotations of power), suddenly goes insane, kills all the hibernating crewmen, and sends one of the active astronauts adrift into space. The remaining astronaut (Keir Dullea) dismantles the mad computer and the voyage proceeds to its destination. A monolith appears and seems to swallow up the spaceship (it is several hundred feet long), and the traveler is swept up in a storm of strange light images and even stranger happenings.

At the end of this sequence, the airman emerges into an eighteenth-century drawing room and surveys the scene. He sees an aged man seated at a table eating some food. The astronaut approaches him to inquire about his destination. However, before he reaches the table, a glass falls to the floor and the sound shatters the mood. In the next instant the viewer learns that the elderly man is an older version of the astronaut himself. The scene shifts to the same individual lying on a bed in the same elegant setting, only he has aged further, appearing even more wizened and shrunken than before. The metamorphosis is complete: a sphere of light rises from the dying man's breast and begins to fill the room, which then dissolves into the vault of the heavens themselves. The bulbous object assumes the outlines of a human embryo and begins a voyage through space toward Earth.

The film ends with this startling sight, and the recurrent theme strikes home with all its force: the creature will perhaps bring life to Earth.

2001: A Space Odyssey is easily the most profound and

philosophic film of the past several decades. Through its use of music (that of Johann and Richard Strauss, as well as the electronic music of Gyorgy Ligeti) and its nearly overpowering visual effects, the film bears its intellectual cargo well. The viewer is able to retain both the visual splendor and the intellectual message. This film far transcends the ordinary "search" and "knowledge is evil" themes of many science fiction films in its near-documentary vividness and its ability both to create and to sustain wonder.

The Andromeda Strain (1970) is the tale of an unknown virus brought from space that threatens to wipe out the human race. Special effects carry a large burden in the treatment of the plot, and the film suffers accordingly. *The Andromeda Strain* fails to achieve a balance between effects and plot, and is thus a far weaker film than *2001* in its failure to exploit terror.

THX:1138 (1971) combines Orwell's *1984* and Aldous Huxley's *Brave New World* to depict a future where men and women are stripped of their individuality and take drugs to control their sex drives. They grope at each other in a nightmare world where everything is seen in white, from their clothing to their dwelling places and their pale, fungoid bodies. It is a world where technology has taken over in every respect, and any attempt to flee results in a life-in-death existence in a psychiatric ward devoted to the care of the "insane." Although exciting at times, the film fails to sustain its mood or fulfill its promises.

Logan's Run (1976), directed by Michael Anderson and starring Michael York, takes place three centuries from now when people are dwelling under opaque, hermetically sealed domes in the midst of devastation. At age 30, the individual has a choice of being recycled or to run for his life. York, who is 29, discovers that recycling is a deception, a means by which the government deals with overpopulation, and so decides to run for it. He and a young girl escape and meet an old man (Peter Ustinov), who reveals his knowledge of the past. York returns to the doomed city, tells the people the secret, and brings about a grand revolt.

In Nicholas Roeg's *The Man Who Fell to Earth* (1976), David Bowie, the rock star, in what is undoubtedly the weirdest makeup of the decade, appears as a chilly, beautifully composed cat-eyed man from outer space. He has come from another planet in search of water for his drought-ridden homeland. Eventually he is exploited by government, big business and friends. Officialdom suspects the androgynous stranger and brings him to his knees. Movie and rock fans cheered Bowie's performance.

The only science fiction film to come near to Kubrick's monumental *2001: A Space Odyssey* (1968) is George Lucas's elaborate and beautifully photographed intergalactic fairy tale, *Star Wars* (1977). The film is a happy combination of fun and fantasy based on early ritualized adventures found in comic books and science fiction serials, all blended with witty observations on a wide range of literature from *The Hardy Boys* to parts of the Bible. Within weeks of the release of *Star Wars*, kids, grownups, and critics pronounced it a grand and glorious hit. Early box office returns assured Twentieth Century-Fox Pictures, that after a long series of inferior movies, they would assuredly be in the black.

Audiences cheer the direct story line of *Star Wars*. Like the old-fashioned films of Douglas Fairbanks and Errol Flynn, the good guys are out to defeat the bad guys in a story of fast pursuit, unexpected encounters, and breathless escapes before sweeping to a happy ending. Lucas offers a tale of suspense and adventure with no message, no sex, and only a superficial sight of blood. He salutes the Western, gangster, and war films, telling his tale with humor, cheerfulness, and affection. In spite of the ludicrous situations, the actors handle their roles with sincerity and solemnity, and the director never takes a condescending attitude toward his material. His respect turns what could have been high camp into a rousing, swashbuckling distinguished film.

The plot (which any ten-year-old SF buff knows by heart) tells of a damsel in distress and three stouthearted friends who go to her aid. Audiences cheer the last-minute rescue and the defeat of dastardly villains. Princess Leia Organa (Carrie Fisher), the leader of the rebellion against the evil Galactic Empire, has been taken prisoner by Darth Vader (David Prowse) and Grand Moff Tarkin (Peter Cushing). They have taken her aboard Death Star, the Empire's mobile command ship, capable of destroying the entire star system with one thrust of energy. Princess Leia has stolen the computerized blueprints of Death Star, and the villains know that if the blueprints reach her rebel friends, the Evil Empire will be destroyed and freedom will once more be enjoyed by all the subjugated revels. Leia's friends, hearing of her plight, set out to rescue her. Like Leia, they are determined to restore justice to the Empire. Luke Skywalker (Mark Hamill), a handsome farmboy, enlists the help of Solo (Harrison Ford), a freelance spaceship captain who accepts any adventure where there's money. Solo's first mate is Chewbacca, a seven-foot monkey-faced anthropoid.

Ben (Obi-Wan) Kenobi (Alec Guinness), is an old mystic who is in possession of "The Force," a mixture of old-fashioned Christian faith and ESP. They are joined by two robots, the Laurel and Hardy of the mechanical world. Along the way Luke Skywalker and his buddies meet imperial storm troops, enemy aliens, rebel fighters, a menagerie of horrific monsters, ray guns, and lethal neon swords.

Star Wars' cinematography and special effects turn it into a screen masterpiece. Stuart Freeborn of the makeup department creates the most nightmarish collection of extraterrestrial freaks yet seen in movies. Freeborn turns people into hideous turtles, apes, pythons, and spiders, creating a terrifying dream of genetic engineering. John Barry, responsible for the production designs along with John Dykstra's special effects, has created a breathtaking series of lunar landscapes and space shots—a world of spaceships, explosions of planets, space battles, and views of outer space that are overwhelming.

In *2001: A Space Odyssey*, Kubrick used composite opticals, in which he placed a spaceship on one part of the film and blacked out the background, then shot the ship; he then covered the spaceship, rolled the film again, and, in the blackout part of the scene, placed his stars and moons behind the spaceships. This multiple exposure process was expensive and took endless time. Lucas and Dykstra's secret was a computerized camera, in which they linked the camera to a calculator which recorded and memorized each shot. Thus they were able to have spaceships crossing over planets all the time. Kubrick's ships were linear and can be seen from only one angle. Dykstra's ships are seen in all conditions and from all angles. Kubrick used 35 different effects; Lucas used 363.

George Lucas, age 33, with only three pictures to his credit (the other two are *THX:1138* and *American Graffiti*), belongs to the new school of young Hollywood directors who are not "angry" but who love movies and are dedicated to cinema. Lucas, if given the chance, may bring more originality and artistic talent to American films that just might return the silver screen to its old magic.

George Lucas's *Star Wars* (1977) is an action-packed movie, peopled with comic book characters, spectacular scenic effects, taking its viewers to faraway planets. Steven Spielberg's *Close Encounters of the Third Kind* (1977) is about people. There are no wars in outer space, no worlds colliding, and no malignant growth threatening our universe. The film, combining theological observations with science fiction, offers homespun characters from Muncie, Indiana, America's heartland, facing a baffling but insistent UFO phenomenon.

A solid suburbanite, repairman Roy Neary (Richard Dreyfuss) works for an electrical power company in Indiana, has a wife and three kids. One day he witnesses a swirling purple cloud near his home and from that moment his life is never the same. Roy's experience with the UFO's sets him off on a series of adventures to an ultimate rendezvous with a ship from outer space. After his eerie experience the hardhat appears to go mad, and spends his time sculpting a coneshaped form in his living room. Eventually the image emerges as Devil's Tower, Wyoming, and Roy realizes where he is destined to meet the spaceship and its occupants. Another person similarly affected by the UFO's is a young mother, Jillian Guiler (Melinda Dillon), whose three-year-old son Barry (Cary Guffy) appears to have some psychic connection with the UFO's and is abducted by the flying saucers. Because of their belief in the UFO's, Roy and Jillian are alienated from their society. They have experienced close encounters of the first and second kind—seeing flying saucers and physical evidence of their existence. Both are prepared for close encounters of the third kind—actual physical contact. They begin their journey to Devil's Tower.

Every good movie has a confrontation scene—a meeting between the hero and villain, a good-bye, a death, or a shoot-out in the saloon. Spielberg's confrontation scene at Devil's Tower, Wyoming, is of epic proportions. An army of official investigators, the crazed repairman and Jillian, seeking her son, break through security and witness the landing and disembarkation of the alien spaceship. The mother is reunited with her child, while Roy, the hardhat, takes the child's place in the spaceship for a journey to outer space.

The last forty minutes of *Close Encounters* give it a historic place in cinema history. The screen lights up with stunning visual and aural sensations. The night skies, blinking lights, and colored shapes offer an extraordinary psychedelic light show. It is a breathtaking sequence, bringing the heavens down to earth when the earthlings and alien creatures come together on a landing field in Wyoming.

Steven Spielberg, with the help of Vilmos Zsigmond, Douglas Trumbull, William Fraker, and a brilliant crew of technical wizards, including John Williams and his exciting and imaginative musical score, have created dazzling effects, motion, luminosity, velocity, and sound to create brilliant scenes. Spielberg's UFO's terrorize, yet enchant. He offers a supercharged humanistic science-fiction film that shows how it just might be when mankind has an encounter of the third kind.

Since the pioneering days of George Méliès and Charles Urban, science fiction has been a genre that draws audiences to the box office. What perhaps remains to be considered is the American attitude toward these films, and how its variations affect our viewing habits. The anti-intellectual archetypal scene might be the one in which the brilliant young scientist and his lady assistant work through the night to discover an antidote for the poison being sprayed about by the Giant Spider from Planet X. Only when the assistant removes her glasses (intellectuals have weak eyes from reading too much) does she become sexually attractive, and the plot is finally launched. The good doctor must eventually show that he really is a normal male by striking the creature and killing it, saving the world from destruction. Similar banalities have long been the bane of the science fiction film, and it is to the credit of such men as Stanley Kubrick that this aspect of things has been mitigated.

The absent-minded professor and the mad scientist are also tiresome stereotypes that have had an all too deleterious effect on the production of such films. The American attitude is mixed: on the one hand is the natural fear of the strange and the unknown, and on the other, the puritanical fear of meddling with what seems to be God's domain, not man's. There is also the absurd theory that virile males and academicians are at opposite ends of the scheme of things, and that technology has produced many blessings for us, despite the omnipresent danger of abuse of atomic power and other powerful forces. Such ambivalent factors are always present when a science fiction film is made, and because these factors are not balanced or properly understood, numerous botches and bad films are the result. All too many films are thinly plotted, depending on their special effects to keep them artistically viable. In addition, many films that pretend they are science fiction films are really crude sex rivalries, lust-for-supreme-power tales, or crackpot scientist stories, only joined together by a laboratory setting. Such films should be exposed as the crudities they are, and attention should be concentrated on such works as *2001* and *Forbidden Planet*. Perhaps the stereotypes are impossible to avoid entirely, but their presence can at least be muted or held to a plausible level—something rarely done in this genre.

In conclusion, the science fiction film offers superb grounds for the production of a masterpiece or a complete and utter botch. As with much else, the choice is the director's, and those who choose to act in a given film. Despite their limitations and feeble plots, the science fiction film can still be both instructive and entertaining, fulfilling two of the purposes of art. The genre may be neither great nor wholly devoid of critical value, but the peaks and valleys are still there for audiences to see—and hopefully enjoy.

Outstanding Science Fiction Films and Their Directors

Destination Moon	(1950)	Irving Pichel
The Thing	(1951)	Howard Hawks and Christian Nyby
The Day the Earth Stood Still	(1951)	Robert Wise
The Creature from the Black Lagoon	(1954)	Jack Arnold
Invasion of the Body Snatchers	(1956)	Don Siegel
Forbidden Planet	(1956)	Fred McLeod Wilcox
2001: A Space Odyssey	(1968)	Stanley Kubrick
The Andromeda Strain	(1970)	Robert Wise
Logan's Run	(1976)	Michael Anderson
The Man Who Fell to Earth	(1976)	Nicholas Roeg
Star Wars	(1977)	George Lucas
Close Encounters of the Third Kind	(1977)	Steven Spielberg

16 / The Musical

IN 1927, when Al Jolson faced the camera and sang "Mammy" in *The Jazz Singer*, the talking picture and the musical were born simultaneously. Warner Brothers, a minor studio at the time, had gambled on a new sound recording device for its production of *The Jazz Singer*, and within months every major studio had its own musical under way.

Like the Western, the musical was wholly an American product, created and developed in Hollywood studios. The prototype of the early musicals was *Broadway Melody* (1929), billed as the first "100% All Talking, 100% All Singing, 100% All Dancing" picture. It tells the story of two sisters from a small town who make it to Broadway and fall in love with a big-time song-and-dance man.

Audiences were delighted with this behind-the-scenes glimpse of show business, and the theme was repeated, with minor variations, in dozens of musicals that followed. Story lines revolved around talented unknowns who finally achieve stardom, "show must go on" themes, and an assortment of backstage crises—interspersed with bright, lavish musical numbers designed solely to entertain. These flamboyant, escapist films were just what audiences wanted, particularly during the grim Depression years.

Among the most popular of the backstage musicals were Warner Brothers' *Gold Diggers of Broadway* (1929); MGM's *Broadway* (1929); Universal's *The King of Jazz* (1930), starring Paul Whiteman; Fox's *Fox-Movietone Follies* (1930); and Paramount's *Paramount on Parade* (1930). Borrowing the title of the first "100% All Talking" film, MGM produced *Broadway Melody of 1936*, *Broadway Melody of 1938*, and *Broadway Melody of 1940*.

Equally popular with film audiences during this period were the all-star revues—an idea that Hollywood borrowed from Broadway. The revues contained vaudeville sketches, gags, songs, and crude production numbers with elaborate settings and gaudy costumes. Even top dramatic stars were recruited to do song-and-dance numbers, backed by flashy chorus lines.

Word reached New York that in Hollywood sound meant music, and dozens of Broadway stage and nightclub performers alighted at the train station in Los Angeles, determined to earn some of the big money. Musical performers recruited for their special talents descended on the movie capital. Rudy Vallee, Texas Guinan, Gertrude Lawrence, Ethel Waters, Fannie Brice, Sophie Tucker, Eddie Cantor, and the sad-eyed Helen Morgan arrived, and many appeared in various musical revues. Feeling superior to the medium, they performed their special acts, packed their bags, and caught the train back to New York. Others remained and entered screen history.

One of the first and biggest of these films is MGM's *The Hollywood Review of 1929*. Everyone under contract at the studio, except Lon Chaney and the aloof Garbo, appeared in this farrago. Grinning with good showmanship (and perhaps some embarrassment) were Joan Crawford, Marion Davies, John Gilbert, Norma Shearer, Buster Keaton, Bessie Love, William Haines, Conrad Nagel, Jack Benny, and Marie Dressler. In an effort to be "arty," Norma Shearer and John Gilbert did the balcony scene from *Romeo and Juliet*. For the big finale, the entire company participated in a skit called "Singin' in the Rain."

Not to be outdone, Warner Brothers displayed the talents of its stars in *Show of Shows* (1929). For the seemingly mandatory "arty" number, John Barrymore did a soliloquy from *Richard III*, and as a finale, the entire cast sang and danced to "Singin' in the Bathtub." Obviously, there wasn't much originality in these early musicals.

One of the first musical comedies written for the screen, *Sunny Side Up* (1929), managed at least to avoid a few of the clichés. Starring the popular team of Charles Farrell and Janet Gaynor, the film was based on a romantic "poor girl, rich boy" plot. Its stunning production number, "Turn on the Heat," was the high point of the DeSylva, Brown, and Henderson musical score.

Several other musical comedies were set on college campuses including such trivial but entertaining films as *Close Harmony* (1929) and *Follow Through* (1930), starring the team of Buddy Rogers and Nancy Carroll. In this type of film, the action would abruptly come to a halt in various places, a song or dance routine would be interjected, then the narrative would continue. Miss Carroll, the belle of these films, had an odd but charming voice, and was the first real star developed by the talkies.

Three directors, experimenting with sound, pushed the musical forward: King Vidor, Rouben Mamoulian, and Ernst Lubitsch. King Vidor, a talented director, made *Hallelujah* (1929), the first full-length film to employ an all-Negro cast, a milestone in music and sound. In Rouben Mamoulian's *Love Me Tonight* (1932), visual and aural experiments offer wit and good humor. It is a masterpiece of light cinema. By expanding our definition of musical, we can include Rouben Mamoulian's *Applause* (1929), a superior film because of pace, movement, and rhythm. *Applause* is not only a captivating story but is also filled with inventive sound techniques—camera mobility, modulated sound, and rhythmic integration of the actors. A tender plot, and superior acting makes Mamoulian's film a screen classic.

Fortunately for the screen, Ernst Lubitsch's early American efforts are light comedies with music. He had the good fortune to select for his performers Jeanette MacDonald, Jack Buchanan, Miriam Hopkins, Claudette Colbert, and Maurice Chevalier. With Lubitsch's clever guidance, they romped through several unforgettable early musicals and clever comedies. He brought to his productions scintillating dialogue, rich photography, touches of sex, and songs that added rather than detracted from the story. His best efforts are *The Love Parade* (1929), *Paramount on Parade* (1930), *Monte Carlo* (1930), and *The Smiling Lieutenant* (1931).

By 1931-32, the screen had discovered the operetta. John Boles sang his way through a highly improbable story in *The Desert Song* (1930); Grace Moore and Lawrence Tibbett warbled duets in *New Moon* (1930); and Bernice Claire and Alexander Gray starred in *No, No, Nanette* (1931). These operettas offered far-fetched stories, ridiculous characters, and improbable situations. The public quickly tired of them. If the genre of the musical was to become a permanent form of entertainment, someone or something was needed to save it.

Something did! Three people, whose names have become synonymous with the Hollywood musical, helped to resurrect the musical's popularity, making it a permanent part of the industry: Busby Berkeley, the choreographer and director, and Ginger Rogers and Fred Astaire, the dance team.

Warner Brothers, usually interested in the contemporary

scene, decided to turn out one more musical, *Forty-Second Street* (1933), choreographed by Busby Berkeley. This musical, the first to take advantage of the flexibility of the camera, reveals how exciting music combined with visual images can be. Berkeley, who established himself as the best director of this type, presents dance routines that are exercises in geometric designs performed by thinly clad chorus girls, twisting and turning, photographed from all angles. He takes his camera up, down, under, and sideways, even rolls it around to catch the spirit of movement. He was the first to liberate the musical film from staginess, and with his innovations, the movie musical at last found itself superior to stage productions.

Although Mervyn LeRoy directed *Gold Diggers of 1933* and Lloyd Bacon handled *Forty-Second Street* and *Footlight Parade* (1933), it is Berkeley's dance routines with their infectious vulgarity that turn these musicals into fun. His annual *Gold Diggers* (1933-1937) pictures, *Footlight Parade* (1933), *Dames* (1934), and *Flirtation Walk* (1934) were his best.

Today, many of Berkeley's early musicals have been rediscovered, delighting those who watch late-night television shows. Various critics and cinema historians claim they are much more than entertainment, examining them in detail, praising them for their artistry and arcane symbolism. Intellectuals study them in detail for "camp," and essays are even written about the Freudian aspects of the Busby Berkeley musical!

Despite this overkill, it is clear that Berkeley's intricate dance patterns established the musical as a special genre, although not all of his ideas were in good taste. At times his large and visually complicated dance numbers can be *too* kaleidoscopic—too abstract and too vulgar; the dancers become dehumanized. But what Berkeley lacked in choreographic talent he more than made up for in imagination and flair.

The public paid its money for the novelty of the productions, and musicals for some time remained profitable. Warners turned out several a year. The studio structured these pictures to a pattern, centering around the backstage musical adventures of a young couple, usually played by Dick Powell and Ruby Keeler. Other regular performers were Joan Blondell, Aline MacMahon, Mina Gombel, Guy Kibbee, and Sterling Holloway. Frequently a young girl dancer in the chorus must at the last moment take over for the temperamental star in a

Broadway musical. The dialogue offered such unforgettable lines as Warner Baxter telling Ruby Keeler in *Forty-Second Street* (1933) that the star (Bebe Daniels) could not go on because she had broken her leg, and Ruby must go out there at the last minute and take over. This was her big chance. Just before pushing her onstage, Baxter encouraged her by saying, "You're going out a youngster, but you've got to come back a STAR!"

If 1933 was a memorable year because of *Forty-Second Street*, it was also remembered as the year the pixie Fred Astaire and the delightful Ginger Rogers first came together in an improbable film, *Flying Down to Rio*. *Rio* would be just another forgotten movie except for the moment Astaire and Rogers stepped on the dance floor together. With enthusiasm, charm, talent, and good taste, these two burst onto the screen with a dance called the "Carioca." From 1933 to 1940, RKO teamed the two in a series of light comedy musicals, and the genre reached its zenith. Astaire and Rogers reshaped the musical. In *The Gay Divorcee* (1934), *Top Hat* (1935), *Swing Time* (1936), *Follow the Fleet* (1936) and *Shall We Dance?* (1937), the debonair Astaire and the graceful Rogers made film history. These magnificent partners danced into the hearts of movie fans to the music of George Gershwin, Cole Porter, Jerome Kern, and Irving Berlin, and for several years their magic feet dominated the musical scene. Eventually Ginger Rogers went on to dramatic roles but the perennially youthful Astaire tapped, strutted, and waltzed his way along with such partners as Judy Garland, Rita Hayworth, Betty Hutton, Eleanor Powell, Cyd Charisse, Leslie Caron, and Audrey Hepburn.

Although Astaire on occasion used elaborate settings, trick props, backup dancers, and optical effects, he scorned the Busby Berkeley style. Instead he brought originality to the dances by insisting that there be no trick shots, that views of the dancers be full-length, and that the full figure of the dancer be on the screen during any dance routine. He was one of the first to integrate the dance properly into the story, and as a result, his films brightened the declining years that musicals faced toward the end of the decade.

Mae West, with her satirical comments on sex, was not strictly a song-and-dance girl but her sly way with lyrics and her physical gyrations kept her fans roaring and carrying money to the box office. Her films had songs and, on occasion, dances; by stretching the definition, we can include them in the musical genre. Usually it was Mae herself who with delightful self-mockery strutted and wiggled her way through suggestive numbers. Batting her mascaraed eyes, and with the perfectly timed delivery of her *double entendres*, she punctuated all her comments with physical movements—a swinging hip, a tiny hand, a rolling eye. West's films were not musicals *per se*, but what she did with songs and a few dance steps helped save the musical from disaster. The public queued up to see her ambulate and sashay through such flimsy scripts as *She Done Him Wrong* (1933), *I'm No Angel* (1933), and *Going to Town* (1934), and exchanging *bon mots* with W. C. Fields in the unforgettable *My Little Chickadee* (1939). Writers and composers realized other vistas for the musical from her roguishness. Her satirical moments foreshadowed the sophisticated musical of the 1950's.

MGM, with its long list of glamorous stars, had no success with the musical until 1935, when Louis B. Mayer launched the arch Jeanette MacDonald and the wooden Nelson Eddy in a series of operettas. Although not strictly song-and-dance performers, the two brought a freshness and gaiety to *Naughty Marietta* (1935), *Rose Marie* (1936), and *Sweethearts* (1938). The same studio later gave birth to *The Broadway Melody* series (1936-38-40) with their dazzling sets, endless chorus lines, and glittering costumes.

Although Judy Garland appeared briefly in *Pigskin Parade* (1936), *The Broadway Melody of 1938* stopped its whirling activities just long enough for this exciting fifteen-year-old girl to step forward and sing "Dear Mr. Gable," and America's greatest musical star was on her way. The following year she made *The Wizard of Oz* (1939), one of the best of the musicals. In spite of decor that today seems vulgar, the film rides to fame on its delightful score by Harold Arlen and E. Y. Harburg and, of course, the voice of Judy Garland. An excellent supporting cast helped turn the film into cinema legend.

During the 1930's, child stars were *de rigueur*. They mimed, sang, danced, and mugged their way through many scripts, and since American audiences—always a pushover for kid performers—had to have merely a glimpse of a curly-haired moppet to bring them to their feet to cheer, a young performer like Shirley Temple was destined only for success. With a wobbly lower lip and tearful eye, she tugged at the heartstrings by singing and dancing in *Stand Up and Cheer* (1934). For four years, 1934 to 1937, she was the world's number-one box office attraction. Her singing and dancing with Bill "Bojangles" Robinson, the great tap dancer, made America forget its money problems. Other child performers to follow were Deanna Durbin, Donald O'Connor, Bobby Breen, Peggy Ryan, Elizabeth Taylor, Jane Powell, and the greatest kiddie team of all, Judy Garland and Mickey Rooney.

Biographies were often a source for musicals, although their stories were so inaccurate that they became jokes. Based loosely on the life of the person presented, who was often a performer, they were really only an excuse to introduce the songs of the performer's career. The music would be good, the movie bad. Some of the better biographical musicals were those of George M. Cohan (*Yankee Doodle Dandy* (1942), danced and played by the strutting James Cagney), Al Jolson, Ruth Etting, Florenz Ziegfeld, Jane Froman, Victor Herbert, and Glenn Miller. Others were disasters. Despite the fact that *Night and Day* (1945)—the biography of Cole Porter—had a promising cast (Cary Grant, Jane Wyman and Ginny Sims) and also included his most memorable songs, the movie was a dismal failure, only remotely resembling Porter's actual life.

The war years made the musical a must. The lonely G.I.'s wanted the gaiety, color, lightness, and escapism offered by song-and-dance films. Studios were hard-put to find talented male performers, since so many had been drafted into the Armed Forces. Talent scouts trooped out younger actors, some good and others bad, who helped fill the places of departed stars. Ginger Rogers, Rita Hayworth, Deanna Durbin, Betty Hutton, Donald O'Connor, Betty Grable, and Gloria Jean tapdanced, sang and strutted. *The Fleet's In* (1942), *For Me and My Gal* (1942), *Lady in the Dark* (1943), and the delightful *Cover Girl* (1944) helped many a homesick G.I. through solitary nights.

The year 1944 was a milestone in musical films, for MGM (a rich studio with much musical talent under contract), in order to please the younger crowds that were gathering at the box office, decided to do musical films on a large scale. Their efforts were so successful that film critics refer to the decade of the late 1940's and early 1950's as the Golden Era of the Musical. Stars Fred Astaire, Judy Garland, Gene Kelly, Cyd Charisse, and Leslie Caron; writers Betty Comden, Adolph

Green, and Arthur Freed; and directors Vincente Minnelli, Stanley Donen, and Gene Kelly were exemplars of this musical renaissance.

In the 1940's and 1950's, surrounded by a talented staff from Broadway and old hands from the prewar cinema, MGM continued to dominate the musical scene, turning out *The Ziegfeld Follies* (1944), *The Band Wagon* (1953), and *Funny Face* (1956). Out of these many musicals came one of the best, Vincente Minnelli's *Meet Me in St. Louis* (1944).

Minnelli's picture changed the song and dance genre and opened new vistas for others that followed. Chuck Walters choreographed the superb musical numbers, and Sam Ayres and Cedric Gibbons did the sets. The songs by Hugh Martin and Ralph Blane and script by Irving Brescher and Fred Finklehoffer all helped to make the film unforgettable. *Meet Me in St. Louis* tells a warm story of an American middle-class family at the turn of the century. Judy Garland as a lovesick teen-ager and her sister Margaret O'Brien do a cakewalk number that underlines the warm affection that was part of the family relationship. Although Garland was the star and sang "The Trolley Song," "The Boy Next Door," and "Have Yourself a Merry Little Christmas," it was the poignant performance of Margaret O'Brien that is best remembered. In an unforgettable scene, the six-year-old girl, Tootie, saddened by the news that the family is to leave St. Louis to live in New York, says goodbye to her snowman. Another memorable moment is the Halloween bonfire celebration when the little girl wants so desperately to be accepted by her companions. Tootie proves her bravery by throwing flour in the face of Mr. Brockhoff, the meanest man in town, and then runs away for dear life.

Minnelli's art is skillfully revealed in the sequence of the child in flight, the menacing trees, the dark sky, and the ominous noises. The fear of supernatural spirits is realized just by Tootie's facial expressions as she hurries back to her friends. The director's creative genius made the scene a moment of great poignancy. His musical gave the screen carefully meshed songs, beautiful sets, music, and dancing all woven together in an artful film.

The Band Wagon (1953) is another Minnelli musical that shows the form at its very best. Technicolor, songs, scenic designs, costumes and camerawork are superb. The choreography (Michael Kidd) is, however, the most important factor. Jack Buchanan, Nanette Fabray, Oscar Levant, and Fred Astaire are whacky, malicious, and delightful. The piece is filled with singable songs and swaying rhythms. The climax of the picture is the "Girl Hunt" ballet with the incomparable Cyd Charisse doing a spoof of Mickey Spillane's gangster thrillers with Astaire. The satire of the private eye, the gangster, and the gun moll, the chorus acrobatics, the use of guns and knives are contemporary dancing at its best. Minnelli's visual images and montage keep dramatic incidents shifting from one locale to another. The picture is filled with evocative imagery, lights, music, and movement that make the American musical top entertainment, and *The Band Wagon* nothing short of sensational.

No view of the musical screen is complete without a note on Gene Kelly, the American actor-dancer-choreographer-director. Kelly left Broadway for *For Me and My Gal* (1942), and from that year he, along with a few others, dominated musical films for two decades. His films had the best box office returns in musical history. In his early films, he was lucky to be supported both by the young Frank Sinatra and by witty scripts from the writing team of Betty Comden and Adolph Green. *Anchors Aweigh* (1945) and *On the Town* (1949) were two of the most original musicals to hit the screen.

On the Town (1949), recognized by some critics as perhaps the funniest screen musical, is a magical film that had top-flight talent working for it. Aided by Adolph Green and Betty Comden, who wrote the lyrics and the script, and Harold Rossen who handled the camera, Gene Kelly and Stanley Donen turned out one of Hollywood's most exhilarating and influential musicals. No one talks in this movie if song and dance will do instead. The sextet of principals in perpetual motion light up the screen with their enthusiasm, vivacity, and talent. The picture has unfaltering pace, rapid humor, and some devastating song-and-tap routines. It is American musical talent at its best.

The story (hardly important) serves as a thread to show off the talents of the performers. Three American sailors (Frank Sinatra, Jules Munshin, and Gene Kelly), on a 24-hour leave in New York pair off with three girls (Vera Ellen, Betty Garrett, and Ann Miller). The picture never lags or ceases to sparkle. The three couples go on the town, laughing, joking, bickering, bantering, and finally kissing goodbye. *On the Town* reflects the exuberance of postwar America. It also is an example of Hollywood's knowhow when it comes to making splendid musicals. Soon after came the exceptional *An American in Paris* (1951), which was directed by Minnelli.

The following year, Stanley Donen and Gene Kelly teamed up to give the screen what is perhaps its greatest musical, *Singin' in the Rain* (1952).

If *Meet Me in St. Louis* was the musical of the 1940's, then *Singin' in the Rain* (1952) was the musical not only of the 1950's but also for all time. Other efforts pale in comparison to this hilariously good-natured satire of the early "talkies"; for sheer fun it has never been surpassed. The plot burlesques the Hollywood of 1927, in the transition period from the silents to sound films. The picture is a delightful romp that affectionately satirizes the industry's awkward efforts to make musicals. Filled with movie vamps, automobiles, flappers, and the glamorous, phony world of Hollywood in the 1920's, *Singin' in the Rain* is an exhilarating musical. Jean Hagen as the brainless movie queen Lina Lamont, who fights the battle of the microphone, gives a deadpan performance that drives the picture to a high pitch of entertaining mayhem. Gene Kelly, Donald O'Connor, and Debbie Reynolds turn *Rain* into not only an enjoyable but also a thoughtful picture. The film is never cloying or overly sentimental but bubbles with vivacity and humor. Adolph Green and Betty Comden, two writers noted for their clever, brittle work on Broadway as well as in film, collaborated on the book, and Gene Kelly and Stanley Donen choreographed and directed. These four, backed up by music from Arthur Freed and Nacio Herb Brown, offered the public an affectionate and witty film.

By 1955, the musical began to lose its popularity and the "Golden Era" was over. The cycle was failing to draw crowds at the box office, and as social problems became increasingly more important, fans were no longer interested in musical films. Some of the biggest names were disappearing from the screen. Fred Astaire and Gene Kelly donned their dancing shoes only on special occasions; Betty Grable was offered few pictures; Rita Hayworth retired from musicals; Leslie Caron and Ginger Rogers turned to drama.

Toward the end of the decade, the screen offered little originality; instead, it presented photographed Broadway hits: *Oklahoma* (1955), *Carousel* (1956), *The Pajama Game* (1957), *South Pacific* (1958), *The King and I* (1956), *Bye,*

Bye, Birdie (1962), and *My Fair Lady* (1964). Although
filmed at tremendous cost, most were tremendous bores. Hollywood appeared to have no one to replace the inventive
Busby Berkeley, Fred Astaire, Gene Kelly, Vincente Minnelli
or Stanley Donen.

The 1960's musicals (if they were not Broadway remakes)
consisted of stereotyped program pictures starring Elvis
Presley, Ann-Margret, Pat Boone, and, later, Frankie Avalon
and Annette Funicello in their *Beach Party* series. A last
magnificent effort was made with *The Sound of Music*
(1965), not really a musical but a movie with music, and
featuring Julie Andrews, but it failed to bring the musical
back to its old status. The picture combined song, scenery,
and politics and made box office history, but for some reason
studios did not follow with similar films. The motion picture
industry had apparently forgotten the formula for its past
successes, namely, musicals written directly for the screen
that banish dull, everyday cares. The Broadway musical was
substituted without much success. As the genre lay neglected,
Cabaret (1972) pumped new life into the changing genre.

Based on a Broadway play, *Cabaret* is an imaginative, dazzling film. Unlike most other musicals, its theme is grim—it
presents a decadent, anti-Semitic Germany on the brink of
Nazism. Bob Fosse's sensual musical numbers and choreography capture the aura of corruption and moral decay, and are
actually commentaries on the end of the Weimar government
and the rise of Hitler's Third Reich.

Set in Berlin in 1931, the story revolves around Sally Bowles
(Liza Minnelli), an ambitious American entertainer who
works in the Kit-Kat Klub, lives in a boarding house, and
meets people from every level of German society. The Kit-
Kat Klub's lewd, mocking and sinister master of ceremonies
—played superbly by Joel Grey—is the personification of de-
cadence, and he joins Sally in several provocative song-and-
dance routines. No other musical in screen history so skillfully
interweaves musical numbers with the story line. *Cabaret* is
hard, unsentimental cinema; it is also an example of the musical at its best.

Mean Streets (1973) and *Taxi Driver* (1976) marked
Martin Scorsese as one of the industry's most creative directors. Each of his films make strong personal statements about
contemporary society. In his most recent film, he turned back

to the 1940's musicals with their big bands, inane comedy, and free-and-easy camaraderie among musicians. *New York, New York* (1977) has no murder, no madness, no ugly look at Gotham. Nostalgia abounds. Scorsese has caught the look, rhythm and feel of the old musicals and has also captured the loneliness and darkness behind this mass-culture fantasy. *New York, New York* is Scorsese's first musical and most original film, filled with feeling, inventiveness, and intelligence.

Jimmy Doyle (Robert DeNiro), boy saxaphonist, and Francine Evans (Liza Minnelli), girl vocalist, meet, are hostile to each other, and then find love. Francine becomes a big star, and the story leads into a love-versus-career conflict. Scorsese sets the tempo with his long epic opening: V-J Day 1945, at a gigantic rooftop night club with all New York below. The movie excels in photography, production design, soundtrack, and sets. Minnelli and DeNiro capture the emotional texture of the old and new. *New York, New York* is a memorable musical, thanks to Martin Scorsese's brilliant direction.

Created and developed in the West Coast studios, the musical, like the Western, is a supremely American contribution to the cinema. Al Jolson singing "Mammy" in *The Jazz Singer* (1927) launched the genre. In the beginning years, Hollywood, in its search for material, leaned heavily on the show-biz backstage formula. By 1929, approximately seventy musical films had appeared, almost all with the same basic story. Broadway performers rushed to the West Coast, but many could not adapt to the demands of the camera, and Hollywood was forced to develop its own musical talent. Buddy Rogers and Nancy Carroll, the first popular musical team, are an example. Musical revues copied from Broadway remained a staple of the early years, reaching their height with Vincente Minnelli's *Ziegfeld Follies* (1946).

During the Depression, economic stringency forced producers to eschew technical innovations, particularly Technicolor. When *The Wizard of Oz* (1939) used color to full effect, color became a necessary ingredient for every production.

By 1933, early film revues and operettas, reflecting the popular Broadway influence, gave way to a distinguished musical film style. *Forty-Second Street* (1933) and *Flying Down to Rio* (1933) introduced a real jazz beat and made tap dancing the basis for choreography. Busby Berkeley, whose formalized dance production numbers were a unique feature of the big Hollywood musical, brought discipline to the genre and saved the musical.

By the 1940's, the industry established the characteristics of the Hollywood musical: lavish but tasteful productions, original screenplays, effective use of color, musical numbers integrated with the story, and, above all, excellent music and dancing. By the end of the 1950's, a declining box office and increasing costs were making elaborate musicals an economic problem. Tastes were changing, too. The storybook exuberance of the musical was replaced by stories that offered intimacy, sentimentality and a kind of realism. In the late 1960's, Hollywood turned to Broadway and transferred theater hits into dull movies. Films such as *Oliver* (1968), *Funny Girl* (1968), *Paint Your Wagon* (1969), and *Hello, Dolly* (1969) may mark the farewell to big stereophonic musicals.

Perhaps *Cabaret* (1972) has re-opened the way, showing how imagination, taste, and a thoughtful theme could be combined to create a musical with wit, style, and political observations. Future productions will have singing and dancing, but the plots will confront such problems as political issues, world affairs, and social problems.

Outstanding Musicals
and Their Directors

Broadway Melody	(1929)	Harry Beaumont
Sunny Side Up	(1929)	David Butler
The Love Parade	(1930)	Ernst Lubitsch
Forty-Second Street	(1933)	Busby Berkeley and Lloyd Bacon
Footlight Parade	(1933)	Busby Berkeley and Lloyd Bacon
Gold Diggers of 1933	(1933)	Busby Berkeley and Mervyn LeRoy
The Gay Divorcee	(1934)	Mark Sandrich
Top Hat	(1935)	Mark Sandrich
Born to Dance	(1936)	Roy Del Ruth
Swing Time	(1936)	George Stevens
The Broadway Melody	(1938)	Roy Del Ruth
The Wizard of Oz	(1939)	Victor Fleming
Meet Me in St. Louis	(1944)	Vincente Minnelli
On the Town	(1949)	Gene Kelly and Stanley Donen
An American in Paris	(1951)	Vincente Minnelli
Singin' in the Rain	(1952)	Gene Kelly and Stanley Donen
The Band Wagon	(1953)	Vincente Minnelli
Cabaret	(1972)	Bob Fosse
New York, New York	(1977)	Martin Scorsese

17 / The Comedy Film

FILM HISTORIANS consider Lumière's *Watering the Gardener* (1896) the first screen comedy. A single sight gag serves as the basis for the story. A mischievous boy stands on a garden hose and stops the flow of water. When the gardener peers into the nozzle to see what's wrong, the boy removes his foot and the curious man is soaked. Audiences laughed at the victim with his wet head and deflated ego. Thus filmmakers discovered two never-failing ingredients for comedy: take any innocent bystander and make him the butt of a physical prank; deflate authority.

By 1905, moviemakers, who had previously been content to photograph belly dancers, circus acts, trains rushing toward the audience, and guns blazing into the faces of spectators, realized that the naughty boy with the garden hose opened the door to slapstick, and through that door came a parade of outstanding movie clowns.

It was the French who first specialized in film humor, excelling at the genre during the first decade of the twentieth century. Many of their films employed trick photography. Fans enjoyed comedies in which old ladies took their protesting husbands to visit museums and then dragged them away from nude female statues.

American studies were initially more interested in melodrama than comedies. But in 1911, Vitagraph introduced one of the first important comic stars, the rotund British actor, John Bunny. With Flora Finch as his partner, Bunny romped through dozens of short but amusing slapstick films based on the fat hero's social blunders. The public kept calling for more, and within a year Bunny was commanding a salary of $1,000 a week.

Other studios followed suit. The Essanay Company produced a series entitled "Snakeville Comedies," with Wallace Beery as the promising star. In 1912, Mack Sennett, America's "King of Comedy," a circus performer, directed his first film at the Keystone Studios, and a year later he introduced the madcap Keystone Kops in *The Bangville Police*. (Mack Sennett and Charlie Chaplin are discussed at length in Part I.)

In the 1920's, Rudolph Valentino tangoed his way into feminine hearts, Greta Garbo lured men to their untimely deaths, Lillian Gish fought her way through a cruel world, and Gloria Swanson simpered in her milk bath, but the fans lined up at the box office to see America's emerging young comedians. These court jesters were permitted outrageous license as they ridiculed social and political institutions, romance, and high society. They particularly enjoyed deflating fellow-actors and their "art" movies. No one could possibly take Rudolph Valentino's *The Sheik* seriously after seeing Ben Turpin's *The Shriek of Araby* (1923). If one half of the world believed in the phony intoxicating romances of Elinor Glyn's *Three Weeks*, the other half laughed at Mack Sennett's burlesque of Ruritania in *Three and a Half Weeks* (1924). Cecil B. DeMille's Biblical epics were brilliantly spoofed by Buster Keaton's *The Three Ages* (1923), and Stan Laurel in *Mud and Sand* (1922) similarly mocked Rudolph Valentino in *Blood and Sand*.

Although Charlie Chaplin was the superstar of the genre, he shared the spotlight with a few other comedians. The best to dominate the screen along with Chaplin until sound came along were Buster Keaton, Harold Lloyd, and Harry Langdon; and although all were creative artists in their own right, these three were destined to work in Chaplin's shadow.

For almost a decade, the one performer to threaten Chaplin's throne for any length of time was Harold Lloyd. After years of searching for a screen image, Lloyd's character emerged as a timid, bespectacled milksop who, in spite of his horn-rimmed glasses and straw hat always managed to overcome any obstacle in his way. Scattering kindness and sunshine wherever he went, Lloyd's comedies pleased many theater managers with high gate receipts.

Charlie Chaplin's tramp was not only whimsical but also cruel. He could whack his opponent over the head with a club, slam doors on fingers, drop anvils on toes, kick other people in the backside, and hurl splattering pies in society women's faces. Harold Lloyd's wholesome young man might accidentally set off a chain of catastrophes, but he never would intentionally harm anyone. He may be the sincere, wide-eyed all-American jerk victimized by con artists, but eventually "Good Old Harold" defeated the rogues and succeeded in every endeavor, no matter how high the odds against him. His "try and win" philosophy seemed sincere, for he believed in himself.

Grandma's Boy (1922) was the first film to present the Lloyd image of the eager, clean-cut, bumbling young man who, despite his awkwardness, goes on to overcome villains and other obstacles and thereby win the pretty but vacuous heroine. Lloyd not only found a screen character but also a certain type of story that rocketed him to the top of the film world. Critics dubbed them "thrill comedies," for various scripts had the hero climbing high buildings, zipping down gridirons past countless opponents to make the saving touchdown, or facing the horror of mirrors in a circus fun house. Lloyd's portrayal of the shy country boy in the "thrill comedies" carried him to the zenith of fame during the 1920's.

Never venturing into the land of fantasy, the films utilized only commonplace material. With skillful editing, the comedies were high cinema. *Safety Last* (1923) contains the ingredients that characterize a Lloyd picture. Wanting to appear as a success to his girlfriend, Harold goes along with a publicity stunt by assuming a friend's role as a human fly. The "fly" must climb to the top of a twenty-story building. Harold, frightened but determined, begins his ascent, and on his perilous way encounters pigeons, mice, flagpoles, swinging windows, a clock, and even a tennis net. Dangling dangerously above the street while still wearing his glasses and a straw hat, our hero reaches the top and wins the girl. The audience cheers his courage. *Grandma's Boy* (1922), *Safety Last* (1923), and *The Freshman* (1925) carried American comedy to new heights.

Harry Langdon's "dumb clown" took him to the top, but, unfortunately, did not keep him there. His first and best full-length comedy was *Tramp, Tramp, Tramp* (1926), directed by Harry Edwards, followed by *The Strong Man* (1926) and *Long Pants* (1927), both directed by Frank Capra. Langdon had the good fortune to be manipulated through his silent comedies by the inventive director Capra. Harry's innocent looks made him resemble a child who could never figure anything out. Although he excelled at subtle pantomime, his comic techniques was very specialized, and the public often misunderstood his humor. After *The Chase* (1929) and *Heart Trouble* (1928) he faded into obscurity.

Buster Keaton, the clown who never smiled, was not a serious threat to Chaplin in his own time. But critics have been reevaluating his efforts, and a few pronounce him superior to the English comedian. Keaton lived in a world of intimidating circumstances. Armed with indomitable courage he succeeds whatever the odds, refusing to be crushed by wind, rain, snow, trains, boats, animals, or men. Charlie Chaplin's little tramp ended up with nothing, but Keaton's stone face and acrobatic skill conquered all problems and often won the girl.

Sherlock Junior (1924) proved just how inventive Keaton's comic genius could be, but *The General* (1927), a radical departure from the comic tradition of the 1920's, is his best film. It is dramatic comedy rather than slapstick, and some critics declare that it is even superior to Chaplin's *The Gold Rush* (1925).

The story concerns the adventures of a Southern engineer who loves his locomotive, the General, as much as his girlfriend Annabelle. During the Civil War, Keaton's engine is hijacked by a band of Union raiders who make a run back to Chattanooga. Annabelle is an unwilling passenger in the heist. When Keaton realizes that his locomotive has been stolen, he sets out into northern territory to find his beloved engine and bring it home. The journey North and the return with Annabelle and the General is the cleverest, longest, and most skillful chase sequence in film, occupying seven of the eight reels. During the rescue, our hero is confronted with machines that think and men who pursue and kill each other. Over battlefields, up mountains, and across bridges, the little engineer and Annabelle bring the locomotive happily to rest on Confederate soil. The ingenious sight gags make this silent film particularly noteworthy, as fewer than fifty subtitles are needed in order to explain the story.

Keaton's reputation grows each year as new generations of fans discover the sophistication beneath the deadpan mask. His best films are *Sherlock Junior* (1924), *The Navigator* (1924), and of course his masterpiece, *The General*.

The invention of sound ended the fun. All four comedians saw their public turn to new talent. Langdon slipped into oblivion and the wealthy Lloyd all but retired. Chaplin, realizing that his "Little Tramp" would lose his charm if he spoke, put the lovable character on the shelf and used the screen to preach instead, at times forgetting to be funny. Keaton slipped from star status to making only guest appear-

ances. The stone-faced comedian, unable to find a suitable
script, and after a series of failures, was gaining a fresh popularity at the time of his death in 1966.

The key mimes, the last examples of the *commedia
dell'arte*, were replaced by Broadway musical talent. The
wonderful world of slapstick gave way to the insinuating Mae
West, the snide remarks of W. C. Fields, the repartee of
Wheeler and Woolsey, the Three Stooges, the effervescent
Eddie Cantor, and the mad world of the Marx Brothers.

With the invention of sound, comedy changed more than
any other film genre. Chaplin, Keaton, Lloyd, and others had
offered sight gags and "the chase." Some of the early sound
comedies relied on sight gags, but sound meant mostly vaudeville routines and songs. Its appeal was principally aural.

The Marx Brothers, a family of the most disreputable figures the screen has ever presented, dominated screen comedy
in the 1930's. After years in vaudeville, the four brothers—
Groucho, Chico, Harpo and Zeppo—brought their crazy
world of mayhem to be captured on film. Their first picture,
The Cocoanuts (1929), bombards moviegoers with sight
gags, props, puns, running comments, and a world in which
normal behavior is stamped upon and ridiculed. Their
routines are made up of zany humor, verbal jokes, and maniacal demolition of the scenery.

In *Duck Soup* (1933), *A Night at the Opera* (1935) and
A Day at the Races (1937), they make viewers accept their
madness as a philosophy of life. Insane dialogue is counter-
balanced and alternated with frantic activity. Every film follows a basic tenet: ridicule everything in life. Armed with
verbal hatchets, they demolish middle-class virtues. With eyes
aflame, heads to the wind, and spouting absurd epigrams,
they pursue and ridicule charlatans in the fields of education,
medicine, politics, and law.

If Sennett's Keystone Kops offered an absurd world to
silent films, then the Marx Brothers, aided by the stately Margaret Dumont, introduced the world of the absurd to sound.
Like the Keystone Kops, they offered a madcap universe of
concentrated anarchy. Like the Mack Sennett clowns, they in-
habited a madcap universe where insanity was normal.

Laurel and Hardy, the Ritz Brothers, The Three Stooges,
Leon Errol, Will Rogers, Jack Benny, Eddie Cantor and Joe
E. Brown clowned and cavorted through the comedies of the
1930's, but along with the Marx Brothers, the best comedians

of the decade were the archetypal sex symbol Mae West and the bulbous-nosed, gravel-voiced misanthrope, W. C. Fields.

The phenomenon of the time was Mae West, the anachronistic embodiment of the Victorian male's erotic dreams carried to comic extremes. West burst upon the American screen at a time it needed both new comedy and new escape. Clever, humorous, and above all, businesslike, she parlayed a single idea, the human sex drive, into a lifetime career. Mae, who came West from road shows and the Broadway stage, wrote her own material, supervised her own costuming, and very shrewdly managed every platinum thread of her larger-than-life-sized image.

When Mae sashayed down the staircase in *Night After Night* (1932), she not only turned a drab movie into a hit but also saved Paramount from bankruptcy. Fans loved the undulating blonde who kept eyeing her leading men and the audience, inviting each and every one in her immoral invitation, "Come up and see me some time." Millions of Americans did. She expressed open pleasure at the embraces of men and was the first star in screen history to brush aside romantic love. There was no pretense to La West. She came to the point, and unlike her movie sisters, who sinned but always suffered—Joan Crawford, Norma Shearer, Barbara Stanwyck, or Constance Bennett—Miss West never gave the idea that she had been tricked into a life of wickedness. What is more, she never denounced her sinful ways but instead gave the impression that she loved the luxury that accompanied them. Mae seemed to enjoy being wicked, wealthy, and popular with men. She was always a character who openly liked furs, motor cars, and diamonds, and admitted the fact that she enjoyed her work. Her dialogue and physical twitching hastened Joseph Breen's censorship council to check what some thought was an advancing tide of pornography. And in order to appease the censors, Mae would at the end of her films (with a sly wink at the audience) admit that she was a good simple girl who really wanted most in life to find a good dependable man. *She Done Him Wrong* (1933) and *I'm No Angel* (1933) broke box office records. The success of these two films helped persuade Paramount not to sell out to MGM.

Teamed with a succession of virile leading men, Mae and her films were and are a minor Camp art form in themselves. She co-starred with that improbable leading man, W. C. Fields, in *My Little Chickadee* (1940), the two stars provided a healthy antidote for Depression aftermath and a fascinating subject for students of the American scene. West, a living parody of the American romantic dream, and Fields, the misogynist, a Dickensian lower-middle-class anachronism, motivated by self-centeredness and cupidity, a forerunner of the "Theater of Cruelty," together offered the talkies blue dialogue, contributed to the tightening of Hays Office censorship, and provided a depressed nation with a chance to laugh at life and, particularly, sex.

W. C. Fields, the screen's nasty old man with the scratchy voice, stood his ground against an intrusive world by uttering clichés and doing some heavy drinking. Fields sputtered, insulted, and threatened enemies who seemed unaware of his very existence. Fields, with his acid wit, helped shred the tattred fabric of the American Dream.

Fans loved Fields best when he enumerated and attacked his pet peeves; children, animals, marriage, helpful old ladies, the law, hard work, anything sweet and sentimental. His long list of screen successes included *It's a Gift* (1934), *The Bank Dick* (1941), and *Never Give a Sucker an Even Break* (1941). Along with Mae West and the Marx Brothers, W. C. Fields brought a gaudy, vulgar type of comedy to the screen that was welcome at a time when the Hollywood dream factory was busy making films with artificial glamour and sentimentality.

In contrast to the slapstick comedy of the 1920's, in the 1930's there appeared the successfully romantic "screwball" comedy. For a decade the lunatic, merry world of gay characters brightened many a dull Depression evening. Frank Capra and Robert Riskin were the creators of this style of comedy. Their film starring Clark Gable and Claudette Colbert, *It Happened One Night* (1934), was replete with funny, romantic, rich, and whimsical characters.

The Capra-Riskin screwball nonsense was followed by a spate of comedies that presented eccentric or fey characters who were both charming and likable, who found the world attractive and enjoyable. These characters created their own type of private fun and offered "in" jokes with subtle, hidden meanings. Amusing situations depended on sight gags, absurd mixups, the unexpected, and, above all, brittle repartee. Not since Lubitsch had the screen enjoyed such clever madness. The farcical situations offered badinage that showed the public just how entertaining words could be.

It Happened One Night is light fluff, but the dialogue, acting and direction are superb. Claudette Colbert (the daughter of a millionaire) travels incognito by bus from Miami to New York, running away from her determined father. Clark Gable, an unemployed newspaperman, recognizes the heiress, and sensing an exclusive story, decides to ride along and gather material for his article on "Rich Society Girl's Flight to Happiness." Colbert and Gable, snarling and pretending to hate each other, are forced to stay overnight in various auto camps. Eventually the chemistry of sex begins to work. The film's theme told what many Americans during the Depression found out to be true: money alone can guarantee neither a good time nor lasting happiness—a theme that was treated seriously by Orson Welles in *Citizen Kane* some seven years later. In the romantic tradition of the 1930's, the two live happily ever after. Capra's film, the best comedy of the decade, earned five Oscars.

Other studios hurried their performers into the screwball comedy cycle, and within a year theaters were inundated with zany comedies filled with absurdly exaggerated characters. The best actress for this type of film was the acid-tongued comedienne Carole Lombard. Her beauty, joined with an often vicious and rapacious wit, made her the paradox of the film world. She proved herself a star with *My Man Godfrey* (1937) and *Nothing Sacred* (1937). Lombard shared the screwball world with Myrna Loy and William Powell, who played a charming man and wife team in *The Thin Man* series directed by W. S. Van Dyke. This series broke the stereotyped pattern of movie couples, showing the public that a man and his very own wife could be witty, human, funny, and madly in love with each other. Katharine Hepburn teamed with debonair Cary Grant to turn out a satirical screwball farce in *Bringing Up Baby* (1938). Henry Fonda and Barbara Stanwyck made *The Mad Miss Manton* (1938), and Rosalind Russell in *Hired Wife* (1940) fought, bickered, and kicked her employer-husband squarely on his backside. *You Can't Take It With You* (1938) revealed the antics of a whole family of screwballs who took ballet lessons, collected snakes, and made fireworks in their basement. By 1938, these racy, witty pictures, concerned with unusually clever Americans, drove the Ernst Lubitsch high-style European comedies off the screen. America came into its own heritage.

During the 1940's, war comedies became springboards for comedy performers. Indulging in what was at that time considered clever repartee and broad slapstick, Paramount, Columbia, and RKO attempted farces with the Andrews Sisters, Martha Raye, Red Skelton, Edgar Bergen and his dummy Charlie McCarthy, Bob Hope and Bing Crosby, Alice Faye, Ray Bolger, Danny Kaye, and Carmen Miranda. The most overrated comedy team for a decade was Bud Abbott and Lou Costello, two knockabout funnymen who relied nearly exclusively on gags, verbal jokes, and slapstick to achieve rather repetitive and boring comic effects.

Writer-director Preston Sturges's comedies dominated the 1940's, but he subsequently lost steam and purpose, leaving behind several intriguing and offbeat satires. In each film he presented his own freewheeling, witty, personal vision of the world. He believed that chance determines success and insecurity was an enforced way of life. His films exploit visual incongruity and humiliation. He mocked social convention, apparently approving amoral standards. Characters with dignity are invariably pulled into slapstick situations—for example, Henry Fonda and Barbara Stanwyck in *The Lady Eve* (1941), and Eddie Bracken, forced to masquerade as a war hero in *Hail the Conquering Hero* (1944). Two of the best examples of the humiliation theme are the hoax played on Dick Powell in *Christmas in July* (1940) and Joel McCrea being stripped of his identity in *Sullivan's Travels* (1942). Sturges's comedies were in marked contrast to the sugary entertainment of wartime.

The Lady Eve (1941), with Barbara Stanwyck, is an amusing trifle of gaiety, lightness, and charm, a scintillating comedy of manners. Sturges's pictures are fast-paced, and often contradictory, polished and well-structured, filled with believable characters.

Comedy was not a major part of the Hollywood scene during the 1950's, although Spencer Tracy and Joan Bennett attempted to be funny in *Father of the Bride* (1950) and Donald O'Connor had a talking mule for a friend in *Francis* (1950). The brightest comedies of the decade were the films of Judy Holliday and Marilyn Monroe. Holliday rose to stardom in a filmed Broadway play *Born Yesterday* (1950), in which she portrayed a daffy dumb blonde. She went on to make *The Solid Gold Cadillac* (1956) and *Bells Are Ringing* (1959). With each picture she demonstrated her agility as a comedienne.

Marilyn Monroe, presented as a cross between the wisecracking Jean Harlow and a young Mae West, pouted and undulated through a series of satirical comedies and musicals. Her superior performance in Billy Wilder's *Some Like It Hot* (1960) helped make this the best screen comedy since World War II. Her co-stars, Jack Lemmon and Tony Curtis, fearing for their lives after witnessing a gangland massacre, masquerade as two girls, joining an all-girl jazz band en route to an engagement in Miami Beach. Aboard a Pullman train, the men share close quarters with the voluptuous girls, and the overnight journey becomes a frantic romp. Wilder sprinkled his story with outlandish slapstick, ridiculous impersonations, sex jokes, and casual eroticism in order to make ironic comments on American mores of the late 1920's.

Aside from Holliday and Monroe's appearances, the decade produced almost no outstanding film comedies. Bob Hope continued in his usual format, Lucille Ball was occupied with television, Danny Kaye made a series of dull films, and Doris Day and Rock Hudson were seldom funny. Jerry Lewis and Dean Martin separated to go their individual ways.

Black Comedy emerged in the 1960's. Harking back to Charlie Chaplin's wicked but funny wife-murderer in *Monsieur Verdoux* (1947), Hollywood came out with outrageously comic films about heretofore serious subjects. Nothing escaped ridicule. Psychoanalysis, brotherhood, love, sexual perversion, mothers, racism, murder—all were fair game for the satirists. The younger generation crowded into the theaters and shouted approval as one tradition after another was shot down.

One of the most startling Black Comedies was Stanley Kubrick's *Dr. Strangelove, or How I Learned to Stop Worrying and Love the Bomb* (1964), a satire about a nuclear holocaust, whose similarities to Sidney Lumet's *Fail Safe* (1964) caused producers to consider a suit for plagiarism. Kubrick's theme was deadly serious, yet he treated it as an enormous cinematic joke. Audiences loved it.

Strangelove concerns a psychotic right-wing general who believes that Communists are poisoning America through fluoridation of the water. In his madness, he orders a nuclear attack on the Soviet Union, and American bombers take off at once. All are recalled by a frantic U. S. President, except for one damaged bomber that doesn't receive the message. The plane keeps heading relentlessly toward Russia, manned by a flight crew that could have come straight out of a 1940's Hollywood war film, including a Negro bombardier, a whooping, hollering Texan, and a Jewish radio operator. Engaging in tough talk, smutty humor, and mushy sentiment about being friends forever, they are determined to destroy the "Commie punks." But once they release their bomb, the Russians' Doomsday Machine is automatically activated, spreading a blanket of atomic fallout over the earth. The film ends as the world vanishes in a mushroom cloud, while a velvety-voiced soprano sings "We'll Meet Again." This final holocaust is actually terrifying because it is so plausible, yet audiences can't help but laugh as the world races headlong to destruction.

In portraying the lunacy of the world situation and the madness of scientists, generals, and politicians, Kubrick created one of the screen's funniest and sickest films—truly a masterpiece of Black Comedy. Other directors soon followed his lead. Tony Richardson's sick satire *The Loved One* (1965) features a wild party at a funeral parlor, where girls leap out of caskets, chalky morticians usher visitors into embalming rooms, and dead military men are shot into space to circle the earth forever. Alan Arkin's *Little Murders* (1971), written by Jules Feiffer, spoofs urban crime and violence. *Putney Swope* (1970) concerns a black man who accidentally becomes president of an all-white advertising agency. He declares he won't rock the boat—just sink it—and then proceeds to place profane commercials on television and otherwise upset the Establishment.

The Graduate (1967), directed by Mike Nichols, presented a minor off-Broadway actor, Dustin Hoffman, in a satire on the tyranny of America's social and sexual customs. The film gave Hollywood its breakthrough into the elusive 18-to-25-year-old market, and needless to say, Hoffman established himself as one of America's best actors.

In *The Graduate*, Hoffman is Benjamin Braddock, just out of college, an inert, inarticulate schlemiel living in a well-to-do suburb of Los Angeles. Ben is the victim of his parents' affluence. Along with their wealth, they parade him as an object before their friends. Mrs. Robinson, a frustrated neighbor, introduces Ben to sex, and he then falls in love with her daughter Elaine.

What made *The Graduate* an influential movie was its witty, brittle dialogue and the scenes filled with hilarious comments on the mores of American life. Its comparative frankness in sexual matters made it a critical and commercial success. The director's outlook on middle-class aspirations gained him a following among young movie audiences, who were anxious to find new myths to replace the old. Nichols's film on the generation gap spawned dozens of imitations.

Robert Altman's *M*A*S*H* (Mobile Army Surgical Hospital) (1970), awarded the Oscar for the year's best screenplay, is a bitter, cynical farce concerning the staff of an Army hospital in Korea during the war. Almost as devastating as Stanley Kubrick's *Strangelove*, Altman's Black Comedy, filled with gags, slapstick, abrasive dialogue, dirty nastiness, and hilarious situations, deals with gruesome situations, blood and gore, cruelty, and zany characters. It openly ridicules belief in God. The film is so anti-military that the U. S. Army, Navy, and Air Force banned it from all service theaters. *M*A*S*H* offers cool wit, emotional freedom, and shocking good sense. The film shows the mad antics of the doctors, nurses, and enlisted men of a medical unit in a field hospital on the 38th Parallel during the war in Korea, hardly the setting for comedy. The heroes are a trio of fun-loving guys with quick wit, who go for their victim's jugular vein.

The main action is in a surgical ward, with doctors working on maimed war casualties making dispassionate observations on sex and life as they saw bones, cut out vital organs, and throw human parts and bloodsoaked rags on the floor. There is a steady processing of bloody meat, slaughterhouse details of operations, wisecracks, and sex. It offers the last bleeding word on doctor-hospital jokes. Bodies are taken from stretchers to operating rooms to coffins. Sex, religion, the medical profession, and, most of all, military life are reduced to shambles. Altman cross-cuts between lunatic sex scenes to a graphically depicted operating room. *M*A*S*H* heads the screen's list as the most hilarious and repugnant comedy to date.

*M*A*S*H* (1970) and *Dr. Strangelove* (1964) and, running a close third, *The Graduate* (1967) push comedy to its blackest limits—films that ridicule every principle that for generations civilization has revered.

The three best things to happen to comedy in the 1970's were Mel Brooks, Elaine May, and Woody Allen. Interestingly, all three are writers-performers-directors.

Elaine May and Mike Nichols were a unique comedy team in the early 1960's; both turned to directing movies, and although Elaine May has only two films to her credit, it is obvious that hers is a talent of distinction. *A New Leaf* (1970) and *The Heartbreak Kid* (1972) are brilliant caricatures that examine the madness of love and the anguish that may follow. In *A New Leaf*, May directs herself in the role of a dull but studious spinster, a botanist who meets a charming, aging, impecunious playboy (Walter Matthau), falls in love, and passes from an awkward individual into an understanding woman.

The Heartbreak Kid is a discomforting character study of a shrewd manipulator (Charles Grodin) who marries a sloppy lower-class Jewish girl (Jeannie Berlin, May's real-life daughter). On his honeymoon in Miami, the groom meets a cool, aloof WASP (Cybill Shepherd), deserts his wife, follows his golden girl to Minnesota, to eventually win her as his wife. Jeannie Berlin's portrayal of the comically ill-fated Lila, who is dumped three days after her marriage, is a brilliant performance of the funny-sad deserted bride. Unfortunately, the public somehow failed to understand the film's subtle observations on the American way of life, and it never received the recognition it deserved.

The comedy of Mel Brooks is the comedy of chaos, outrageous puns, wild burlesque, shouting insults, and weird sounds. *The Producers* (1968) tells of a Broadway producer hoping to do a musical on the life of Adolph Hitler.

Blazing Saddles (1974) demolishes the Western myth with sight gags, occasional obnoxious sounds, broad remarks, and several hilarious performances. It tells the story of a black sheriff in a Western town in the 1860's. Madeline Kahn and Cleavon Little, spoofing Marlene Dietrich and James Stewart, are satire at its best.

In *Silent Movie* (1976), Mel Brooks, Dom De Luise and Marty Feldman try to outsmart a conglomerate (Engulf and Devour) by making a silent movie. Muted voices, subtitles, burly humor, and sight gags, along with guest appearances by Paul Newman, Anne Bancroft, and Liza Minnelli, turn the picture into hilarious mayhem.

The most versatile talent in films today is Woody Allen, who reigns as the top comedian in American movies. Allen writes his own scripts, directs his films, and plays the leading role; on occasion, he composed the musical score. From TV comedy writer and night club monologist, Allen has climbed to the top of the comedy heap.

Allen's success is in the intellectual nature of his comedy. He appeals to the hard-to-please fan, particularly the college audience. His films have the structure of collage—blackout sketches, old newsreel footage, parodies of old movies, sight gags, fake interviews, going from bad gags to good ones. He delivers very funny, very zany comments on the contemporary scene. He is a mold-breaker. *Play It Again, Sam* (1972) is a fantasy structured around the character Humphrey Bogart played in *Casablanca* (1943).

Bananas (1971) tells, in a way, of a revolution in a Latin-American banana republic. Allen talks of Kierkegaard, mumbles comments on present-day society and plays Christ. *Sleeper* (1974), the most sustained of his comedies, has Woody awakening to discover he's two hundred years into the future. The film offers sight gags, puns, funny lines, and absurd situations. He goes from Mack Sennett slapstick to the most sophisticated screwball comedy.

Annie Hall (1977) examines the complex relationship of a modern couple. With the simplest conversation, wisecracks, telling scenes, and nervous gestures, the film pierces through to anxiety, hope, despair, and, above all, caring. The love of Allen, a Jewish New York comic, and Diane Keaton, a WASP cabaret singer from Wisconsin, reaches out for understanding to the most mature audiences. The give and take and the struggle of the lovers to understand each other is heartbreaking. *Annie Hall* displays Woody Allen's exceptional talent as an actor and supreme sensitivity as a film director.

Both Mel Brooks and Paul Morrissey have met up with the doctor-trying-to-be-God. Brooks's version, *Young Frankenstein* (1974) is a kind of craziness found in the Abbott and Costello movies. Gene Wilder, young Frankenstein, creates an excruciatingly funny operation on Liam Dunn. The movie is a farce-parody of the Hollywood mad-doctor films, and at times reaches maniacal peaks. It aspires to be entertainment.

Andy Warhol's *Frankenstein* (1974) is something else. Paul Morrissey, an underground director who has surfaced, presents a (bloody) valentine to his mentor Andy Warhol. The movie may be unsteady and unsettling, part put-on and part serious, but it has sober observations to offer its audience. Udo Kier as the Baron Frankenstein, German accent and all, brings the touch of Pygmalion to his lady monster. Beneath the cliché of the scientist-gone-mad, Morrissey shows his disgust with mainstream culture, its sexual shams, death machines and the young generation. Within this bleak, angry version there are beheadings, buckets of blood and innards pushed into the viewer's face (like a throwback to the movies of the 1950's, when audiences with special 3-D glasses watched blood and guts scenes). Perversely fascinating, the movie is the first original variation on the theme in years.

For seventy-five years, comedy has been king of the silver screen. From the first day when Edison photographed Fred Ott's crazy sneeze to the outrageous films of Mel Brooks, audiences have applauded and approved the world of laughter.

In the early days, Mack Sennett, Charlie Chaplin, Fatty Arbuckle, Buster Keaton, Mabel Normand, Chester Conklin, and dozens of others heaved custard pies, kicked policemen in the pants, and led their co-stars in a mad dance of comedy routines. Theirs was the world of the absurd.

When sound took over, the slapstick world of Buster Keaton, Larry Simon, the Keystone Kops, and Harold Lloyd ended, only to be replaced by the wisecracks of Leon Errol, W. C Fields, Eddie Cantor, and Laurel and Hardy. The high peak of comedy during the 1930's was the entrance into the studios of the greatest family comedy team of all—the Marx Brothers. Holding on to the mad world of Sennett, they helped the public for a time to forget the Depression. Mae West and W. C. Fields bolstered sagging box office receipts, raised eyebrows, and had censors back at work.

During the 1930's Frank Capra introduced fans to a world of grownups who behaved in a completely irresponsible way. Mr. Deeds, filled with small-town idealism, went to town and gave away his money; the Vanderhof family set off fireworks in the basement and paid no income tax; and Mr. Smith, honest to the point of madness, persuaded men to vote for honest government. Myrna Loy and William Powell upheld domestic virtues; the beautiful Carole Lombard, a whacky, kooky heroine, confessed to a fake murder and pretended to be dying of a rare disease. Constance Bennett and Cary Grant were sophisticated ghosts in the *Topper* series, and even the remote Garbo, with Ernst Lubitsch as her director, tried comedy. *Ninotchka* (1939) was a clever satire on Communist discipline versus the pleasures of Paris.

The 1940's offered the gag factory of Bob Hope and Bing Crosby, Olsen and Johnson, and Dean Martin and Jerry Lewis. Comedy films were turned out in mechanical fashion to help the public forget the dark war years. Fans had to be content with the uninspired shenanigans of Abbott and Costello or the raucous Judy Canova. In 1947, Charlie Chaplin's *Monsieur Verdoux*, the comical, ironic story of a bluebeard who murders his wives for money, may have repulsed the public, but it is the screen's first Black Comedy.

If the 1940's and 1950's offered a long list of dull comedies, the movies played a different tune by the 1960's. Directors working independently turned their cameras on all the sacred cows, not only milking them but blowing them apart! Black Comedy was what the public, particularly the young kids, wanted. They went into gales of laughter as each sacred tenet was smashed. Sex, religion, big business, momism, education, and Madison Avenue were targets of ridicule. *Dr. Strangelove* led the mad dance and others followed. Comedy has come full cycle from the surrealistic cruelty of the Sennett two-reelers to the realistic cruelty of *M*A*S*H*. Both were determined to be destructive as the audience died laughing.

Outstanding Comedy Films
and Their Directors

Tillie's Punctured Romance	(1914)	Mack Sennett
Safety Last	(1923)	Fred Newmayer and Sam Taylor
The Gold Rush	(1925)	Charlie Chaplin
The General	(1927)	Buster Keaton and Clyde Bruckman
Trouble in Paradise	(1932)	Ernst Lubitsch
It Happened One Night	(1934)	Frank Capra
The Lady Eve	(1941)	Preston Sturges
Monsieur Verdoux	(1947)	Charlie Chaplin
Some Like It Hot	(1959)	Billie Wilder
Dr. Strangelove, or How I Learned to Stop Worrying and Love the Bomb	(1964)	Stanley Kubrick
The Graduate	(1967)	Mike Nichols
M*A*S*H	(1970)	Robert Altman
The Heartbreak Kid	(1972)	Elaine May
Sleeper	(1974)	Woody Allen
Blazing Saddles	(1974)	Mel Brooks
Silent Movie	(1976)	Mel Brooks
Annie Hall	(1977)	Woody Allen

18 / The War Film

OF ALL the facets of life subject to the camera's interpretation, none is more horrible and more awesome to an audience (and more challenging to the cameraman) than war. The studios during the 1940's, in trying to capture this horror, turned out more pictures on this subject than at any other time in film history. Treatments of war ranged from actual documentations of overseas conflict to lighthearted portrayals of life on the home front to studio reproductions of the heroics of land combat, aerial bombing, and ocean warfare.

Any discussion of war films should begin with D. W. Griffith's monumental melodrama *The Birth of a Nation* (1915), the first American epic, concerning the Civil War and its tragic aftermath. There is only one battle sequence in the film, but that one based on Matthew Brady's photographs of actual battles; it is so graphic and devastating that few films today can equal its impact on an audience. The picture abounds with troop manipulation, exploding cannons, prancing horses, and daring deeds, and even though Griffith tended to underplay the horror of war in favor of melodrama, with officers in grand histrionic fashion rushing forward to catch a falling flag, a soldier embracing his enemy as he falls dying, a boy clutching a photograph of mother or sweetheart, the film stands as prototype for all war films.

In 1917, after America's entry into the war, the Committee on Public Information created a division of films whose purpose was to sell the war to America. Hollywood became part of that effort, turning out pictures that emphasized Prussian atrocities. These movies were made by men far removed from the actual fighting who had little practical knowledge of modern warfare. Yet their synthetic versions of conflict were more popular than the real-life war documentaries and newsreels that were reaching the United States.

Among the earliest of the propaganda films was *The Little American* (1917), which came out shortly after the Germans sank the British liner *Lusitania*. The film stars "Little Mary" Pickford, who battles the Huns and pleads for America to enter the war. As a passenger who survives the sinking of the ship (impressively staged in the film), Little Mary says, via titles: "I was neutral until I saw your men attack innocent women and murder old men. Then I stopped being neutral and I became human."

A formula for these films emerged quickly. The villain was always a fiendish, sadistic Prussian who wanted to commit unspeakable acts against the virtuous young heroine. But she was protected by the hero (an American, or perhaps, an ally), who always triumphed in the end. Battlefield heroics, behind-the-lines humor, and beautiful spies were also standard features of these movies. Walter Long and Erich von Stroheim often played the dastardly Germans (von Stroheim, in particular, became the German everyone loved to hate).

Just before the Armistice, two films appeared—Griffith's *Hearts of the World* (1918) and Chaplin's *Shoulder Arms* (1918). Griffith's moving film describes the horrors of Prussian militarism in much less simplistic fashion than other propaganda films. One heartbreaking scene takes place in a small French village overrun by the enemy. A woman has been killed, and her three young children, who are too terrified to venture outside the home, bury her in the cellar.

In the Chaplin film, a satirical, corrosive comment on war, Charlie Chaplin goes off to fight and ends up by bringing the Kaiser to London single-handedly. Chaplin offers incisive, witty observations on life in the trenches, distilled into a hard, black comic fantasy.

Most studios decided with the end of the Great War that America was not interested in a serious picture of that event. Irving Thalberg at MGM thought that the war theme might be material for yet another type of epic, and he produced *The Big Parade* (1925), with King Vidor as director. Laurence Stallings, the author of the script, offered a serious treatment of the horrors of war by presenting the action from the point of view of a young infantryman caught up in inevitable death. Stallings's script, Vidor's controlled direction, and John Gilbert's acting contributed to an inspirational film. The picture made MGM a top studio.

Unlike previous films, *The Big Parade* depicted war as neither romantic nor heroic, but as a hellhole filled with pain, terror, loneliness, and death. The film's outlook was neutral, although frequently sentimental, since it showed war through the eyes of the common soldier who was not especially concerned with moral issues. Vidor's film captured the authenticity of battle, the comradeship among the soldiers, and the anguish of the women as their men marched off to possible death.

The combat scenes are outstanding. As the camera travels slowly across acres of battlefields, the viewer gets the feeling he is actually a participant in the holocaust.

After the box office success of *The Big Parade*, war became a popular subject for epic treatment, almost on a par with the Bible and the Old West.

The next commercial hit was Raoul Walsh's *What Price Glory?* (1926). Based on an earthy, powerful Broadway play by Maxwell Anderson and Laurence Stallings, the film was so heavily censored that the play's original force was destroyed. The watered-down screen version of *What Price Glory?* recalls mainly the lighter moments of one of the most destructive wars in human history. It is also notorious for its historical discrepancies.

By the mid-1920's, Hollywood discovered the spectacular possibilities of airplane combat. Dogfights between camouflaged planes added pictorial excitement, while groundfighting provided additional thrills. Several of these films were scripted by J. M. Saunders and directed by William Wellman, with D. Grace performing all the daring stunts. From these romanticized experiences on the screen, the public learned that World War I aviators were mostly young boys who expected and accepted death, drowned their anxieties in drink, and kept a sober face when a fellow pilot's name was erased from the flying list. Such were the thin plot lines of *The Power of Wings* (1922), *Lilac Time* (1928), and *The Dawn Patrol* (1930). *Hell's Angels* (1927-30) is remembered today for its dramatic combat scenes, including a zeppelin raid over London and a hilarious performance by Jean Harlow.

In *Wings* (1927), a massive war and air film, the epic treatment was transferred from the Western plains and Biblical deserts to the wild blue yonder. William Wellman's film mixed sex, war, and airplanes and featured some exciting flying scenes. The aerial dogfights are thrilling, as balloons, planes, and men go down in flames. When his camera is not aloft, Wellman fills the screen with columns of troops moving over a battle-scarred countryside, bristling with gun entrenchments. He recreates in the Battle of Saint Michel one of the most realistic yet lyrical sequences in the film. The director's awesome scale of battle scenes, the excitment of the aerial dogfights, the death, destruction, and holocaust of war made *Wings* a top-notch war film.

Lewis Milestone's *All Quiet on the Western Front* (1930) is a scathing condemnation of war that focuses on the dreadful waste of human life. Milestone, his cinematographer Arthur Edeson, and composer David Brockman put aside sentimentality and chauvinism to reveal that the glories of war were buried in mud, suffering, and death.

Milestone's film was the first to show the war from the viewpoint of ordinary German soldiers. The director never relents in his determination as we follow from the very beginning the mute faces of soldiers marching by in endless file until the ending where Paul, thinking that he is safe, reaches out to catch a butterfly and is hit by a sniper's bullet, making audiences realize the loss of a young and unfulfilled life. Audiences seldom forgot the scene in the trenches when Paul (Lew Ayres) stabs a French soldier (Raymond Griffith). As the Frenchman lies dying, the terrified and bewildered young German scoops up water for him and there finds a snapshot of the doomed man's family. This poignant scene underscores the contrast between the theoretical ideal of patriotism with the tragic reality of battle.

American audiences who hated the Germans in countless other movies came face to face with one of the basic contradictions of war, that young men kill other young men who are basically no different from themselves. The seemingly organized slaughter of men and the moments of low comedy, coupled with periods of boredom, undeniably presented aspects of war never before shown on any screen.

Despite the success of *All Quiet*, audiences in the 1930's were not interested in war films. By the end of the decade, however, another war was looming. This time, Hollywood was quick to seize the historical moment. Even before the United States entered the conflict in December, 1941, anti-Nazi films were being churned out by the studios. These films ranged from documentaries about the European conflict to light-hearted portrayals of life on the home front to studio reproductions of the combat. For the most part, Hollywood's "meaningful" war films degenerated into sloppily sentimental love stories or glamorized versions of events.

Among these films was *The Mortal Storm* (1941), a grossly contrived and sentimentalized movie which purported to examine the impact of Nazism on a family of brothers. Such films were passionately propagandistic.

Charlie Chaplin parodied Hitler in *The Great Dictator* (1940). In his savage satire on fascism, Chaplin exposes the Nazi leader's megalomania. But Chaplin's direct, heavy-handed pleas for human decency interrupt the flow of the film. In addition, many viewers felt that Hitler and Nazism were not a laughing matter. The film helped send Chaplin into eclipse.

Hollywood's misrepresentation of Germany reached its wild-est flights of fancy after the U. S. entered the war, in such films as *Address Unknown* (1944). The top Nazis in the movie occupied huge offices draped with colossal swastikas and portraits of Hitler and were viewed as cultured swine. They enjoyed chamber music, drama, and good food and wine, but would not hesitate to shoot women and children. The heroes and the people in the occupied country were presented as square-jawed Resistance fighters who listened to the BBC in cellars while planning fantastic acts of sabotage. Such were the stereotypes that dominated most anti-Nazi films. Elizabeth Bergner, the renowned Austrian actress, sent coded messages to the Allies in *Paris Calling* (1941). Paul Muni, as a heroic Norwegian, blew up German submarines in *Commandos Strike at Dawn* (1942); Bonita Granville in *Hitler's Children* (1943) was flogged by Prussian supermen. With the exception of *Guadalcanal Diary* (1943), these films seldom depicted authentic war conditions. Warner Brothers was undoubtedly the war propaganda film studio, in terms of both quantity and quality.

When the United States declared war on Japan, Hollywood faced a dilemma: it knew even less about the Japanese than about Germans. As a result, the Japanese were portrayed as snarling little men with horn-rimmed glasses and buck teeth who liked to torture, rape, and pillage. The "heroes" who fought them were equally unbelievable, and the story lines were contrived. Erroll Flynn saved Burma from invasion; Katharine Hepburn poisoned the enemy; Gary Cooper almost single-handedly evacuated the wounded under Japanese attack.

Thirty Seconds Over Tokyo (1944), was basically a mo-rale-booster that showed the cooperation between Army and Navy forces. Filmed on a large scale, the picture had some scenes of genuine power and sincerity. The flying sequence from the aircraft carrier to Tokyo is technically remarkable.

One important development was the use of Chinese who were not professional actors among the supporting players.

Also worthy of attention is *The Story of G. I. Joe* (1945), one of a rash of mid-1940's films aimed at telling Americans what was happening to their sons and husbands far from home. Based on the news stories of war correspondent Ernie Pyle, the action in the film seems natural, not histrionic. The movie is marred, to be sure, but Director William Wellman approaches documentary quality while simultaneously prodding the imagination.

The war documentaries of Frank Capra, Anatole Litvak, John Huston, Eric Knight, and several others were effective. These directors looked at the war from a personal point of view, filming actual battles and using them in movies such as *Memphis Belle* (1944) and the outstanding *The Battle of San Pietro* (1945). John Huston wrote and narrated *The Battle of San Pietro*, the true, dynamic story of how a regiment of infantrymen captured a 700-year-old village. Despite their success, the regiment was decimated; a thousand replacements were needed. Huston's narration of this 30-minute film, unlike many documentaries, conveys neither optimism, pomp, nor bitterness.

Frank Capra's documentary series, *Why We Fight*, was intended mainly for the soldier in training who was still unfamiliar with what was happening in the war.

America's potential to produce a truly great film about World War II was limited by the national obsession for heroics, adventure, and romance. Hollywood seemed unwilling to study the totality of actual warfare, and was thus unable to distinguish between "the real thing" and the well-meaning but overly professionalized and overly expressive imagination of it.

The stereotypes in most Hollywood war films miseducated the American public, leaving viewers with a distorted concept of "the enemy" and of historical events. Germans and Japanese appeared to lack any vestiges of humanity; cruelty was depicted as a national trait. Of course, such propaganda was designed to reassure the public that we were the "good guys" and that God was on our side.

One could not help but be moved by the martial music, drum rolling, and the calm heroics. But the false, synthetic image of Germany and Japan did a great deal of damage when the postwar era arrived and the cinema vision no longer reflected reality. The problems of postwar readjustment in a radically changed world could not be solved as easily as they were in war films.

The postwar era gave rise to a new group of films that dealt with the problems of readjustment in a radically changed world. Though technically not war films, at least one should be mentioned here—William Wyler's *The Best Years of Our Lives* (1946). This unpretentious story concerns three ex-G.I.'s of diverse backgrounds who return to the same home town and have difficulty fitting in again after their war experiences. The decorated bombardier (Dana Andrews) can no longer be content as a drugstore clerk. The wounded Navy machinist (Harold Russell), who lost both hands, has to learn how to live with two "hooks." The banker (Fredric March), must grapple with new business ideas under the handicap of being an "older executive" in a youth-oriented society.

Wyler not only evokes compassion for the three veterans, but makes meaningful comments about America's short memory toward its heroes. The film just misses being great because its sentimentality is a bit too obvious, its music too romantic, and its situations a little contrived. Nevertheless, it ranks high for its basic theme, the splendid performances of the stars (especially the amputee. Harold Russell, a nonprofessional actor), and the fine photography.

The so-called "police action" in Korea from 1950 to 1953 inspired a revival of war films. Those that were produced while the conflict was going on were as synthetic and propagandistic as the typical World War I and II films. In later years, however, after wartime passions had abated, a much more realistic movie about the Korean fighting came out—*Pork Chop Hill* (1959), directed by Lewis Milestone. The story recounts the efforts of several hundred G.I.'s to recapture a worthless hill in Korea while truce talks are in progress. The bloody, brutal battle scenes are a sharp contrast to the dilatory peace talk sequences—underscoring the fact that men are dying needlessly while politicians squabble over petty details.

Unlike most war films, there is little flamboyance or grace in the way the troops charge the hill; they simply seem frightened and bewildered. The heavy loss of lives becomes totally meaningless when the politicians eventually decide to neutralize the territory and make it a no-man's land. Although the film lacks the impact of Milestone's *All Quiet on the Western Front*, it still must be considered a superior war movie.

More realistic films about the two world wars also emerged with the passage of time and the cooling of emotions. In *The Desert Fox* (1951), German officers and soldiers of World War II are depicted as real, complex human beings. The film takes a sympathetic look at the German Afrika Korps Commander Rommel, played by James Mason.

David Lean's *Bridge on the River Kwai* (1957) is an ambitious antiheroic war film showing the tangled motives and emotions of both Japanese and British officers. Neither the Japanese prison camp commander (Sessue Hayakawa) nor his British captive, Colonel Nicholson (Alec Guinness) are stereotypes. They are both complex characters with good and bad traits. Thus, the dichotomy between the ally and the enemy is blurred.

Another sensitive war film, *The Enemy Below* (1958), pits an American destroyer captain against a German submarine captain. Curt Jurgens, as the enemy commander, emerges as a man of understanding and sympathy.

Stanley Kubrick's magnificent *Paths of Glory* (1957) brought World War I to the screen again, from a radically different perspective. Kubrick offers a pitiless and devastating study of deceit and corruption in the French army. The short film concerns a French colonel (Kirk Douglas) who opposes his superiors when they court-martial three innocent soldiers. Avoiding cheap sentiment, Kubrick's picture holds up to scorn the generals who offer false encouragement to doomed men.

In the 1960's, several adventure movies appeared which subtly perverted history by having "good Nazis" as the heroes. Among these films are *Up from the Beach* (1965), featuring a German Occupation officer who saves French civilians from air raids; *Battle of the Bulge* (1965), with a shrewd Panzer commander who loses faith in the Nazi regime; and *The Bedford Incident* (1965), with its postwar "good Nazi" who helps the American against the Russians. These films are rather good thrillers, but some critics fear that the pendulum has swung too far away from earlier images of the enemy without offering any deeper understanding.

Merrill's Marauders (1966), a low-key film that was skillfully directed from a tight script, turned out to be one of the better war pictures of the 1960's. It concerns men at war in a suffocating Asian jungle without artillery support. They fight quietly and die quietly. There are no subplots and no beautiful girls appearing from nowhere; there are only little victories, long marches, and the constant threat of disease. For once the star, Jeff Chandler, embodies the person he is playing and gives an unforgettable characterization of General Merrill.

However, during the 1960's, one of the standard plots of the war film vanished completely, the simple story of a group of men under pressure in a deadly situation. Directors began to explore new areas of interest. The screen presented large-scale spectaculars and antiwar films with a Black Comedy touch.

In *The Longest Day* (1962), Darryl F. Zanuck scrupulously restaged the D-Day landings of 1944 and offered spectacle and drama. The film had some brilliantly handled action sequences, but was neither a hit with the public nor the critics. *The Heroes of Telemark* (1966), the story of the Allied Ski Commandos raiding a Norwegian heavy-water plant, consisted of frequent explosions and childish violence. It motivated a cycle of graphic war adventures featuring knifing, garrotting and demolition. *Where Eagles Dare* (1969) and *Kelly's Heroes* (1970) excel in murder, bomb bursts, and demolitions as homes, churches, office buildings and bridges are blown sky-high. David Lean with his two films *Lawrence of Arabia* (1962) and *Dr. Zhivago* (1965) improved the quality of story and production, lifting films out of their epic rut into the realm of serious cinema. Robert Aldrich, who went from gritty realism to inflated medodrama, loaded his film *The Dirty Dozen* (1967) with violence which places this film as a landmark in the violence cycle of the 1960's.

Stanley Kubrick's *Dr. Strangelove* (1964), a nightmare comedy on the global balance of terror, opened the way for ridiculing war (see "The Comedy Film"). Mike Nichols's *Catch-22* failed to capture Yossarian's (Alan Arkin) perpetual epic panic. However, *M*A*S*H* (see "The Comedy Film") not only caught the gore, blood and cruelty of the book, but managed to present the emotional freedom, cool wit, and good sense.

In the 1970's directors avoided the Hollywood stereotyped "war film" and were contemptuous of anything military. Characters scorned discipline, criticized the government, made fun of officers and ridiculed battlefield heroics. The horrors of war were turned into Black Comedy, yet none of these directors really questioned the validity of war. Hollywood had not yet become bold enough to attempt truly pacifist movies. Its primary goal has always been to entertain.

Patton (1970) probes the career of the controversial general, George S. Patton, exposing his ruthlessness, his delusions of grandeur, and his egotism, but portraying him as a moving figure nevertheless. *Patton* may be the most brutally honest portrayal of an American general in screen history. The General is seen as an anti-Establishment figure in his own way; "hawks" can see the film as a tribute to their belief that unyielding aggressiveness pays off; "doves" can see the work as a portrayal of bloodthirsty militancy at least somewhat subdued in the end.

At one time Patton muses on the theme of reincarnation and imagines that he is the descendant of Hannibal, only he is now fighting the Nazis as the Carthaginian leader once struggled against Scipio and the Romans. It is a macabre touch, but a profoundly absorbing one. The photography and film music make it difficult to not respect Patton, at least, despite his shortcomings. Yet, his ruthlessness, his delusions of grandeur, and his egotism make him appear demonically driven. Unfortunately for the viewer, Patton's psyche (according to L. Farrago's biography of him) is much more complex than it appears in the movie. In the film, he also lacks any real opposition to his plans. The occasional setbacks that he suffers seem more contrived in retrospect than anything else. One wonders if wars create war lovers or if war lovers create war. No one who sees this film can remain unmoved.

By the mid-1970's the big war blockbuster was once more back in fashion. *Midway* (1976) is a mundane story of a World War II carrier battle. *MacArthur* (1977), the story of the brilliant and egotistical general, leans more on lengthy discussions of military and political strategy than a sense of battle and dramatic human incidents. Beginning on Corregidor three months after Pearl Harbor, it continues through the defeat and occupation of Japan, "police action" in Korea, and President Truman's firing MacArthur.

In *A Bridge Too Far* (1977) the director Richard Attenborough tells of a maneuver to parachute 35,000 men behind the German lines in Holland in an attempt to block the retreating German troops at crucial bridges. Airborne troops, tank, and infantry divisions were to meet, march on the industrial Ruhr, and end the war before Christmas. Masterminded by General Montgomery and sanctioned by Eisenhower, the project failed because of a crucial mistake in planning, faulty intelligence, battlefield politics, bad weather, miscalculation, and bad luck. When the men dropped at the farthest bridge they were surprised by two SS Panzer Divisions and were massacred by the thousands.

Cross of Iron (1977), the German retreat from Russia after Stalingrad, is a paradox of revulsion-attraction. Sam Peckinpah's delight in violence dominates the film. In almost unremitting horror there is shooting, explosions, screaming, and dying. The only good feeling in the film is the bond that develops among men in the trenches.

The Eagle Has Landed (1977) is a suspense drama of a German attempt to kidnap Winston Churchill. However, for the present it appears as though World War II has ended on the American screen. Hollywood is pointing its cameras toward Vietnam.

Soon to be relieased are Francis Ford Coppola's *Apocalypse Now*, Jeremy Paul Kagan's *Heroes*, Hal Ashby's *Coming Home*, and others.

In retrospect most Hollywood films depicting war in Europe and the conduct of people seem grotesquely unreal. War films date more noticeably than those of any other genre. The smooth Nazi villains, the downtrodden peasants, the multiracial Allied platoons—how contrived they all appear to be now. The snarling Japanese gibbering their way through studio jungles are far removed from actuality. Hollywood only reinforced the public's stereotypes and traditional expectations for war movies. Unfortunately, from the beginning, the industry has tried to produce entertainment far more than art. For every film "above" the others, there are hundreds of "B" and "C" movies.

From Hollywood came a small collection of war film masterpieces—*The Birth of a Nation*, *The Big Parade*, *All Quiet on the Western Front*, and a few others—but far more often there were cheap scenarios that offered false heroics, fake sets, and mathematically timed explosions. Yet the war film, unlike the gangster film, appears not to have run its course. The public continues to ask for more of this genre even if it is presented as mockery.

Hollywood is rarely in the vanguard of political thought. Perhaps when a larger segment of the population becomes pacifist, Hollywood will produce some truly pacifist movies. Although many of the films discussed portray the horrors of war, none really question the validity of war.

Outstanding War Films
and Their Directors

The Birth of a Nation	(1915)	D. W. Griffith
The Big Parade	(1926)	King Vidor
All Quiet on the Western Front	(1930)	Lewis Milestone
The Road to Glory	(1936)	Howard Hawks
Sergeant York	(1941)	Howard Hawks
Thirty Seconds over Tokyo	(1944)	Mervyn LeRoy
The Battle of San Pietro	(1945)	John Huston
The Story of G. I. Joe	(1945)	William Wellman
The Best Years of Our Lives	(1946)	William Wyler
From Here to Eternity	(1953)	Fred Zinnemann
Paths of Glory	(1957)	Stanley Kubrick
The Bridge on the River Kwai	(1957)	David Lean
The Guns of Navarone	(1961)	Carl Foreman
The Longest Day	(1962)	Andrew Marton
		Ken Annakin
		Bernhard Wicky
Dr. Strangelove	(1964)	Stanley Kubrick
Patton	(1970)	Franklin Schaffner
M*A*S*H	(1970)	Robert Altman
A Bridge Too Far	(1977)	Richard Attenborough
The Eagle Has Landed	(1977)	John Sturges

19 / The Western Film

EDWIN S. PORTER'S *The Great Train Robbery* (1903), the first dramatically creative film, set the pattern for Western films with its crime, pursuit, and retribution. Porter had all the elements right there in the beginning: bad characters performing dastardly deeds, pursued and vanquished by the good guys representing law and order; horses, guns, and a moving train.

After appearing as a bandit in *The Great Train Robbery*, Max Aaronson, a vaudeville performer, headed West to become the screen's first cowboy, "Broncho Billy." Between 1908 and 1915 Aaronson, who changed his name to Gilbert Anderson, appeared in a series of short but profitable shoot-em-ups that helped establish the Western as America's favorite type of movie.

Cecil B. DeMille's *The Squaw Man* (1914), the first major film to be produced in Hollywood, was also the first full-length Western. Always the keen showman, DeMille filled the screen with Indians, cattle rustlers, villains, and barroom brawlers. His success prompted other directors to follow the same formula.

The Western utilizes a few simple ingredients: fast action, clear-cut conflicts between good and evil, and uncomplicated heroes who project virility, courage, physical dexterity, and loyalty. The women, too, are simple, steadfast, and true, while the villains are invariably cruel and amoral. Minor characters include the townspeople, the bar habitués, and perhaps a rural comic or two. Comments on the action may come from a ranch hand, a drunk, or a stagecoach driver, who serve as a kind of Greek chorus. Inevitably, the hero reaches a decisive moment, his supreme test of loyalty and courage, when he must confront the villain in a battle to the death. In the end, evil is destroyed; the hero triumphs by killing.

Between 1865 and 1890, the "Wild West" gave birth to more legends than any other time and place in American history. The reason for the widespread interest in these stories was the dime novel. These "penny dreadfuls" exploited the deeds of the Western characters and enlarged them beyond real-life happenings. The "golden days" of the badman and the cowboy lasted only a few years (thirty at the most), and there was very little about either their work or their deeds to make them attractive, but the pulp writers implanted in the minds of their readers the idea that life in the "Wild West" was exciting and that these lawless territories offered endless adventures.

The deeds of famous bandits, law-abiding men, snivelling cowards, brave women, and dastardly Indians were exploited in print. Billy the Kid, the Dalton Brothers, the James Family, the Younger brothers, Wyatt Earp, Calamity Jane, Annie Oakley, and Belle Starr walked into legend through the popular dime novel.

Producers watched the climbing gate receipts of DeMille's *The Squaw Man* and realized what the fans wanted. Every big and little company put their actors on horseback.

Writers turned to the dime novels for characters and plots and simply rewrote or repeated the old story with an occasionally different slant. At least ten films have been based on the character of Jesse James. Seven films have dealt with the young killer Billy the Kid; Wyatt Earp, the famous sheriff, has been portrayed in five films. Women also receive their share of attention: Calamity Jane has been a major character in five movies, and Annie Oakley has appeared several times, including a Technicolor musical.

Psychologists explain that the Western appeals to certain aspects of human nature, particularly the American admiration for rugged individualism. Viewers participate vicariously in the adventures on the silver screen. Migrating to the West represented for many an escape from the mundane world, a return to primitive innocence. Yearning for the violent but attractive world of Wild Bill Hickock, Bat Masterson, the Younger brothers, or the Ringo Kid, audiences dream of adventures in the wide open spaces with these daring characters. Western films release these feelings just as the dime novels and the Wild West traveling shows released them for an earlier generation.

By 1914, W. S. Hart, after several films, emerged with a basic screen character that fans loved, replacing "Broncho Billy" as the public's favorite Western hero. Bill Hart outrode and outshot all his enemies. His strong stone face and blazing guns made audiences feel that either justice was once more established or at least the social code was saved. Hart's screen portrayals were more psychologically sound, more sincere, and deeper than those of his contemporaries.* He was eventually succeeded by the dashing Tom Mix.

Mix was the best horseman in cinema history. Although he started in pictures in 1910, he received little attention from the public until the decline of Hart. His Westerns were well written, with three-dimensional characters, sensible motivation, and imaginative plots. Offscreen he fascinated his fans with beautiful white cowboy suits, sports cars, and high living. After a decade of top billing, by 1935, his popularity faded and he was replaced by the young John Wayne. Mix retired from the screen, the last of the big cowboy stars of the silent era.

In the early years, Westerns were churned out with such speed that virtually all the director could do was stick to the formula; there was little room for originality. It wasn't until 1923 that the first outstanding Western hit the screen—*The Covered Wagon.*

This was not the traditional Western but an epic about the crossing of America in 1849 by the biggest wagon train in history. The director, James Cruze, captured the majestic sweep of the plains and the determined spirit and deep-rooted convictions of the pioneers. Cruze shot the movie on location, filming such spectacles as a full-scale Indian attack and the caravan crossing a rushing river. Produced at a cost of

---

* As early as 1923, French critics said that Hart's was the first genuine characterization to be established by cinema. From the early days of moviemaking, the French critics have been interested in the American Western. In France, cults form around various pictures, directors, and actors; the French see films repeatedly to study technique, hunt for symbols, dissect motivations, or look for Freudian touches. They first discovered and organized the Bogart *mystique,* later extended to the films of Howard Hawks and Greta Garbo. The French intellectual can even compare the Western to Greek tragedy. Influenced by the novels of James Fenimore Cooper, Frenchmen have long been attracted to the lonely Leatherstocking and his Indian companion living the life of the "noble savage." In the 1920's (and occasionally today), the ordinary Frenchman's knowledge of America was still so vague that he thought William S. Hart and his heroines were contemporary types living on the frontier; that guns, Indians, and the rush for land were still part of the American way of life, and that all one had to do was board a train and get off at Pittsburgh to begin the life of the romantic cowboy. Although confused with characters and time, the French were, however, the first to see the serious aspects of Hart's films and to point out that the materials of the Western are epic and mythic.

$750,000, *The Covered Wagon* grossed $4 million, and ran for fifty-nine weeks at the Criterion Theater in New York, surpassing the record that had been set by *The Birth of a Nation*.

After the success of the Cruze film, John Ford, a young director with an established reputation, made *The Iron Horse* (1924), a drama about the construction of the first American transcontinental railroad. Like *The Covered Wagon*, it contains magnificent outdoor photography. Ford's superb action sequences and the obligatory romance embellish the film's historical theme without ever obscuring it.

Both Cruze and Ford use symbols in their Westerns. In *The Covered Wagon*, the Indians refer to the plow as a "weapon" that will kill the buffalo. (The plow represents the white man's encroachment on the buffalo's grazing lands.) In *The Iron Horse*, the train symbolizes Eastern progress about to conquer the West.

Although many Westerns were produced in the 1920's, the two already mentioned were by far the best. *North of 36* (1924), *The Pony Express* (1925), *The Thundering Herd* (1925), and *Three Bad Men* (1926), were popular but offered little originality. William S. Hart, Ken Maynard, Harry Carey, Buck Jones, Fred Thompson, and Hoot Gibson continued the Western tradition and helped maintain the cowboy's popularity.

With the advent of the talkies, however, the Western film seemed doomed. How could sound be recorded in the wide open spaces? What mechanism could follow dialogue on horseback? The technical problems were quickly solved, however, permitting the Western to survive and flourish in the sound era. Among the most successful of the early talking Westerns were *The Virginian, Billy the Kid,* and *The Big Trail*, all produced in 1930, and *Cimarron* (1931). John Wayne, who played the young cowboy in *The Big Trail*, subsequently became the quintessential Western hero. By 1975, his films had grossed about $400 million.

Most Westerns were relegated to "B" picture status, but when Universal decided to make its first big Western, it went all out. To direct its production of *Sutter's Gold* (1936), the studio brought in the famous Russian director, Sergei Eisenstein. (The virtual inventor of montage, Eisenstein had come to Hollywood to study American film techniques.) At the last moment, Universal capitulated to political pressures and gave the final script to James Cruze, prompting a disillusioned

Eisenstein to depart for Mexico and home. Cruze, meanwhile, didn't fare too well with the assignment; *Sutter's Gold* was a failure.

After *The Big Trail* (1930), Westerns in general languished for almost a decade until DeMille, John Ford, and a collection of superstars, Tyrone Power, Henry Fonda, James Stewart, and others returned the genre to popularity.

In 1939, three important Westerns reached the theaters: Henry King's *Jesse James*, which made heroes of badmen; DeMille's *Union Pacific;* and John Ford's *Stagecoach*. DeMille, always alert to what the public wanted, selected Gary Cooper and Jean Arthur for his first super-Western, *The Plainsman* (1936), and followed this in 1939 with another spectacular, *Union Pacific*, starring Barbara Stanwyck. The film offered the theme of empire-building and featured a train holdup, a barroom fight, an Indian attack, a train wreck, and a climactic street shootout. *The Plainsman* and *Union Pacific* may not have been great art, but they swelled box office returns.

John Ford is without a doubt the most celebrated director of this genre. He began working in pictures in 1914 when the industry started, made over 125 features (many of these silent Westerns), and won six Academy Awards and four New York Film Critics' Awards. His name is linked almost automatically with the Western. His pictures are concerned with courage, honesty, pride, and loyalty—primary human virtues. His films reveal the folk history of our land.

Ford's outstanding Western is *Stagecoach* (1939), universally acclaimed by critics as an all-time great.* Based on Ernest Haycock's short story "Stage to Lordsburg," *Stagecoach* takes several key motifs—a motley collection of characters, Indians versus the cavalry, the good badman—and presents them in an exciting story. The film sweeps across the plains and mesas of Arizona, at the same time focusing sharply on the individuals caught up in the action. Tension and suspense are present throughout.

The story concerns nine passengers traveling on a stage from Tonto to Lordsburg in the 1870's, when Geronimo and

* Orson Welles has said that before he went to RKO Studios in 1940 to make his now-celebrated *Citizen Kane*, he spent hours in the Museum of Modern Art observing directing techniques. Welles acknowledges John Ford as his master, noting that he saw *Stagecoach* more than forty times. (The *London Sunday Times*, February 3, 1963.)

his Apaches are on the warpath. Among the passengers are an outlaw (John Wayne), who is being brought back to prison by a marshal; a woman of questionable reputation; an alcoholic doctor; a mysterious gambler; an expectant mother; a respectable banker (actually an embezzler); a timid salesman; and the stagecoach driver. Their lives hang in the balance while the marauding Indians pursue the stage relentlessly. As the drama progresses, the passengers emerge as clearly defined individuals. There is nothing very original in this idea, but Ford's techniques make it work. The scenery, the photography, the lighting, and, above all, the rhythmic editing, are superb.

No one has so consistently captured the American Southwest's sweeping landscape, lonely frontier towns, and colorful characters as John Ford. William Wyler, Howard Hawks, Raoul Walsh, Fritz Lang, King Vidor, Cecil B. DeMille, Henry King, and Michael Curtiz brought forth Western epics but the genre belongs to Ford. His noble characters, facing both badmen and a hostile landscape, have given entertainment to movie fans for almost sixty years. His glorious history of daring pioneers who even in their defeat are dignified make the Western adventure film compelling art and a particularly moving form of film.

New themes, complex characters, and more important roles for women were introduced in the Western in the period during and after World War II. The earliest of these "new wave" Westerns was *The Ox-Bow Incident* (1942), a somber and atmospheric film that broke with tradition insofar as it portrayed frontier life in proper perspective. This quiet film was praised by critics but ignored by the public; nevertheless, it had an enormous impact on the Western genre. Henry Fonda and Dana Andrews headed the cast, Lamar Trotti wrote the script, and William Wellman directed.

The story concerns an incident that supposedly occurred in Nevada in 1885. Three strangers—a young cowboy, a Mexican, and an old man—are accused of murdering a rancher and stealing his livestock. The townspeople lynch them, only to discover later that they have hanged innocent men.

Like the films of William S. Hart, *Ox-Bow* offers an uncompromising portrait of the harsh frontier. Wellman, taking an unsentimental and realistic view of an ugly episode, makes a strong plea for justice and respect for law. He also presents a convincing psychological study of a sadistic ex-officer who sweeps the townspeople along in his craze to hang the men, mainly for the pleasure of the act. This short film stands as a minor masterpiece.

The postwar period produced many of the most enduring Western classics. Howard Hawks's *Red River* (1948) is one of the most thoughtful of the genre. John Wayne as the cattle baron prods his men and herds beyond endurance. Montgomery Clift made a deft impression as the youngster who rebels against Wayne's twisted sense of power.

Another powerful Western is Henry King's *The Gunfighter* (1950), the story of an outlaw's last hours. A young upstart sets out to make a name for himself by killing Jimmy Ringo, a feared gunman. Ringo kills the boy instead, and the boy's three brothers set out to avenge his death. When one of the brothers succeeds in killing Ringo, the boy realizes that he has exchanged places with the doomed man. He himself is now the hunted.

Two westerns that deserve special mention are *High Noon* (1952) and *Shane* (1953). Neither picture sacrificed the traditional action and suspense, yet each dealt intelligently with life-and-death confrontations.

High Noon, directed by Fred Zinnemann, has been one of the most influential post-World War II Westerns, resembling classic tragedy. It is a tale of revenge, honor, and integrity. The outlaw friends of a dead bandit are bent on avenging his murder. Their target is the sheriff of a small town, who seeks help in fending them off. But it soon becomes painfully clear that the townspeople don't want to get involved; they won't help the sheriff make a stand against the criminals. In the end, he chooses to face the outlaws alone, rather than run away.

In *Shane,* considered by some critics to be the best of the genre, director George Stevens did not tamper with the accepted Western pattern. The hero, Shane, is a quiet, mysterious stranger who emerges out of nowhere to help the oppressed homesteaders. When Joey, a young, wide-eyed boy, first sees Shane, he rushes to his father, shouting, "Pa, he's like God." Shane stays at a local farm and quickly earns the respect of the people as he helps them battle the cattle barons and their hired killers. Basically peace-loving but true to the ritual code, Shane must eventually strap on his gun, mount his horse, and set out to kill in order to bring justice and honor to the community.

The action is seen through the eyes of the idealistic little boy, Joey, to whom Shane is a larger-than-life figure, skilled with both fists and guns yet quietly dignified and understanding. Joey follows Shane and witnesses the final showdown between his hero and the killer. After triumphing, Shane rides off into the unknown, and the little boy stands with tears in his eyes, shouting, "Come back, Shane." True to the Hollywood code of the West, the demigod rides off into legend.

What makes *Shane* superior is its original treatment of the battle between good and evil—from the perspective of a child. Skillfully edited, the film sustains its tension and momentum throughout. Lloyd Griggs' color photography of mountains, plains, streams, and town gives the film an epic sweep that enhances its power.

By the 1960's, the Western turned to symbolism. In *Giant* (1956), Rock Hudson, dressed in traditional cowboy garb, is contrasted with James Dean in modern dress, who represents the new generation—interested not in tilling the soil but in amassing a fortune in oil. David Miller's *Lonely Are the Brave* (1962) develops an offbeat story about a solitary cowboy who realizes that he is useless to present-day society. In John Huston's *The Misfits* (1960), Clark Gable, Montgomery Clift, and Eli Wallach, the "last" cowboys, are reduced to hunting wild mustangs and killing these noble beasts to make canned dog food.

Several modern films deviated markedly from the traditional Western: *The Misfits* (1961), *Hud* (1963), directed by Martin Ritt, *The Wild Bunch* (1970), directed by Sam Peckinpah, and *Little Big Man* (1971), directed by Arthur Penn.

The playwright Arthur Miller wrote the script of *The Misfits*, John Huston directed, and three superstars played the leads. *The Misfits*, with Clark Gable, Marilyn Monroe, and Montgomery Clift, supported by Eli Wallach and Thelma Ritter, is an exceptional horse-opera. Three lonely failures trying to retain some shred of honor and follow the ideals of the West take up with a vivacious divorcee and her friend and set off to round up horses to be slaughtered for pet food. Roslyn (Marilyn Monroe), repelled by the killing of the beasts, shows them how far from the ideals of the West they have strayed. She confronts the killers with her plea for humanism.

The film has superb rodeo riding sequences, an exciting hunt for the wild horses, moments of tenderness and compassion. Clark Gable, Marilyn Monroe, and Montgomery Clift brought brilliant insight to their complex characters.

In *Hud,* the noble hero is replaced by an antihero—a sensual, hard-drinking, fornicating Texan who prefers a Cadillac to a horse and doesn't give a damn for social values, justice, honesty, or people. He's out solely for himself. Hud has no villain to gun down because he has no cause worth fighting for. In his world, cowboys listen to transistor radios and while away their time in beer joints. Hud's shiftless, amoral way of life is a torment to his father; the clash between the old man's lifestyle and that of his son is probed deftly.

As in *Shane,* much of the action is seen through the eyes of a youngster—in this case, Lon, Hud's teen-age nephew. Lon worships Hud, until he finally realizes that the object of his admiration is not worth anyone's respect. In the end, he rejects Hud's corrupt way of life.

James Wong Howe's camera captures the dry, flat, unromantic Texas landscape in all its loneliness and emptiness—a reflection of Hud's character. The fast-moving trucks, endless highways, blaring radios, and monotonous ranch houses are also signs of spiritual desolation.

The amoral antihero of *Hud* is neither removed from society nor punished; good does not necessarily conquer evil. Life simply flows on as always, with injustice still rampant. Hud inherits the ranch but faces an empty, selfish life. There are no last-minute rescues, no heavy moralizing. The realism of *Hud* is diametrically opposed to the heroics of *Shane.* When Melvyn Douglas shoots his last two Texas longhorns, it signifies the end of the Old West.

The Wild Bunch (1970) is a shocker that ushered in the decade of the 1970's. Never has a Western aroused such critical damnation and praise; its highly graphic violence both fascinates and repulses. *The Wild Bunch* does not present the usual theme of good versus evil, but of bad versus bad. The film depicts the actions of a ruthless gang of killers pursued by an equally ruthless gang of bounty hunters avidly seeking human corpses. For them money is more important than men.

Peckinpah relies heavily on camera tricks to emphasize the violence. Through the use of slow motion he turns bloodbaths into ballets, so that vicious killings appear almost beautiful. Yet the gore is horrifying—blood spurts from wounds, faces disintegrate, and heads are blown off. The film was praised for its fine direction, realism, and spectacular visual effects, while at the same time deplored for its brutality.

Arthur Penn's multilayered epic, *Little Big Man* (1971), one of the more original Westerns, offering not only the standard ingredients—Indians, cowboys, guns, and chase sequences—but vitriolic social criticism as well. Its main target is the white man who slaughters Indians and desecrates the land. Yet the film is not deadly serious or preachy. Outrageous touches of black comedy and farce abound.

Little Big Man is a tall tale about Jack Crabb, (Dustin Hoffman) the crusty narrator who claims to be 121 years old. In a series of flashbacks, Crabb recalls his tragicomic peregrinations in search of his identity. After his parents are massacred by Indians, young Jack is captured and reared as a brave by the Cheyenne tribe. He is renamed "Little Big Man." Because of his white birth and Indian upbringing, he shuttles back and forth between the two societies.

In amusing, mock epic style, the film follows the hero as he travels around the West and meets such legendary characters as Wild Bill Hickock, Calamity Jane, Wyatt Earp, and General George Armstrong Custer. In striving to make a place for himself in the world, he becomes, in turn, a religious disciple, a mule skinner, a swindler, an Indian scout, a hero, a drunkard, a gunfighter, and a hermit. In each role, however, he soon fails. He remains an outsider, neither Indian nor white, belonging nowhere.

The film sharply denounces the mythic Western heroes and presents a new interpretation of the West. Bill Hickock dies among indifferent gamblers; General Custer is a vainglorious psychopath, an egotistical, strutting, preening maniac. The massacre of his troops at Little Big Horn is a filmic gem, combining graphic realism and high humor. Another superb episode is the massacre of the Indians at Washita. U.S. troops emerge from a mist-enshrouded, snow-covered landscape to attack and butcher the unsuspecting Indians. Penn cuts rapidly from shots of the avenging soldiers to their bewildered, dying victims. As in *The Wild Bunch,* beauty and death are fused; the bloody massacre is choreographed with the grace of a ballet.

By the late 1960's, Hollywood was back in the saddle once more. *Butch Cassidy and the Sundance Kid* (1969), *True Grit* (1969), *A Man Called Horse* (1970), *McCabe and Mrs. Miller* (1971), and *High Plains Drifter* (1973) kept the genre alive. In *Blazing Saddles* (1974) Mel Brooks rode roughshod over the whole Western genre.

In 1976 there was a spate of Westerns: *Breakheart Pass, The Missouri Breaks, Buffalo Bill and the Indians, The Shootist, The Outlaw Josey Wales,* and *The Return of a Man Called Horse.*

This latest revival gives new weight to the belief of some critics and writers that the saga of the American frontier is our most enduring myth. The Western has been, of course, our most popular narrative form, and movies capture the image of a man and his style which expresses itself in violence. Some of the latest films satisfy the nation's longing for the old-time, uncompromising loner-hero, while other films debunk that monumental screen creation. *Buffalo Bill and the Indians* presents the legendary scout as a drunken, sleazy, philandering showman. *The Shootist* offers John Wayne as a turn-of-the-century gunfighter who has nothing to do but die in style. These Westerns present more psychologically complex heroes than earlier films, but they are still meant to emerge as heroes in spite of their complexes. The Western revival is again offering enjoyable male stars riding over the Western landscape in a form that never disappoints its audiences.

Outstanding Western Films
and Their Directors

The Great Train Robbery	(1903)	Edwin S. Porter
The Covered Wagon	(1923)	James Cruze
The Iron Horse	(1924)	John Ford
Cimarron	(1931)	Wesley Ruggles
Stagecoach	(1939)	John Ford
The Ox-Bow Incident	(1943)	William Wellman
Red River	(1948)	Howard Hawks
The Gunfighter	(1950)	Henry King
Winchester 73	(1950)	Anthony Mann
High Noon	(1952)	Fred Zinnemann
Shane	(1953)	George Stevens
The Searchers	(1956)	John Ford
The Misfits	(1961)	John Huston
Hud	(1963)	Martin Ritt
Butch Cassidy and the Sundance Kid	(1969)	George Roy Hill
True Grit	(1969)	Henry Hathaway
The Wild Bunch	(1970)	Sam Peckinpah
Little Big Man	(1971)	Arthur Penn
McCabe and Mrs. Miller	(1972)	Robert Altman
Bad Company	(1973)	Robert Benton

20 / The Romance Film

FROM Mary Pickford in *The Mending of the Nets* (1912) to Robert DeNiro in *The Last Tycoon* (1977), romance has been as much a part of cinema's history as the camera itself. The movies quickly learned to package and distribute this product, and the public found the commodity irresistible. For decades the name Hollywood meant romance and the movie screen was the face of love.

For the first half of the century, the movies managed to show life as it could be lived in the imagination. The camera, a magic mystery box that unfolded endless stories of glamorous romance, explored every avenue known to script writers: boy meets girl, a cowboy may leave behind a sad heroine and prefer his horse, beauty may select the beast, a scientist may prefer his laboratory, a mother may sell her soul to educate a son or buy medicine for a sick husband, and a self-sacrificing demimondaine may give all for love. These are the basis of movie legends. Romance in the cinema begins with "once upon a time."

The greatest technical contribution to the romance genre has been the closeup. Early directors, moving their camera ever closer to the performers, used closeups and dolly shots as a means of communicating to the audience the most minute gestures and the sublest emotion. The camera, capturing these emotions, projected the erotic power of the face on the screen into the minds of the audience, and audiences caught the simulation of passion that could be turned off and on by the camera. D. W. Griffith, Erich von Stroheim, Thomas H. Ince, and others, realizing the public wanted to see their favorite star entangled in emotional problems of love, turned to romance.

The 1920's was an era of wonderful nonsense, the heyday of romance. Women were the leading scriptwriters. Anita Loos, Frances Marion, Bess Meredyth, Jeanie MacPherson, and Lenore Coffee wrote stories for certain stars. Their ranks rapidly expanded to include June Mathis, Dorothy Parker, and Sonya Levien. Two other writers Vincente Blasco Ibanez and Elinor Glyn excelled in exotic scenarios, taking audiences to Paris, Spain, Monte Carlo, the desert and the pampas. In Glyn's world, no girl was raped or seduced, and no man was ever a brute. In Ibanez's torrid stories of bull-fighters and passion, someone had to pay for breaking the moral code and might meet death at the end of the film. To satisfy the fans, there was always a haunting epilogue to reu-nite the lovers.

Theda Bara, Rudolph Valentino, Douglas Fairbanks, Charles Farrell, Janet Gaynor, Ramon Novarro, and Ronald Colman brought to the screen moments of tenderness, passion, and romance. John Gilbert and Great Garbo in *Flesh and the Devil* (1927) established their position as the screen's most romantic couple. John Barrymore and Camilla Horn in *The Tempest* (1928) offered love to clamoring fans, while Ronald Colman and Vilma Banky in *Night of Love* (1927) kindled sparks between them. How far could romance go? In *The Woman Disputed* (1928), Norma Talmadge as a prosti-tute has given herself to a Russian officer in exchange for the freedom of a captured Austrian spy. The information the spy has procured frees the town, but Norma's lover Paul, hearing of Norma's role in the proceedings, leaves her. Only when 10,000 Austrian soldiers gratefully kneel at her feet in thanks does Paul reconsider.

Sam Goldwyn's *Stella Dallas* (1925) and *The Dark Angel* (1925) set standards for the romantic genre. In *Mare Nos-trum* (1925), Alice Terry in her execution scene had fans weeping. In *La Boheme* (1925), the queen of sentiment, Lil-lian Gish, gave an affecting portrayal of tremulous pathos as Mimi, who dies of tuberculosis. Mae Murray in *The Merry Widow* (1925), dancing with John Gilbert, carried make-be-lieve and romanticism to its silent-era heights. On the sound stage next door, Greta Garbo in her first American film *The Torrent* (1925) would become within a few years (along with Marlene Dietrich) a legend of glamor and the greatest romantic actress in cinema history.

Seventy-seven million fans went to the movies every week, and for the first time "just folks" could see gilded society lilies, nightclubs, Graustark, motor cars, beautiful clothes, the vamp and the pure heroine. Romance sold tickets.

By 1928 there were changes. The romantic women in *The Garden of Allah* (1927), *The Road to Romance* (1927), and

Dream of Love (1928) were being edged off the screen by
Colleen Moore, Joan Crawford, and Clara Bow, the modern
American girls of the jazz age. Two others opened avenues.
The somber Evelyn Brent in *Underworld* (1927), hard as
nails and soft as feathers, the perfect gunman's woman, was a
forerunner of the straight-from-the-shoulder no-nonsense
heroine who came to full bloom in the 1930's gangster films.
The erotic Louise Brooks, an actress of rare intelligence, in *A
Girl in Every Port* (1927) and *Beggars of Life* (1928) also
showed audiences realistic characters who opened the door
for the down-to-earth gal of the talkies. The microphone was
soon to banish a fair amount of romantic grace from the
screen. Mary Pickford, Gloria Swanson, Vilma Banky, and
Pola Negri faded out. The chorus girl stepped forward to be
the leading lady.

When the screen learned to talk, with the exception of the
comedies of Ernst Lubitsch and the romantic stories of Josef
von Sternberg, romance lacked humor and good taste. The
moonlight, flowers, and frills were replaced for a time by a
more realistic and sometimes brutal approach to love. The
talkies put the melo into drama, and the stories of struggle,
sacrifice, and redemption were concerned with small people
with small problems. Women may have become flesh and
blood, attainable and real, but perhaps too real. Jean Harlow,
Mae West, Jean Arthur, Bette Davis, Miriam Hopkins, and
Constance Bennett changed the romantic screen heroine into
a brassy, brittle, freewheeling sexy blonde. Marlene Dietrich
and Greta Garbo alone held on to the woman-of-mystery
image.

The studios in the 1930's structured stories to capture the
matinee trade, and for a while, the romantic tradition fell
into the confession tale, or as the industry called them,
"hankie pictures." These stories were peopled by two types—
a waif buffeted about by the winds of a cruel world or a
scheming minx who eventually gets her comeuppance. They
were stenographers, shopgirls, parlor maids, or innocent
small-town girls who trusted the wrong man and ended up
pregnant but unmarried. Helen Twelvetrees, groomed as a
threat to Mary Pickford, was often a popular shopgirl (Little
Nell) who cried her way through dozens of mediocre pictures. Ann Harding, usually a woman doctor, made momen-
tous decisions concerning her career and true love. Kay
Francis sipped champagne and took long trips on tramp
steamers in order to forget the cruel blow fate had dealt her.

The undisputed queen of the New York theater, Helen Hayes, agreed to appear in the manufactured melodrama *The Sin of Madelon Claudet* (1931). Madelon, an unmarried mother turned prostitute, educates her son to be a doctor, then dies under the wheels of his car, unrecognized and unmourned. Not only the public but also the industry hoodwinked itself into believing these trite but sad films. Only the art of Miss Hayes could have transformed such material into an Academy Award-winning performance.

The queen of the sob-circuit, however, was the sophisticated Constance Bennett. In 1930, she was the highest paid actress in films. The public apparently considered her lacquered looks, clipped speech, and fashionable hairdo's appropriate for such incongruous roles as stenographer, shopgirl, or housemaid. In *Son of the Gods, Rich People, Common Clay, Three Faces East* and *Sin Takes a Holiday*, all made in 1930, Miss Bennett was seduced and abandoned by the scion of one wealthy family or another. In 1931 she made four pictures: *Bought, The Easiest Way, The Common Law,* and *Born to Love*. In these, too, her trust in men was betrayed.

Constance Bennett's rival, Joan Crawford, eventually surpassed Miss Bennett, if not in acting ability at least in popularity. This ambitious actress appeared in dozens of films based on a theme of "rags-to-riches without happiness." Usually cast as a hard-as-nails shopgirl, Miss Crawford always met a rich man who offered her jewels, furs, and a penthouse, but seldom marriage. Striding about in Adrian gowns and mingling with the wealthy, she had everything she had always yearned for but was more miserable than ever. After suffering, weeping, and recognizing her errors, Crawford would eventually find true happiness by spurning wealth and sin for some poor but honest young man. Miss Crawford sought happiness in *Sadie McKee* (1934), *No More Ladies* (1935), and *I Live My Life* (1935).

The 1930's may have seen the freewheeling, wisecracking heroine bringing realistic stories to the screen, but the movies also presented sentimental tales and romantic comedies. Irene Dunne admirably portrayed a gallery of self-sustaining wives, mothers, sweethearts, and mistresses in *Back Street* (1931), *Magnificent Obsession* (1935), and *When Tomorrow Comes* (1941). In *Love Affair* (1939), playing opposite the magnetic Charles Boyer in the ultimate love story, two people meet on a luxury cruise, fall in love, then separate, but agree to meet in six months. On her way to the rendezvous the girl is hit by a car and crippled. She doesn't tell the man, refusing to be a burden. Months later they meet again when he comes to her apartment to bring a gift from his grandmother and discovers she is crippled. Audiences wept and laughed with the actress in this beautifully acted tale. The background was perfect for the story—Naples, the French Riviera, ocean liners, New York. Leo McCarey directed a near-perfect romantic film.

Tear jerkers were carried to a higher level of cinema art with the appearance of the shrewd and attractive Norma Shearer. Irving Thalberg, an MGM executive, decided to star his wife in several elegant women's pictures. Miss Shearer worked the sob-circuit in such pictures as *The Divorcee* (1929), *The Trail of Mary Dugan* (1929), and *The Last of Mrs. Cheyney* (1930). Later she had the intelligence to select more challenging roles, and eventually proved her ability in such romantic films as the doomed Elizabeth Moonyean in *Smilin' Through* (1932) and Elizabeth Barrett Browning in *The Barretts of Wimpole Street* (1934). With her patrician bearing and sharpened aristocratic air she was the last word in feminine sophistication. Her regal courage as she goes to meet her death in *Marie Antoinette* (1938) reveals her as a dramatically versatile actress.

Dietrich and Garbo are the actresses who excelled in the romantic film. Their last pictures signaled the end of the genre. By the 1940's the screen turned to the American career girl.

Marlene Dietrich in *The Garden of Allah* (1936) becomes the screen's purest romantic transfiguration. In *Shanghai Express* (1932), most of the action takes place aboard a train as Shanghai Lily and her former lover Captain Harvey (Clive Brook) are held up by a gang of revolutionaries. The sets, lighting, costumes, and acting made this Sternberg's greatest popular success of the early 1930's. In *Dishonored* (1931), she is a Viennese streetwalker recruited to be a spy, who then falls in love with her Russian enemy. In *The Blue Angel* (1930), *Scarlet Empress* (1934), and *The Devil is a Woman* (1935) she presents a subtle put-down of the romantic as sentimental fool. Her films are all nuance, shadows, and suggestion—and above all, romantic.

Garbo's allure, like Dietrich's, lay in her denial of the humdrum world reserved for other women. Divinely untouchable, as a *femme fatale* she draws men like a magnet and is eventually victimized by love. In *Susan Lenox* (1931), desolate and in love, she follows her man into the steamy tropics to beg forgiveness. In *Grand Hotel* (1932) she prepares for an assignation with her lover, not knowing he has been killed. In *Queen Christina* (1933), she sets off for a solitary life. Her lover has been killed in a duel. In *Anna Karenina* (1935) she forsakes her child, husband, and reputation to run off with a military officer. When he tires of her she throws herself under a train.

Her performance in *Camille* (1937) has been pointed out by critics as the single most beautiful performance in the American sound film. As the demimondaine reformed by love, Camille excels at self-sacrificing love. Her luminous beauty, extraordinary sensuality, and disciplined acting override the banal material and carry it to great heights in screen entertainment. *Camille* proves how the romantic film can be high art. Women admired the actress for her willingness to acknowledge her sensuality. Garbo was an adult woman caught in the web of love, and audiences, especially women, paid to see her suffer. Her many films offer adventure, love, romance, and disaster.

Dorothy McGuire, Margaret Sullavan, and Joan Fontaine brought class, refinement, and art to the romantic genre. Audiences recognized and admired these heroines as a breed apart. Their films projected their beauty and goodness, down to the last detail. All three women brought unobtrusive good taste to sometimes overly sentimental stories.

Dorothy McGuire, whose quiet and appealing charm could breathe intelligence and beauty into the dullest housewife, proved in *Claudia* (1943) her superior talent as an actress. Her gentle, sympathetic characterization of the mute in the suspense thriller *The Spiral Staircase* (1945) was an affecting performance. In *The Enchanted Cottage* (1945), as the ugly wife she was magically transformed into a beautiful person through other people's love and affection. Dorothy McGuire made a soap opera believable.

The most romantic heroine of the talkies, Margaret Sullavan, made no secret of the fact that she was embarrassed by making movies. This did not stop her from turning *Only Yesterday* (1933), a soapy weeper, into an above-average film. Director Frank Borzage, one of Hollywood's great romanticists, exploited her romantically innocent quality in four films: *Little Man, What Now* (1934), *Three Comrades* (1938), *The Shining Hour* (1938), and *The Mortal Storm* (1940). Her best performance is in Ernst Lubitsch's enchanting *The Shop Around the Corner* (1940). Sullavan's face, her instinctive grace, her honey-husked voice, and special magic gave the movies some enchantingly beautiful performances. She raised the sentimentality inherent in the love-and-suffer theme to a creative level.

Actresses used to complain in the 1940's that all the good roles went to Ingrid Bergman, but Joan Fontaine had no reason to complain. She may have been cast in the same role over and over again, but to each she added a delicate touch, a romantic flair that distinguished her characterizations. Fontaine excelled as the wide-eyed innocent shy English rose threatened on all sides by approaching danger. Her films demanded no real thought on the part of the audience, but most at least offered an evening of excellent make-believe. She excelled in her sensitive portrait of the young girl in Alfred Hitchcock's screen adaptation of Daphne DuMaurier's popular novel, *Rebecca* (1940), the story of a shy wife who feels that her new husband (Laurence Olivier) does not love her and thinks her a poor substitute for his dead spouse. Without getting maudlin, the movie evokes just the right touch of sympathy for the unhappy wife.

Fontaine won an Academy Award in Hitchcock's *Suspicion* (1941), the story of an heiress who fears that her husband (Cary Grant) is out to murder her. *Jane Eyre* (1943) successfully reworked the pattern of a genteel young woman who almost falls apart as inexplicable events terrorize her.

No discussion of romance is complete without a glance at the contributions of Ingrid Bergman. Introduced to American audiences in *Intermezzo* (1936), the Swedish beauty was an instant success. In *Casablanca* (1943), she and Bogart, in a film geared to the romantic tradition, created a miraculous aura. Bergman will always be remembered by this film. *Gaslight* (1944), in which she and Charles Boyer are cast against type as criminal and victim in a study of Victorian villainy, is a pungent production. As the distraught wife, Bergman offers an emotional characterization marked by superior acting. In *Spellbound* (1945) she is the intense psychiatrist, awakened to love by her new chief Gregory Peck. Her performance convinced the audience of the sincerity of this rare film. In *For Whom the Bell Tolls* (1943), she adds an earthiness and sensual beauty as the Spanish Loyalist peasant girl, and in *Notorious* (1946), the story of spies in Buenos Aires, her characterization is charged with intensity and warm appeal. Ingrid Bergman excelled in roles of spiritual quality; she went from one successful film to another, creating a gallery of characters of winning personality, lustrous looks and ardent sincerity.

By the mid-1930's, the "hankie" and costume romance pictures were giving way to a more sophisticated type of woman's picture. Writers discovered the career girl. With skillful studio publicity and stronger roles, women emerged as superstars. Claudette Colbert, Carole Lombard, Rosalind Russell, Norma Shearer, Bette Davis, Katharine Hepburn, Barbara Stanwyck, and Ginger Rogers were valuable studio "properties."

In 1938 and 1939, two films were released that helped push the woman's picture into more prominence. Warner Brothers, wanting to cash in on the advance publicity of *Gone With the Wind* rushed into production and released *Jezebel* (1938), the story of a rebellious Southern beauty. Deliberately structured to the talents of Bette Davis, the film found an eager public. The following year the success of the epic *Gone With the Wind*, and particularly the performance of Vivien Leigh, induced studios to seek out scenarios with strong roles for women.

By 1942, eleven million men were in uniform, and a great percentage of the movie audiences consisted of women. To the box office came the mothers, wives, sweethearts, and sisters of men at war; the movies depicted women's problems and emotions, and female camaraderie, displaying women against an array of job backgrounds—Rosie the Riveter, government girls, and women in uniform. The pictures were usually concerned with a woman's constant search for happiness, self-sacrifice, or the woes of the beautiful heroine in love with a married man, torn between sin and virtue. Many were emancipated girls, fighting for a safe and secure world.

The genre began in earnest when MGM executive Louis B. Mayer persuaded Greer Garson and Walter Pidgeon to make a series of sentimental war stories. *Mrs. Miniver* (1942) was laughed at by the British facing Nazi bombs, but it affected American audiences. The industry went to work in earnest to propagandize for the Allies, and various aspects of war dominated the themes of 80 percent of the films that followed.

Every studio was quick to see the potential box office appeal in women's problems, but Warner Brothers and MGM worked hardest. Warner's studio fared best, for they had such stars as Bette Davis, Joan Crawford, Ann Sheridan, and Barbara Stanwyck under contract. MGM offered Irene Dunne, Greer Garson, Katharine Hepburn, Lana Turner, and Ava Gardner. Columbia's ace was Rita Hayworth; Twentieth Century-Fox exhibited Betty Grable; RKO found comedy material for Alice Faye and Rosalind Russell.

MGM produced a series of battle-of-the-sexes comedies with Katharine Hepburn and Spencer Tracy. When *Woman of the Year* (1942), directed by George Cukor, was critically and financially successful, MGM put the two in tandem for eight more pictures. The Tracy/Hepburn films deserve special mention, for they are today the screen's best examples of sophisticated comedy, appealing to men as well as women. Tracy, usually a sports writer or promoter, newspaper reporter, scientist, or district attoney, is confonted by the headstong Hepburn with her cultured accent, upper-crust confidence, and elegant mannerisms. Audiences loved it when the level-headed and acid-tongued Tracy got the better of the suave and uppity society girl, the aristocrat willing to leave her social level and indulge in democratic fun.

There were other movie couples: Jeanette MacDonald and Nelson Eddy smiling at each other, warbling duets; Veronica Lake and Alan Ladd in trenchcoats, slinking through foreign streets; Greer Garson and Walter Pidgeon braving the buzz bombs; Myrna Loy and William Powell dressed in impeccable evening clothes solving endless crimes. But Tracy and Hepburn were *the* romantic American couple. Their combination of wit and elegant earthiness brought dignity, beauty, and idealism to the screen comedy. For over a decade the two starred in slick, amusing stories noted for witty dialogue and finished acting. Their best films were *Woman of the Year* (1941), *Without Love* (1945), *State of the Union* (1948), *Adam's Rib* (1949), and *Pat and Mike* (1952).

Bette Davis's films can hardly be classified as romantic. Love is seldom an emotion projected in her films, and although in the 1940's, when women came to grips with a manless existence and Hollywood offered tear-jerking plots, bitchery and frivolity gave way to female strength, particularly between women—but not Davis. With the exception of *Dark Victory* (1939), *The Old Maid* (1939), *Now Voyager* (1942) and *Old Acquaintance* (1943), which she balanced with compassion, she is the quintessential evil woman. Davis rode to stardom on malevolence. Not commercially beautiful, with startling eyes and a disdainful mouth, she projects anger, cruelty, pain, and evil.

As empress of Warner Brothers and queen of the neurotics,

Bette Davis starred in a series of improbable melodramas in which she shot men, killed her sister, ran down a mother and her child, and opposed fascism. Several times she even played a double role.

Davis enjoyed one box office success after another in *Jezebel* (1938), *The Letter* (1940), *The Great Lie* (1941), *A Stolen Life* (1946), and *All About Eve* (1950). She lived in a studio dream world, filming unbelievable stories and building up a tremendous public following. Always surrounded by dependable performers such as Claude Rains, Gladys Cooper, Geraldine FitzGerald or Mary Astor, she emerged as the greatest dramatic star and box office queen from 1937 to 1947. Her best performances are *Of Human Bondage* (1934), *Jezebel* (1938), and *All About Eve* (1950). During the 1930's and 1940's she entrenched herself in unsympathetic roles but in her gallery of psychotic characters she managed to pick up two Academy Awards. Her films helped propel the romantic films of Dietrich and Garbo into obsolescence.

Joan Crawford followed closely behind Davis. Both stars knew all the techniques of moviemaking, both knew how they should be lighted and dressed to show off their physical aspects, and both knew the kind of scripts that would reveal their talents. Crawford's best roles were *Grand Hotel* (1932), *A Woman's Face* (1941), in which she led a band of crooks in Stockholm, and *Mildred Pierce* (1945), which garnered her an Academy Award.

Mildred Pierce, a beautifully photographed soap opera, could be considered the typical woman's film of the 1940's. The plot is a far-fetched melodrama, telling the story of an outraged mother's revenge on her second husband who has switched his affection to Mildred's daughter.

The picture has all the characteristics of the genre—illicit love, sex, murder, self-sacrifice, and the dastardly deeds of a selfish man. Audiences were willing to forget the empty contrived plot, because the shoddy story was enhanced by skillful lighting, fine clothes, elegant settings and convincing characterizations. The public loved Mildred—her warmth, her sacrifices for her children, and her final triumph. Crawford brought expertise to the role and gave the screen her best perfomance as the ambitious mother.

Before the woman's picture lost its appeal, there were two superior productions worthy of attention, both proving that the genre can be a work of art when handled by experts. The

first, *Letter from an Unknown Woman* (1948), stands today
as a pictorial classic. Howard Koch turned a novelette by Ste-
fan Zweig into a scenario, and Universal invited Max Ophuls,
the international director, to translate the romantic story into
filmic form. Joan Fontaine played the lead, supported by
Louis Jourdan. Told in flashbacks, the film is a character
study of a girl trapped in her romantic dreams, a victim of
her illusions. Overcome by nostalgia, she is unable to move
forward in her life, preferring to live only for the moment in
time she spent with a pianist.

The film overflows with the rich black-and-white photography of Franz Planer. In lyrical beauty, the long tracking
shots catch the spirit of the lovers and the beauty of the city.
Ophuls uses camera angles, romantic images, ironic situations, and various repeated sequences to hint at the futility of
the love affair. His direction, the photography, and the beauty
of Joan Fontaine—her breathless delivery of lines and her restrained acting—elevate the picture into an unforgettable
movie. Everything works in this film to show how powerful
the romance picture could be.

The second film, *The Heiress* (1949), excels because of the
masterful direction of the distinguished William Wyler, the
superb acting of Olivia de Havilland and Ralph Richardson,
and the skillfully crafted script by Ruth and August Goetz.
Leo Tover's photography catches not only the anguish of
characters but also the austere background of the Sloper's
home on Washington Square.

When the war ended, perceptive producers turned to sociological themes, shooting realistic crime thrillers on actual
location. The American woman, her man returned, was no
longer seeking to escape from her own reality into someone
else's larger-than-life-size problems while American men,
fresh from Normandy and Iwo Jima, preferred stories that
concerned the contemporary world.

The genre did not end abruptly, however, but trailed on
into a more subdued, secondary level. Joan Crawford continued with *Possessed* (1947) and *The Damned Don't Cry*
(1950); Jennifer Jones made *Love Letters* (1945), *Portrait
of Jennie* (1948), and *Madame Bovary* (1949). Mention
should be made of two films with Susan Hayward, as the alcoholic in *I'll Cry Tomorrow* (1955) and the murderess in *I
Want to Live* (1958), showing how far from romance the
woman's picture had ventured. Barbara Stanwyck, Bette

Davis, Greer Garson, and Lana Turner tried to pump life into empty scripts, but the genre was waning.

Ross Hunter made one last effort to recapture a dwindling audience as late as 1966. Dusting off one of the most badly battered scripts ever to be filmed (six times), he produced *Madame X*. Like *Back Street*, *Smilin' Through*, and *Stella Dallas*, this film had been a perennial favorite with matinee matrons. Hunter's version, directed by David Lowell Rich and starring Lana Turner, was the sixth remake, and without a doubt the worst.

By the middle of the 1950's many of the woman stars were released from their contracts and went their separate ways. Some realized that age had caught up with them and retired; others tried Broadway; a few continued to make inferior films. Others disappeared or turned up in touring companies of Broadway shows. The only actress whose star ascended in the 1950's was Marilyn Monroe. Physically attractive, charming, beautiful and talented, she was one of the new performers to rise to the status of superstar. Marilyn went from one success to another. Unfortunately the stress of the star system was her downfall.

For two decades, the woman's picture did not fare too well. McCarthyism, atomic weapons, the Korean and Cold War, juvenile delinquency, the rise of the drug problem, and television demanded the attention of the public. The 1950's had little to offer. *Peyton Place* (1957) was an unsatisfying version of a best-seller, offering one woman's viewpoint on the moral hypocrisy and sexual maladjustments of Middle America. The autonomous 1940's heroine was left behind. Marriage was a popular institution. Women slipped into masculine shadows and wore aprons, had kids, worked. The independent, career-minded girls of the 1940's were out. Bright and witty women with style and self-importance ended. Few female stars could bear a picture on their own shoulders. *A Star is Born* (1954) was the best of the romance pictures of the 1950's. Judy Garland found herself torn between two great loves—her man and her career. Katharine Hepburn kept the flickering flame of romance alive in *The African Queen* (1951), *Summertime* (1955), *The Rainmaker* (1956), and *The Desk Set* (1957). With intelligence, energy, and stoicism, Hepburn, facing life as a middle-aged unmarried female, finds love and happiness.

The torments of love as depicted in the novels of Fannie Hurst, Faith Baldwin, Kathleen Norris, and Edna Ferber gave way to the sordid worlds of Tennessee Williams and William Inge. The lush romantic scores of Erich Wolfgang Korngold, Frederick Hollander, Max Steiner, and Alfred Newman gave way to soundtrack engineers who found their inspiration in the classical music of Maurice Ravel, Richard Strauss, or Igor Stravinsky, jazz, rock and pop, and preexisting popular music.

Tennessee Williams's plays, with their deftly structured, passionate plots, were concerned with sleazy, sexy situations in which delicate heroines, driven by loneliness and archaic romantic ideals, are sex-starved, ranting bitches or traumatized by collapsing love affairs. Between the 1950's and the 1960's, nine of his plays (one novel) kept Gertrude Lawrence, Vivien Leigh, Katharine Hepburn, Anna Magnani, Elizabeth Taylor, and Geraldine Page before an appreciative public. *The Glass Menagerie* (1950), *A Streetcar Named Desire* (1951), *The Rose Tattoo* (1955), *The Fugitive Kind* (1958), *Cat on a Hot Tin Roof* (1958), *Suddenly Last Summer* (1959), *The Roman Spring of Mrs. Stone* (1961), *Summer and Smoke* (1961), and *Sweet Bird of Youth* (1962) gave actresses an opportunity to try for classical heroic stature.

While films of the 1930's and 1940's romanticized life in small-town America, films of the 1950's criticized it. William Inge's plays do not offer violence but portray sympathetically the aspirations and thwarted ambitions of small-town life in the Midwest. Inhabitants live behind a facade, are empty, unsatisfied people, often sexually frustrated. *Picnic* (1956) is filled with emotional battles and brings into the open the interpersonal conflicts of normal American people. A drifter (William Holden) awakens sexual desires and changes the lives of various women. *Come Back Little Sheba* (1952), *Dark at the Top of the Stairs* (1960), and *Splendor in the Grass* (1961) present a sure eye for character and views of sexual conflict.

The era of the Love Goddess virtually ended with the death of Marilyn Monroe in 1962. The trend toward self-expression, youth and liberation gave the screen actresses but no new heroines, sirens, or ladies. In the 1960's and early 1970's, directors were too busy turning violence into money and feeding the public a steady stream of buddy-buddy movies, with male teams replacing the boy-girl romance. But by 1975, the industry took a new direction. Human relationships have not been a basic theme for many movies lately, and particularly deep friendship with or between women. However, the rising importance of women has made studios turn their cameras on their problems and present them as people with feelings, fantasies, and fates of their own. Movies are discovering that relationships can exist between women as well as men.

Martin Scorsese's *Alice Doesn't Live Here Anymore* (1974) initiates a new direction for the self-determination of women. It tells the story of a woman who is deprived of her husband's support and protection and is forced to take the road of independence. Ellen Burstyn never once loses her femininity as Alice. She handles the uncertainty and self-doubt of her situation with humor, wit, and gritty determination. Alice will survive against all odds. The film mirrors both the problems and the joys of searching for self-fulfillment.

In Robert Altman's *Three Women* (1977), the setting is a rehabilitation center for old people in Palm Springs. The inmates are attended by white-clad girls who come and go according to a time clock, a therapeutic assembly line. The approach is clinical. To this desert spa comes Millie (Shelley Duvall), looking for love. Pinky (Sissy Spacek) arrives at this hygienic limbo and moves in with Millie, and the two, living in this desert wasteland, share emptiness and the absence of love. A third woman, Willie (Janice Rule), their landlady, is an artist. After a horrific climax, the three form a female trinity, each assuming a role that had been denied her in individual life. Altman's movie captures the innermost world of the three women, telling us in his paradoxical film of light and heat, sorrow and joy, together and alone, that people are becoming more vulnerable to pain, cruelty, loss, and betrayal. The film with its searching insight and beauty of form has three performers who evoke acting at its deepest expressive level.

Fred Zinnemann's *Julia* (1977), the story of friendship between two women, is a moving recollection of that profound bond of feeling that can exist between women as well as men. Julia (Vanessa Redgrave), an Englishwoman, a rebel since childhood, is now an anti-Fascist in Berlin. Lillian (Jane Fonda), her friend, smuggles a large sum of money into Germany to help Julia in her fight against oppression. The picture has a touch of cloak-and-dagger, world history (Hitler's Berlin), and political observations. Jane Fonda and Vanessa Redgrave offer characterizations that are marvelous and true.

Zinnemann's film is another step toward recognizing women and the problems they face.

Kathleen Quinlan as a schizophrenic patient and Bibi Andersson as her psychiatrist in *I Never Promised You a Rose Garden* (1977) received critical acclaim. Jane Fonda in *Coming Home* (1977), Diane Keaton in *Looking for Mr. Goodbar* (1977), and Liza Minnelli in *New York, New York* (1977) are Hollywood's extensions of problems that concern women. Paul Mazursky's *An Unmarried Woman* (1978) and Herbert Ross's *The Turning Point* (1977) reveal women as no longer satellites to man put planets in their own right.

Following a long spell of small parts, actresses at last are emerging into prominence again. After a decade in which sex roles in American society have undergone some irreversible changes or modifications, the old family movie stereotypes are unusable. The old-fashioned female is no longer of interest to the public. The clinging vine, shrinking violet type is passing away.

Where does the woman's picture go? What exactly is the woman's role in society? The effects of the Women's Liberation movement make trying to place her in society increasingly difficult for screenwriters. Movies can no longer offer the self-sacrificing or the decorative woman as sex objects, or at best subservient to men. As man and woman move toward meeting each other on mutual territory, the number of divorces mounts and the family shrinks to the basic unit of a couple. (In an equal world, the hunt for greater freedom may have lasting results. Warren Beatty's *Shampoo* (1975) reveals this facet.) Are serial marriages to be accepted as patterns of life? The family in its traditional structure, surrounded by its relatives and community ties as reflected in the *Andy Hardy* series, *Meet Me in St. Louis,* and the penultimate *The Grapes of Wrath.* is disappearing. What will be the image of the modern woman? Will she be a mere extension of a career girl, an equal partner to her man, a policewoman, or a bionic invention?

Outstanding Romance Films
Their Directors and Stars

Only Yesterday	(1933)	John Stahl (Margaret Sullavan)
The Barrets of Wimpole Street	(1934)	Sidney Franklin (Norma Shearer)
Alice Adams	(1935)	George Stevens (Katharine Hepburn)
Anna Karenina	(1935)	Clarence Brown (Greta Garbo)
Camille	(1936)	George Cukor (Greta Garbo)
Jezebel	(1938)	William Wyler (Bette Davis)
Wuthering Heights	(1939)	William Wyler (Merle Oberon)
Love Affair	(1939)	Leo McCarey (Irene Dunne)
Rebecca	(1940)	Alfred Hitchcock (Joan Fontaine)
The Letter	(1940)	William Wyler (Bette Davis)
Kitty Foyle	(1940)	Sam Wood (Ginger Rogers)
The Little Foxes	(1941)	William Wyler (Bette Davis)
Suspicion	(1941)	Alfred Hitchcock (Joan Fontaine)
Mrs. Miniver	(1942)	William Wyler (Greer Garson)
The Constant Nymph	(1943)	Edmund Goulding (Joan Fontaine)
Old Acquaintance	(1943)	Vincent Sherman (Bette Davis)
Gaslight	(1944)	George Cukor (Ingrid Bergman)
Mildred Pierce	(1945)	Michael Curtiz (Joan Crawford)
To Each His Own	(1946)	Mitchell Leisen (Olivia de Havilland)
Letter from an Unknown Woman	(1948)	Max Ophuls (Joan Fontaine)

The Heiress	(1949)	William Wyler (Olivia de Havilland)
Summertime	(1955)	David Lean (Katharine Hepburn)
Alice Doesn't Live Here Any More	(1974)	Martin Scorsese (Ellen Burstyn)
Three Women	(1977)	Robert Altman (Janice Rule, Sissy Spacek, Shelley Duvall)
Julia	(1977)	Fred Zinnemann (Jane Fonda, Vanessa Redgrave)

21 / Novels into Film

IN ITS development, the screen has been an all-devouring monster, and moviemakers had to search everywhere for food to put into the hungry invention. Thus a close relationship has existed between the novel and the film from the beginning of the film industry. The reciprocity is clear from many points of view: the number of films based on novels; the effect of adaptations on reading; a built-in audience that assures box office receipts. The industry's own appraisal of its work shows a persistent, steady preference for films derived from novels. When the film went from the animation of stills to telling a story, it was inevitable that the novel would become an invaluable source of material.

In 1903, Edwin S. Porter of the Edison Company filmed Harriet Beecher Stowe's *Uncle Tom's Cabin* as a series of tableaux, with little attempt at continuity. Topsy, without any introduction, dances a jig, St. Claire is killed in a saloon brawl while defending Uncle Tom and Mark shoots Simon Legree.

But the Italians were among the first to seize upon and make full use of the novel as a source of material for films. In 1908, Luigi Maggi filmed his interpretation of Sir Edward Bulwer-Lytton's *The Last Days of Pompeii*. By 1909 the American screen offered Mary Pickford in *The Violin Maker of Cremona*. Novels into film had become a part of the industry.

By 1910, Vitagraph, a studio operating in Brooklyn, attempted to lure big names from the theater by offering them roles in literary classics. Their most successful effort was *A Tale of Two Cities* (1911), starring Maurice Costello as Sydney Carton and Florence Turner as Lucy Manette. Norma Talmadge was the little seamstress who rode to her death with Carton. Miss Turner appeared as Viola in Shakespeare's *Twelfth Night*, later as Hetty in an adaptation of James Fenimore Cooper's *The Deerslayer*. In 1908, director Francis

Boggs turned out a one-reel version of Alexandre Dumas' *The Count of Monte Cristo* (1908).

D. W. Griffith was one of the most important earlier directors to use novels as bases for film art. During his first years as a director, he adapted a number of literary works, among them Jack London's *Just Meat (For Love of Gold)* (1908), Frank Norris's *A Corner in Wheat* (1909), and Helen Hunt Jackson's popular novel of the noble Indian girl, *Ramona* (1910).

One of Griffith's greatest successes, *Broken Blossoms* (1919), was based on the short story "The Chink and the Child" from Thomas Burke's *Limehouse Nights*. Completed in eighteen days of shooting, the film concerns a poignant love story set in London's East End, reminiscent of Charles Dickens's novels at their most graphic level. Griffith's editing, authentic sets and, above all, the quality of the performances in *Broken Blossoms* made the work a screen classic. The film, telling of brutality, prejudice, and impossible love, deserved its lasting screen success. The early scenes are filled with the velvety, almost phosphorescent photographic effects later hailed as revolutionary in the films of Joseph von Sternberg.

Nathaniel Hawthorne's *The Scarlet Letter* (1926), was filmed no fewer than five times, but Lillian Gish's impersonation of Hester Prynne remains the best. Directed by the Swedish Victor Seastrom (Sjostrom), the film contains characteristic elements of the Scandinavian artist's work: an austere theme, brooding skies, dark landscapes, the intermingling of beauty and sensitivity, and stark tragedy.

Miss Gish at last was cast in the role of a mature woman, in sharp contrast to the innocent and girlish characters presented to her under Griffith's direction. Her performance, coupled with Seastrom's brilliant direction, makes this one of the most skillful literary adaptations for the screen.

For twenty-three years, Mary Pickford, the undisputed queen of the cinema, was America's Sweetheart. She appeared in a number of adaptations of popular but minor works of literature. Her early successes were *Poor Little Rich Girl* (1917), from the Eleanor Gates novel, and *Rebecca of Sunnybrook Farm* (1919), the popular novel by Kate Douglas Wiggin. In 1920 she appeared as Eleanor H. Porter's fatuous optimist *Pollyanna*. In Frances Hodgson Burnett's *Little Lord Fauntleroy* (1921), she enjoyed one of the most successful roles in her lengthy career.

In contrast to the innocent world of Kate Douglas Wiggin,

Eleanor H. Porter and Frances Hodgson Burnett, Hollywood by 1924 discovered the fictional world of Elinor Glyn. "Madame" Glyn's best-sellers, peopled with sentimental characters, dealt daringly with adultery in a prewar world of Ruritania's glittering royalty, hunting parties, and never-ending romance, often seen through the eyes of a servant girl. This world had ended by 1918, but Madame Glyn, like Erich von Stroheim, was smart enough to realize that innocent Americans were still awed by titles and imagined European nobility wallowing in luxury and depravity. For an industry in its infancy, Elinor Glyn provided an added spark of life.

Madame Glyn's official masterpiece, *Three Weeks* (1924), involves a beautiful queen of a faraway kingdom who foresakes her loveless existence for a stolen holiday with a young British aristocrat. She then sorrowfully renounces him and returns to assume her royal duties. By the end of the 1920's, however, the studios and public had had enough of Glyn trivia.

During the same decade, there were other outstanding adaptations of novels. Robert Louis Stevenson's classic thriller *Dr. Jekyll and Mr. Hyde* (1920) presented John Barrymore enjoying the horrific role of the dangerous, unpredictable doctor. Douglas Fairbanks changed Johnson McCulley's story "The Curse of Capistrano" into a swashbuckling drama, *The Mark of Zorro* (1920). Joseph Hergesheimer's story of simple mountain folk, *Tol'able David* (1921), emerged as one of the most beautiful films of rural American life. *The Covered Wagon* (1923), based on the novel by Emerson Hough, was brought to the screen by director James Cruze. Victor Hugo's classic novel *The Hunchback of Notre Dame* (1923), directed by Wallace Worsley, offered Lon Chaney in a striking and vivid characterization.

The industry reached everywhere to find material to feed its ever-hungry cameras; and producers, realizing that best-sellers already had a built-in audience, paid high prices for popular publications. The 1930's more than any other decade found the novel a great fount for screenplays.

All Quiet on the Western Front (1930), adopted from Erich Remarque's best-seller, was turned into a milestone of cinema history. Directed by Lewis Milestone, it is an outstanding condemnation of war and ranks among the finest motion pictures on this theme (see "War Films").

Under the regime of decency, inaugurated by the New Production Code of Administration, supervised by Joseph

Breen, Hollywood focused its cameras away from the harsher aspects of contemporary life towards the events of a sweeter and safer day. Charles Dickens, William Shakespeare, William Makepeace Thackeray, Leo Tolstoy, Louisa May Alcott, and Sir James Barrie were the spiritual, and often the actual, authors of the stories on which the screenplays of 1934, 1935, and 1936 were based. Literary greats replaced the gangster and the shady lady. Favorable box office responses to these literary classics caused the industry to reflect that perhaps the public might be forsaking Frankenstein, Al Capone, the Wolf Man and Billy the Kid.

Charles Dickens and James M. Barrie dominated Hollywood in the mid-1930's. Dickens was a natural for films, with his eccentric characters and intricate plot-weaving novels. *Dombey and Son* (retitled *Rich Man's Folly*) (1931); *David Copperfield* (1934); *Great Expectations* (1934); and *The Mystery of Edwin Drood* (1935) were all public favorites. The fey characters from Barrie's novels and plays made audiences happy. *The Little Minister* (1934), *What Every Woman Knows* (1934) and *Quality Street* (1937) entertained the public and offered stardom to players. Movies transported audiences out of harsh America into tranquil nineteenth-century England.

Moviemakers reworked the Dickens story *A Tale of Two Cities* at least seven times. Jack Conway's 1935 version remains the best. No film has captured so accurately Sydney Carton's melancholy fatalism (brilliantly portrayed by Ronald Colman) or the moral necessities which can drive a man to self-destruction. There are memorable scenes: Carton in the snow at Christmas watching the carollers and churchgoers hurry past to the warmth of the home which he does not possess, the courtroom scene, the ride to the guillotine, and Carton standing on the edge of death delivering his famous speech, " 'Tis a far, far better thing I do today than I have ever done before . . ."

Continuing to work the vein of nostalgia and innocence, George Cukor directed Louisa May Alcott's *Little Women* (1933). With its flawless Hobe Erwin designs and a competent performance by the angular and athletic Katharine Hepburn in the role of tomboy Jo March, it is today a viewable if slightly saccharine romance.

John Ford's adaptation of Liam O'Flaherty's *The Informer* (1935) is one of the decade's best achievements and deserves attention not only because it transgressed the rules of Hollywood, but also because the director was able to turn melodrama into something close to tragedy. The picture cost very little and required only three weeks to shoot. Because he believed so deeply in his production, Ford worked without salary, settling instead for a percentage of the profits.

Set in Ireland at the time of the Black and Tan Rebellion (1921), it tells the story of a man's temptation, fears and remorse; his fall, retribution, forgiveness and death. An Irish rebel, Gypo Nolan (Victor McLaglen), betrays his friend to the British for the reward of a mere twenty pounds. The hero/villain picks up his blood money, spends it on fish and chips and gives part of it away to a needy girl, is captured, and goes to his death. Stories that necessitated the killing of a likeable character and emphasized human weaknesses were not usually tolerated by Hollywood, but Ford was determined not to provide a last-minute rescue.

Usually men who betray their buddies are villains deserving death. Ford's development of Gypo's character is the crux of the picture's greatness. McLaglen's torment, anguish, and blustering ways make him an ambivalent villain. His suffering and redemption assume tragic overtones as he stumbles along to his inevitable doom.

Brilliant performances, Max Steiner's musical score, and Ford's sensitive direction and editing turned the picture into a classic.

MGM Studios appears to have had the most elaborate library. In *Mutiny on the Bounty* (1935), the story of Captain Bligh cast adrift in an open boat in 1789, Charles Laughton's performance is superior screen acting. *Captains Courageous* (1937), by Rudyard Kipling, was faithfully adapted for the screen. The Kipling tale excells with two famous performances, Freddie Bartholomew as the rich spoiled brat who emerges into an honorable and decent fellow, and Spencer Tracy as Manuel, the Portuguese sailor. Victor Fleming and his cameraman Hal Rossen give their documentary quality, enriched with breathtaking shots of the fishing fleet, heaving seas and unfurling sails.

Frank Capra's *Lost Horizon* (1937), from the James Hilton novel, is a splendid fantasy, one of the most impressive films of the 1930's. A group of travelers fleeing from the revolution in China is forced to land their plane in the hidden kingdom of Shangri-La, a Tibetan utopia. The English explorer is delighted with the tranquil city, but his fellow travelers become restless and want to return home. On the trail over a high mountain pass, the travelers are killed; Colman alone survives. The film ends with his struggling back across the mountain, an infinitesimal figure crawling up a sheer cliff in a violent storm, determined to reach again the paradise of Shangri-La.

Pearl Buck's novel *The Good Earth* (1937), filmed by Sidney Franklin, recreates Chinese history at the turn of the century as seen through the eyes of a peasant farmer and his family. Farmer Wang Lung and his wife O-Lan work the land, rear a family, and despite plagues, famine, and other misfortunes endure a cycle of work, success, failure, and eventually, happiness. The film is an example of superb studio teamwork. A stream of writers worked on the script, three directors contributed ideas, a first-rate cast excelled at characterizations, skillful craftsmen produced authentic sets and costumes, and the special effects department helped push the film into a screen classic, with what appeared to be authentic swarms of locusts, fires, earthquakes, and revolutions. Franklin's film epitomizes what made American pictures of the 1930's so technically brilliant.

In 1939 William Wyler turned Emily Brontë's powerful and atmospheric classic *Wuthering Heights* into one of his most highly rated films, despite substantial defects in concept and execution. Wyler's interpretation of the brooding, Gothic novel may not satisfy fastidious literary critics, but no matter—the public loved it. Like *Gone With the Wind*, made in the same year, *Wuthering Heights* is American moviemaking at its best. The newspapermen-screenwriters Ben Hecht and Charles MacArthur were an odd selection to adapt the Brontë novel, for both were creators of hardnosed, snarling, contemporary characters, hardly the artists to bring to the screen the tormented Yorkshire characters. They made daring changes in the script, cutting out the whole second generation of characters, omitting many situations in the book's first half, and concentrating on the Heathcliff-Cathy romance. Their creative screenplay caught much of the torment, cruelty, and beauty of the original.

A demanding director, Wyler insisted on authentic sets, costumes, and music, and James Basevi's designs added to the film's magnificence. Laurence Olivier was magnificent as the uncouth, brooding, passionate Heathcliff. His portrayal dominated the film. The fragile Merle Oberon as Catherine Earnshaw was a perfect foil for the tempestuous Olivier. Their portrayal of the doomed lovers set amidst the Yorkshire moors brought cinema to great heights. Greg Toland's photography, the excellent scenario, lighting, acting, and setting, along with Wellman's editing, made *Wuthering Heights* one of the screen's major achievements of the decade.

The Civil War epic *Gone With the Wind* (1939), one of the largest-grossing films in cinema history, provided a superb capstone for the films of these years. Directed for the most part by Victor Fleming, the film sealed David O. Selznick's reputation as a producer of spectacular pictures. Vivien Leigh gave her most convincing performance as Scarlett O'Hara. (See "The Epic Spectacular" for details.)

Studio executives pronounced John Steinbeck's novel *The Grapes of Wrath* too controversial for film material. Some critics called it a Communist document, an attack on America; others pronounced it a masterpiece. John Ford staked his reputation on the controversial book, and today his film stands as one of the most moving and beautiful ever to come out of Hollywood.

The Joads, driven from their homestead in the Oklahoma Dust Bowl, journey westward to California, looking for the Promised Land and discover the exploitation which awaited them there. Ford's film is one of the first to reveal a genuine social conscience and to attempt a realistic treatment of ordinary people. It was Hollywood's strongest stand against social injustice. The compassionate and magnificent characters found in the novel are captured faithfully on film. Steinbeck's Okies emerge as the greatest family portrait ever seen on the screen. Their struggles, happiness, disappointment, problems, and eventual breakdown stand as the finest study of the Depression Years.

Ford's film differs slightly from Steinbeck's novel, but basically captures the book's message. Political radicalism and religious satire are muted but family loyalty, affinity for the land, and human dignity are poignantly revealed.

Orson Welles in 1942 turned an ordinary novel by Booth Tarkington into a grandoise and eloquent film. Forsaking the cynicism of *Citizen Kane,* Welles takes a gentle, affectionate, and even considerate approach to his story (*The Magnificent Ambersons*), and in Proustian fashion dissects the bitter conflict in a Midwest town between a rapidly decaying landed aristocracy and an industrial *bourgeoisie* anxious to gain control of society.

In *The Magnificent Ambersons,* Welles refuses to make concessions to popular appeal and the film shines with his brilliant directorial touches. Stanley Cortez's photography helps raise the film into the level of art with its soft focus, frames, shadowed rooms, and beautiful winter scenes.

Filmed dramatizations of other novels followed. Charlotte Brontë's romantic melodrama *Jane Eyre* (1943) had been screened several times, but Robert Stevenson's version was undoubtedly the best. Orson Welles as Rochester was proud and satanic, while Joan Fontaine as Jane brought precisely the right touch of fear and strength to the character. John P. Marquand's *The Late George Apley* (1946), a film satirizing Boston manners and directed by Joseph L. Mankiewicz, featured a beautiful stellar performance by Ronald Colman.

Hollywood, which has never placed much faith in its own creative artistic abilities, again utilized fictional material in the years following World War II. During these postwar years, the studios relied heavily on books which stressed psychological characters and social realism. *The Lost Weekend* (1945), based on a novel by Charles Jackson and directed by Billy Wilder, told of a single weekend in an alcoholic's life. Ray Milland portrayed Don, an intellectual who lacks the fiber to finish his stories. His craving for drink, lying, stealing, desire for suicide, stay in a hospital ward, and descent into an alcoholic hell are all vividly captured in a terrifying picture.

Robert Penn Warren's popular novel *All the King's Men* (the rise and fall of the late Huey Long), came to the screen in 1949 as an ironic and cynical political exposé directed by Robert Rossen. Broderick Crawford gave an Academy Award-winning performance as Willie Stark, the small-town hick who rose to political importance by trading integrity for votes. A self-styled redneck trampling on tradition, Stark sweeps nearly everyone along on his evil trail with his brand of bluff, egotism, and corruption. His increasing use of blackmail and bribery inevitably lead to his assassination by a common gunman.

In the late 1940's a sudden spate of films arguing for racial justice continued the trend of social realism. These films showed that Hollywood was beginning to present a greater degree of courage. Although these films were at times not completely honest with their subject matter they were at least an initial attempt to deal with previously highly emotional issues. Several tried to make forthright social statements. In 1946, Dore Schary offered Richard Brooks's wartime novel, *The Brick Foxhole*, dealing with anti-Semitism. Edward Dymtryk's *Crossfire* (1947), one of the first American antiracist films, was a tough melodrama about the murder of a Jew. The film helped break traditional taboos against public discussion of racial and religious injustice to minority groups. The studios seized upon these newly freed themes with an almost religious zeal.

During the 1950's, filmmakers adapted larger numbers of best-selling and commercially popular novels in efforts to bring greater numbers to the public into the theater.

John Huston made a valiant attempt to transfer the novel *The Red Badge of Courage* (1951) by Stephen Crane to the screen. The production was undermined, Huston lost interest, and audiences were not yet interested in the antihero. *The Caine Mutiny* (1954), from Herman Wouk's popular book, gave Humphrey Bogart one of his best screen roles as Queeg, the pathetic victim of combat fatigue.

Elizabeth Taylor and Montgomery Clift starred in *A Place in the Sun* (1951), an adaptation of Theodore Dreiser's novel *An American Tragedy* (1925). Dreiser's tale told the story of a young Midwesterner seeking to escape from the monotony, poverty and emptiness of his family background. After a rich girl introduces him to the glitter of the wealthy class, his love for money and the glamorous life persuade him to murder his first sweetheart, now pregnant. George Stevens's touching and memorable screen treatment preserves the novel's beauty, insight, and tenderness, but Dreiser's social comments were neglected. The director downplayed Dreiser's relentless cynical observations on the malaise of American society, and on occasion lost sight of Dreiser's basic theme that all men are not created equal. Stevens turns the story into a straightforward Hollywood romance.

Viva Zapata! (1952) presents Marlon Brando in one of his most impressive and strangely eloquent roles in cinema. Directed by Elia Kazan, the picture was based on the book *Zapata, the Unconquerable* by Edgcomb Pichon. The director achieves an authentic recreation of Mexico and invests his film with a sense of gathering destiny. Brando, giving a performance marked by simplicity, forever chides himself for his weakness, illiteracy, and dependence on horse and rifle. The picture overflows with brilliant characters who fight against oppression and discover their own insufficiencies. The exceptionally fine black-and-white photography is the work of Joseph MacDonald; the excellent script is John Steinbeck's.

James Jones's *From Here to Eternity* (1953), the angry and compassionate Army novel of World War II, was filmed by

Fred Zinnemann. While attempting fidelity to the book's cynical, brutalized view of humanity, Zinnemann was unable to fully capture the drama of military life as depicted in this 430,000-word novel. Although the characterizations are somewhat superficial, the outbreaks of violence and hatred are skillfully handled, and Zinnemann does manage to capture the mood of the muscular male society dominating the novel.

The Blackboard Jungle (1955), directed by Richard Brooks, was one of the first taut, violent films about American schools and the problems of teen-age hoodlums. As the harassed teacher, Glenn Ford found this role perfectly suited to his image of integrity and quiet resolution. Elia Kazan and John Steinbeck joined forces once more to produce *East of Eden* (1955). The film, notable for introducing James Dean as the outsider teen-ager who rebels against his father and his brother, achieved a considerable degree of success because of Dean's performance and the distinguished acting of Julie Harris, Jo Van Fleet, and Raymond Massey.

David Lean's spectacular film *The Bridge on the River Kwai* (1957), based on the Pierre Bouille book, is a powerful antiheroic war film concerned with the absurdity of military behavior in a Burmese prison camp during World War II. The film has superior performances by Alec Guinness and Sessue Hayakawa, splendid photography, and is long and expensively produced. It epitomizes the industry's effort to entertain the declining audiences of the period.

A sharp difference between the traditional "movies" and the "new cinema" arose during the 1960's with the proliferation of young and highly creative filmmakers. Yet independent companies and the studios continued to draw on the novel for screen material.

With increased freedom in the treatment of theme, plots, sex, and language, directors sought novels which would provide material for the exploration of these areas. The writings of D. H. Lawrence were one of the richest sources for such material.

In the 1950's a few American films had timidly broken parts of the Production Code, but with *The Fox* (1968), director Mark Rydell gave a liberal treatment of the Lawrence story with much nudity, Lesbianism, masturbation, autoeroticism, straight sex, and a catalogue of phallic symbols. The director and screenwriter changed the story, seriously distorting Lawrence's philosophy and intent. In the novella, Lawrence only hints at the Lesbian nature of the two girls, but the movie spells it out, including an explicit love scene.

Richard Brooks's dramatization of Sinclair Lewis's *Elmer Gantry* (1960) is a revealing study of smugness, bigotry, and the vulgarity embodied in the Midwestern Protestant clergy. Burt Lancaster as the hellfire Bible-pounding salesman gives an admirable performance, but the picture fails to capture the flamboyant emotions and Lewis's scathing satire. Brooks overloaded his film with racing crowds, roaring fires, and spectacular sets. Stanley Kubrick's adaptation of Vladimir Nabokov's *Lolita* (1961), a novel about a middle-aged man's infatuation with a prepubescent girl, is a slyly tragic black comedy.

Orson Welles's *The Trial* (1962), based on Franz Kafka's novel, is perhaps one of the most remarkable failures of the decade. Anthony Perkins as Joseph K. the clerk who is arraigned and condemned for an undisclosed offense, symbolizes for Welles the numerous dilemmas and problems that afflict modern society. Perkins's lack of artistic maturity for the title role faulted the film. The director was overwhelmed by Kafka's theme of man's alienation from himself and the world around him.

Jospeh Losey's English production of *The Servant* (1963), written for the screen by Harold Pinter, based on a novel by Robin Maugham, offers the recurrent theme in Losey's films: human frailty and the temptations that encourage deviant behavior. The film mounts in horror at the changing master-servant relationship, with final victory passing to the servant's corrupt world.

Ulysses (1965), directed by Joseph Strick, was a sincere and uncompromising, though obviously abridged, version of James Joyce's complex novel. Martin Ritt's *The Spy Who Came in From the Cold* (1966) offered a wintry version of John LeCarre's novel, with Richard Burton as a down-and-out cynical spy forced to betray both his girl and himself. The Greek director Michael Cacoyannis brought Nikos Kazantzakis's lusty, hedonist hero to the cinema with *Zorba the Greek* (1964). Anthony Quinn's brilliant performance as Zorba filled the screen with the title character's exuberant zest for life. His abundant energies find full release in a series of grand-scale adventures. Walter Lassally's scenes of harsh landscapes, crowded villages, rocky shorelines and windswept hills represent photography at its best.

In the 1960's, the admirable hero gave way to the antihero. The most he could hope for was pity. The hero as misfit appealed to the young who sought more relevant experiences and were beginning to find them in film. The antihero in his searching, frustrations, alienation and anti-Establishment attitudes began to receive much attention from the medium. These loners, emotionally charged, in conflict with society, revealing racial, sociological and ideological tensions, set box office records.

Perhaps the most successful of these antiheroic films was Mike Nichols's *The Graduate* (1967), based on Charles Webb's novel. Within two years of its release it grossed $43 million. Nichols offered a fresh, touching and hilarious film, eloquently depicted the love pangs of a twenty-one-year-old modern kid who refuses to conform. The film viciously satirizes the older generation's sexual hypocrisy while revealing the amorality and coarse stupidity of modern society.

Stanley Kubrick's *A Clockwork Orange* (1971), an English production based on the Anthony Burgess novel, builds upon tendencies already existing in today's society. Kubrick's statements on the growth of youthful violence, the drug culture, and the extraordinary increase in eroticism sometimes revolted the public but received praise from the critics. The film is filled with scenes seasoned with touches of satire, mordant humor, and the sinister, giving a rather terrifying glimpse into society of the future. Fully as unique, eloquent and shocking as the book, the picture is an even more extraordinary accomplishment in itself. Kubrick's slow-motion sequences are done with rare grace and sinister beauty. When he speeds up Alex's orgiastic session with two young girls picked up in the Record Bootick, the scene becomes an insanely comic ballet. For Kubrick, the film medium appears to be an instrument with an almost infinite variety of pedals and stops.

If directors like Antonioni, Nichols, Kubrick and Losey take us into a world of terror, violence, lust and absurdity, other directors prefer to capture a more romantic world. A number of films returning audiences to the nostalgia of the 1930's and 1940's filled the screen at the opening of the 1970's. Arthur Hiller's *Love Story* (1970), an adaptation of Erich Segal's best-selling novel, concerned the romance between a rich Harvard jock and a poor but bright Radcliffe girl. The film describes their love affair and marriage (she later dies of leukemia) in such oversentimental and saccharine fashion that the critics panned it unmercifully. *Summer of*

'42 (1971), based on the novel of Herman Raucher, deals with the sexual awakening of three young men. Seen through the reminiscing eyes of one of the three youths, the film tenderly recreates the initiation into manhood of one of them. David Lean's *Ryan's Daughter* (1971), set against the romantic background of the Dingle Peninsula in Ireland, deals with another doomed love affair.

Mark Twain's novels *The Adventures of Tom Sawyer* and *The Adventures of Huckleberry Finn,* masterpieces of humor, characterizations and realism, are considered to be the author's best works, containing his most representative humorous sketches, vigor, high-spirited exaggerations and native idioms.

The best *Huckleberry Finn* (1939), directed by Richard Thorpe, starred Mickey Rooney as the resourceful, unconventional boy with an innate sense of humor. Rooney dropped his Andy Hardy gimmicks to give a fine performance, ably partnered by the black actor Rex Ingram. However, the film, played for laughs, fails to capture Twain's wry, humorous, and cynical comments on American society.

David O. Selznick's production of *The Adventures of Tom Sawyer* (1938), directed by Norman Taurog, manages to evoke rural life in the age of American innocence and the fun, adventure and provincial background of the Twain classic. Tom Kelly's acting, the photography of James Wong Howe, and particularly the decor by William Cameron Menzies make this a distinguished film.

When *Reader's Digest* entered the motion picture industry and decided to eschew violence, sex, and profanity and instead give sweetness and light, beauty and wholesomeness to audiences, they agreed that *The Adventures of Tom Sawyer* (1971) offered a clean bill-of-fare. This time the classic was set to music. Tom (Johnny Whitaker) with his commonplace virtues lives in a world of fishing, picnics, family gatherings and grave robbers. Tom's friend Huckleberry (Jeff East), the free spirit, the essense of adventuresome America, gives the picture vigor, freshness and animation. The film captures the beauty and strength of rural America and presents the river as a powerful metaphor.

In the last few years at least six novels have received serious screen treatment. *Deliverance* (1972), directed by John Boorman, based on the novel by James Dickey, is the best outdoor drama of the 1970's. Four city men on a weekend outing canoe down river rapids. The trek turns into a nightmare. The film presents contemporary man against man and nature and his instincts to survive. The picture is stylishly paced and may have raised arguments over the concentrated dosage of violence, but the film stands as a first-rate thriller. F. Scott Fitzgerald's *The Great Gatsby* (1974), directed by Jack Clayton, is the story of Daisy who smashed up things and people and then retreated behind her money. Acting, dialogue, sets, costumes and photography made this an above-average picture. Mia Farrow captures Daisy's cynicism and carelessness. Peter Bogdanovich's *Daisy Miller* (1974) turned Henry James' novel into a dull and undistinguished movie. Cybill Shepherd failed to capture the vulnerable Daisy, the innocent American girl adrift in Roman society.

John Schlesinger's *The Day of The Locust* (1975) is concerned with little people living on and off the fringes of the film industry. It is a devastating probe of the Middle American soul and is a study of frustration and bitterness. The picture presents fools, freaks and dreamers who have come to know the meaning of loneliness. Schlesinger's film stands as a bristling, glittering contemporary comment. *The Day of the Locust* not only mirrors the weaknesses in our society but tells what is the matter with the American dream.

Stanley Kubrick's *Barry Lyndon* (1975), based on a novel by William Thackeray, tells the story of an Irish rogue (Ryan O'Neal), a swashbuckling scoundrel faking and hacking his way to the top of the social ladder, using the rigidly stratified British aristocracy as a stepping-stone. Kubrick's film, unfortunately, lacks the irony found in the novel, but the picture offers stunning photography, lavish costumes, beautiful sets, golden lighting, and powerful music. The movie is an epic of esthetic delight.

Another film of the movie industry, *The Last Tycoon* (1976), directed by Elia Kazan, offers a faithful, lavish, and, unfortunately, bloodless transcription of the Scott Fitzgerald novel. Robert DeNiro as Monroe Stahr, has earned well-deserved praise for his work in the title role. The movie fails to capture the spirit of the novel and, although many of the small parts are handled by outstanding performers, the strength and fire of the Fitzgerald novel never comes through.

In transferring novels into film, numerous differences exist. Faint praise and searing criticism often result when those already familiar with the novel view the film version. The novel depends upon individual creation and language, and often has a limited audience. The film, on the other hand, depends upon a moving image and industrial production to achieve its effects; it must appeal to a mass audience. It makes its appeal to the perceiving senses and is free to work with the endless variations of physical reality, while literature is a symbolic medium that stands between the perceiver and the idea.

Changes are inevitable the moment one abandons a verbal medium for a visual one. The director undertakes the adaptation of a novel, offering his idea of the book, his paraphrase of the printed word. He views a book as raw material and looks not to the organic novel, whose language is inseparable from its theme, but rather to characters and incidents which have somehow detached themselves from language and have achieved a life of their own.

Thus, there is often no necessary likeness between the excellence of a novel and the quality of the film based on that particular book. In short, the film in spite of certain resemblances inevitably becomes a different artistic entity from the novel on which it is based.

But as long as films are made, the motion picture industry will draw on novels as a source for screen material. Many books have been used toward widening the spectrum of film subjects, and particularly when creative talent is employed, have enhanced our film enjoyment. What a pleasure it is to see *Pride and Prejudice* (1940) with the graceful acting of Laurence Olivier and Greer Garson, and to hear the delightful dialogue that Aldous Huxley has gleaned from the novel. Across the screen march many a literary character that sent fans joyously out of the theaters: Tolstoy's novel of the unhappy *Anna Karenina* (1935) with the enigmatic and romantic Garbo, Gary Cooper guarding the ramparts in *Beau Geste* (1939), Joan Fontaine as *Jane Eyre* (1944) standing up to the flamboyant Rochester of Orson Welles. Creative talent collaborated to bring to the screen the powerful *Les Miserables* (1935) with Fredric March as the escaped convict, being hounded by the sly and determined police inspector Charles Laughton; and Booth Tarkington's *Alice Adams* (1935) has Katharine Hepburn sparkling in her interpretation of the Midwestern heroine. The list is long and impressive.

About one-half of all films made have been adaptations of

novels, plays, or stories. The novel has provided the filmmaker with exciting stories, interesting and original characters, and meaningful and urgent themes. Bringing the novel to the screen, the filmmaker has given a new dimension to the printed word. The word has been allowed to live in new ways for those who have encountered it previously on the printed page. To those who have not read the novel, the filmmaker has introduced new stories, people, and ideas.

Outstanding Novels into Film
And Their Directors

The Four Horsemen of the Apocalypse	(1921)	Rex Ingram
The Hunchback of Notre Dame	(1923)	Wallace Worsley
Greed	(1924)	Erich von Stroheim
Ben Hur	(1926)	Fred Niblo
The Scarlet Letter	(1926)	Victor Seastrom
The Wind	(1928)	Victor Seastrom
All Quiet on the Western Front	(1930)	Lewis Milestone
Little Women	(1933)	George Cukor
The Informer	(1935)	John Ford
Mutiny on the Bounty	(1935)	Frank Lloyd
The Good Earth	(1937)	Sidney Franklin
Drums Along the Mohawk	(1939)	John Ford
Gone With the Wind	(1939)	Victor Fleming
Wuthering Heights	(1939)	William Wyler
The Grapes of Wrath	(1940)	John Ford
The Magnificent Ambersons	(1942)	Orson Welles
The Maltese Falcon	(1941)	John Huston
The Lost Weekend	(1945)	Billy Wilder
All the King's Men	(1949)	Robert Rossen
Intruder in the Dust	(1950)	Clarence Brown
A Place in the Sun	(1951)	George Stevens
The African Queen	(1952)	John Huston
Shane	(1953)	George Stevens
East of Eden	(1955)	Elia Kazan
The Bridge on the River Kwai	(1957)	David Lean

Vertigo	(1958)	Alfred Hitchcock
Paths of Glory	(1958)	Stanley Kubrick
Psycho	(1960)	Alfred Hitchcock
Inside Daisy Clover	(1966)	Robert Mulligan
Deliverance	(1972)	John Boorman
The Great Gatsby	(1974)	Jack Clayton
The Day of the Locust	(1975)	John Schlesinger
Barry Lyndon	(1975)	Stanley Kubrick
The Last Tycoon	(1976)	Elia Kazan

22/The Documentary and Direct Cinema

THE DOCUMENTARY, or actuality film, sometimes called factual or nonfiction films, a term first coined in the 1920's, is the filming of actual events as they happen, or the simulation of particular occurrences of a distant or proximate historical period. Its basic purposes are to supply background material and unbiased factual information. Directors of documentaries prefer to record an event rather than create it. The form eventually came to designate those films that contain some degree of social commentary. This type of film may present and explore contemporary lifestyles, past cultures, traditions and customs of distant places, or the real world's events and people. It can be a dramatic factual film presenting fact instead of fiction. Newsreels, travel, nature, propaganda, sociological, and scientific films comprise the documentary film genre.

The actuality film dominated the cinema in the very first years. By 1908, the actuality film had become a subsidiary part of movie programs, mostly taking the form of newsreels. In 1909 Charles Pathé founded the *Pathé-Journal (Pathé-News)*, releasing his newsreels on a commercial basis. By 1912, Hearst and Universal had made newsreels while Paramount and Fox followed suit in 1916 and 1918 respectively. As early as 1911 various branches of the Federal Government produced factual films, but interest soon waned and the genre was forgotten. During the First World War the newsreel was important in turning out propaganda treatment. Often these early efforts were presented without cutting, editing, or structuring the material. One of the first movements toward structuring actuality film was in the Soviet Union, where Dziga Vertov and Sergei Eisenstein experimented with the form; their silent films had far-reaching influence on documentary filmmakers in other countries.

Robert Flaherty, an American educated in Canada, considered to be the father of the full-length nonfiction documentary and its best director, presented *Nanook of the North* (1920). Flaherty's film, a study of the Eskimo people, combined the energetic, didactic style of the Russian films with a reflective, lyrical style of his own, creating the first significant documentary in the history of cinema.

Flaherty had no preconceived concepts about his characters, settings, or situations; his approach was to explore the subject and let the material shape the film. He spent months on research, traveling to the Hudson Bay Territory and Baffin Island to photograph the Eskimo and his family. Above all, Flaherty wanted his film to be a simple statement of primitive existence. Following Nanook and his family, Flaherty's camera captured the weather, the search for food, the community, and the family circle, showing how the Eskimo existed in a cruel and often heartless world. The result was a short anthropological film, accompanied by a few titles which describe the circle of seasons and the life of the Eskimo Nanook and his family. In this film Flaherty found his basic theme for other documentaries that followed—a simplified world in which the only conflict is that of man against nature. Flaherty's fluid camerawork, sharp editing, and extraordinarily beautiful photography turned *Nanook* into a film classic.

In the early years, Hollywood missed its chances to develop the documentary. Even though *Nanook* had been a popular and critical success, Flaherty was not encouraged to continue his work; the studios were not interested in capturing primitive human life within its natural environment. Eventually Paramount sent Flaherty to Samoa to make a Nanook of the South Seas, entitled *Moana*. After completing *Moana* (1926), MGM engaged Flaherty to work as collaborator on *White Shadows of the South Seas* (1928). But Flaherty was not content with either assignment, for he was unable to bring his style of filming to the finished products.

F.W. Murnau, the German director under contract to Fox, quarreled with his studio and, in 1928, joined with Robert Flaherty to form an independent documentary film company. Flaherty, after completing *Moana,* realized there was a powerful film to be made with a South Seas setting, and he and Muranu set out for Tahiti. They, too, quarreled with each other, and Flaherty withdrew from the production. The completed film *Tabu* (1931), credited to Murnau, is a fictionalized story using natives in their natural setting. The breathtaking photography earned a national release for the product.

Its popularity at the box office encouraged other directors to continue work in film reportage, but unfortunately only a few films of this type followed.

Discouraged with Hollywood's lack of interest, Flaherty went to England, where John Grierson,* considered the country's leading director of the social documentary, was a leader of the British film industry. Flaherty made two pictures—*Industrial Britain* (1933) and *Man of Aran* (1934). In *Aran,* he followed the tenets of *Nanook* and presented the inhabitants of the island of Aran struggling against nature. Thus Flaherty, by refusing to adhere to the dictates of the big West Coast studios, worked independently and became one of the first to offer personal cinema.

Merian C. Cooper and Ernest Schoedsack followed in Flaherty's footsteps with two superior films, *Grass* (1925) and *Chang* (1927). The former tells of a Persian tribe's twice-yearly migration in search of grass; the latter describes how Siamese tribesmen struggle against vegetation and wild animals to protect their families. Both pictures were successful at the box office.

America may have launched the first popular structured documentary, but it was the Russians who turned the genre into propaganda. Communist authorities in the Soviet Union realized this type of film could easily serve to bring Marxist-Leninist ideology to the masses. Sergei Eisenstein's fiction film, *The Battleship Potemkin* (1925), based on broad historical events of the preceding twenty years, was one of the most successful produced by the Russians. Its creative editing, compositional stylization, and use of montage (collision of images) created a tremendously successful film. Dziga Vertov, whose real name was Denis Kaufman, excelled at newsreel techniques. He opposed fictionalized reconstruction in his films, and rejected exotic settings and professional performances in favor of "candid camera" shots. Instead, his films attempted to capture the spirit and movement of cities, people, and machinery. His best film is *Man with the Movie Camera* (1928). Filmmakers still follow many basic concepts formulated by Eisenstein and Vertov.

Leni Riefenstahl, German actress and director, had a strong influence on the documentary film. She made, at the invitation of Adolf Hitler, propaganda films for the Third

---

* Critic John Grierson gave the documentary its name, defining it as a "creative treatment of actuality."

Reich. Two of her films, *Triumph of the Will* (1934) and *Olympiad* (1936), are noted for their editing and photography, establishing her as master of the spectacle. *Triumph of the Will* was the official record of the Nazi Party Congress in Nuremberg, and *Olympiad* that of the Berlin Olympics of 1936. In the latter, she poeticized the human form and the German political scene. Both of these pictures, organized and supervised by Riefenstahl, put her into the front ranks of German directors. She proved (like Eisenstein) that propaganda could be art. Her rhythmic editing and brilliant photography had a worldwide influence on others interested in the documentary. Because her work deified Adolf Hitler, Riefenstahl has been persecuted for having made such effective films about so unworthy a subject.

If Flaherty was the outstanding American director of the documentary, Pare Lorentz was a close second. Lorentz went to work for the United States Resettlement Administration in 1935 (part of President Franklin D. Roosevelt's New Deal), and the office asked him to make a film that would dramatize the problems of the Dust Bowl area. Lorentz' picture was designed to show how agricultural overdevelopment had led to the great dust storms that were ruining the fertile land of the overplowed plains. The authorities thought that if Lorentz' film received wide distribution, perhaps the public could learn a lesson for the future.

The Plow That Broke the Plains (1936) presents a sharp, graphic treatment of land, dust, and poor people. Lorentz' photography manages the difficult task of combining harsh reality with eloquent lyricism. He brings meaning, emotion, and depth to the treatment of his subject. His rhythmic editing, matching the narrative and images to Virgil Thomson's music created a superior film. Lorentz subsequently made *The River* (1937) and *The Fight for Life* (1940). However, the Federal Government lost interest in these factual films when politicians thought that Washington should stay out of filmmaking. Finding his funds cut off, Lorentz was forced to give up his splendid efforts.

For various reasons, the documentary film was not too popular with movie audiences. Independent producers and directors found it difficult to obtain outlets in which to show their efforts. It appeared that the public did not want to be taught lessons or to see harsh realities. They preferred to be entertained. When local theaters presented documentaries, bored audiences complained at the box office.

During the 1930's, American documentary films turned chiefly to travelogues. These films were repetitive in form; the camera took a tourist's view of various countries while the soundtrack mouthed clichés, such as ". . . and as the sun sinks slowly in the West, we leave . . ." Hollywood instead channeled its social comments and reformist energy into the gangster and the social-conscience films. The left-wing Film and Photo League made the only activist films of the period. From this background came filmmakers such as Seymour Stern, Ralph Steiner, Leo Hurwitz, Paul Strand, and Willard Van Dyke. However, their films lacked effective distribution methods.

Some critics claimed that Hollywood lobbyists were the ones who had brought pressure against the Federal Government's sponsorship of documentary films; still others blamed commercial film distributors for refusing to give screen time to such pictures. By the late 1930's, however, *Time* magazine took an interest in such films, and produced a series called *The March of Time*. Directed by Louis de Rochemont, these films were monthly newsmagazines, and because they were handled so professionally, the documentary film found a receptive audience. The series ran from 1934 to 1951, with de Rochemont producing the regular issues until 1943.

When war came, both the British and Germans realized the effectiveness of the documentary for training soldiers and keeping up civilian morale, and their films stand today as a superb record of World War II. When America realized the impact of such films, Hollywood's best talents were sought out. Frank Capra, an outstanding Hollywood director, was asked by the Federal Government in 1942 to make propaganda documentaries for the war effort, and his *Why We Fight* series (1942-45) was, like the Flaherty and Lorentz films, a landmark in documentary style. John Ford, John Huston, and William Wyler made propaganda films for national release. Huston's *The Battle of San Pietro* (1945) stands as one of the best of the war efforts. It is a frightening account, showing for the first time real infantry combat conditions with the American G.I.s.

The ending of the war appeared to signal the ending of the documentary as well. The movie industry, with its newly enlarged screens, turned out blockbusters and spectaculars, leaving no time for audiences to sit through a documentary. Just when the genre appeared to give its last gasp, it found a new and fertile field in television. And instead of being relegated to the cinema archives, it took another direction and grew into a powerful force, particularly in T.V. By the 1960's, the term "documentary" was considered too imprecise, and a new group of American directors working with a diffused style of documentary, named their filmmaking Direct Cinéma (Free Cinema in Britain, and Cinéma Verité in France).

Direct Cinema

After World War II, a group of young experimental directors rejected the lyrical and semirealistic approach used by Robert Flaherty, Pare Lorentz, the Russians Sergei Eisenstein and Alexander Dovzhenko, the Englishman John Grierson, and the German Leni Riefenstahl. They continued to work with documentary film, but made certain changes in the style, and there evolved a new approach called Now or Direct Cinema. Like its European cousin Cinéma Verité, Direct or Now Cinema is a diffused style of the documentary. The name was coined by Albert Maysles, explaining the directorial approach to movies during the early 1960's by such directors as Robert Drew, Richard Leacock, Donn Alan Pennebaker, and the Maysles brothers. Direct Cinema is direct in the sense that technical professionalism is secondary to the recording of the actual event or situation. There is often erratic camerawork and lighting, no structured narrative, and very little interpretive editing. It is often characterized by long takes.

The films of Direct Cinema tell semi-truths, because the unacknowledged presence of the camera forces an unreality in the behavior of the performers. This school gained prominence in the 1950's when several directors, particularly Richard Leacock (who had worked with Flaherty) and the Maysles brothers sought a different film style. Rejecting structured narratives, established stories, studio techniques, and name stars, these directors concentrated on films capturing a complete experience of a factual story, photographed and recorded with mobile equipment, then edited into a social document. Their basic tenet was to offer some slice of life that others might see, understand, enjoy, and learn from.

This group of directors could be said to have their beginnings in 1948 when Sidney Meyers directed a film called *The Quiet One*, a story concerning the problems of a Negro boy.

Meyers's film was followed by Morris Engel's *Little Fugitive* (1953), *Lovers and Lollipops* (1956), and *Weddings and Babies* (1958). All films were made on location with a low budget, portable equipment, no name stars, and a small camera crew. The success of Engel's films encouraged other artists to try their hand at offbeat projects.

Lionel Rogosin's *On the Bowery* (1957) is concerned with lost lives on the New York streets and is in its way a melancholy, terrifying film. In 1959, Rogosin made *Come Back, Africa*, which set forth the problems of Blacks living in South Africa. In each of his pictures, he adheres to a narrative, while taking his camera to actual places and presenting actual people and their problems. Alfred Leslie made a dramatic short called *Pull My Daisy* (1958) based on the third act of a play by Jack Kerouac, a film of exceptional merit.

About 1958, a young French anthropologist journeyed to Africa to make authentic films of life there. Carrying a 16mm hand-held camera and a microphone, he traveled everywhere, recording whatever he saw. His pictures and soundtrack consisted of natural, unrehearsed reactions from the people who participated in the scene. These people told in simple terms their feelings concerning questions that Jean Rouch asked.

When the Robert Flaherty Foundation heard of Rouch, he was invited in 1959 to come to America to show his films. Other directors saw the results and were struck by Rouch's photographic and recording techniques. The French critics named his documentary style Cinéma Verité. (Actually, Cinéma Verité, or "Film Truth," evolved from the Russian Dziga Vertov, only the term was first used to describe Rouch's technique.) Direct Cinéma and Cinéma Verité spring from the same genre and have many similarities.

In the 1960's, the imaginative Shirley Clarke filmed two plays, *The Connection* (1960), a story of drug addiction, and *The Cool World* (1963), which deals with the frustrating ghetto life of a young black. Clarke incorporated into these fiction films many of the techniques of Direct Cinema. There were long takes, with characters appearing to improvise dialogue and action, and very little editing. Bert Stern in 1961 shot the outstanding *Jazz on a Summer's Day*. These and a few others launched Direct Cinema commercially, and documentaries in this style flooded the market.

Direct Cinema bloomed in the 1960's. Robert Drew and Richard Leacock produced a documentary for the Democratic nomination called *Primary*, then turned their "living camera" on the attempt to integrate the public schools in New Orleans in *The Children Were Watching* (1960). *David* (1962) is the story of a group of ex-drug addicts. *Football* (1962) and *The Chair* (1963) were praised by critics and audiences. *Happy Mother's Day* (1964) is a scathing study of American publicity on the mother of quintuplets.

A young actor named John Cassavetes persuaded one of the studios into permitting him to make an experimental film, and the result was *Shadows* (1960), a picture that gained a great deal of attention (certain critics tagged it the first Underground film to surface). Cassavetes rejected the well-written scenario, composing only an elementary plot line (a colored girl is seduced by a white boy, who does not know that she is colored), and simply *improvised* action and words before the camera. The work was done under amateurish conditions, with poor lighting and primitive equipment, but this was the effect Cassavertes wanted. Another of his films, *Faces* (1969), because of its story, photography, and acting, received critical acclaim; it is an uncompromising examination of personal relationships. So far Cassavetes has been able to combine successfully Direct Cinema with narrative.

In Direct Cinema, directors were making films not to entertain but rather to stimulate, to make people see and think, even to be repulsed by what they saw. They wanted to fully describe slums, juvenile delinquents, protest marches, drug problems, civil rights struggles, police brutality, and bigotry. They were determined to capture contemporary problems and the turmoil of the world.

Other creative directors now took the Direct Cinema approach to their films. Norman Mailer's *Beyond the Law* (1965), the Canadian director Allen King's *Warrendale* (1967), and Frederic Wiseman's *Titicut Follies* (1968) are frightening films telling brutal stories about inmates in prison, public asylums, and medical institutions. *Warrendale* is a shocking jolt that all too painfully reveals the world of the mentally disturbed. Many viewers disliked the film for its raw study of an asylum for disturbed children.

Albert and David Maysles, two brothers involved with Direct Cinema, are determined to record their views of the contemporary world. They believe that nothing must stand between the audience and an event being recorded. Editing is important, but there must be no star, no script, and no staged sequences—only the true happening. The Maysles brothers, who went on to make *Gimme Shelter* (1970) and most recently *Grey Gardens* (1976), completed *Salesman* (1969), a film that tells in newsreel-documentary-realistic fashion the events in the lives of four men who sell Bibles. The two brothers lived with these men for six months, carefully photographing all their actions as salesmen, and then spent fifteen more months editing the finished film into a penetrating view of American life.

Frederic Wiseman's film *Primate* (1974) explores the animal behavior studies at the Yerkes Regional Primate Research Center in Atlanta, Georgia. It is in many ways a shocking view, not only of institutional abuses of animals in the search for scientific knowledge but also of the scientists themselves.

Direct Cinema, like its French cousin Cinéma Verité, pulls no punches and contains little fakery or deception. With hand-held cameras, directors enter streets, private apartments, marketplaces, institutions, and jungles in their search for reality. They offer a vision of reality that the movies seldom had the courage to present before. Their stories gave the screen realistic studies of dope pushers, misfits, pimps, and twisted personalities. These experimental films sometimes show the movie public the more brutal and vicious sides of life.

By the 1960's, experimental cinema directors introduced documentary techniques into a relatively new genre—the rock festival. The American film audience is youth-oriented, and the purpose of the rock film is to translate a live musical performance onto film so young movie fans can enjoy closeups of their musical idols. Donn Alan Pennebaker's *Monterey Pop* (1968) set the direction for others to take—emphasizing the power of the music. Michael Wadleigh's *Woodstock* (1969), in presenting Joan Baez, Country Joe, Arlo Guthrie, Jimi Hendrix, and many others in concert on a 600-acre farm near Bethel, New York, uses optical effects such as split screen and superimpositions, many closeups, and various loudspeakers for "surround" effect. In *Gimme Shelter* (1970), the Maysles's film not only caught the frenzy of the Rolling Stones' musical production and the rage of the crowd, but also, when they turned their cameras on the audience, the sight of a young man being stomped to death by Hell's Angels. *Celebration at Big Sur* (1971) offers pop music, celebrated performers, and the joys of a music festival. In a related youth-oriented genre, audiences swelled box office receipts to see Bruce Brown's motorcycle saga *On Any Sunday* (1972).

The French also pumped new life into the documentary in recent years. In 1969, Marcel Ophuls, son of the famous director Max Ophuls, created a considerable stir when he released his documentary *Le Chagrin et la Pitié (The Sorrow and the Pity)*, which was four and a half hours long. He uses Direct Cinema or Cinéma Verité to tell his story, and shows with as much objectivity as possible that not all Frenchmen were against the Germans, but that many were active in collaborating with their enemy. The picture caused a furore and became a *succès de scandale* when it opened in Paris. Ophuls documentary destroyed the myth of universal French resistance to the Nazis.

By the 1970's, young Americans were once more interested in taking their portable but sophisticated equipment to all places, examining social problems in the richest country in the world. Barbara Kopple's *Harlan County U.S.A.* (1977) is a passionate essay about a thirteen-month strike in Kentucky coal mines. James Klein, Julia Reichert, and Miles Mogelscu offer a stirring picture of America's downtrodden in *Union Maids* (1977). The directors have three women tell their story of the labor movement in Chicago in the 1930's. Each recalls her agony of participating in the battle of the shops and picket lines. Barbara Margolis filmed *On the Line* (1977) and found an appreciative audience for it; the film is a cry for collective action to fight impersonal capitalism and its injustices.

Direct Cinema has found a public, for the serious moviegoer is attending and encouraging the genre. It is perhaps the best means of capturing and explaining the political and moral issues of our society, since it involves a search for certain truths that are rarely found in films of the past. With its sophisticated machinery, videotape adjuncts, lighting equipment, and ability to capture live dialogue, the Direct Cinema can capture many phases of the complexity, contradictions, and mysteries of the human condition.

Outstanding Documentary Films
and Directors

Nanook of the North	(1922)	Robert Flaherty
Grass	(1925)	Merian Cooper, Ernest Schoedsack
Moana	(1926)	Robert Flaherty
Chang	(1927)	Merian Cooper, Ernest Schoedsack
Man of Aran	(1934)	Robert Flaherty
The Plow That Broke the Plains	(1936)	Pare Lorentz
The River	(1937)	Pare Lorentz
The City	(1939)	Willard Van Dyke
The Fight for Life	(1940)	Pare Lorentz
The March of Time Series	(1934–45)	Louis de Rochemont
Battle of Midway	(1942)	John Ford
Why We Fight	(1942–45)	Frank Capra
Memphis Belle	(1944)	William Wyler
The Battle of San Pietro	(1945)	John Huston
The True Glory	(1945)	edited by Carol Reed, Garson Kanin
Louisiana Story	(1948)	Robert Flaherty
Benjy	(1951)	Fred Zinnemann
Kon-Tiki	(1951)	Thor Heyerdahl
The Sea Around Us	(1953)	Jacques-Yves Cousteau
Blue Water, White Death	(1971)	Peter Gimbel
Georgia O'Keeffe	(1977)	Perry Miller Adato
The Last Resort	(1977)	Daniel Keller
The Ona People	(1977)	Anne Chapman and Ana Montes
Life and Other Anxieties	(1978)	Steven Ascher and Ed Pincus

Outstanding Direct Cinema Films and Directors

All My Babies	(1952)	George Stoney
The Chair	(1962)	Richard Leacock, Donn Alan Pennebaker
Happy Mother's Day	(1963)	Richard Leacock
Don't Look Back	(1966)	Donn Alan Pennebaker
Warrendale	(1967)	Allen King
Titicut Follies	(1967)	Frederic Wiseman
High School	(1968)	Frederic Wiseman
Monterey Pop	(1968)	Donn Alan Pennebaker, Richard Leacock
Law and Order	(1969)	Frederic Wiseman
Medium Cool	(1969)	Haskell Wexler
Salesman	(1969)	Albert and David Maysles
Hospital	(1970)	Frederic Wiseman
Woodstock	(1970)	Michael Wadleigh
Gimme Shelter	(1971)	Albert and David Maysles
Primate	(1974)	Frederic Wiseman
Welfare	(1975)	Frederic Wiseman

23/Experimental Cinema: The Avant-Garde

THE TERM "avant-garde" loosely describes any experimental movement in the arts, working outside accepted forms. Avant-garde films are works produced usually by small groups or individuals who desire to explore untouched areas of the medium in a particularly self-expressive manner. The radical experimentalists making these films were active in Europe from 1918 to 1930.

By the early 1920's, European society had drastically altered from its prewar condition. The upheaval and turmoil of this conflict shattered one's traditional viewpoint of society and its beliefs. Art, for example, broke away from established traditions, and more painters worked in the areas of Dadaism, Cubism, Futurism, and Expressionism. Literature, too, had changed. The romantic novel's contrived situations and stereotyped characters gave way to the styles of realism and naturalism, and eventually, stream of consciousness. Montmartre and Montparnasse were spawning new forms in painting, literature, and film. Filmmakers, discontented with the products from Hollywood and the Paris studios, rebelled against commercial films. The time was ripe for artists to attempt avant-garde cinema.

Although the movement began in Germany, it quickly spread to many European cities; however, Paris in the 1920's became its fountainhead. The early turn-of-the-century short films of Géorgès Méliès (one of the spiritual fathers of surrealism) and Louis Feuillade, whose early serials liberated artists to explore hitherto unknown aspects of the unconscious, could be considered forerunners of this school's later efflorescence. Just as their films were interested in illusion, poetry, trick photography, slow and fast action, so too did these devices capture the interests of the avant-garde directors. Like Méliès and Feuillade, these experimental artists of the 1920's mingled dreams, fantasies, and recurring images with puzzling objects, then placed their absurd characters in weird situations in order to tell their stories.

Realizing that film could be used in various ways, French painters left their easels and experimented with movies. Their films received private screenings but several were released to the Paris theaters. Audiences were enraged, puzzled, or delighted at what these artists had done with their absurd stories, strange images, bizarre characters, and trick photography. Critics, amused at these shorts, dubbed them avant-garde, an adjective used to describe an art form ahead of its time. Several artists, such as Fernand Leger, Man Ray, Marcel Duchamp, Salvador Dali, Luis Buñuel, Germaine Dulac, and Dimitri Kirsanoff, realizing that film could reflect one's personal artistic views, turned to the movie short as a new medium of self-expression.

When World War I ended, certain German films dealing with the occult were released in Paris; young painters were captivated by these imported films with their stories of vampires, zombies, demons, and devils. These characters in their mad world embodied everything the surrealist artists came to revere—dreams, madness, hysteria, and black humor. The avant-garde film received a thrust forward with *The Cabinet of Dr. Caligari* (1919), a German film revealing the dark passions of tormented characters. When the picture was released in France, the Paris film world was enthusiastic over its expressionistic sets, somnambulistic characters, the use of hypnotism, and the theme of one man controlling another's mind. The demons and devils in *The Golem* (1920), *Nosferatu* (1922), *The Student of Prague* (1926) and *Metropolis* (1926) were also welcomed by the surrealist painters. Paris was impressed with Walter Ruttmann's art films, particularly *Berlin, the Symphony of a Big City* (1927). Viewers were delighted too with the German cinematographer's treatment of his subject through an abstract eye. These German pictures carried experimental film into areas where the commercial documentary and narrative film had left off.

Germaine Dulac, an established artist, enthralled by these foreign films, directed *Ames de Fous* (1918) and *Le Diable dans La Ville* (1924). Her most popular film, *The Seashell and the Clergyman* (1928), was one example of the cinema's first venture into surrealism. Dulac's short surrealistic fantasy filled with sexual symbols was strenuously attacked by critics, public, and censors alike. In turn, her films gave impetus to

Dmitri Kirsanoff's avant-garde film *Menilmontant* (1925), with its remarkable use of free cutting and poetic images. By 1928 Jean Epstein's *La Chute de la Maison Usher (The Fall of the House of Usher)*, showing the German influence in sets, costumes and characters was one of the best of the genre. By 1928, such world-famous artists and directors as René Clair, Salvador Dali, Luis Buñuel, Claude Autant-Lara, Jean Renoir, and Abel Gance were experimenting with art films.

If the Germans were preoccupied with the supernatural and the documentary approach, the French, as in the early days of filmmaking, were engrossed by "trick" techniques in their films, often with a wild sense of humor. Many of these efforts rejected structured narratives and pictorial material, stressing plastic and rhythmic aspects. These films treated all kinds of topics; some lacked meaning, while others were heavily laden with influences from German films; still others suggested Freudian concepts with strange, surrealistic overtones. The films of Man Ray and Fernand Leger provide noteworthy examples.

Ray, an American living in Paris, was one of the original Dadaists and a founder of surrealism. Between 1923 and 1929, he made four avant-garde films. Two of them, *Le Retour a la Raison* (1923), *(The Return to Reason)* and *Emak-Bakia* (1927), showing aspects of surrealism, are abstract and provocative. Fernand Leger's *Le Ballet Mechanique* (1924) was a popular breakthrough. The picture was applauded by an amused public who laughed at the dancing pots and pans and the repeated images of a very fat woman climbing a flight of stairs.

Ray and Leger's films impressed other avant-garde filmmakers, but it was not until 1928 that two Spanish artists living in Paris—Luis Buñuel and Salvador Dali—made the best and most popular avant-garde film of all time, the surrealistic *Un Chien Andalou (An Andalusian Dog)*.

Both men had seen avant-garde films and decided that since the directors were taking themselves too seriously, it was time to make a picture that would satirize the absurd aspects of the genre. The two conceived their film as a series of jokes. Nothing was to have rational explanation but have the logic of a dream. Hoping to set up a reaction against this type, with tongue in cheek the pair made *An Andalusian Dog*. Despite their initial attempt to burlesque the entire avant-garde movement, the film was hailed as a minor masterpiece, and the two were declared the high priests of the movement.

Un Chien Andalou, only twenty-five minutes long, is a screen classic. The story is a series of vicious images into which one can read all types of meanings. The film is filled with dream fantasies, puzzling characters, and enigmatic action. Many mystifying scenes occur; swarms of ants appear out of a hole in a man's palm; two dead and decaying jack-asses are dragged across a living room; a man clutches at a nude woman; a cyclist keeps falling off his machine; strange beach scenes appear; and, the most memorable scene of all—a man (Buñuel) very slowly opens a woman's eye, slashes her eyeball with a razor, and the eye's gelatinous contents ooze onto her cheek.

The film angered, perplexed, and pleased audiences. Disciples of Sigmund Freud had a field day trying to catalogue its symbols and meaning. Possibly it is Buñuel and Dali's filmic revolt against a society that stifles mankind's conscious and unconscious sexual needs. It powerfully impressed many would-be directors of the 1920's and is today one of the best and most influential of the short art films.

If *Un Chien Andalou* is *the* avant-garde film of the 1920's, then Jean Cocteau's *Le Sang d'un Poète (The Blood of a Poet)* (1930) is the best of the 1930's. After the furor caused by the Buñuel-Dali picture, public attention turned to the Cocteau film, a short enigmatic picture written, directed, and edited by the artist himself. Jean Cocteau—famous as a poet, painter and playwright—had been impressed with the Buñuel-Dali film and decided to attempt something similar. His picture rejects the world of ordinary appearances and carries the viewer into a surrealistic world filled with erotic images, where statues turn into people and people into statues, characters play a mysterious card game, and chimneys come tumbling down. The film overflows with free association, visual symbolism, and abstract effects. By shifting from actuality to fantasy, Cocteau's film represents a unique example of the genre. Both public and press applauded.

By 1929, fans had taken such an interest in avant-garde films that a festival was held in Switzerland for the best independent film of the year. However, the growing popularity of the type was abruptly cut short. Social, political, and economic forces changed the madcap, carefree 1920's into the somber mood of the Depression. The invention of sound also ended avant-garde filmmaking. Money was hard to raise and making personal films with sound equipment was too costly; artists were forced to give up their experimentation.

Independent artists who advanced the art sought other areas in order to make a living. Luis Buñuel, René Clair, Jean Renoir, and Claude Autant-Lara established themselves as directors of commercial films. Paul Fejos (*The Last Moment*, 1929), and Robert Florey (*Life and Death of a Hollywood Extra*, 1927), worked in Hollywood on comedy, gangster, and horror films. Gregg Toland photographed for the big studios and eventually distinguished himself as a leading cinematographer. Ralph Steiner, Paul Strand, and Charles Klein found their independent films curtailed by the Depression, and they too had to forsake experimental films. For a time, experimental films ceased to be made.

By the end of the 1930's, companies making photographic equipment began to manufacture a cheaper 16mm camera, and artists once more turned to making personal films. However, it was not in France but in America—particularly on the West Coast—where the avant-garde film enjoyed its renaissance. By the 1940's, personal, independent films, showing strong influences of the French avant-garde and abstract films, came into full bloom. Hans Richter, Kenneth Anger, Ian Hugo, James Broughton, Sidney Peterson, Curtis Harrington, Marie Menken, Willard Maas, Mylon Meriam, Christopher Young, Maya Deren, and Alexander Hammid tried their hand at turning out experimental pictures. Influenced by German expressionism, Russian rhythmic cutting, and above all, by French trick photography, their surrealistic films were concerned with dreams, poetic images, psychological abnormalities, erotic symbols, and sexual fantasies. These films—sometimes presenting a narrative but more often offering an imaginative motif—found a receptive audience. Maya Deren's *Meshes of the Afternoon* (1943) tells of a surrealistic nightmare. Curtis Harrington in *Fragments of Seeking* (1946) and *Picnic* (1948) offers essays on personal, psychological experiences. James Broughton's *Mother's Day* (1948) is a subtle exploration of a child's behavior. By the 1950's the avant-garde genre was metamorphosed into the Underground film.

The Underground Film

Certain sociological changes in America contributed to the development of the genre known as "Underground" film. After World War II, a demand for political reforms, liberation movements, relative sexual freedom, the struggle against war, the eventual introduction of hallucinatory drugs, and an outright revolt by younger people against social taboos found their way into various art forms. The Underground films reflect and examine these feelings and ideas. The films themselves became part of the social upheaval and dissent that they so faithfully mirror.

Certain directors had something very personal to say, and using film media, they shattered social taboos, language barriers, and religious and sexual restrictions. Some of their films can be characterized as pop, camp, and trivia, but are worthy of attention because of the directors' personal concern with an artistic experience or a social comment. Because of censors and public protest, many of these productions were refused theater bookings and were confined to private clubs, hence the term "Underground."

Among the first to offer their filmic experiments were four independent producers-directors, Maya Deren (*A Study in Choreography for the Camera*, 1945), Kenneth Anger (*Fireworks*, 1947), Curtis Harrington (*On the Edge*, 1949, and *Fragments of Seeking*, 1946) and Gregory Markopoulous (*Psyche*, 1948). Their pictures were self-financed, personal, daring, and concerned with sexual dreams and adolescent visions. Each expressed the anxieties of the decade—the frantic times, sexual freedom, political views, personal dreams, and philosophical comments on the world around them. In the 1950's others followed—Jonas Mekas, Kenneth Jacobs, Ron Rice, Stan Brakhage, and Marie Menken. They were succeeded in the 1960's by Bruce Baillie, Carl Linder, Ben Van Meter and Robert Nelson. Each artist used cinema to capture abstract beauty, design, visual forms, movement, time and space. Refusing to submit to public taste or defer to censorship, Underground filmmakers ignored existing taboos and presented puzzling objects, calculated insanity, sex orgies, and nudity.

Because each director financed his own films, he remained unconcerned with studio controls, production restrictions, or the temper tantrums of a star. He followed no set rules, particularly with regard to either subject matter or cinema techniques.

Like the French directors who founded the *nouvelle vague* cinema, the directors of the nonnarrative, imagistic films issued edicts, announcements and proclamations in the press and at public forums, declaring their intentions in their pictures. Their films were to be different, individual, and select. Some declared that they wanted no public audiences to see their finished products, since their films were for a chosen few. Others invited one and all to see their efforts.

One of the best and most representative of the Underground films is Kenneth Anger's *Scorpio Rising* (1962-64). The story, photography, and soundtrack characterize the Underground films of the early 1960's. Anger's film, a study of violence, (thirty-one minutes long) presents motorcycle cultists, pop songs, drugs, and homosexual orgies. These elements represent for him the driving forces of society. His picture is an emotional study of youth, death, and black humor.

What makes this film superior is its editing, use of the jump cut, and raucous musical score. There are glimpses of young boys strapping on motorcycle costumes as though they were sacred robes. We see flashing shots of belts, buckles, bracelets, helmets, phallic symbols, comic strips, iron helmets, and Nazi flags as the motorcycle cult prepares for a party. The wild orgy—a rough all-male sex party—is interposed with scenes of Christ and His disciples entering Jerusalem.

The hero "Scorpio," developed by montage shots, combines character traits of Hitler, Marlon Brando and James Dean. Faces flash on and off, accompanied by a blaring soundtrack that creates a tremendous tension as the characters leap on their cycles and race to their doom. The film found wide public acclaim and influenced significantly other films that followed.

Stan Brakhage's films provide considerable influence on the Underground genre. Brakhage avoids surrealism and pure excitement, but nonetheless gives his pictures a "personal" touch. He makes films about his own life that represent poetic versions of that life—for example, *Window Water Baby Moving* (1959), a vivid film of the birth of his child. His best film is considered to be *Dog Star Man* (1959-64), a complicated film, seventy-eight minutes in length, filled with intricate actions, symbols, and cutbacks.

The best-known director of this genre is probably Andy Warhol, who is a major figure in the American Pop Art movement and only tangentially part of this group. His sometimes annoying films have managed to obtain a wider release than others. *Sleep* (1963) is six hours long and shows a man asleep. With a female impersonator, he made *Harlot* (1965) and in *My Hustler* (1965) he presented homosexuals, transvestites, sadists, and drug addicts who improvised their dialogue before the camera; in 1966 he completed *The Chelsea Girls*, the most popular of all the Underground films. Using a split screen, Warhol telescopes seven hours of material into three and a half. The film had a national release in at least 100 theaters and grossed nearly $1,000,000. It contains monotonous monologues and various comments on religion, society, and sex. Some critics damned it; others praised it; much of the public thought that they had paid their money to be bored.

By 1960, a group of filmmakers and producers calling themselves the New American Cinema published statements that outlined the organization's rebellion against constraints on social and political attitudes and the restriction of subject matter permitted in films. The group, which included Lionel Rogosin, Peter Bogdanovich, Jonas Mekas, Shirley Clarke, Robert Frank, and Alfred Leslie, gave encouragement to the independent filmmaker of the future.

Audiences sometimes object to the experimental, avant-garde, Underground films because of their indiscriminate selection of subjects. Some think the films are sexually too explicit; many object to their amateurish editing and cheap photography. Others are bewildered because often there is no story to follow, only flashes of people and objects. Many claim the films *are* immature, self-conscious, childish, and deliberately sensational. The films have been accused of being revolting, showing subjects that repel the viewer. Many contain not only poor photography and atrocious acting but also bad soundtracks. Some offer sordid surroundings with disreputable characters sitting about telling long, boring, and repulsive tales. Often the camera is jiggled or turned upside down; the film is scratched, bleached, overexposed, or underexposed.

In the 1960's, Underground films that were once considered pornographic with their daring subjects, explicit photography, and profanity received more and more public showings. Producers challenged the censorship code and offered their wares to all. The public in a way was ready for this change. European imports had helped pave the way for their acceptance. After being exposed to Italian neorealists and the French New Wave, the American public had become sophisticated enough to accept the Underground films with their unconventional approaches and their forthright treatments of sex. Eventually the genre surfaced and was there for all to see. The Underground, a heretofore concealed product of the avant-garde, emerged as public entertainment and was subsequently a part of the Hollywood commercial products. By the 1960's, nudity, profanity, sexual fantasies, and daring themes—long considered provocative by the Hollywood Establishment—were now part of the popular contemporary cinema scene. There was no longer any reason for selective pictures to be shown "Underground." Today's films link all film genres together. Various aspects of the avant-garde, experimental, and Underground films are being expanded into structured and commercial films.

Outstanding Avant-Garde Films and Directors

La Fête Espagnole	(1919)	Germaine Dulac
Le Ballet Méchanique	(1924)	Fernand Leger
Le Diable dans la Ville	(1924)	Germaine Dulac
La Chute de la Maison Usher	(1928)	Jean Epstein
Menilmontant	(1926)	Dmitri Kirsanov
Berlin—Rhythm of a City	(1927)	Walter Ruttmann
Un Chien Andalou	(1928)	Luis Buñuel, Salvador Dali
Le Sang d'un Poète	(1930)	Jean Cocteau
Meshes of the Afternoon	(1943)	Maya Deren
Geography of the Body	(1943)	Willard Maas
Fragment of Seeking	(1946)	Curtis Harrington
Fireworks	(1947)	Kenneth Anger
Mother's Day	(1948)	James Broughton
Window Water Baby Moving	(1959)	Stan Brakhage
Flaming Creatures	(1962)	Jack Smith
Scorpio Rising	(1962-64)	Kenneth Anger
Hallelujah, the Hills	(1963)	Adolfás Mekas
Sleep	(1963)	Andy Warhol
The Chelsea Girls	(1966)	Andy Warhol
Galaxie	(1966)	Gregory Makropoulous
Tom, Tom	(1969)	Ken Jacobs

APPENDIX

Glossary of Film Terms

Absurd: A genre of drama in which the world is an incomprehensible place, where traditional meanings seem to have been revoked, and the laws of probability are suspended. Characters live in a world of isolation and anxiety and there are no fixed beliefs. The playwrights who best represent the genre are Samuel Becket, Eugene Ionesco, and Jean Genêt.

angle shot: camera in such a position that a line from the lens to the scene forms an acute or obtuse angle rather than a right angle; a slanting shot; a high-angle shot looks down on the subject; a low-angle shot looks up at the subject.

art house (or art theater):   small movie house whose management usually specializes in showing intellectual, offbeat, or artistic foreign films.

auteur: literally French for author. Coined by François Truffaut in 1954 in the film periodical *Cahiers du Cinéma*. The term was somewhat clarified by André Bazin in the same publication in 1957. It emphasizes the director as the dominant creator and author of the film. Particular stress is placed on the "tension" between the director's personality and the requirements of an externally imposed script. His film contains qualities that are characteristic of his personal technique and vision as they appear in his total sum of films. *Auteur* directors are François Truffaut, Jean-Luc Godard, John Ford, Alfred Hitchcock, Fritz Lang, and Howard Hawks.

Cahiers du Cinéma: French cinema magazine founded in 1951 by the French film critic André Bazin and producer Jacques Doniol-Valcroze. Many of the writers included the major New Wave directors: Jean-Luc Godard, François Truffaut, Erich Rohmer, Claude Chabrol, and others. They presented their concepts of filmmaking in various articles published in the magazine.

camera angle: the area of sight that a camera takes in when it is set up to shoot. The norm is arbitrarily based on a 35mm camera with a 2-inch lens pointed at a scene from shoulder height. From this norm, deviations of high, low, and wide can be determined.

camera boom: a mechanized crane with a platform to house cameras; extends upward to photograph high shots.

cinéma verité: a method of documentary filming that emphasizes reality by fast film stock, and a minimum of equipment; uses especially the hand-held camera and portable sound apparatus. It avoids when possible the technical and formal means of moviemaking.

closeup: a scene where the actor or object is close to the camera. With an individual, only the face, or face and shoulders, are usually seen. The purpose is to show emotion.

continuity cutting: the smooth and uninterrupted style of cutting film, giving the impression that the action is continuous. The result is a fluidity of motion.

crab dolly: a platform with wheels on which a camera is set; able to move in any direction; usually positioned and operated by hand.

credit titles: a list of those people involved in creating a particular film. Usually rolled at the beginning of a film.

cross-cutting: the alternating of shots to suggest two or more events occurring at the same time. D. W. Griffith used this to arouse strong emotion in his audiences.

cut: the splicing of two shots together in such a way as to produce an instantaneous transition. Creating time and space in films is largely due to the style of the cutting. The two most often used are jump cut and match cut.

cutback: an abrupt stop to take the viewer back to a previously shown action. The purpose is to show lapse of time or parallel action.

cutting room: where separate portions of the film are cut according to the desired effect required and spliced together.

deep focus: a technique in photography which enables all distances to remain clearly in focus, from closeup ranges to infinity; was especially effective in Orson Welles's *Citizen Kane*.

depth of field: the limit for distancing of objects from the camera in which they are still seen clearly and distinctly. This limit is reached when a "circle of confusion of greatest acceptable size" is produced.

director: the person who superintends the actual production of the motion picture. It is his interpretation of the script and adaptive technique that give the film its character and polish.

dissolve: the superimposition of two shots on the screen, whereby the first shot fades away as, simultaneously, the second shot comes into view.

documentary: the genre that presents factual, political, historical, or social events objectively. These events may be real or staged. Technically, these films have a realistic approach, roles may be played by nonactors, use natural lighting, and adopt a newsreel approach to the story, all of which enhances the film's acceptance as an actual account of the issues. This style of filmmaking was used by early Russian directors to record the progress of the Red Army (Dziga Vertov).

dolly shot (tracking shot, trucking shot, traveling shot): the camera on a truck or dolly moves in relation to that which is being filmed. It can move in close to the subject or retreat from it. Orignally, tracks were laid on the set and the camera was rolled along. It was harnessed in a stand on wheels, called a dolly.

double exposure: shooting two pictures on the same strip of film before the film is developed. This results in having two scenes appear on the screen at the same time.

dubbing: adding the sound to a film after the visual portion has been completed. It can be either synchronous or nonsynchronous. Sometimes, foreign language films are dubbed in English for American audiences. One technique of dubbing is called voiceover. This involves maintaining the original soundtrack in the background, and merely adding the new one in "over" the original one. An example of this is in the political speeches made by the black worker in Jean-Luc Godard's *Weekend*.

dunning process: the visual technique where objects which are out of focus of one another, having diverse depths of field, can be photographed in the same shot and both be seen clearly. In such shots the various levels seem to be compressed closely and sit on top of one another.

dynamic cutting: a style of cutting which places contrasting shots or sequences in juxtaposition in order to imply a similarity of themes, which has not been previously established.

editing:　the process of joining distinct and individual pieces of film in meaningful juxtaposition.

editor:　the person who superintends the joining of one shot (strip of film) to another.

epic:　the film genre characterized by bold sweeping themes, usually in heroic proportion. The tone in most epics is dignified and things are treated as being larger than life. There are usually messages to be given by characters of an idealistic, noble nature. Cecil B. DeMille is considered America's foremost director of this genre.

extreme closeup (detail shot):　a minutely detailed view of an object or a person. Such a shot of an actor usually includes only a view of his eyes or mouth.

extreme long shot:　a panoramic view of an exterior location, taken from a long distance.

fade:　the gradual appearance of an image from the darkness, or a gradual disappearance of an image into the darkness, leaving the screen blank.

faking:　the cinematic process by which unrealistic interpretations are seen as reality. This effect makes use of special scenic, mechanical, camera, and laboratory devices.

fast motion (accelerated motion):　technique achieved by photographing a subject at a slower rate than 24 frames per second, then projecting the image at the standard 24 frames per second. The result is rapid, jerky movements, which give humans an automaton quality.

feature:　the name given to the main event in any given showing at a movie theater. It is several reels long and tells the main story. Two such films playing on the same bill, is called a double feature.

filters:　pieces of glass or plastic which, when placed over the aperture of a camera lens, distort the light entering the camera, and produce, therefore, distortions on the film, when developed.

fish-eye lens:　an extreme wide-angle lens, that causes such a radical distortion in the light entering the camera that the print of the image seems to have its edges wrapped into a sphere.

flash:　a short strip of film used to give a brief impression, usually used to show a lapse of time or emotional reaction.

flashback: a technique in editing that juxtaposes a shot taken in the present with one that has already taken place. The shots that represent the past seem to come as interruptions in the action of the present.

flash-forward: technique in editing that juxtaposes a shot of present action with one that takes place in the future. The future shots are seen as interruptions in the present action.

follow shots: shots in which the camera moves around to give a mobile account of a scene.

frame: a single image appearing on a strip of film; also, the name given to the dark line on the strip of film, which separates one single image from the next one.

freeze frame (freeze shot): an image from a single frame which is reprinted a number of times on the filmstrip (in sequence) and which, when projected on the screen, gives the effect of a still photograph.

genre: types of film which include certain established conventions of that particular style of film, i.e., Westerns, thrillers, musicals, spectacles, dramas, melodramas, comedies, documentaries, biographies, mysteries.

glass shot: a shot taken partly of a constructed set and partly of a representation of the desired effect on a sheet of glass, which is placed in front of the lens of the camera so as to coincide with the perspective of the built-up set.

grip: man who is responsible for rigging up the equipment (lights, hanging scenery, props, etc.) and for their operation.

high angle shot: a shot in which the subject is photographed from above.

independent film: a film made outside the aegis of a big-name studio, backed by either the director and members of the crew, or wealthy friends. These films usually don't have elaborate sets, techniques, or big stars in the leading roles. They are ventures which are close to the director and so encompass much of his style and thought.

iris: a masking device that blackens part of the screen. Only part of the image is seen, usually through a circular or oval section of light which can be expanded or contracted.

jump cut: an abrupt transition between shots that is disorienting in terms of spatial and/or temporal continuity. It is achieved by cutting out a section of the mid-portion of a shot, and splicing the two ends of the shot together.

lap dissolve: a shot in which the scene gradually fades and in fading blends with the next scene, which gradually becomes more prominent. For a brief time the film is double exposed. The lapse of time is a little longer than in a straight dissolve.

lighting: flat—the light, in coming from behind the camera, falls in front of actor.

           back—light proceeds from in back of the object photographed and into the camera.

           side—the light is thrown from the right or left of the object.

           top—a spot is thrown from above to focus on the chief actor of the scene.

long shot: a scene taken with a camera using the entire angle of view of the camera lens, with lens focused on objects a long distance away.

mise-en-scène: the staging of a film; considering the movements of the actors in relation to setting, lighting, etc.

montage: coined from the French "to mount," "to assemble." Used by Sergei Eisenstein to show the difference between the Russian style of editing and that of the Americans. It is assembling, arranging, or editing the film; making a composite picture by bringing together into a single composition a number of different pictures or parts of pictures and arranging these so that they form a blended whole. Montage for Eisenstein was the fundamental creative process in filmmaking. His method was to combine shots of unrelated objects or persons to create in the minds of the audience meaningful relationships. This is sometimes called *dynamic cutting*.

Moviola: a one-person movie-viewing machine, used by editors in cutting rooms.

Mutoscope: a peephole machine showing a series of moving photographs to a single viewer.

neorealism: an Italian film movement which produced its best works from 1945-55. Strongly realistic in its story, action, and sets, neorealism emphasizes the documentary aspects of film art, stressing loose, episodic plots, ordinary events and characters, natural lighting and location settings, amateur actors, a preoccupation with poverty and social problems, and an emphasis on humanistic and democratic ideals. The term has also been used to describe any film which reflects the technical and thematic aspects of Italian neorealism. It was a reaction against the artificialities and propaganda of the Fascist films. The major directors of this school were Roberto Rossellini, Giuseppi de Santis, Vittorio de Sica, and Luchino Visconti.

negative image: the reversal of lights and darks of the subject photographed—blacks are white and whites are black.

nonsynchronous sound: sound and image are not recorded simultaneously, or the sound is detached from its source in the film image.

nouvelle vague (new wave): a term coined by journalist Françoise Giroud to describe a technique in French films of the late 1950's and 1960's. The new wave directors were those French filmmakers who came into prominence during the 1950's (Jean-Luc Godard, François Truffaut, Claude Chabrol, and others). These directors had control of all aspects of filmmaking involved with their movie.

overexposure: often used in fantasy or nightmare shots. It occurs when too much light enters the aperture of the camera lens, causing the images to be exceedingly bright.

overlap: a technique in dialogue cutting, in which the sound track is carried over into a shot which did not begin the sound. Usually, this is seen when, instead of seeing the speaker, we get a shot of the person being addressed.

pan: movement of the camera in a horizontal plane.

panorama: a scene in which the camera is rotated without changing the position of the tripod. The effect is the same as looking from the window of a moving train.

process shots: first shots are taken of desired background (often distant countries), then another shot is made in the studio of players going through the actions of the scene. The two films are blended by trick camera projection.

producer: the person finally responsible for the shaping and outcome of a film. He is in charge of business and often is responsible for the commercial success or failure of a film.

pullback dolly: a technique used to surprise the viewer by dollying back from a scene to reveal an object which was previously off frame.

rough cut: the total footage of the film which has been put together before the editor has tightened up on scene transition. A sort of rough draft of a film before it is polished into the final print.

scenario:　the outline of the story, indicating the action in order of its development, the scenes, the cast of characters and their appearance, etc.

scene:　a unit of film, composed of a number of interrelated shots, unified by a central concern—a location, an incident, or a minor dramatic climax.

script person:　the person in charge of the written scenario of a film, and who reads along with the action to check on dialogue and interpretation of a particular scene.

sequence:　a section of film that is relatively complete in itself and which begins and ends with fades, dissolves, and cuts.

shot:　those images which are recorded from the time the camera starts to the time it stops, that is, an unedited, uncut strip of film.

slow motion:　shots of a subject photographed at a faster rate than 24 frames per second, then projected at 24 frames per second. The effect is a dreamy, graceful, dancelike slowness of motion.

soft focus (gauze shot):　a scene taken through gauze or a focus disk, which gives the scene a soft hazy appearance.

star system:　performers in demand by the public given special film roles. This was the way Hollywood functioned when the big studios controlled the market. In order to get these names to work, each studio outbid one another in salary promises until famous actors were being paid unbelievable amounts of money, just for their name.

stock footage:　usually found in studio film libraries; it consists of historical shots and other footage which is applicable and likely to be used in the future on another production.

stock shots:　film footage kept in stock for general use, including things that it would be inadvisable to reshoot, such as historical events, famous places, etc.

styles:　a. *expressionism*: a style of film making which distorts time and space as it is seen in reality. The essential aspects of objects and people are emphasized rather than their surface appearance. The techniques which are involved are fragmentary editing, variety of shots (particularly closeups), extreme angles, lighting effects, distortions caused by different lenses.

b. *naturalism*: the variety of realism based on the principles and methods of a group of 19th-century writers (Emile Zola, Gustave Flaubert, Guy de Maupassant), who believed that the artist should apply scientific objectivity and precision in his observation and treatment of life, *without* idealizing, imposing value judgments, or *avoiding what is regarded as repulsive*. In films, this effect is achieved through use of naturalistic sets, natural lighting, real-life soundtrack, cameras used as part of the action (as a third person).

c. *realism*: a recording of life as it is, refraining from imposing a predetermined pattern upon the materials; details are to be presented as they actually are. The main concerns of such a genre are with the activities encountered in everyday life. It is an attempt to give an interpretation of reality with a little more freedom of expression than naturalism allows. It is an attempt to preserve the space-time continuum by emphasizing long shots, lengthy takes, eye-level camera placement, and a minimum of editing and special effect photography.

d. *romanticism*: a movement in the arts characterized by freedom in form and subject matter, emphasis of sympathetic feelings and use of imaginative suggestion. These films are often marked by an unrestrained sensuousness, vague imagery, lack of logical precision, escape from the realities of life. Technically, reality is seen not as it is, but as the artist would have it seen. Films of this type (such as Bo Widerberg's *Elvira Madigan*) are characterized by very beautiful, stylized landscapes, long shots, interesting uses of color, symbolism, idealistic plot, emphasis on emotions, vivid soundtrack.

e. *surrealism*: a movement in modern art and literature which attempts to portray or interpret the workings of the subconscious mental activities by means of incongruous, fantastic imagery. It is characterized by unnatural juxtapositions of objects and variations of combinations. Every possible cinematic device, technique and experiment is used to recreate this subconscious view of the world. No order or reason is present, time and space have no permanence.

swish pan: panning shot in which the camera is swung on its vertical axis, producing a blurred sensation on film.

synchronous sound: the correspondence of image and sound, which are recorded simultaneously, or seem to be. The sound corresponds precisely with the action on the screen.

take: each performance before a camera which is recorded on film.

Underground film: an avant-garde movement, which emphasizes film as pure form and stresses the filmmaker's self-expression over considerations of content and narrative.

wide-angle lens: a lens which permits the camera to photograph a wider area than a normal lens. As a side effect, it intensifies perspective.

wipe: a modern screen device which is used to replace certain types of dissolves. It involves two succeeding shots on the screen in which the second appears to wipe the first off the screen along a visible line, and which runs from top to bottom, bottom to top, left to right, right to left, diagonally, circularly, split screen panels, or any number of designs. *Pushover wipe*: the first image moves horizontally across the screen as if propelled by the second image which immediately follows it.

zoom shot: permits the lens to change focal distances very rapidly; a real or apparent movement of the camera toward the object being photographed.

Bibliography

The following books have been consulted by the author and are recommended for further reading:

Agee, James	Agee on Film: Reviews and Comments	Boston:	Beacon Press,	1964
Battrock, Gregory	The New American Cinema	New York:	Dutton,	1967
Baxter, John	Hollywood in the Sixties	New York:	Barnes,	1972
Baxter, John	Hollywood in the Thirties	New York:	Barnes,	1968
Bessie, Alvah	Inquisition in Eden	New York:	Macmillan,	1965
Blum, Daniel	A Pictorial History of the Silent Screen	New York:	Putnam's Sons,	1951
Blum, Daniel	A Pictorial History of the Talkies	New York:	Putnam's Sons,	1968
Bogdanovich, Peter	John Ford	New York:	Dutton-Vista,	1968
Brownlow, Kevin	The Parades Gone By	New York:	A. K. Knopf,	1968
Cameron, Ian (ed.)	The Films of Jean-Luc Godard	New York:	Dutton-Vista,	1967
Clarens, Carlos	An Illustrated History of the Horror Film	New York:	Capricorn,	1967
Cowie, Peter	70 Years of Cinema	New York:	Barnes,	1968
Cowie, Peter	Swedish Cinema	New York:	Barnes,	1969
Crowther, Bosley	The Great Films	New York:	Putnam's Sons,	1964
Crowther, Bosley	The Lion's Share	New York:	E. P. Dutton & Co.	1957
Eisner, Lotte L.	The Haunted Screen	Berkeley:	U. of Cal. Press,	1969
Everson, William	A Pictorial History of the Western Film	New York:	Citadel Press,	1969
Eyles, Allen	The Western	New York:	Barnes,	1967
Finler, Joel	Stroheim	Berkeley:	U. of Cal. Press,	1968

311

312 | An Introduction to American Movies

Franklin, Joe	Classics of the Silent Screen	New York:	Citadel Press,	1967
Gifford, Dennis	Movie Monsters	New York:	E. P. Dutton & Co.	1969
Gish, Lillian	The Movies, Mr. Griffith, and Me	Englewood Cliffs, NJ:	Prentice-Hall,	1969
Graham, Peter	The New Wave	New York:	Doubleday,	1968
Griffith, Richard, & Mayer, Arthur	The Movies	New York:	Simon & Schuster,	1957
Halliwell, Leslie	The Filmgoers Companion	New York:	Hill & Wang,	1966
Higham, Charles & Greenberg, Joel	Hollywood in the Forties		Barnes,	1968
Houston, Penelope	The Contemporary Cinema	New York: Baltimore:	Pelican,	1963
Kael, Pauline	I Lost It at the Movies	Boston:	Little, Brown & Co.,	1954
Knight, Arthur	The Liveliest Art	New York:	Macmillan,	1957
MacGowan, Kenneth	Behind the Screen: The History and Techniques of the Motion Picture	New York:	Delta (Dial),	1967
Madsen, Axel	Billy Wilder	New York:	Doubleday,	1969
Manvell, Roger	New Cinema in Europe	New York:	E. P. Dutton (Pic.)	1965
McVay, Douglas	The Musical Film	New York:	Barnes,	1967
Montague, Ivor	With Eisenstein in Hollywood	Berlin:	Seven Seas,	1968
Ramsaye, Terry	A Million & One Nights	New York:	Simon & Schuster,	1964
Renan, Sheldon	An Introduction to the American Underground Film	New York:	Dutton,	1967
Robinson, David	Hollywood in the Twenties	New York:	Barnes,	1968
Rondi, Gian Luigi	Italian Cinema Today	London:	Dennis Dobson,	1966

Rude, Richard	*Godard*	New York:	Doubleday,	1968
Schickel, Richard	*The Stars*	New York:	Dial,	1962
Schumach, Murray	*The Face on the Cuttingroom Floor*	New York:	Wm. Morrow,	1964
Sarris, Andrew (Ed.)	*Interview with Film Directors*	New York:	Bobbs-Merrill,	1967
Sarris, Andrew	*The American Cinema*	New York:	E. P. Dutton,	1968
Springer, John	*All Talking, All Singing, All Dancing*	New York:	Citadel Press,	1966
Tyler, Parker	*Classics of the Foreign Films*	New York:	Citadel Press,	1967
Vidor, King	*A Tree is a Tree*	New York:	Harcourt-Brace,	1953
Walker, Alexander	*Sex in the Movies*	Baltimore:	Penguin,	1969
Wollen, Peter	*Signs and Meaning in the Cinema*	New York:	Jarrold & Sons, Limited,	1969
Wiseman, Thomas	*Cinema*	London:	Cassell,	1964
Wood, Robin	*Arthur Penn*	New York:	Dutton-Vista,	1967

Suggested Reading List

Author	Title	City	Publisher	Year
Agee, James	Agee on Film: Reviews and Comments	Boston:	McDowell, Oblensky,	1941
Agel, Jerome	The Making of Kubrick's 2001	New York:	New American Library,	1970
Armes, Roy	Film & Reality	Louisiana:	Pelican,	1974
Bawden, Liz-Anne (Ed.)	The Oxford Companion to Film		Oxford University Press,	1976
Baxter, John	Hollywood in the Sixties	New York:	A. S. Barnes & Co.	1972
Bohn, Thomas W. & Richard L. Stromgren	Light & Shadows	New York:	Alfred,	1975
Brownlow, Kevin	The Parades Gone By	New York:	A. K. Knopf,	1968
Casty, Alan	Development of the Film	New York:	Harcourt, Brace, Jovanovich,	1973
Cavell, Stanley	The World Viewed	New York:	Viking,	1971
Clarens, Carlos	An Illustrated History of the Horror Film	New York:	Capricorn,	1967
Crowther, Bosley	The Great Films	New York:	G. P. Putnam's Sons,	1967
Curtiss, Thomas Quinn	Von Stroheim	London:	Angus & Robertson,	1971
DeNitto, Dennis & William Herman	Film & the Critical Eye	New York:	Macmillan,	1975
Dickinson, Thorold	A Discovery of Cinema		Oxford,	1971
Fell, John L.	Film: An Introduction		Praeger,	1975
Halliwell, Leslie (Ed.)	The Filmgoers Companion (4th ed.)	London:	Hart-Davis MacGibbon,	1974
Huss, Roy & Nathan Silverstein	The Film Experience	New York:	Harper & Row,	1968

Johnson, Lincoln F.	*Film, Space, Time, Light & Sound*	New York:	Holt, Rhinehart,	1974
Kael, Pauline	*I Lost It at the Movies*	Boston	Little, Brown & Co.,	1965
Knight, Arthur	*The Liveliest Art*	New York:	Macmillan,	1957
Kuhns, William	*Movies in America*		Pflaum,	1972
Linden, George W.	*Reflections on the Screen*	Belmont, Cal.:	Wadsworth,	1970
MacGowan, Kenneth	*Behind the Screen*	New York:	Delta (Dial),	1967
Madsen, Roy P.	*The Impact of Film*	New York:	Macmillan,	1973
Solomon, Stanley J.	*The Film Idea*	New York:	Harcourt, Brace, Jovanovich,	1972
Thomson, David	*Movie Man*	New York:	Stein & Day	1967
Taylor, John Russell	*Directors & Directions: Cinema for the Seventies*	New York:	Hill and Wang,	1977
Zinman, David	*Fifty Classic Motion Pictures*	New York:	Crown,	1970

Major 16mm Film Distributors

Feature Films on 8mm and 16mm, 5th edition (New York: R. R. Bowker, 1977), by James L. Limbacker, is the best source for locating distributors of particular films. *Mass Media*, a bi-weekly newsletter available from Mass Media Associates, 2116 N. Charles Street, Baltimore, Maryland 21218, offers up-to-date listings of important 16mm films.

AMERICA'S FILMS
> 1735 NW Seventh Street, Miami, Fla. 33125

AUDIO BRANDON
> 34 MacQuestern Parkway So., Mount Vernon, N. Y. 10550
> 3868 Piedmont Avenue, Oakland, Calif. 94611
> 1619 North Cherokee, Los Angeles, Calif. 90028
> 2512 Program Drive, Dallas, Texas 75220
> 400 Brookfield Avenue, Brookfield, Ill. 60513

AVCO EMBASSY PICTURES CORP.
> 750 Third Avenue, New York, N. Y. 10017

BUDGET FILMS
> 4590 Santa Monica Boulevard, Los Angeles, Calif. 90029

CANYON CINEMA FILMMAKERS' COOPERATIVE
> Room 220
> Industrial Center Bldg., Sausalito, Calif. 94965

CENTER CINEMA CO-OP
> S. Michigan & E. Adams, Chicago, Ill. 60603

CINEMA 5 LTD.
> 595 Madison Avenue, New York, N. Y. 10022

CINE WORLD
13 Arcadia Road, Old Greenwich, Conn. 06870

CLEM WILLIAMS FILMS
2240 Noblestown Road, Pittsburgh, Pa. 15205
1277 Spring N.W., Atlanta, Ga. 30309
5424 W. North Avenue, Chicago, Ill. 60639
2170 Portsmouth, Houston, Texas 77098

CONTEMPORARY/McGRAW-HILL FILMS
1221 Avenue of the Americas, New York, N. Y. 10020

CORONET INSTRUCTIONAL MEDIA
65 East South Water Street, Chicago, Ill. 60601

FILM CLASSIC EXCHANGE
1914 S. Vermont Avenue, Los Angeles, Calif. 90007

FILM-MAKER'S COOPERATIVE
175 Lexington Avenue, New York, N. Y. 10016

FILMS INCORPORATED—a subsidiary of Encyclopedia
Britannica Films, Inc.
440 Park Avenue, New York, N. Y. 10016
476 Placemour Drive N.E., Atlanta, Ga. 30324
625 Mt. Auburn Street, Cambridge, Mass.
5625 Hollywood Boulevard, Hollywood, Calif. 90028
8124 N. Central Park Avenue, Skokie, Ill. 60076
1144 Wilmette Avenue, Wilmette, Ill. 60091

GROVE PRESS FILM DIVISION
196 W. Houston Street, New York, N. Y. 10014

INSTITUTIONAL CINEMA SERVICE
915 Broadway, New York, N.Y. 10010

JANUS FILMS
745 Fifth Avenue, New York, N. Y. 10022

MASS MEDIA MINISTRIES
2116 N. Charles Street, Baltimore, Md. 21218

MASS MEDIA ASSOC.
1720 Chouteau Avenue, St. Louis, Mo. 63103

MAYSLES FILMS
1697 Broadway, New York, N. Y. 10019

MODERN SOUND PICTURES
1402 Howard Street, Omaha, Neb. 68102

MUSEUM OF MODERN ART FILM LIBRARY
11 West 53rd Street, New York, N. Y. 10019

NATIONAL CINEMA SERVICE
333 West 57th Street, New York, N.Y. 10019

NEW LINE CINEMA
853 Broadway, New York, N.Y. 10003

NEWSREEL
630 Natona Street, San Francisco, Calif. 94102

NEW YORKER FILMS
16 West 61st Street, New York, N. Y. 10023

PICTURA FILMS DISTRIBUTION CORP.
111 Eighth Avenue, New York, N. Y. 10011

PYRAMID FILMS
Box 1048, Santa Monica, Calif. 90406

SWANK AUDIO-VISUALS, INC.
2800 Market Street, St. Louis, Mo. 63166

SWANK MOTION PICTURES
393 Front Street, Hempstead, N. Y. 11550

TRANS-AMERICAN FILM CORP.
Hollywood Taft Bldg., Hollywood & Vine Streets, Hollywood, Calif. 90028

TRICONTINENTAL FILM CENTER
333 Sixth Avenue, New York, N. Y. 10014

TRANS-WORLD FILMS
332 S. Michigan Avenue, Chicago, Ill. 60604

TWYMAN FILMS
329 Salem Avenue, Dayton, Ohio 45401

UNITED ARTISTS 16
729 Seventh Avenue, New York, N. Y. 10019

UNITED FILMS
6555 E. Skelly Drive, Tulsa, Okla. 74145

UNIVERSAL-16
445 Park Avenue, New York, N. Y. 10022

WALTER READE 16
241 East 34th Street, New York, N. Y. 10016

WARNER BROS., INC.
Non-Theatrical Div., 4000 Warner Boulevard, Burbank,
Calif. 91522

Index

Bacall, Lauren, 73
Bachelor Party, The, 76
Back Street, 249
Bacon, Lloyd, 56, 195, 205
Bad, 117
Bad Company, 117, 245
Bad Day at Black Rock, 84
Bad News Bears, The, 119
Badlands, 116
Ball, Lucille, 75, 215
Balsam, Martin, 168
Bananas, 112, 219
Bancroft, Anne, 120
Bancroft, George, 131
Band Wagon, The, 199-200, 205
Bankhead, Tallulah, 49
Banky, Vilma, 34, 39, 49, 247
Bara, Theda, 26, 28-29
Bardot, Brigitte, 29
Barretts of Wimpole Street, The, 250, 261
Barrie, James M., 32, 266
Barry Lyndon, 276, 279
Barrymore, Ethel, 49
Barrymore, John, 33, 163, 193, 247, 265
Barrymore, Lionel, 14, 49
Barthelmess, Richard, 18, 35, 45, 130
Bartholomew, Freddie, 120, 267
Bat, The, 163
Batman, 177
Battle of San Pietro, The, 227, 233, 284
Baxter, Warner, 196
Bazin, André, 92, 129n
Beatty, Warren, 132-133, 260
Beaumont, Harry, 36, 205
Beery, Wallace, 57, 206
Ben Hur, 32, 79, 149-150, 155-156, 160, 161, 279
Bennett, Constance, 49, 249
Benny, Jack, 210
Benton, Robert, 117, 143, 144, 145, 245
Bergen, Edgar, 214
Bergman, Ingmar, 95-96
Bergman, Ingrid, 64, 67, 252-253, 261

Bergner, Elizabeth, 226
Berkeley, Busby, 56, 136, 194-195, 203-205
Berlin, Irving, 196
Berlin, Jeannie, 218
Bertolucci, Bernardo, 107
Best Years of Our Lives, 68, 228, 233
Biblical films, 38, 78-79, 147-148, 154-156
Bicycle Thief, 72, 90
Big Heat, The, 64, 141, 195
Big Parade, The, 36, 223-224, 232, 233
Big Sleep, The, 139-140, 195
Big Trail, The, 237-238
Biograph Company, 10-11, 14, 31
Birth of a Nation, The, 7, 15-17, 146, 160, 222, 232, 233
Bitzer, "Billy," 14, 15, 32
Black Cinema or *film noir,* 61, 64, 138-145
Black Comedy, 23, 106-107, 115, 183, 215-217, 221, 230
Black Legion, 58
Black Orpheus (Orfeu Negre), 92
Blackboard Jungle, The, 105, 272
Blacklist, of Communist sympathizers, 73-74, 76
Blacks in films, 112-113
Blair, Linda, 121, 169, 170
Blasco Ibanez, Vincente, 44, 247
Blazing Saddles, 112, 218, 244
Block booking system, 25, 71-72
Blockbusters, 78, 113, 115, 118
   See also Epic/Spectaculars
Blondell, Joan, 52, 56, 132, 195
Blood and Sand, 32
Bloom, Claire, 169
Blow-Up, 106
Body and Soul, 144
Body Snatchers, The, 167, 171

Carrie, 117, 170

Carroll, Nancy, 193-194, 203

Casablanca, 62, 67-68, 252

Cassavetes, John, 84, 100, 287

Cat and the Canary, The, 112

Cat from Outer Space, The, 171

Cat on a Hot Tin Roof, 85

Cat People, 61, 167, 171

Censorship, 37, 54-55, 102, 103
  See also Production Code

Chabrol, Claude, 92, 93

Chandler, Jeff, 230

Chandler, Raymond, 139-140, 144

Chaney, Lon, 34, 162-163

Chaney, Lon, Jr., 165-166

Chaplin, Charlie, 13, 20-24, 25, 29-30, 31, 35, 52, 53, 66, 67, 93, 176, 207, 209, 215, 221, 223, 226

Charisse, Cyd, 196, 200

Chatterton, Ruth, 49

Chayefsky, Paddy, 76

Chevalier, Maurice, 40, 49, 55, 194

Child and teen-age stars, 53-54, 120-121, 197, 198

Chinatown, 143, 145

Christie, Julie, 70, 88, 121

Cimarron, 150, 161, 237, 245

Cinemascope, 77

Cinerama, 77, 154

Circus, The, 23

Citizen Kane, 7, 60, 65-67, 269, 270

City Lights, 23

Clair, René, 296

Claire, Ina, 49

Clansman, The, 15

Clarke, Arthur C., 178, 184

Clarke, Mae, 130, 132

Clarke, Shirley, 100, 286, 299

Clayton, Jack, 88, 168, 171, 276, 279

Cleopatra, 150, 158-159, 161

Clift, Montgomery, 70, 82-83, 106, 154, 240-243, 271

Clive, Colin, 49, 165, 166

Clockwork Orange, A, 274

Close Encounters of the Third Kind, 170, 189-201

Clouzot, Henri-Georges, 92, 112

Clurman, Harold, 79

Cobb, Lee J., 80

Cocoanuts, The, 210

Cocteau, Jean, 295

Code and Rating Administration (CARA), 104

Cohan, George M., 198

Colbert, Claudette, 40, 52, 55, 150, 194, 212-213

Colman, Ronald, 34, 247, 266, 270

Columbia Pictures, 31, 55, 56, 62, 159

Comden, Betty, 198, 200-201

Comedy films, 19-21, 52-56, 61, 112, 206-221
  black, *see* Black Comedy

Comics, films based on, 117

Coming Home, 119

Communist "witch hunt," 68, 73-74, 84

Conklin, Chester, 20, 21

Connection, The, 100, 286

Constant Nymph, The, 261

Conversation, The, 117

Coogan, Jackie, 53

Cool World, The, 100

Cooper, Gary, 52, 55, 70, 238

Cooper, Jackie, 53, 120

Cooper, Merian C., 282

Coppola, Francis Ford, 101, 115, 119, 134-135, 137, 232

Cops-and-robbers films, 130-131

Corman, Roger, 141, 145, 167-168

Costello, Lou, 214, 220

Count of Monte Cristo, The, 10

Countess from Hong Kong, A, 23

Cover Girl, 63, 198

Covered Wagon, The, 32, 148-149, 161, 236-237, 245, 265

Coward, Noel, 72

Crawford, Broderick, 270